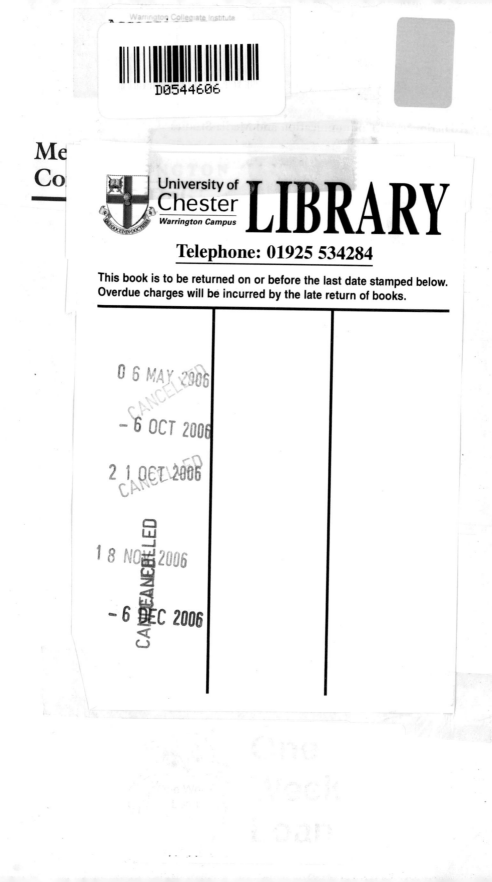

Also by James Watson

A Dictionary of Communication and Media Studies
FOURTH EDITION, 1996
with Anne Hill

Media Communication

An Introduction to Theory and Process

JAMES WATSON

First published 1998 by
MACMILLAN PRESS LTD
Houndmills, Basingstoke, Hampshire RG21 6XS
and London
Companies and representatives throughout the world

ISBN 0–333–68399–4 hardcover
ISBN 0–333–68400–1 paperback

A catalogue record for this book is available
from the British Library.

This book is printed on paper suitable for recycling and
made from fully managed and sustained forest sources.

10   9   8   7   6   5   4
07 06 05 04 03 02 01 00

Editing and origination by
Aardvark Editorial, Mendham, Suffolk

Printed in China

Contents

Introduction   1

1. **Setting the Scene: Media in Context**   11
    Communication, culture, power   12
    Culture and hierarchy   16
    Hegemony: an overview   18
    The modern face of hegemony   21

2. **The Language of Study**   33
    The language of transmission   34
    Signs, codes, texts   40
    The semiological approach to analysis   51
    Audience: the language of reception   53

3. **Audience: the Uses We Make of Media**   60
    Identifying the complexities of audience response to media 61
    Uses and gratifications theory   62
    Issues of dependency   65
    The emancipatory use of media   66
    Cultivation theory   67
    The resistive audience   68
    Ethnographic perspectives   74
    Corporate intrusions   78

4.	**Media in Society: Purpose and Performance**	**83**
	Propaganda, profit, power	84
	The public service model: technology and competition	86
	Classifications of purpose revisited	89
	Functioning according to roles	94
	Principles of media performance: possibilities and problems	96
	Media performance and human rights	99
5.	**The News: Gates, Agendas and Values**	**105**
	The cultural orientation of news	106
	Selecting the news: gatekeeping	108
	Setting the agendas of news	112
	Amplification of issues	113
	New values	117
	Ideology and the news	124
6.	**Narrative: the Media as Storytellers**	**130**
	Homo narrens: the storytelling animal	131
	Narrative frames	134
	Genre, codes and character	137
	Newsworthiness: fictionworthiness	142
	News as narrative	146
7.	**Pressures and Constraints in Media Production**	**152**
	Media communication and the 'project of self'	153
	The dilemmas of professionalism	162
	News management and the hazards of source	165
	Uneven playing fields 1: gender imbalance	169
	Uneven playing fields 2: ethnic imbalance	172
8.	**In the Wake of Magellan: Research as Exploration**	**179**
	Engaging the truth: perspectives on research	180
	Approaches to research 1: content analysis	182
	Approaches to research 2: ethnography	184
	Approaches to research 3: focus groups	190
	Researching audience use of media technology	195

Segmentation: the marketplace approach to
consumer research   198

9. Ownership and Control: Ongoing Issues   207
Information, disinformation, 'mythinformation'   208
Struggles for dominance: private sector *v.* public sector   212
Corporate power and the media   216
Global imbalances in informational and cultural exchange   227

10. Prising Open the Black Box: Media Effects Revisited   233
The spectrum of rival effects: perspectives   234
Cultivation position 1: a consumerist effects story   236
Cultivation position 2: violence, order, control   238
Ethnographic position: resistance through appropriation   242
Technology, surveillance and privacy   247

11. Cyberspace Calling?   258
Global opportunities: research and the Internet   259
Cybervisions: new frontiers, new worlds   262
Personal encounters in cyberspace   265
Virtual reality and real world dilemmas   270
Networking and the vulnerability of data   274
Ongoing questions, ongoing issues   275

Concluding Remarks   281

Notes   282
Glossary of Terms   298
Index   308

List of Figures

1.1	Socio-cultural pyramid	16
1.2	Features of hegemony	18
1.3	The advance of media technology	27
2.1	Shannon & Weaver's model (1949)	35
2.2	Two of Wilbur Schramm's models (1954)	37
2.3	Gerbner's model of communication (1956)	39
2.4	Signifier-signified	41
2.5	Front page of *Daily Star*, Monday 24 June 1996	47
2.6	Advertisement for Ellesse watches	49
2.7	British youth, 1977	57
2.8	A semiological model	58
3.1	One-step, two-step, multi-step flow models of communication	72
4.1	'Knowledge is power'	84
4.3	Criteria of public service communication	98
5.1	White's simple gatekeeping model (1950)	108
5.2	McNelly's model of news flow (1959)	110
5.3	Bass's 'double action' model of internal news flow (1969)	111
5.4	McCombs and Shaw's agenda-setting model of media effects (1976)	113
5.5	Rogers and Dearing's model of the agenda-setting process (1988)	114
5.6	Tripolar model of agendas: policy, corporate and media	115
5.7	Galtung and Ruge's model of selective gatekeeping (1965)	117
5.8	Westerståhl and Johansson's model of news factors in foreign news (1994)	125

5.9   Cartoon published in *Index on Censorship*, 3, 1994   127

7.1   The 'communicator arm' of Maletzke's model of the mass
      communication process (1963)   154
7.2   Maletzke's full model of the mass communication process (1963)   157
7.3   Another example of police prejudice   173

8.1   Research as coorientation   201

9.1   Global moguls   215
9.2   The dynamics of public agenda setting   216

Acknowledgements

The author and publishers wish to thank the following for permission to use copyright material:

Addison Wesley Longman Ltd for Figure 3.1 from Sven Windahl and Denis McQuail, *Communication Models for the Study of Mass Communications*, 2nd edn, Longman (1992).

Association for Education in Journalism and Mass Communication for Figure 5.1 from D.M. White, 'The gatekeepers: a case study in the selection of news', *Journalism Quarterly*, **27** (1950); and Figure 5.3 from A.Z. Bass in *Journalism Quarterly*, **46** (1969).

Peter Clarke for Figure 9.1, cartoons of Silvio Berlusconi, Ted Turner and Rupert Murdoch included in *Index on Censorship*, Sept/Oct 1994.

Daily Star for Figure 2.5, front page of the *Daily Star*, 24 June 1996 editon.

Oxford University Press for Figure 5.2 from J.T. McNelly, '"Intermediary" communicators in the international news', *Journal of Communication*, Spring (1976).

Ellesse for the advertisement reproduced in Figure 2.6.

Getty Images for the photograph reproduced in Figure 2.7.

The London Metropolitan Police for the photograph reproduced in Figure 7.3.

Sage Publications Ltd for Figure 5.9 from Jörgen Westerståhl and Folke Johansson, 'Foreign news: news values and ideologies', *European Journal of Communication*, **9**:1 (1994).

Sage Publications Inc for Figure 5.5 from E.M. Rogers and J.W. Dearing, 'Agenda-setting: where has it been, where is it going?' in *Communication Yearbook*, vol. 11, J.A. Anderson ed. (1987).

The University of Chicago Press for Figure 5.4 from McCombs and Shaw, 'Agenda setting model of media effects', *Public Opinion Quarterly,* **36** (1972).

The University of Illinois Press for Figure 2.2 from Wilbur Schramm, *How Communication Works*, W. Schramm ed. (1954); and Figure 2.1 from Shannon and Weaver, *Mathematical Theory of Communication* (1949).

Every effort has been made to trace the copyright holders but if any have been inadvertently overlooked the publishers will be pleased to make the necessary arrangement at the first opportunity.

Introduction

Target readership

The readers I have had in mind while writing this book have been those like my own students, starting out on degrees or other higher education courses in communication, media and cultural studies. Some will already have academic qualifications in media-related subjects. Others will be studying the subject for the first time.

Though some will be straight from school or college, hopefully still academically sharp despite their long lay-off from June till September (where they have been struggling in low-paid jobs for the means to continue their studies), others will be returning to study via access to higher education courses or coming direct from years in the workplace.

All will be eager for the challenge of a subject which has proved immensely popular at all levels of education. Most will be keen to learn new skills such as video and radio production, desk-top publishing or photography. They will readily appreciate that practice needs to be supported by theory, that understanding must guide practice as practice must reinforce theory.

Content

This book provides a detailed overview of the 'study' part of courses in media communication. Throughout my teaching over many years I have urged a first principle in the study of communication, that it can be meaningfully explored and understood only if the contexts in which it takes place are taken into account. In Chapter 1, Setting the Scene: Media in Context, I have attempted to map, albeit briefly, the terrain where media operate.

Increasingly the media have found themselves positioned at the heart of cultural, social, political and economic contexts; and these contexts both influence media performance and are influenced by it. The media are part of trends, responsive to them and often instrumental in publicising, and therefore influencing the direction and extent of such trends.

It is vital to recognise that events have antecedents: they have a history as does the manner in which the media cover those events. Although it has not been within the scope of this volume to investigate historical developments in the media, the importance of these – for further research on the part of the student – is frequently stressed; and this presupposes a view that students of media count among their communication skills competence in research methods.

Terminology: friend not foe

Study itself is situated in contexts, one of which, focused on in Chapter 2, The Language of Study, is that part of the linguistic map which shows signs and symbols; in our case, the terminology (some say jargon) of the subject. Unless the student is familiar with the special terms that have evolved in the study of communication, and then makes it common scholarly practice to discuss, describe and analyse, access to anything more than a superficial 'reading' of media texts, media processes and audience responses to those texts and process will be limited.

At first sight terminology – in any specialist subject – can appear off-putting. Yet familiarity and practice soon prove its usefulness. I have already used one term basic to our studies – *reading*. For the student of communication this means more than a simple exercise in reading words. It may include the reading of advertise-ments, for example, and in the context of such an exercise it implies skills in observation and analysis – of meaning-making – worthy of Sherlock Holmes. Indeed it might be argued that Holmes is not a bad role model for the study of communication (so long, I suppose, as his cocaine habit is overlooked).

The terminology of communication study is catholic and has been imported from a number of disciplines – philosophy, psychology, sociology, cultural studies, political science and linguistics. It permits users to refer to concepts, theories and practices without having to explain them repeatedly, or have them explained, which would be the case if no readily recognisable terms existed.

We may, in discussing the news, refer to *gatekeeping* and *agenda setting*, terms employed to describe complex media processes (see Chapter 5, The News: Gates, Agendas and Values). Their use is as unavoidable, and as necessary, as labelling your possessions, knowing people's names or having a number on your door. Hikers lost on the moors in a fog are more likely to progress to safety if they understand the symbols (the terminology) on the map of the terrain.

The special language of communication offers more than mere signposting. It serves, also, as a framework for the development of understanding and a mechanism for critical analysis. It helps, for instance, to separate out, at least initially, the *denotational* aspects of any text from the *connotational*, the level of description, of identification, from the level of analysis: that is, it prompts us to recognise the difference while at the same time suggesting that in any analysis it is advisable to set the scene (by working at the denotational level) before plunging into the more subjective realms of intepretation (the connotational level). As in all the best academic practices, theory works hand in hand with skills.

In brief, then, the language of study enables us to operate with confidence by reminding us what to look out for, whether we are studying the front pages of the tabloids, advertisements, TV soaps, movies, party political broadcasts or the latest fashions. It enables us probe behind the surfaces of things, to 'unmask' appearances; to spot what isn't said as well as what is – the hidden agendas of mass communication.

Starting with audience

Because the subject of media communication is so vast it is inevitable that media courses will vary in their structure and content. I have tried to take this into account, although most courses will deal with the five basic elements of media:

- *Production:* the processes of message-making; of narratives and representation
- *Texts*
- *Contexts:* social, political, economic; and involving *institutions*
- *Reception*
- *Technology*

Ideally these ought not be studied separately because they are obviously interactive and interdependent, but there is no getting away from the fact that study is inevitably *sequenced* and so is a book on study.

In a sense the study of media communication can be said to resemble a circular building with a number of entrances. You can start with the nature of the medium itself or, as I have done, after presenting a contextual and terminological frame to study, gone through the Audience/Reception entrance (Chapter 3, Audience: the Uses We Make of Media).

This allows us to begin where 'the student is at', for everyone born in this Age of Information is a consumer of media, and has been since childhood. Students do not come to the subject, as they might if they were to take a course in nuclear physics, with little previous knowledge. They arrive with a history of media experience that is part of their own history and that of their family and friends.

It would seem productive to build on this knowledge, experience and awareness; and if motivation were needed, then the pleasure of consumption is likely to stir the necessary interest (after all, there are not many subjects where homework might comprise a visit to the cinema or watching your favourite sitcom on TV).

Another reason for beginning with audience is the shift in emphasis which has taken place over the years in the study of media. At one time the focus was exclusively on the production side of media. Then attention switched to the examination of texts. Then interest moved on to the ways in which audiences deal with media texts.

From being seen as a 'mass', generally consuming messages as they were intended to be consumed – that is, acceptingly – audiences were credited with a degree of independence of thought and judgment. The mass became a composite of individuals with individual needs and responses; and those individuals were members of families, peer groups, work groups, communities; not dupes of media but capable of using media for their own ends; in short, the *active audience*.

Nothing in media, or its study, stands still: reception by audience has to be analysed in relationship to the increased role institutions play in mass communcation – their reach, and their power to influence (an issue I return to in Chapter 9, Ownership and Control: Ongoing Issues).

The communicators and their world

If students are first and foremost consumers of media many of them may also eventually become producers of media and Chapter 4, Media in Society: Purpose and Performance, seeks to identify the functions of media in the community – to inform, educate, entertain, and what else? The media are so prominent in any modern state, and their influence extends far beyond local and national boundaries, that everyone, from presidents and prime ministers to pressure groups concerned about the impact of media on human attitudes and behaviour, insists on having a say in defining the purpose of media.

Essentially the media operate in what is defined as *public space* or the *public sphere*. In fact, in modern times, they arguably embody that space by being 'the voice of the people'. Chapter 4 seeks to examine functions through the public roles which the media cast themselves in, and those which society affirms or questions.

Expectations about these roles are regularly, unavoidably, in conflict, and this conflict is best examined by focusing on how media actually perform: do the tabloids keep us fully informed? Of course in some things they keep us more than fully informed; but in other matters they are curiously silent. The task of the student of media communication is to ask why.

The importance of the News

So far the media scene will have been looked at through a wide-angle lens. We are at the point when we need to switch to the operational level of media production. In Chapter 5, The News: Gates, Agendas and Values, I have set out to examine, in close-up, the processes through which the raw material of news passes on its way to the public, via the press and broadcasting.

The news is important to us because it purports to represent 'the world out there'; its realities. We need only pause for a moment to assess just how much of our knowledge of the world is *mediated* by newspapers, radio and TV. The pictures in our heads are pictures for the most part put there by the media; and our attitudes towards those pictures, our definition of their meaning – our recognition of their reality – owes much to what the media have selected, omitted, shaped and interpreted.

Perhaps more than any other media format, the news claims to represent reality, the way things are; and in that representation there is the underpinning assumption that some of those things represented are the way they should be. That underpinning we call *ideology*, a term defined in Chapter 1, and revisited in Chapter 2.

In our studies we will readily come to recognise the complexity of realities and that the media impose frames or grids upon those realities. They offer 'versions' of reality. In some cases, an active audience reponse may reject the media's definition of reality or at least question it. The student of media soon appreciates that while news may look 'natural', that naturalness is 'constructed'; and such constructs require careful examination.

Telling stories

It is not merely a quaint habit that journalists refer to 'writing stories'. One might say that the world we recognise is made up of stories of one kind or another. It follows that central to the study of communication at any level is exploration of *narrative*. In everything we do or say, in everything we wear, we are narrating a story about ourselves.

From morn till night we are addressed by messages in story form. Stories attempt to sell us washing powder or perfume, cars or holidays. By telling us what we ought to wear or what car we ought to be seen driving, the tales spun by commercials also hint at what we are or what we might become. They often constitute the parables of our time.

Chapter 6, Narrative: the Media as Storytellers, looks at how narrative formats and devices are employed in order to attract and sustain the attention of audience and evoke responses in terms of attitude and behaviour. We react to stories in many ways: they touch us rationally and emotionally. Often they come with sermons built in. They position us culturally, morally and politically.

When we watch TV soaps we may get a strong feeling that we are being preached at: we may be cynical about this, or we may be grateful for the message which is being conveyed. What we can be certain about is that the message is there. This chapter sets out to assist the process of unpicking narrative. It may also provide students with handy hints to guide their own storytelling – news reporting, script writing, storyboarding and the creation of advertisements. *De*construction should, in any media course, be balanced by *con*struction.

Not shooting the messenger

In olden days bringers of bad news often got punished as though they were somehow personally responsible for it. Today we blame the media for many things, in some cases justifiably. Damning the messenger, however, gets us nowhere; attempting to understand the predicament of the journalist, photographer, film maker and broadcaster is, however, necessary – for study but also for those ambitious to work in the media.

Chapter 7, Pressures and Constraints in Media Production, discusses the social, cultural, political, legal and institutional constraints which are part of the day-to-day experience of the media practitioner. Many hazards lie in the path of best practice (assuming, of course, that best practice can be satisfactorily defined). For example, the pursuit of truth may be obstructed by the red light of laws such as, in

Britain, the Official Secrets Act; or a politically sensitive investigation may be halted by those in high places who own or control the means of communication.

Striving after objectivity, balance or impartiality (assuming that these too can be convincingly defined) may also hit buffers institutionally erected. A newspaper whose owner is committed to supporting political Party X is unlikely to encourage journalists wishing to write, without bias (assuming that too can be defined!), about the policies of rival Party Y.

The student as researcher

A practice shared by students and journalists alike is researching and reporting. Their aim is to find things out. The research methods which the student may use to gather information for an essay, project or dissertation will rarely be confined only to books and periodicals. Student researchers will become familiar with many forms of researching – creating and conducting questionnaires and interviewing being prominent among them. Interview skills developed by the student will transfer usefully to skills employed by the journalist.

At the same time much may be learnt from the research methods of media scholars and this is a justification for Chapter 8, In the Wake of Magellan: Research as Exploration. How such researchers have gone about their work investigating aspects of media should provide plenty of ideas for the student researcher. Most importantly, the findings of scholars down the years have shaped and reshaped our understanding of media.

Whether the subject of enquiry has been the role of new technology in the processes of production and reception, the impact of TV on family life or the alleged desensitisation of society by exposure to images of violence, research findings have brought us new insights while at the same time generally cautioning us against rushing to judgment.

Some readers of this book may well become the Ferdinand Magellans of the future. A Portuguese seaman, Magellan (1480–1521) is considered the first to have circumnavigated the globe. His exploit is known to us through the efforts of a voyager of another kind, John of Gutenberg (c.1400–68), who introduced the printing press to Europe around 1450.

Through the printed word Magellan's exploits were celebrated – publicised – for subsequent generations. Today of course, exploration relies less on reading the signs of wind and weather, and more on navigation through computer-mediation systems. The objectives – to find things out, to understand things more thoroughly – are equally vital in an age when the sheer volume of information, the complexity of sources and outlets, can confuse as much as clarify.

The media is always in the news

The media love controversy and are perpetually involved in it. When they sensationalise or pursue dubious methods of enquiry they run the risk of public rebuke. Politicians call for new restraints on the freedom of the press. In turn the media invoke constitutions, written or unwritten, defending the liberty of expression. One set of rights (freedom to speak out) conflicts with another set of rights (the individual privacy of the citizen). In Chapter 9, Ownership and Control: Ongoing Issues I return from the *micro*-level of operations to the *macro*-level of themes, selecting a number of issues at the forefront of concern. These are less to do with what worries the media than with what are defined as 'problems' by commentators on and critics of the media.

For example, the implications for performance of media resulting from corporate and transnational ownership receives little analysis outside of academic literature; yet what has been termed the 'enculturalisation' of society, in harness with its 'consumerisation', is arguably one of the most pressing issues of our time. This is a core theme of Chapter 8 which is intended as a starting-point for further study. There are, of course, issues aplenty. These increase and decrease according to changing circumstances and today's 'burning issues' will in time fade from prominence to be replaced by others.

Questioning media power

Sooner or later every student of media communication will encounter two metaphors used to describe the effects of media on audience – the magic bullet and the hypodermic needle. In one, the message scores a bullseye (end of argument); the second suggests media messages are injected into the accepting arm of the public. In each case, the public is victim.

Both images have the power which emanates from simplicity combined with vividness; and both, at least in media study circles, are regarded as gross oversimplifications. That does not necessarily diminish their currency as ways of expressing 'strong effects' opinions about the media.

Views on the effects of media on audience have on occasion, if not regularly, resembled the swing of a pendulum: the effects are strong, the effects are weak. Close observation and research complicates matters further, suggesting that media power may be strong and weak at the same time, depending on circumstances.

Chapter 10, Prising Open the Black Box: Media Effects Revisited, approaches the nature and extent of media influence upon the perceptions, opinions, attitudes, beliefs, values and behaviour of audience with caution. 'Media Effects? – It All Depends' could be a fitting subtitle of this chapter..

This is not to downsize the substance of effect, merely to admit that the territory abounds in uncertainties. Yet despite these uncertainties, these misgivings, issues of media power have to be addressed by investigation and reinvestigation. The student, as a member of audience, as a practitioner in media production of one sort or another, and as a researcher, is in a good position to compile evidence, examine it, reflect upon it and draw tentative conclusions from it.

Micro-level surveys of audience responses to media can be useful and revealing. Groups of my own students have conducted modest yet often illuminating investigations into many aspects of audience use of media; and not a few of these have run wholly counter to expectations, confirming more discerning, more critical perspectives on the part of audience than are often credited to it.

The view from Cyberspace

Chapter 11, Cyberspace Calling?, also suggests a degree of uncertainty and not just because the future is obviously difficult to predict. After all, technologically speaking, the future is already with us. The doubt springs from that eternal mystery, human behaviour. Such questions as: how have people responded, how do they respond and how will they respond; and in what circumstances have, do and will responses be modified? – these are sufficient to sow seeds of humility in most of us.

Those embarking on media study are advised that doubt is as likely to increase with further learning as diminish. The comfort is that you are better informed about *why* than you were before! The advice is to stay cool: doubting things may not make you happy but as sure as hell beats being made a fool of.

Many exciting visions of present and future have accompanied the giant leap of New Age Communication into Cyberspace. Again, the metaphors have allure: we 'surf' the Internet; we roar, unchecked by speed limits, free from the risk of being pursued by blue lights and screaming sirens, along the 'superhighways' of information.

It is the language of speculation if not of romance which, for the now deeply cynical student of the three Ps, publicity, persuasion and propaganda, inevitably provokes questions about how romantic, how grand, how super cyberactivity really is; and how far realities match up to vision.

In this final chapter I outline contending claims for the Net world and for the growth in numerous forms of that alternative to the 'actual', virtual reality. As part of their own investigation of cyberclaims students will need to examine the nature of the changes in the production, transmission and reception of messages in the light of computer-mediated communication.

They will study the details, the intricacies, of this 'new' mode of instant exchange between individuals sometimes separated by thousands of miles. At the same time they might explore the possibilities for groups, even whole communities of interest, to create new spheres of interaction, free of geographical limits and liberated from reliance on traditional media communication.

As researchers, students will generally have had access to the Internet, the World Wide Web and the myriad other services constantly coming on line. Only by direct experience will they be able to decide what the advantages and disadvantages are of computer-aided 'talk' and whether this supplements, or utterly supplants, the teacher, the classroom, even the college or the campus itself.

Using this book

An introduction to the subject, *Media Communication* anticipates broader and deeper study, using many references which are designed to send the reader out on further explorations. The NOTES at the back of the book, while basically documenting references, also extend points made in the text and can be used to trail more specialist aspects of the field.

As well as an introduction and summary, three features round off each chapter:

1. For recap purposes, a list of KEY TERMS used in the chapter is provided. These can be quickly checked again by looking up the GLOSSARY printed after the Notes.
2. SUGGESTED ACTIVITIES. Modest tasks in research and analysis are proposed here, offering the reader a chance to practice a range of communicative skills appropriate to the study of media.
3. NOW READ ON gives a very brief selection of notable texts which reach out beyond the limits of what has been covered in each chapter and which may prove useful in research for essays, seminar presentations and dissertations.

The occasional use of boxes in the main text serves a number of purposes – to insert supplementary information, explanations or viewpoints; to give prominence to notable quotations and to highlight important definitions. Boxes also help to break up the text, thus making it more manageable. They assist readers by signposting places in the book which they may wish to return to.

Postscript

One of the world's best-known scholars of media, Umberto Eco, writes in the Preface to *Travels in Hyperreality* (translated from the Italian by William Weaver and published in Britain by Picador, 1986), 'I believe it is my job as a scholar and a citizen to show how we are surrounded by "messages", products of political power, of economic power, of the entertainment industry and...to say that we must know how to analyse and criticise them'.

Eco admits that while he is capable of writing learned volumes, 'work that demands time, peace of mind, patience' he also feels compelled in journalism and in teaching to communicate his ideas now rather than later:

> That is why I like to teach, to expound still imperfect ideas and hear the students' reaction. That is why I like to write for the newspapers, to retread myself the next day, and to read the reaction of others.

Eco is declaring that nothing is for sure but that whatever the theory, wholly or only partially formed, it must be subject to regular questioning and that the ideas and opinions of others are vital in the ongoing exploration of meaning. He confesses that this is a difficult game, 'because it does not always consist of being reassured when you meet with agreement and having doubts when you are faced with dissent'.

For Eco 'There is no rule; there is only the risk of contradiction'. Such a point of view may, for the student, compound uncertainty with uncertainty, but it helps define the nature of the study of communication, which is as much about feelings as the working of the intellect, as much about values as knowledge.

Sometimes, Eco argues, 'you have to speak because you feel the moral obligation to say something, not because you have the "scientific" certainty that you are saying it in an unassailable way'. I would venture to suggest that Eco might have added that sooner or later everything boils down to how we *perceive* the world. To this end I shall round off with the comments of a very cynical canary, which I shall place in a box for want of a cage.

In a short story by the 19th-century Brazilian writer Machado de Assis called *A Canary's Ideas*, a man finds a canary in a junk shop and is astonished to discover that the bird can not only talk but speaks with philosophical eloquence.

When the man asks, 'Has your master always been the man sitting over there?' the bird answers reprovingly, 'What master? The man over there is my servant... .' Amazed at the nature of the bird's perception of its existence, the man says, 'But pardon me, what do you think of this world? What is the world to you?'

'The world,' retorts the canary with a certain professional air, 'is a secondhand shop with a small rectangular bamboo cage hanging from a nail. The canary is lord of the cage it lives in and the shop that surrounds it. Beyond that, everything is illusion and deception.'

Acknowledgments

I am indebted to scores of authors, present and past, whose work has helped immensely in my own teaching and writing; to hundreds of students over the years who shared their uncertainties with me; to my colleagues whose friendship and support have kept me human (though I have no evidence they would agree with this) and to my family whose forbearance, like the imagination, has (to date) known no limits.

For transforming my hand-drawn models into printable shape, my thanks go to Barry Feist and Stephen Ellwood, learning support staff at the West Kent College. The resolute interest and extremely helpful advice of my editor, Catherine Gray of Macmillan, are greatly appreciated.

James Watson

1 Setting the Scene: Media in Context

AIMS OF THE CHAPTER

■ To make the case that the study of media communication cannot be isolated from an understanding of wider social, cultural, political and economic contexts.

■ Briefly to describe and explain some of the most significant of these contexts.

■ To explore the idea that social realities are determined by language and those with dominant influence over its public use; and to link communication with notions of power and the ordering of socio-cultural activities.

■ To introduce the concepts of ideology and hegemony and to relate these to four interacting trends in the modern world – rapid advances in media technology, the convergence of ownership and control, the globalisation of media operations and the decline of the public sphere.

This chapter presents an overview of the contexts – cultural and social – in which the media operate. Without a grasp of the influences which have shaped media, study of it at the micro-level – newspapers, films, TV programmes, advertising – is to risk falling into a trap, which the media often do themselves, of portraying realities as though they exist only in the present, disconnected from the past. To see the wood as a whole we must step back from the trees a little. The media as we know them are only the latest in a long line of message systems, beginning with marks on cave walls, the evolution of non-verbal and spoken language and eventually becoming the core activity of communities, societies and nations. Here the role of language as a definer of reality is examined.

Notions of ideology, hegemony and consumerisation are introduced and related to communicative practices and the increasingly dominant part played in modern society by the great corporations; in particular concerning the rivalry between public and private spheres of communication. Also seen as contextual factors are time and space, each subject to transformations by new technologies. Finally, global competition between forces of centralisation and decentralisation, of progress and reaction to progress, are identified as significant trends.

Communication, culture and power

Sometimes we have words for things which continue, regardless, to evade total definition. One of these is 'culture'. Just as the Eskimo has a number of words for 'snow' to fulfil instrumental necessity within a physical context of eternal ice, so we have a number of words and phrases in which 'culture' features. We 'cultivate' the earth and we 'cultivate' relationships.

Societies are said to 'enculturalise', that is cultivate people by various means such as education and persuasion through art and public address to enter, be part of, contributory to, existing cultures.

Occasionally when I ask students to define *socialisation* they give the answer, 'It's going out with your friends and enjoying yourself'. This is, of course, 'socialising'; but it is certainly a feature of most cultures. It is a useful mistake, helping us to mark the difference: socialisation is generally what other people do to us – shaping us to fit into society; while socialising is what we do for ourselves.

Such behaviour is acceptable and encouraged, so long as it is not considered *antisocial*. In which case, society may take action to bring us 'back into line'. As we shall see, the media are prominent among the public arbiters of our behaviour. They, as it were, 'speak society's lines', claiming for themselves the role of a community's conscience as well as performing as its ever-vigilant guard dog. At this early stage, we may view them as an agency of order.

To varying degrees, all societies enculturalise those who belong in them with social *values* out of which have sprung, perhaps over centuries, *norms* or rules, some written and clear-cut, others inferred rather than being explicit, all pointing in the direction of expected patterns of behaviour. Language is the primary means by which the values, norms and acceptable/not acceptable patterns of society are formed, expressed and reinforced. Also, it is the primary means of defining our realities.

Krishan Kumar, in his chapter 'Sociology' in *Exploring Reality*,[1] writes that 'in using language, or other kinds of signs such as gestures, we impose a sort of grid on reality. Since language and other symbolic systems are social products, this is a socially constructed grid. So our reality is a social reality'.

Kumar continues:

> A physical gesture such as a raised hand can be a threat or a greeting. We have no way of knowing which, unless we have learned to understand the place such a 'sign' has in the culture of the person or people concerned. Until we know that – and it could be fairly important that we know it fast – the gesture remains literally empty, devoid of all meaning or significance. Language places it and gives it

meaning. Without a word to describe a thing, it remains unintelligible – to all intents and purposes, non-existent.

It follows that those whose words – and therefore definitions – can effectively reach the largest number of people have the greatest potential to define what is what; to say *this* is reality, to declare *this* is how things are or how they must be. The media, of course, along with other social agencies such as the family and education, are at the centre of this process, influenced by, and influencing, the others.

When the former British Prime Minister Margaret Thatcher made her historic remark that there 'is no such thing as society, only individuals and their families' she was, some critics argued, using language in an Orwellian sense: Winston Smith, George Orwell's hero in the novel *Nineteen Eighty-Four* (1949), is employed in the Ministry of Truth. His job is to slim down the language so that meaningful words, once removed from the nation's vocabulary, would also remove that which was meant. Thus the word 'free' was retained – in what Orwell appropriately terms 'newspeak' – only in the sense of 'this dog is free from lice'.

Commonality and difference

For the moment let us put our trust in the existence of society, however difficult it might be to define. Society speaks of itself, acquires a sense of *commonality* (of things shared) through its culture – its language, laws and customs, geography, history, technology and even the weather. Without commonality, and the means to sustain that commonality, a society may fall apart.

What holds together the many disparate and often conflicting parts of a society is communication. It has the power to unite, to forge the spirit of union, of belonging in community and nation. Equally communication can serve as an instrument of demarcation between individuals and communities. National anthems exist to remind us that their purpose is to unite 'us' in the face of 'them', whether this is on the field of battle or on the field of sport.

Students of media communication will be well aware that in wartime the media generally urge national cohesion and speak with a united voice (against the enemy). They are responsible for trying to sustain the 'feel-good factor'. In peacetime, however, conflict 'within' – between rival political parties, between employers and workers, between religions, between majorities and minorities – may often rule the headlines.

All too often language is used as a weapon that widens divisions, nurtures alienation, provokes social, ethnic or racial hatreds. While communication may be a path to the truth it can also be used to obscure it. What is beyond debate is that communication has 'power value': it has long been classified as a *form* of power which those who possess power seek to control and those who do not possess power seek to acquire.

Communication has the power to define, persuade, inform and to disinform. An analysis of communication at the level of community and nation is obliged to recognise that truth is not necessarily separated from falsehood; rather, the process of *propaganda* blurs the elements in order to be persuasive.

The capacity of words and images to be distorted, bent to purposes which have have little or no connection with the truth, is seemingly limitless. We are aware of this. 'Economising with the truth' (that is, using language to conceal rather than reveal) is such a common practice in everyday life that plain honest speaking often comes as a shock. It is advisable, therefore, in our response to the use of language for us to assess the 'truthworthiness' of the source as well as the content and form of the message.

In *Munitions of the Mind: A History of Propaganda From the Ancient World to the Present Day*,[2] Philip M. Taylor puts the matter succinctly:

> Communication with a view to persuasion is an inherent human quality. It can take place in a private conversation or a mass rally, in a church or cinema, as well as on a battlefield. It can manifest itself in the form of a statue or a building, a coin or a painting, a flag or a postage stamp.

To the above list Taylor adds 'speech, sermons, songs, art, radio waves, television pictures'. Whether they operate between individuals or people in millions, the task of the analyst remains the same – to investigate the *intent* of the act of communication and the ways in which members of the intended audience respond to that communication.

It is arguable that most mass communication, whether it is a party political broadcast, the TV news, a pop song, a soap opera or sitcom is in some way or another, to a greater or lesser extent, an exercise in propaganda (of preaching, if you like). Taylor writes:

> Propaganda uses communication to convey a message, an idea, an ideology [see later in the chapter for definitions of ideology] that is designed primarily to serve the self-interests of the person or people doing the communicating.

As we shall see in Chapter 3, this does not necessarily mean that those who receive messages, propaganda or otherwise, actually welcome the communication, believe it or accept it: they have their own self-interests, their own values. No enculturalisation is irresistible.

Power forms in society

Whatever aspects of culture we explore we invariably return to questions concerning the nature and exercise of power, for power makes things change, or prevents things changing. Whether defined as the ability to make decisions and to have those decisions carried out, to influence hearts and minds, to alter states of being or simply to hire and fire workers, power is the key factor in the dynamics of any culture.

In *The Media and Modernity: A Social Theory of the Media*,[3] John B. Thompson identifies four forms of power exercised in society – ecomomic, political, coercive and symbolic. Economic power emanates from the possession of wealth or the means by which wealth is generated; political power rests in decision-making arising from being in a position of elected, appointed or inherited authority; coercive power springs from the use of, or potential use of, superior strength. Invasion of one country by another is an example of coercive power. Symbolic power works through images (linguistic, pictorial, aural) to create and mobilise support for a cause and it is integral to the operation of the other power forms.

Other classifications include *position*, *resource* and *charismatic* (or personality) power, each overlapping with Thompson's categories and each one somehow connected with communication processes. A case can be made for recognising *technological* power, what Karl Marx referred to as the *means of production*, as a category in its own right. John of Gutenberg's invention of the printing press in around 1450 was not substantially the result of either economic or political imperatives, but it soon proved to be a winner economically. Politically and culturally it brought about profound and far-reaching changes.

By symbolising knowledge as something potentially accessible to all and rendering the act of reading an exercise in individualism and a possible source of subversion, printing transformed the known world by becoming 'a power in the land'. In easily reproducible, and permanent form, it spread knowledge and ideas beyond the traditional boundary fence of the privileged to the 'common people'. In doing so, it offered them glimpses (and sometimes visions) of their own potential power.

Yet the media have never been either separate from or independent of the forces which create them and which in turn they shape and influence. They work, as Thompson points out, within institutional frameworks. As such they operate as forms of *cultural apparatus*, part of the machinery of state or of powerful interest groups within the state. Historically the media have more often served as the voice of the powerful than of the people. They have been classified by the French philosopher Louis Althusser[4] as one of the prime ISAs, *Ideological State Apparatuses*, along with religion, family structures and education: that is, they are crucially important channels for the transmission of 'rules of conduct' in society; the guardians of a culture's dominant norms and values. They play a part in all power forms, including – in a contributory sense – coercive power.

Coercion, the exercise of power by force, manifests itself through what Althusser terms RSAs, *Repressive State Apparatuses* – army, police, prisons. It is never physically absent but it is in the main culturally concealed. Its visible and tangible presence depends on whether the other power forms are considered to be under threat. In wartime, of course, coercive power moves from the back region to the front region of our lives; and at no other time is symbolic power exercised by the media so graphically, so blatantly or so persuasively.

The media in time of war – with exceptions – become the trumpeters of conflict with the enemy. They do not fire the guns but their clamour for the guns to be fired is an essential part of the process of gathering the people's support for the war effort. ISAs and RSAs conflate, become one and the media speak with a single voice; their task, to create consensus and unity at home, to identify and target the enemy; their role, that of mobilisers of opinion, boosters of national morale.

Culture and hierarchy

Cultures have the capacity for nurturing social equality but their most familiar structural pattern is hierarchical. Figure 1.1 portrays a pyramid structure divided according to social class. Traditionally those at the top of the socio-cultural pyramid have more money, more property and in theory more (or better) education than those classes below them. As a result, they have privileged access to information and knowledge; and to the means by which that information and knowledge is transmitted.

Those at the pinnacle of hierarchy possess what has been termed *cultural capital* by the French philosper Pierre Bourdieu in *Distinction: A Social Critique of the Judgment of Taste*.[5] This, like cash in the bank, or property, is a means of obtaining credit. Cultural capital can take the form of education, knowledge of history and the arts, awareness of conduct and tastes which can be of socio-cultural benefit. Bourdieu talks of 'an economy of social goods' governed by a hierarchy of taste. Cultural capital is a form of property which serves to differentiate between those who possess it and those who do not.

Put quite simply, a child whose home is full of books, its walls hung with pictures of the great masters of art, possesses cultural capital. This may in future 'open doors' which may be shut to others less fortunate. In this sense, culture is an agent of selection, of demarcation, an instrument of inequality. Wealthy (and sometimes not-so-wealthy) parents 'purchase' the cultural capital of a fee-charging education because it is perceived to constitute an *investment* which will eventually accrue *profit*.

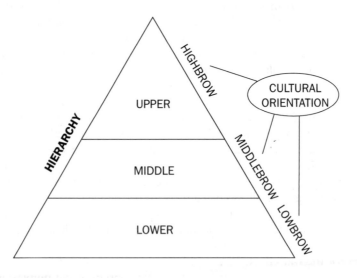

Figure 1.1   Socio-cultural pyramid

Hierarchies of taste

In the past a nation's internal conflicts have largely arisen out of religious and class differences and concerned the unequal distribution of rights and resources. Such conflicts can be viewed as clashes over *value*, between commonality and hierarchy, the one emphasising that which binds – the sharing, the other that which distinguishes by division. In the language of marketing and advertising, this process is called *segmentation*, dividing people according to their actual or potential purchasing habits.

Hierarchy is a dominant feature of most societies not only in terms of the power to command others but in matters of taste and conduct as the notion of cultural capital indicates. For example, the expressions *highbrow*, *middlebrow* and *lowbrow* shown in Figure 1.1 imply, and seem to replicate, social and educational division. Culture is commandeered by structure.

Traditionally, for those privileged people near the top of the hierarchy, culture has been embodied in fine paintings or classical music. For those at the base of the hierarchy there is the kind of TV programme which the Pilkington Committee Report on Broadcasting[6] so deplored, characterised – in Pilkington's judgment – by triviality; or what George Orwell termed 'prolefeed'.

Culture can be seen to have been redefined – appropriated – in order to serve the perceptions of a dominant order. The 1962 Pilkington Report on British TV is of interest to us now not because of the reliability of its judgment but because of the way it reveals the *stratification* of culture along lines of class difference. It interests the student of media because of the assumptions underlying the Committee's judgments: popular meant trivial; trivial meant 'bad' or inferior.

Today things are much more fluid: academics in universities across the globe now dedicate their working lives to the study of this 'trivia'. There must be almost as many academic tomes analysing the significance of soaps, sitcoms, comics and other manifestations of 'popular culture' as there are volumes on the highbrow culture represented by Shakespeare or Mozart.

HISTORY: THE PROPAGANDA OF THE PRIVILEGED?

History automatically discarded everything that smelled of the people. History books told us about how the rich dressed, what they ate, their taste in music, and how they organised their homes.

All they told about the poor was their stupidity, uprisings, exploitations and revolts.

Jésus Martín-Barbero, *Communication, Culture and Hegemony: From the Media to Mediations*
(UK: Sage, 1993)

Social class continues to be an important component of hierarchy, but if the opinions of today's advertisers are a useful indicator, our 'class' is more flexibly defined by our lifestyle, or the lifestyle we aspire to, and of course the occupation that provides us with our spending power.

Hegemony: an overview

Discussion of cultural apparatuses, the shaping of norms and values and the forging of consensus brings us to one of the most important concepts in the theory of culture and the exercise of power. For most people, life can be lived quite happily and fulfillingly without their ever having the slightest idea what *hegemony* might mean. Yet the word, and what the word stands for, what it attempts to explain, is critical to the study of culture, communication, history, anthropology, sociology, politics and economics.

In its simplest sense, hegemony means 'control over'; yet in referring to 'hegemonic control' we are not repeating the same thing using another phrase, but describing a special *form* of control, one based not upon coercion or force, but resulting from successful persuasion or enculturalisation. Hegemony is working when there is general consensus, that is when the mass of the population (or most of it) accepts the controlling influence and decision-making of that part of society termed, by the American writer C. Wright Mills,[7] the *Power Elite* – those members of a community who hold or influence the holding of the reins of power.

Hegemony is rule by won consent. Of all the agencies of hegemonic control the media are generally perceived to be the most powerful, hence the requirement for the Power Elite to exert pressure if not control over the media: better still, to own it.

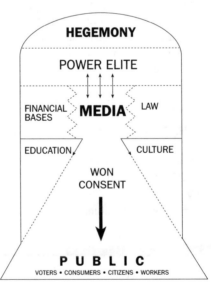

Figure 1.2   Features of hegemony

Hegemony works through ideological state apparatuses (education, the church, the arts, media) and operates best when those apparatuses are speaking in harmony with one another.

We attribute the theory of hegemony to the Italian philosopher Antonio Gramsci (1899–1937) who argued that a state of hegemony is achieved when a provisional alliance of certain groups exerts a consensus which makes the power of the dominant group appear natural and legitimate.[8] It can only be sustained by the won consent of the dominated.

Hegemony works most smoothly when there is a substantial degree of social, economic, political and cultural security in a society. When security is undermined, social division rampant, hegemony is at risk and Althusser's repressive state apparatuses are brought into action. Hegemony serves to provide the Power Elite with the consent of the ruled. A conjectural model of the constituents of hegemony is illustrated in Figure 1.2.

Hegemonies differ at different times and in different circumstances, but what is common to all of them is the governing influence of *ideology*, the public expression of what in personal terms we describe as values. This is an appropriate moment, then, to cite a few opinions on ideology which, in one form or another, underpins and sustains the exercise of hegemony.

IDEOLOGY

- Karl Marx (1818–83) believed that the term applied to any form of thought which underpins the social structure of a society; in other words, ideology is a social construct. Further, Marx believed that ideology upholds the position of the ruling classes, that is, the *status quo*.

- V.L. Allen in *Social Analysis: A Marxist Critique and Alternative*[9] writes that 'ideology is a process through which ideas, values and purposes act to influence behaviour... therefore it is present in all societies at all times'.

- Alan O'Connor in 'Culture and communication' in *Questioning the Media: A Critical Introduction*[10] says ideology is 'both as seemingly natural and as basic as the cement that holds everything together'.

- Gregory McLennan in *The Power of Ideology*[11] suggests three conditions for the operation of ideology in society:

  1. that ideas and beliefs must be *shared* by a significant number of people

  2. that the ideology must underpin some form of coherent *system*

  3. that ideology must connect in some way to *power* and its use in society

Ideology, then, is ever present; and every power form is suffused by it. From a position of dominance it is impatient of competitors. It provides the conceptual 'cement' which upholds the structures of the powerful, defends their interests and is instrumental in helping to preserve the *status quo* – the way things are; they way they are ordered.

Rival hegemonies

On a world scale, the 20th century has witnessed two giant hegemonic systems eyeballing one another – capitalism versus communism; and no event has had a more powerful impact on the structures, attitudes and practices of hegemony on both sides of the ideological fence than the ending of the Cold War.

No historical occurrence has obliged the media to rewrite their stories so fundamentally. For generations since the partition of Germany following the Second World War (1939–45) and the building of the Berlin Wall, the portrait of history showed two mighty warriors, sparring yet never actually exchanging blows directly.

These were, to oversimplify for a moment to the point of being defamatory, the West (the Good Guys of Western mythology) and the East, the Soviet Union and its Iron Curtain satellites (the Bad Guys); the Land of the Free (America) versus the 'Evil Empire' (President Reagan's description of Russia).

From this stand to, this ideological confrontation backed by nuclear arsenals capable of destroying Mother Earth a thousand times over, emanated cultural, political, economic and geographical forces which shaped world society. The risks to survival were colossal, as we were endlessly warned by the media in their role as sentinels and guard dogs of the Western way of life.

What the world witnessed were two ideologies, so dramatically different in principle and practice they would chance the termination of life on earth rather than suffer compromise. Yet so long as the confrontation between the ideologies of capitalism and communism remained a cold rather than a hot war, the phenomenon of Us and Them proved a political convenience and even a comfort. In a world so neatly divided, people knew which side they were on and so big was the divide that other divisions – cultural or ethnic – were often obscured.

When we peered across the ideological gulf between West and East we saw only Russians, some saw Reds; we did not spy Estonians, Azerbaijanis, Latvians, Georgians or Chechens. We ignored the fact, or were unaware of it, that Russia was an amalgam of many nations, many races, many languages; indeed the most multicultural society on earth: communism had recognised no colour but red, no religion but Marxism, no gods but Lenin.

Then came Glasnost.[12] The Iron Curtain turned to velvet. The Berlin Wall was dismantled. With the end of the Cold War surely the global order would be characterised from now on by peace, serenity and cooperation? Alas, no. The old order melted away, but it melted into turbulences which were not new but reactivations of supressed conflicts, many of them ethnic in nature.

The modern face of hegemony

For the most part we expect the powerful institutions in society – the commercial, industrial and media corporations – to subscribe to and support the hegemonic 'alliance'; though evidence of such an alliance is rarely made publicly explicit. That is part of its strength. What *is* made publicly explicit is that institutions support – sponsor – features of the cultural scene, such as sport, the arts and entertainment, which confer prestige by assocation and in doing so nurture public approval.

At the same time it might be claimed that sport, the arts and entertainment have consequently become instrumental in sustaining the hegemonic process. The 1996 Olympics in Atlanta were emblazoned less with golden moments of sporting excellence (though Georgia had its fair share of these, in spite of the bomb) than with the logos of Coca-Cola, McDonalds, Nike and Reebok.

Also, there were numerous criticisms of the American media whose concentration on the exploits of their own athletes, to the neglect of those of other nations, was deemed to be selective negligence of an 'unsporting' nature. It could also be seen as evidence of hegemony at work on a world scale, with the American media defining their country as the power elite among nations.

Todd Gitlin in a chapter in *Television: The Critical View*, edited by Horace Newcomb[13] argues that in liberal capitalism 'hegemonic ideology develops by domesticating opposition, absorbing it into forms compatible with the core ideological structure. Consent is managed by absorption as well as exclusion'.

He adds, crucially, that hegemony survives because its ideology is flexible: 'The hegemonic ideology changes in order to remain hegemonic; that is the particular nature of the dominant ideology of liberal capitalism.' Having stressed that the hegemonic system is 'not cut-and-dried, not definitive', Gitlin offers us a portrait of hegemony in its current state:

> In the twentieth century, the dominant ideology has shifted toward sanctifying consumer satisfaction as the premium definition of 'the pursuit of happiness', in this way justifying corporate domination of the economy. What is hegemonic in consumer capitalist ideology is precisely the notion that happiness, or liberty, or equality, or fraternity can be affirmed through the existing private commodity forms, under the benign, protective eye of the national security state.

Before moving on, let us be clear what Gitlin is saying here. First, he is defining hegemonic practice within the framework of capitalism. Happiness is defined as pleasure through spending (as contrasted, say, with *saving*). Because the great corporations are so central to the provision of this happiness, what has become an indisputable fact – their dominance of national and international economies – has come to be presented as, and largely accepted as, the natural order of things. Their propaganda dwells centrally in consumer satisfaction, aided and abetted by the magic wand of advertising.

The latest commercials from Renault, Castlemaine XXXX, British Airways or Pepsi-Cola are as familiar to us – to the entire population and beyond – as is the Lord's Prayer. Some might even claim that they were its substitute, a religion of pleasure through spending. Yet Gitlin sees rather more than pleasure on the supermarket shelf of the corporations: liberty, equality and fraternity, features of human existence not traditionally associated with getting and spending, are also for sale.

Or rather such qualities are *commodified*; presented in symbolic forms and promoted in commercial terms. By ensuring consumer choice, capitalism has made possible the *liberty* to chose. By bringing down prices in the marketplace, the corporations faciliate equality of opportunity.

By abolishing the deprivations which split society, the corporations hasten, if not entirely achieve, fraternity among individuals and nations. This is not to say that there are no exclusions. Indeed, as will be noted in Chapter 9, the rosy picture painted by the commercials is only seriously intended for a minority of the world's population.

Culture incorporated

As Gitlin makes clear, in the modern world hegemony's greatest institutional exponents and its staunchest defenders are the national and transnational corporations. At the same time they are the most powerful modifiers of hegemony, shaping it to their own needs – their own *intents* – to the point of having state governments, as it were, in their pockets.

It is difficult to avoid corporate involvement in our lives. We study in organisations and we work for them. Potentially they control the water we drink, the food we eat, the clothes we wear, the music we listen to, the sports we watch and the information we rely on.

Corporations dominate the visual landscape of our cities: their skyscraper office blocks remind us, symbolically, of the awesome presence of powers which can be exerted beyond the ballot box and beyond national boundaries. We refer to Captains of Industry and sometimes to Princes, just as we talk about 'Press Barons' and 'Media Moguls'.

Unlike individuals, a corporation does not require a passport to travel the world. It does not require permission to transfer manufacture from one part of the globe to another, bringing fresh employment opportunities to the new, leaving unemployment in the old. At least, we might say, corporations still do not have the vote; but they do have what Herbert Schiller in *Culture Inc. The Corporate Takeover of Public Expression*[14] calls a 'para-electoral' power; a 'factor which has accounted for the essential features and direction of the times' – far more, in fact, than the styles of the American political parties.

Schiller writes:

> This deep and underlying element, long predating the Second World War but becoming more pronounced after it, has been the phenomenal growth and expanding influence of the private business corporation. Through all the political and social changes of the last fifty years, the private corporate sector in the American economy has widened its economic, political, and cultural role in domestic and international activities.

Schiller argues that the rise and rise of corporations has been matched by the decline in the power of – in the case of America – independent farmers, organised labour and a strong urban consciousness.

From our point of view as observers of the media scene, we note the dramatic extent to which transnational corporations have absorbed into their business porfolios newspapers, film companies, advertising agencies, radio and TV stations, music publishers, telecommunication systems, news agencies – you name it, they've got it!

Also, by means of sponsorship, the great corporations promote their name through 'good works', helping to finance libraries, universities, museums, art galleries, orchestras, festivals (on the condition that nothing damages the corporate image of the sponsor).

Before we conclude that we have reached, as it were, the 'end of history' with the arrival of transnational control over cultures local, national and global, acknowledgment needs to be made that Schiller's vision has met with serious criticism. The *appropriation* of culture which Schiller discusses is viewed as also appropriating the hearts and minds of the consumers of culture. Many commentators argue that the public is also capable of appropriating culture, not for corporate purposes: audiences are active, not docile.

APPROPRIATING VELASQUEZ

An exhibition, *Velasquez in Seville*, mounted by the National Gallery of Scotland during the annual Edinburgh Festival was subjected to a strongly worded complaint by *Guardian* critic Adrian Searle[15] for the way the Spanish artist and his work had been 'shopped' as the review's headline declared.

Searle protests about the *consumerisation* of the artist. He writes, 'Decked on the temporary ticket stand... is a Fortnum and Mason's style display of Velasquezabilia: jars of Velasquez-label designer marmalade, set about with fresh oranges in wicker baskets; Velasquez fridge magnets; Velaquez own-brand Spanish plonk and kitchen aprons; Velasquez artisanal brown jugs and nests of rustic ceramic bowls (just like in the paintings!); and for all I know (I was reeling by this time) Velasquez-flavoured novelty condoms'.

Searle's complain is not merely about the consumerisation of culture. The emphasis on things – the still life objects Velasquez painted, and which commerce can produce in profitable numbers – evades the point. It reduces Velasquez to a painter of objects, whereas he was essentially 'a painter of people, of the opacity of living subjects' and his skill 'with the texture of things is engaged in order to focus on the texture of precisely what we cannot fathom – the interaction of his living subjects and the spaces between them'.

John B. Thompson is one of those who challenges Schiller's reading of the world scene, questioning his assumptions about American cultural triumphalism. In the 'sphere of information and communication as well as in the domain of economic activity,' argues Thompson in *The Media and Modernity*,[3] 'the global patterns and relations of power do not fit neatly into the framework of unrivalled American dominance'.

New power orientations

The bases of economic and industrial power, Thompson points out, are shifting eastwards to the nations of the Pacific basin, the so-called Tiger economies. As if to symbolise this challenge to traditional American dominance, Malaysia in 1996, not content with boasting the tallest building in the world, Petronas Towers, commissioned the longest, the £1.3 billion Giga World, a mile and a half of offices, theatres and malls complete with monorail, and standing on stilts above the Klang river. American hegemony watch out!

Thompson also queries Schiller's views on the way American culture 'colonises' the cultures of other countries, thus tending to pollute and displace indigenous cultures. The assumption is that such cultures were pure and unadulterated at some recent point in history. Thompson describes this as 'a somewhat romantic view which, in many cases, does not stand up to careful scrutiny':

> The issues addressed by Schiller should be placed... in a much broader historical perspective. Rather than assuming that prior to the importation of Western TV programmes and so on, many Third World countries had indigenous traditions and cultural heritages which were largely unaffected by external pressures, we should see instead that the globalisation of communication through electronic media is only the most recent of a series of cultural encounters, in some cases stretching back many centuries, through which values, beliefs and symbolic forms of different groups have been superimposed on one another, often in conjunction with the use of coercive, political and economic power.

In Schiller's defence it might be argued that while TV may be only the latest in a long line of weapons of cultural imperialism, its global penetration exceeds all previous forms of communication. Even so, Thompson maintains, the media-imperialist position underestimates the power of audiences to make their own meanings from what they read, listen to or watch. 'Through the localised process of appropriation,' Thompson believes, 'media products are embedded in sets of practices which shape and alter their significance.'

Current world trends in media communication

One of the changes brought about by the advance of consumerism as a central public value has been the abolition of Sundays; or to be more precise, the transformation of Sunday into just another day of the week. This was good news for many, especially the supermarket chains, but perhaps less good for those who – having had a sacrosanct 'day of rest' – came under pressure to work on it.

Naturally a legal right was established for a shop worker to refuse to work on Sundays; yet in an age of persistent unemployment and competition for jobs who could legislate against the employer who says to his Sunday abstainer, 'If you won't work Sundays, I know somebody who will'? The point here concerns time. This, like space itself, seems to have been appropriated – that word again – by a partnership of technology and commerce.

In many industrialised societies people work longer hours than they did twenty years ago. Curious this, when that magnificent piece of work-saving technology, the computer, releases us from so much repetitive and time-consuming drudgery. Or does it? The computer processes information so rapidly that it 'makes' time and having made it, stands idle unless given more work to do – by humans.

The more powerful the computer, the more work it can do. The more work it can do, the more it demands. It is, therefore, a 'make-work' piece of technology because until it ceases to require human labour to feed it data, the computer will always be capable of standing idle, with its mouth open ready for more. The faster the computer works, the faster people have to work to keep up with it.

But not all the people. While the computer makes more and more work for some it does away with the jobs of others. It creates two parallel forms of time – one for those in employment, a time which even the stopwatch often has difficulty keeping up with, and the time for those whose lives are slowed to a snail's pace in queues at the Social Security office.

No industry has been more speeded up or more slimmed down than newspaper publishing. Technology in the form of Frederick Koenig's steam press, installed at the London *Times* in 1814, followed by a host of new inventions to accelerate the manufacture of paper for printing, the composition of type and to multiply the number of newspaper copies that could be printed per hour, helped shape the contexts of the 19th century. Information, along with cotton, coal, steel and ship-building, became big business.

Time, of course, did not speed up, but what could be done within a span of time did, particularly with the coming of telegraphy in the 1840s and 50s. This all seems old hat now for we tend to think of telegraphy as one of those technological curios to be located in the boot sale of history along with steam trains and clattery typewriters. But pause for a moment: telegraphy changed the world; it both altered time and conquered space and we are still living through the legacy of that achievement.

Prior to telegraphy, communication, unless it was between people in direct contact with one another, was reliant on transportation. It is significant that in the early days of the British Associated Examining Board's A Level in Communication Studies there were questions on the exam paper dealing with transport as communication.

Telegraphy (and later telephony in the 1870s) demolished distance as a 'barrier' to communication. As far as the passing on of information was concerned it no longer mattered how far away London was from New York or Sydney. Telegraphy made it possible to ignore time zones. This had far-reaching effects upon the world of commerce, colonialism and a whole array of ways of doing things.

Further, as James W. Carey argues,[16] the telegraphic facility became 'an agency for the alteration of ideas'.

Cultural impact

Paradoxically, while re-defining time and distance, telegraphy also placed distance between people. In the past, business had been conducted face to face. Carey writes that with the coming of telegraphy 'the volume and speed of transactions demanded a new form of organisation of essentially impersonal relations – that is, relations not among known persons but among buyers and sellers whose only relation was mediated through an organisation and a structure of management'.

A second ideological feature given emphasis by telegraphy and the miracle of electricity concerns the notion of unity, of communities being brought closer by instant transmission and receipt of information, a concept turned into the headline phrase 'global village' by Marshall McLuhan, yet even earlier summarised in verse by Martin F. Typper in 1875:[17]

> Yes, this electric chain from East to West
> More than mere metal, more than mammon can
> Binds us together – kinsmen, in the best,
> As most affectionate and frankest bond;
> Brethren as one; and looking far beyond
> The world in an Electric Union blest!

Also arising out of this electronic union were implications for the *control* of time which in turn was to serve as social and linguistic control. Telegraphy facilitated control by making it possible to impose a technology-made grid on time. Admittedly this was a grid which could not switch day into night, could not prevent people down under being abed when people on the other side of the globe were up and ready for business, but it made systems of global communication possible. It clarified the prospect of time being a commodity as much as space. As Carey says, 'The control of time allows for the coordination of activity and, therefore, effective social control'. Sundays, one might say, don't live here any more.

Convergences

I began this chapter by sketching in the crucial role of language as a delineator of context. Technology in the form of telegraphy had a profound impact on the use of language and the knowledge which that language transmitted. James Carey writes that the wire services demanded 'a form of language stripped of the local, the regional, and colloquial... something closer to a "scientific" language' and under '"rigid control"'.

Suddenly words were time and time was money. The telegraph created modern journalism and indeed influenced other forms of writing. The novelist Ernest Hemingway confessed the influence of *telegraphese* on his own style, calling it 'the lingo of the cable'. Today, the nature of transmitted language is even more subject to mediation by the advance of computer digitalisation by which all data – words, images and sound – is broken down into 0-1 codes. This technological convergence (or coming together) is paralleled by another convergence witnessed in recent years, that of the concentration of the ownership and control of mass communication.

Although the style of that which was transmitted by telegraph used words economically, and thus represented a step towards simpler, more direct communication, it is another story when the *number* of those transmissions is considered. Telegraphy was the first direct highway of information. If we could think of the transformation the telegraph brought about in terms of traffic it would have been like stepping from a country cart track into a ten-lane motorway at rush-hour; rush-hour being every hour of every day.

Practically every technological change in the field of communications has had what one might describe as a hands-around-the-globe effect. Computers, by operating digitially, have overridden the differences of national languages. Cables and satellite are networked with computers to cross national boundaries. What were originally separate communication systems – telecommunications and broadcasting – have converged along the same fibre-optic wires to offer multiple services. The same box of tricks can offer us telephonic, televisual, computing, games-playing facilities, each of them linked to a wired world which advocates of the new technologies claim will be limitless in scope (see Figure 1.3).

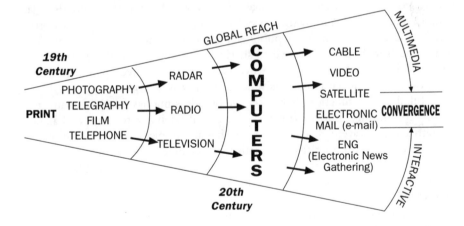

Figure 1.3   The advance of media technology. In 1450 Gutenberg introduced the printing press to Europe. Media technology was slow to diversify until the 19th century. Steam power and then electric power accelerated the number and extent of media forms. With the development of computers in the period following the Second World War technological convergence was made possible. The 1990s saw this process dramatically speeded up with transformations brought about by digitalisation. Technological convergence has been matched, worldwide, by convergence in terms of ownership and control.

We are heading for the 'One-Button' culture. You want pornography? – what machinery is there to censor it when such programmes come in from space? (For a few words about the V-chip, the 'spy in the TV', see Note 18.) You want Sumo wrestling direct from Japan or the latest news of Wall Street's Dow-Jones Index? You want to order a pizza from around the corner? – activate the mouse.

Such developments are largely initiated and operated by the global corporations mentioned earlier who are inscribing on world geography new kinds of 'territoryless' boundaries, one being *access* and the other *control*. These developments need to be viewed in the light of what has been happening to more traditional forms of communications access and control.

The decline of public service broadcasting

During the 1980s and 90s in the Western world public service communication, in particular, broadcasting, has been under siege. The principle of PSB – Public Service Broadcasting – has been challenged by private sector interests; and in practice the beseigers have everywhere subverted if not destroyed the walls of what has by generally common consent the closest formulation to a *public sphere* in the history of communication.

Since the 1920s in Britain PSB has been a central feature of public life, first wholly represented by the BBC and later taking the form of a duopoly with the Independent Broadcasting Authority. The key to both these public services has been – *service*. Even when commercial TV was launched in Britain in 1955 (in America commercial stations had been running since 1941), the goal of profit was balanced by principles of public service empowered by regulation. As a nation the British have been used to sharing, via radio or TV, the great cultural and sporting events which – however tenuously, however patchily – have contributed to their sense of cohesiveness, of unity as a people.

In fulfilling this function, public service broadcasting has provided many gifts to the community, informational and cultural, striving to achieve balance, breadth and innovation. The private sector has also to please audiences, and often does so without the sacrifice of quality. Nevertheless the prime objective of private sector mass communication is profit. If service is profitable then the private sector will provide it; if it is not, the imperatives of the marketplace must be responded to.

As with reporting on the visions held by some authors concerning enculturalisation of society by the transnationals, a cautionary word needs to be added here that PSB is far from one-and-the-same thing as the public sphere. Indeed Hans Verstraeten in a *European Journal of Commmunication* article, 'The media and the transformation of the public sphere'[19] warns that:

> the concept of the 'public sphere'... should on no account be confused with the statute of public broadcasting... . On the contrary, the brief history of Western European public broadcasting supplies us with numerous examples of how public broadcasting companies in political reality contributed to the control of the public sphere rather than its dynamic expansion.

True; and if we identify features of the public sphere as being full public access to the means of communication, as providing meaningful forums of debate, of rational discussion, of a plurality of ideas and standpoints, and perhaps most importantly the systematic opportunity to scrutinise and criticise government policies, then PSB has often fallen short of the ideal. But supporters of PSB argue that it is all we have got; and its demise would leave the public sphere entirely at the mercy of private enterprise.

The debate about public versus private is prominent and ongoing and highlights serious differences of opinion – of ideology – about the functions, role and performance of mass communication. Throughout the Thatcher and Major years in Britain, and in the United States during the presidencies of Ronald Reagan, George Bush and even Democrat president Bill Clinton, the private has been esteemed and privileged over the public, the one triumphal, the other in retreat; hence the dominant trends of deregulation and privatisation.

New world 'dysorder'

Majid Tehranian uses the term 'dysorder' in his chapter, 'Ethnic discourse and the new world dysorder', in *Communication and Culture in War and Peace*, edited by Colleen Roach.[20] He conflates 'disorder' with 'dysfunction', or breakdown. He perceives this condition to be the result both of the ending of the Cold War, 'which has unleased centrifugal [tending away from the centre], ethnic and tribal forces within nation-states' and modern, centralising trends in global culture and communication.

On the one hand corporations and the communication systems which they largely control work towards global centralisation, on the other groups of people within broader communities struggle for independence, demanding demarcation rather than unification. The story of the Balkan countries in the 1990s, of conflict between Serbs, Croats and Moslems over the once-unified Yugoslavia is a tragic example of the 'dysorderly power' of centrifugal forces.

Tehranian conjectures that 'Modernisation as a process of universal levelling of societies into relatively homogenous entities has encountered four great reactions in modern history'. He labels these as:

- Countermodernisation
- Hypermodernisation
- Demodernisation
- Postmodernisation

By 'homogeneous' we mean 'sameness', uniformity. In global terms this homogeneity relates to the cultural forms disseminated by transnational corporations employing new communications technology. This levelling out, Tehranian argues, is more apparent than real. In fact the 'levelling' has camouflaged 'a hegemonic project by a new modern, technocratic, internationalist elite' speaking 'the language of a new international, a new world order': that is, one dominated

---

GLOBAL TRENDS ACCORDING TO TEHRANIAN

Countermodernisation can be seen in the way pressure groups such as some traditional religions react against modern ideas and dominant ideologies – the resurgence, for example, of fundamentalist religion in the face of scientific and technological 'truths'.

Hypermodernisation is represented by the imperatives of rapid industrialisation, working through nationalism and the mobilising of resources in the interests of state power.

Demodernisation is expressed by the voices of environmentalists or feminists; and by those 'localites' (as contrasted with 'cosmopolites') whose advocacy is inspired by the notion that 'small is beautiful'.

Postmodernisation ventures further in its critique of modernity: it denies it while concurrently treating all other models of reality as shifting sands, so many imponderables. (For a further comment on Postmodernism, see Note 21.)

---

by the West and Western capitalism. Tehranian perceives the 'periphery' reacting against the 'core' in a number of potentially conflictual, even explosive, ways.

This, then, is the contemporary context in which the study of media communication must be conducted: there is the centripetal force – that is, drawing to the centre, the core, and the centrifugal force, pulling away from the centre as represented by dissent and sometimes revolt.

Context and study

Obviously it is beyond the scope of an introductory chapter to attempt more than a cursory view of the cultural web of which the media are such an integral part. The ways in which the media address matters such as gender, sex, race, religion, law and order; the way they respond to key issues such as women's rights and racial equality; their disposition towards dissidents, foreigners, the socially disadvantaged and minorities of all kinds are likely to be the bread and butter of media study. Above all we are interested in the ways in which audiences 'make sense' of media and that is the theme of Chapter 3.

The study of media communication is itself not free of ideological frameworks; and every approach to study has its ideological angle, its shaping motive. For me, study of communication is both a scrutiny of the ways in which humans interact communicatively within socio-cultural contexts and an examination of the role of communication in relation to human rights and responsibilities; hence the recurring link made in this book between communcation and democracy, and communication's key function as an agency of change.

In this sense, the study of media might be considered a democratic right and a democratic duty. It should be a central part of a nation's educational curriculum and if it is not, a useful early essay question might be to ask why. James Carey's case for the subject's breadth and depth is equally ambitious in its aims. In *Communication as Culture*[15] he writes:

> The analysis of mass communication will have to examine the several cultural worlds in which people simultaneously exist – the tensions, often radical tension, between them, the patterns of mood and motivation distinctive to each, and the interpenetration among them...

He goes on:

> The task now for students of mass communication or contemporary culture is to turn... advances in the science of culture towards the characteristic products of contemporary life: news stories, bureacratic language, love songs, political rhetoric, daytime serials, scientific reports, television drama, talk shows, and the wider world of contemporary leisure, ritual, and information.

A tall order – but a compelling one.

SUMMARY

This chapter attempts to emphasise and expand on the point that communication can only be meaningfully studied in relation to its cultural contexts. We need to pay due attention to the power of language to define our world, to encapsulate commonality and difference. The role of organisations in communities, nationally and internationally is linked to the workings of hegemony of which ideology is a key component.

While technology has not altered time and space it has had a profound impact on how we view and use them; in particular the nature of our communication. Contextual trends are identified as convergence, both technological and in terms of media control, yet also of divergence in terms of the conflict over public and private. While communications are becoming more global in character, world societies seem to be shifting in the opposite direction, towards fragmentation from the centre and the demand by localite peoples to have more control over their lives.

KEY TERMS

hierarchy ■ cohesion ■ commonality ■ segmentation

cultural apparatus ■ cultural capital ■ ideology ■ hegemony

ideological/repressive state apparatuses ■ consumerisation of society

public service broadcasting (PSB) ■ public sphere/private sector

convergence ■ countermodernisation; hypermodernisation;

demodernisation; postmodernisation

========= **SUGGESTED ACTIVITIES** =========

1. Discussion points:
   (a) Culture is communication;
   (b) Ideology is inescapable;
   (c) The study of media is also the study of politics.

2. Follow up the theme that 'language defines our world'. How far do you agree with this in an age when pictures compete with words for attention and influence? You might wish to jot down notes for an article which argues that in contemporary society words are losing out to images.

3. Draw up a list of sources from which information on the ownership of media might be compiled. It will be important to know not only which corporations own which media but what other industrial and commercial interests those corporations have. Focus on possible conficts of interest, for example a newspaper's right to publish in face of the mother company's desire for commercial confidentiality.

4. You have been asked to take part in a debate on the privatisation of broadcasting. Your brief is to make a case for the protection of Public Service Broadcasting. Prepare a 5-minute speech on the merits of PSB.

========= **NOW READ ON** =========

James Carey's *Communication as Culture: Essays in Media and Society* (UK: Routledge, 1992) quoted in this chapter is warmly recommended and is generally considered a prime text in the study of culture and media. Two more recently published volumes deserve atttention although they will require extra concentration – Peter Dahlgren's *Television and the Public Sphere: Citizenship, Democracy and the Media* and Nick Stevenson's *Understanding Media Cultures*, both published in the UK by Sage in 1995.

In terms of gender perspectives on world media, try *Women Transforming Communications: Global Perspectives* edited by Donna Allen, Ramona R. Rush and Susan J. Kaufman (US: Sage, 1996).

2 The Language of Study

AIMS

- To provide an overview, with explanations and illustrations, of the core terms used in the study of media communication.
- To locate terminology under three related headings – transmission, text and reception and in doing so note a number of landmarks of study which have generated specialist terms.
- At the same time to assist recognition that terminology reflects different 'points of entry' into the study of the subject, differences of approach, emphasis and intepretation.

The study of communication is an amalgam of many disciplines and this is reflected in its diverse terminology. In some ways it resembles the contents of a magpie's nest. It could hardly be otherwise in what is still often referred to as a latecomer in academic studies whose content is drawn from fields as diverse as telecommunications, anthropology, psychology, sociology, linguistics and political science.

Here I focus on terms which, at least in a general way, reflect the evolution of the subject. In the early days the emphasis of study was on mass communication as propaganda, then as mainly one-way transmission. The terminology was essentially of an instrumental, a mechanical nature – identifying the 'parts' which constitute the workings of mass communication.

From a long tradition of linguistic analysis emerged study focusing on the language of signs and codes, and a concentration on the content or text of communication. In turn, and inevitably, attention widened to take in the 'reading' of these texts by audience, and response theory became a dominant mode of communication study.

It is all too easy to oversimplify the evolutionary map of studies. Scholars in different countries work to different timescales and have differing preoccupations. Here then I confess to certain generalisations which specialists in the field may question. However, just as some commentators query the existence of *meaning* as a meaningful term in the study of communication, I would suggest that the meaning of terms undergoes endless modification.

If it suits the purpose of achieving clarity of understanding, if it aids exchanges of 'meaning' then terminology must lend itself to flexible use; and sometimes we may wish to 'borrow' a term from its academic field of origin and employ it in a new and interesting way. I would make the case that different approaches to analysis often interact, overlap and work to mutual benefit: so does the terminology which we should regard as the servant of our studies, not the master. Its usefulness diminishes if it locks us into hard and fast ways of approaching the subject.

The language of transmission

The terminology of study is most readily located in *models* of communication, usually diagrams attempting to illustrate the interconnections and interactions of elements in the process of communicating. Such models reflect the preoccupations of those who design and define them. The term 'model' is also used to describe aspects of communication as a whole; and there are rival models springing from differing interpretations of process.

We refer, for example, to a *propagandist* or *mass manipulative model*, originating with scholarly interest in the mass persuasion techniques employed by the Nazi propaganda machine in Germany before and during the Second World War. Introducing a Symposium on the historical tributaries of media research in the *Journal of Communication*,[1] John Durham Peters writes, 'Hitler, in a curious way, presided over the birth of mass communications research, and not only by chasing so much scholarly talent to the United States and elsewhere'.

During the post-war period when relations between the West and Soviet Russia cooled into Cold War and conflicting ideologies drew upon mass communication to urge their case, the propagandist model remained a focus of study, particularly in the United States. It was giving ground, however, to two rival perspectives: the model of *transmission* and that of *ritual* or *symbol* which we associate with cultural studies.

The transmission model emphasises the process of communicating information from A to B, from Sender to Receiver; the ritual/symbolic model stresses the process of *exchange*. The one is in the main, instrumental; it is linear in direction and technological in orientation; the other is circular or spiral in nature and is couched in the interactive practices of people in cultural situations. One might also term it a socio-cultural model.

The men from Bell Telephones

In 1949 two engineers, Claude Shannon and Warren Weaver, researching for the Bell Telephone Laboratories, produced what they termed the *Mathematical Theory of Communication.* Their findings were published by the University of Illinois Press[2] and gave to the world some of the first specialist terminology of the study of communications.

Shannon and Weaver set in progress lines of investigation and theorising which focused on the production, or supply side, of mass communication. Their remit from Bell Telephones was to find out just how much interference could be tolerated on the telephone line before the message became difficult or impossible to understand (see Figure 2.1). In the model, the sender of the telephone message is termed the Information Source, the receiver is the Destination: it is a very 'depersonalised' approach. In this case the transmitter and receiver are telephones and telephone lines.

What interested Shannon and Weaver, and for us it is the most useful part of the model, is the Noise Source; and the part *noise* plays in the communicative process remains of key interest to study, whether we are approaching it from a transmissional or a socio-cultural direction. The authors of the *Mathematical Theory of Communication* identified three modes of noise, or message interference.

Level A concerned *technical* or *mechanical* noise. Later users of the term have broadened this definition to include many other aspects of message impedence, such as hot (or cold) days in the classroom, distractions such as late-afternoon lessons, things of interest happening outside the window. Level B, *semantic* noise, concerned the meaning of an exchange: was it understood? Once again, Shannon and Weaver's term has become common currency and by regular use widened in terminological scope.

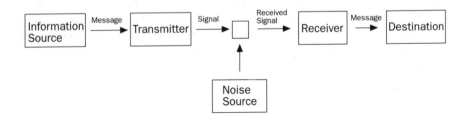

Figure 2.1   Shannon and Weaver's Model (1949). Essentially the authors of this, the first classic model of communication, were studying the nature of communication by telephone, here denoted as *Transmitter* and *Receiver*. The term *Noise source* has come to describe a whole range of factors which 'get in the way' of the clarity of the message. Just the same, the authors found that despite as much as 50 per cent information loss through interference, the basics of a message could still be understood. This capacity they put down to the habit humans have of building into their exchanges *redundancy*, a sort of cushioning of the message with non-essential comment or repetition.

If we acknowledge 'semantic problems' we are talking of ways in which meaning is not clear or is varyingly interpreted. Perhaps we do not understand the language through which a message is expressed. Even when the encoder and decoder share a common language the use of particular expressions, or of specialist terminology, may prove a barrier to effective communication. We may of course use the same words – 'freedom' for instance – but, as a result of our different political standpoints, differ semantically, that is in our definition of the word.

Level C concerns the effectiveness of the communication in terms of its reception. Later scholars have chosen to define Level C as *psychological* noise: you are worried, preoccupied, you have received bad news; you dislike or distrust the communicator – these factors can cause noise at the psychological level.

Shannon and Weaver were able to report to Bell on a key feature of message sending and reception in relation to noise, which they referred to as *redundancy*. They gauged that even with substantial interference on the telephone line a person could reliably pick up the gist of the sender's message; and this was because redundancy – that which is strictly inessential to the core message – was built in to the exchange.

In its relation to work situations, to be redundant is to be out of a job, surplus to requirements. In communication that which is surplus to the requirements of the message remains essential to message reception while also serving a vital role in terms of the quality of the interactive exchange. It may comprise greetings, references to the weather, repetition, rephrasing, checking, digressions or simply pauses.

Indeed, the absence of the use of customary greetings and exchange (what have been termed 'idiot salutations') can not only result in information loss – perhaps because essential data has been delivered too swiftly – but could also create psychological noise. An abrupt manner – on or off the telephone – may signal to the receiver an impression of unfriendliness, even of dismissiveness, which may not be the sender's intention.

The steersman

Today we refer to the Shannon and Weaver model chiefly to identify what it omits. Transmission works best when it is two-way and therefore no model should exclude reference to *feedback*, the most critical feature of any model of transmission, and a field of study in its own right. The Greek word for steersman was adopted in 1947 by Norbert Weiner, an American mathematician, and Arturo Rosenbleuth, a physician, to coin a term to describe the science of cybernetics, the study of feedback systems in humans, animals and machines.

The steersman metaphor is an apt one for examining the nature of communicative interactions. The success of the steersman's voyage depends on the keen observation of wind and tide, on adjusting sails and steering as conditions change. Weiner's books[3] became famous and cybernetics developed into an essentially interdisciplinary study, ranging in its interest from the control systems of the body, the information flow in business and industrial organisations to the monitoring of space missions and the ultimate world of feedback, computer science.

All models of process include, or imply, feedback. Just as it may be said that, without recall, nothing has been learnt, so we might claim that without feedback communication cannot progress. This is truer of interpersonal than mass media communication, of course, but over the long term feedback from audience – gained through market research – is a prime element of the survival or success of every form of media. In any event, our study of feedback should explore its different manifestations – positive, negative, instant, delayed and intermittent, short term and long term.

Wilbur Schramm: steps towards the interactive

Another pioneer, Wilbur Schramm,[4] in 1954 posed the two models reproduced in Figure 2.2. In the first of these Shannon and Weaver's Source and Destination are replicated, but transmitter and receiver become Encoder and Decoder. In the second model a significant transformation takes place: people have become the encoders and decoders of messages.

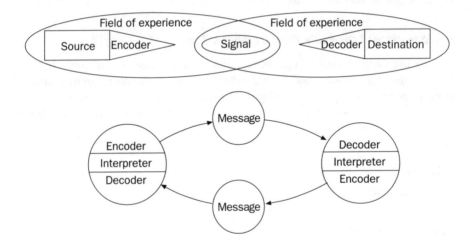

Figure 2.2   Two of Wilbur Schramm's models (1954). The distinctive feature of the first model is the recognition of the importance of the *fields of experience* which communicators inhabit. The signal occurs where the fields of experience overlap. We could elaborate on this by affirming the notion that where we have things in common – our language, culture, attitudes, beliefs and values – the chances of successful communication are enhanced.

Schramm's second model attempts to break with the linear nature of transmission models. The encoder is also the decoder. As we decode, we interpret, thus the message is sent, received, interpreted, modified, extended.

The first model is still mechanistic but it includes an important personal dimension, what Schramm calls *fields of experience*. Where the encoder's field of experience overlaps with that of the decoder communication is likely to be at its most effective. In the second model linearity is abandoned in recognition of the *interactive* nature of the communicative act.

The message has first to be assembled, encoded, and then interpreted or decoded; and the process of interpretation is constant and endless. True, both Schramm's models concern essentially interpersonal communication but it does not require a great stretch of the imagination to extend their use to include media as encoder-interpreters and audience as decoder-interpreters.

Where fields of experience do not overlap we are likely to locate, as cause or effect, semantic and psychological noise, for that experience may be deeply embedded in cultural norms and values. Where these conflict, within countries or between them, divisions arise which may be beyond the power of communication to bridge. American Indians, Australian aboriginees, immigrants to Britain, France and Germany, Moslem communities in 'greater' Serbia, Christian groups in Saudi Arabia will all have recognised the significance of 'overlap' or its absence in community relations. And the narrowing or widening of socio-cultural divisions will to a considerable extent depend upon the attitudes and performance of the voices of community and nation, the mass media.

Key questions: Lasswell's Five, Gerbner's Ten

Not all the early models of communication are diagrammatic in form. Indeed perhaps the best-known model (and arguably one of the most useful) simply comprises five key questions. Harold Lasswell, in a 1948 publication, *The Communication of Ideas*,[5] suggests we might interrogate the mass communication process as follows, asking:

Who

Says *what*

In which *channel*

To *whom*

And with what *effect?*

While not extending the vocabulary of study, the Lasswell model offers us a simple structure of analysis. *Who* are the communicators, *What* is the content, the message of the communicators. The *channel* comprises the means of communication, the technology and the mode or *medium* into which the message is encoded and transmitted. *Whom* is audience and one aim of analysis is to gauge the nature of reception. New terminology has tended to cluster and evolve around those five features of process.

Lasswell was a leading light of the propagandist phase of scholarly interest in media, yet in the 1950s he called for more research into whether propaganda had the effect on the public which had been claimed for it. In 1956 another American,

George Gerbner, whose influence as a commentator on mass communication has spanned several generations, extended Lasswell's five questions to ten:[6]

1. Someone
2. perceives an event
3. and reacts
4. in a situation
5. through some means
6. to make available materials
7. in some form
8. and context
9. conveying content
10. with some consequence.

We can welcome here simple but essential additions to our repertoire of terms. An *event*, something perhaps which may eventually be turned into news, has to be *perceived* as such, as something worth reporting. This suggests the familar and unavoidable process of *selection*. Events get reported, it can be said, only if someone somewhere perceives them to be 'worthy', or to be specific, *newsworthy* – a term which will be examined later in Chapter 5. Gerbner recognises a difference between *situation*, that is, the situation the reporters or photographers might find themselves in, and the *context* in which the processing of the content-message takes place.

Gerbner then presents us with a more complex model of mass communication (Figure 2.3). At first sight the model is forbidding but it rewards close attention.

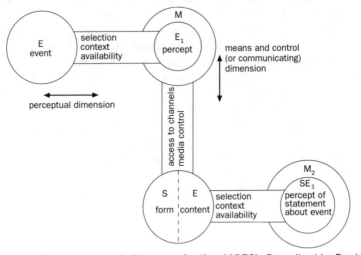

Figure 2.3   Gerbner's model of communication (1956). Described by Denis McQuail in *Communication* (UK: Longman, 1975) as perhaps 'the most comprehensive attempt yet to specify all the component stages and activities of communication'.

M is the responder to an event, the Mediator, and once that event traverses the horizontal axis, it has become a *percept*, an event perceived (E_1).

It is the perception of the event which conditions its processing into message form. In turn the message undergoes modification as it progresses through the *means* of production, which itself is subject to the institutional nature and workings of the newspaper or broadcasting company responsible for transmission.

The difference between the content of a message (E) and its style (S) or form is importantly made clear. The lower horizontal axis concerns the nature of reception. Just as communicators select, and in selecting are influenced by context and limited by *availability* (of information, for example), similar criteria operate as far as audience is concerned. The percept of the mediator meets with the percept (SE_1) of audience (M_2) and becomes ground for interpretation; of confirming, discomfirming, neutrality or indifference.

Gerbner's model identifies the processing of an event from origin to reception. What it does not do is elaborate on the complexity of the message itself; an omission scholars coming to the subject from different directions have attempted to redress.

Signs, codes, texts

What Gerbner has called style-content, semiology (or semiotics), the scientific study of signs and sign systems, describes as text and it is the text, and its meaning, which become the focus of interest. The theories of the pioneers of semiology/ semiotics such as the Swiss linguist Ferdinand de Saussure (1857–1913), the American philosopher and logician, Charles Peirce (1834–1914) and the French cultural critic Roland Barthes (1915–80) have become deeply embedded in the precepts, practices and language of communication study.

De Saussure[7] spoke of language as a 'profusion of signs'. This was not just a picturesque way of describing things. It proposed that we see the whole of communication and behaviour as assemblies of signs, governed by *codes*, or sets of rules, which by careful observation and analysis furnish cues to the decipherment of meaning. The relationship of signs, the interaction between them, called by de Saussure, *valeur*, was the determinant of meaning.

Whereas the study of the process of mass communication has generally taken a sweeping, *macroscopic* view, semiology prefers a more *microscopic* approach, often dissecting (or *deconstructing*) texts, and the language they are expressed in, with the precision of a surgeon. At the same time semiology opens up possiblities for employing the same analytical tools for examining all forms of communication, and at ,all levels – interpersonal, group, organisational or in relation to mass communication.

Signs: signifiers and signified

Some years ago, on a visit to the Greek island of Crete, I was walking a remote path which seemed to lead to nowhere when I came upon a sign – a small wooden

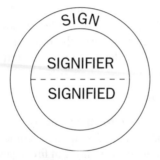

Figure 2.4   Signifier-signified. Each communicative sign comprises what we see or hear (the signifier) and what it stands for, or means (that which is signified).

board nailed to a post stuck in the ground. It bore an advertisement for General Accident Assurance. The sign and its message seemed so out of place – so out of context – that I could not help seeing it as *surreal* rather than real; a message entirely altered in its meaning by the context in which the sign appeared.

The example is cited in order to suggest the importance of the differentiation made in Figure 2.4. The sign is made up of two components, the *signifier* (de Saussure's term) and the *signified*. The second is the 'idea' (Gerbner's *percept*, if you like) of the first. Charles Peirce[8] called the signifier *object* and British scholars C.K. Ogden and I.A. Richards, the *referent*.[9]

As far as the General Accident advertisment was concerned, the notice itself was the signifier. That which was signified, however, is open to interpretation. Quite clearly General Accident's intention was that signifier and signified should be one and the same – a promotional device for General Accident Assurance services. However for me, as 'reader' of the sign, that which was signified was conditioned by when, where and how I saw the sign.

John Fiske puts the matter neatly in his *Introduction to Communication Studies:*[10]

> The signifier is the sign's image as we perceive it – the marks on the paper or the sounds in the air, the signified is the mental concept to which it refers. This mental concept is broadly common to all members of the same culture who share the same language.

At first sight this may seem to be splitting hairs, until we recognise how easily that which is meant can be separated from the signs, or sign system to which it may have initially belonged. Take a sign out of its familiar context – like the General Accident advertisement, release it from its conventional use, and it may undergo a transformation of meaning. Everything depends on the situation and on a range of contextual factors; and everything stresses what has been termed the 'multi-accentuality' of the sign.

All this implies that meaning is something which does not reside in the sign, or assemblage of signs, but is *negotiable*; that is, meaning may be *assigned* by consumers of the sign. This position represents a substantial shift from the transmissional model of communicative interaction: the message emanating from the sender/encoder is no longer a 'property', like a parcel mailed in the post and simply received and responded to; rather, the receiver/decoder is *empowered* more forthrightly in this alternative model of communication.

Iconic, indexical, symbolic

Charles Peirce assembled signs into three categories. The *iconic* resembles that which it describes. Photographs and maps are iconic. *Indexical* signs work by asssociation: smoke, for example, is an index of fire; a jacket over a chair may be an index of someone's presence or absence; the close-up of a revolver in a film usually has the indexical purpose of hinting that the gun is about to be be used.

The *symbol* may have no resemblance to what it purports to signify. The letters of the alphabet are symbols. Their meaningfulness as signs exists through common consent and their use is governed by codes such as grammatical rules. As Edmund Leach points out in *Culture and Communication*,[11] 'a sign is always a member of a set of contrasting signs which function within a specific cultural context'. We may feel inclined to mix, for example, letters, numbers and musical notes in random order. The signs are all genuine but in combination they are meaningless (unless, of course, they have been assembled according to a secret code).

SAYING IT WITH ROSES

Gillian Dyer in *Advertising as Communication*[12] writes: 'A rose is a symbol of love or passion not because a rose looks like love or passion or even because the flower causes it. It is just that members of some cultures have over the years used the rose in certain circumstances to mean love'. In most cases, says Dyer, 'there are the rudiments of a "natural" bond between signifiers and signified in many symbols.

An example of a pure symbol, with no such bond, would be that of the white horse used by White Horse Whisky, where the horse standing in a bar or on top of a mountain or at a building site stands for the bottle of whisky itself, although there is no "logical" connection between the bottle and the sign horse.'

A sign can be simultaneously iconic, indexical and symbolic. The colour red resembles blood, indicates danger, symbolises dominance, strength, the warlike. Equally a sign can pass from one category to another according to time and circumstance. The swastika is an example: it has been – in its clockwise format – a sign of good luck, a decorative sign employed in Roman mosaic pavements; in anti-clockwise format, the emblem of Nazi Germany and, consequently, the symbol of racial genocide.

This capacity of the signified to alter in meaning according to the situation in which the signifier is encountered keys in with a basic premise of cultural studies, that reality is a social construct brought about by the uses of language (that is, symbols). In short, symbols not objects govern our world; hence the power of signs within a process of symbolic exchange.

Codes

Signs rarely work singly. For the most part they are assembled into texts acccording to codes, or sets of observances, rules or guidelines; and these codes range between those which are arbitrary, or fixed, and those of a more flexible nature. For example, the Morse Code is arbitrary. The use of the dots and dashes representing letters of the alphabet is governed by strict rules and if they are not employed according to the rules the 'transmission' becomes meaningless.

Presentational codes – 'rules' of dress and appearance, can themselves range between the strict and the permissive. When Michael Foot, a former leader of the British Labour party, appeared at the Cenotaph in London on Armistice Day wearing a donkey jacket (it was a bitterly cold day) he was taken to task in the media. He was perceived to have breached a code of presentation which demands that public figures signify by their clothing their respect for the dead of two world wars. The signifier here was an item of clothing worn to keep out the cold: the signified, however – according to the media (particularly those papers antipathetic to Labour Party policies) was disrespect.

In the media there are numerous codes of an ethical and legal nature relating to professional practice, but in particular we are interested in *operational* codes, that is governing norms and practices – *conventions* – of production. We will examine these in Chapter 5 on the News. In Chapter 6 on Narrative, we will explore codes at work in both fictional and news stories. With specific reference to television, John Fiske, in *Television Culture*[13] identifies four operational codes. *Natural* codes relate to our lived, socio-cultural world; they could also be termed codes of realism. *Technical* codes are concerned with the modes of operation of the medium; and *ideological* codes work towards the shaping of collective perceptions.

We refer also to *aesthetic* codes which apply to the *appreciation* of artefacts – literature, music, art, architecture, design. What is considered aesthetic – of 'quality' – is arbitrated by conventions which generally reflect the dominance of those 'opinion leaders of taste' in any given society at a given time. Such conventions provoke innovators to breach them; and in turn the innovative becomes convention.

Today, it could be argued, we make our own aesthetic judgments from the vast plurality of signifiers available to us; and what matters is not the 'aesthetic', or pleasure-giving property of that which is 'encoded' but how we make use of it – whether it is a painting or a pair of Armani shoes – in our lives; and we might remind ourselves here that our response is rarely just an individual one. It is influenced by those around us – Significant Others – who importantly influence our tastes, choices and judgment.

Paradigms and syntagms

De Saussure made a distinction between *la langue* and *la parole,* the one describing language as a complete system of forms and contrasts represented in the brains of communicators – their potential for speech; the other by language in action, as it is specifically assembled and employed.

In the analysis of language and language use we discriminate between the *paradigm* and the *syntagm*. An example of a paradigm is the alphabet, the available 26 individual letters from which the syntagm – words and sentences – are constructed. Each message, then, is selected from a paradigm and assembled into a syntagm. In culinary terms, the ingredients are paradigmatic, the meal itself is the syntagm. Coherence if not meaning depends upon 'meaningful' juxtaposition, when the symbols are placed together.

Artists of the Surrealist movement in the first half of the 20th century delighted in breaking paradigmatic rules in order create syntagms which either eluded meaning making or somehow strove for new possibilities of meaning. So long as chefs remain within the rules of edibility (that is, avoid poisoning us), they too may wish to break with convention, to dabble with paradigms by, for example, alternating sweets and savouries or serving them up together.

Paradigms are sets of possibilities from which choices are made. In film making, for example, we might describe close-ups, panning shots, the zoom or rapid cutting as visual paradigms, and sound effects, atmospheric music and silence as aural paradigms. The putting together of those devices in a 'meaningful' order or narrative is the syntagm. We work towards meaning through a process of making choices; and just as important are the choices we have not made. Meaning is about omission as well as commission.

We can see this paradigmatic–syntagmatic process going on every day in mass communication. We wonder why this piece of news footage is used to make a point rather than possible alternatives. We wonder why some news items have been selected and others rejected and why those chosen are placed in the order in which they are reported. A different paradigmatic selection might have produced a different syntagmatic combination, or 'story', and therefore an altogether different meaning.

All the world's a text

Codes govern signs which, assembled, become texts. Roland Barthes[14] makes a useful distinction between what he calls the *work*, that which the encoder or encoders have produced, and the *text* which is what the decoders experience and interpret: you take a photograph (the work); you show it to me and what I 'read' is the text.

The distinction echoes one posed by Erving Goffman[15] in his studies of self-presentation in everyday life. He talks of signs – impressions – which are *given,* that is intended, and those which are *given off*, over which the individual has little or no control and may even be completely unaware of, but which are interpreted by others. In mass communication there is acute awareness that the message transmitted is not guaranteed to be either interpreted as intended or interpreted at all. As we shall see later, audiences may be watching TV but they may not be paying attention despite the encoder's efforts to command it.

Just as there are fixed and flexible codes, so there are *closed* and *open* texts. A party political broadcast is an example of a closed text. Every effort is made in production and presentation to close down alternative readings of the programme. To this end, facts which do not fit in to the propagandist message are omitted, and facts which fit are given emphasis.

News presentation comes under the closed text heading. Its intention is to sufficiently impress us by the professionalism of production – and the 'closure' which the use of newsreaders and the voice-overs of reporters helps determine – into believing that what The News tells us *is* the news. No-one ever appears before the introductory music and the headlines waving a red flag and warning us that The News is a highly selective *version* of what has happened.

A work of art such as a painting, piece of sculpture or a photograph may constitute a more open text, allowing us room for free analysis and interpretation. Visiting the National Museum of Photography, Film and Television one of my students complained there was no literature to explain the photographs in an exhibition of scenes from family life. The student decided that the show was therefore meaningless. What was missing was *anchorage*, the kind of closure we are so familiar with, and often dependent upon, in media practice – the picture in the context of a page, beneath a headline and with an explanatory caption. Open texts can be sources of anxiety, it would seem, as well potentially liberating.

Metonym and metaphor

Linguistics have contributed much to the ways in which we analyse texts, cultures and media practices; not the least we have been made watchfully aware of the use in media of *metonym* and *metaphor*. The first is indexical in nature. A metonym is a figure of speech in which the thing really meant is represented by something synonymous or closely associated with it.

The word 'press' is a metonym standing for all newspapers; the word 'stage' is a metonym for all aspects of the theatre. A photograph of starving African children may be read as *standing for* the general African situation. The news, whether in newspapers or on TV is metonymic because it conveys the real, while at the same suggesting that the specifics of what is being reported are typical of the wider picture.

Metonymy can be seen as an agent of propaganda and of *stereotyping*: protesting crowds are all the same; striking workers? street beggars? social security 'scroungers'? – typical! In contrast, metaphors work by expressing something belonging to one paradigm, or plane, in terms of another plane. The English *Times* during the 19th century was nicknamed The Thunderer. The metaphor had great resonance. In our mind's ear we imagine the thunderclap that commands attention, shakes the earth – and politicians in their shoes. The metaphor might distance us from reality, but creates pictures in our head that carry their own conviction.

Once activated, metaphors are difficult to control: plain truth often shrinks before them. After all, we might ask, did the *Times* really earn its resounding title? If metonyms have the semblance of reality then metaphors glory in symbols. Thunder symbolises outspokenness, power to command attention. The effectiveness of the metaphor lies in its vivid impact and also its imprecision. What, for instance, occurs after thunder; and what does the lightning symbolise? Arguably it could stand for retribution by an angry government.

Metaphors can be deeply enriching, allowing us to see things in new and unexpected ways. Without them poetry would scarcely exist; and without them newspaper headline writers would live a duller working life. Metaphors can inspire us, entertain us, unite us and, of course, serve to divide us because of their emotive potential. To present the conflicts of interest which inevitably arise in society using metaphors of war for example ('attack', 'victory', 'retreat', 'defeat', 'the enemy') has the potential to arouse strong feelings (whether of loyalty or hostility) in the reader.

Cry God for Football, England and St George

On the morning of Monday 24 June 1996, prior to the European Cup match between those two old rivals of the Somme (World War I), the Normandy Landings (World War II) and Wembley (World Cup 1996), Germany and Great Britain, two popular British newspapers sought to rally the British people by a 'call to arms'. Signifiers drawn from this history of conflicts between the two nations were assembled into a grand metaphor of battle in order to mobilise support for the home team and to disarm the opposition.

As can be seen in Figure 2.5, the *Daily Star* pictured Terry Venables (dubbed with a pun 'Jerry') on their front cover, dressed in the peaked cap of the recruiting officer in a famous first world war poster and pointing at the reader with the old summons: 'Join Your Country's Army!'. The *Daily Mirror*, in comparison, portrayed two of the England players, both well known for their fierce combativeness on the field of play, in helmets like those worn by the British 'Tommies' in the second world war. Just as the *Daily Star* played for effect with snatches of the German language ('Herr we go', it announed), so the *Daily Mirror* printed 'Achtung! Surrender! For you Fritz, ze Eur '96 Championship is over' in large letters above and below its picture of the two players. The letter S in *Daily Star* underwent transformation into England's cross of St George while the *Daily Mirror*'s front page editorial recalled in its phraseology the speech made by the British Prime Minister Neville Chamberlain in his declaration of war on Adolph Hitler and Nazi Germany in 1936: 'It is with a heavy heart that we therefore print this public declaration of hostilities'.

Figure 2.5   Front page of *Daily Star,* **Monday 24 June 1996.** The tabloids proved more persuasive on paper than the English football team did on the pitch. The 'battle' was lost to the Germans after a penalty 'shoot-out'.

One might constructively ask why winning in sport was attributed such importance by both these large-circulation newspapers. After all, sport is only a game – or is it? The *Star* was quite open about playing the politics of cohesion, declaring that victory over the Germans would be but one of several positive signs of national regeneration: 'inflation is down and still falling... Living standards are modestly improving... *Coronation Street* is set to go out four nights a week... Fergie has been kicked out of the royal family.' The *Star* recognises a 'new-found "communal enthusiasm". In plain language, we have a common cause, similar to times of war...'.

The sexual connection

Perhaps the most potent metaphorical signifier is sex; by imaginative association, the play on words, the use of innuendo, and most of all the enticing use of images of beautiful bodies, advertisers locate sexual attraction and sexual potency in a limitless range of products, from cars to ice-cream. In the advertisement for ellesse (see Figure 2.6) published in the *Guardian weekend*, 11 March 1995, for example, our attention is drawn to a couple of lovers flanking, in the foreground, a 'stunningly good-looking' watch. The caption, 'designed to perform... anytime... anywhere', is ambiguously, and suggestively, positioned under the pictures of both the lovers in their two different situations and the watch, as though applicable to both or either.

In the first picture the couple, elegantly dressed, seem oblivious of our presence as witnesses, instead gazing raptly into each other's eyes, the man's right hand (which rests possessively on the woman's thigh) handsomely clad in an ellesse watch. In the third picture, the viewer is treated to the lovers ready for a swim, reflecting the fact that the ellesse Liberte 420 series is water resistant to 100 metres. Both pictures would seem to encapsulate the 'perfect balance of strength and style' that the advertisers proffer as a description of the watch. The implied message is that if you have the good taste, and the means, to buy an ellesse watch, you are likely also to be the sort of person who will live the pleasurable lifestyle and attract the kind of partner shown in the pictures. Possession of an ellesse may, indeed, have the power to transform you into the sort of person who attracts the ideal. The watch somehow empowers the hands, whether in a position of possession or desire; it thus becomes a signifier of the sensual, the erotic and the proprietorial.

However, the lovers are not permitted by the image-makers to be so wrapped up in each other that the viewer, and potential customer, is shut out of the interaction. For the intimacy of the first picture is interrupted in the third as if the woman has suddenly become aware that the couple are being watched. Calm and self-possessed rather than surprised, she gazes confidently out at the viewer, as though her lover has been excluded momentarily from her thoughts. We might surmise that the advertiser has not forgotten the primary purpose of the images, to sell a product. Contact (with the consumer and potential customer), not closure (in an intimate embrace), is the key message here.

DESIGNED to PERFORM...

...*anytime...anywhere*

Liberté 420 series, water resistant to 100 metres. With stunning good looks, Liberté is a perfect balance of strength and style. The watch features a Swiss Quartz movement and solid steel bracelet with concealed clasp, and date.

Available from Harrods Fine Watch Department. Selfridges, Goldsmiths, Walker & Hall, Beaverbrooks and selected branches of Watches of Switzerland, Zeus, H Samuel, John Lewis Partnership, F Hinds, Hendersons and other leading Jewellers throughout the United Kingdom & Ireland. For further information Telephone: 01543 414211 Models featured Gents £225.00, Ladies £255.00 Also in Stainless Steel £195.00

Figure 2.6   Advertisement for Ellesse watches.

The interactivity of texts

From the point of view of reception, media texts rarely come singly. They comprise what Madan Sarup describes in his *Introductory Guide to Post-Structuralism and Postmodernism*[16] as 'intersecting an infinitely expandable web called intertextuality'. Texts interconnect and interact with each other, serving to modify, alter or reinforce textual meaning.

Images from films and TV are endlessly recycled in commercials, posters, magazine advertisements to the point where we are not sure where those images came from originally or what their primary purpose was. And when we do encounter the images in their primary setting we carry with us mental traces of their secondary, tertiary or millennial activation.

For the French cultural critic Jean Baudrillard[17] the sheer volume of signifiers in the contemporary world of mass communication is less a web than a blizzard. In fact so confusing is the situation, so detached from their original signification are the myriad signifiers we are bombarded with throughout our waking day that Baudrillard pessimistically conjectures that meaning is too lost in the blizzard to be worth the trouble of attempting to define it.

The metaphor of the blizzard suggests a condition – blinding and confusing – which is not obviously the result of any deliberate shaping or structuring. Yet we should not, as students of media, underestimate the capacity of the agencies of mass communication for, as it were, blizzard control or conclude in the confusion of the storm that ideology is absent.

In 1996 BBC Television screened an interesting commercial (one of a series using its most popular programmes and artistes) to publicise itself as a worldwide broadcasting service. It used the cast of the long-running TV soap, *Eastenders*. At first sight all the familiar signifiers are present – the characters, their chief venue (the *Queen Vic*) and a typical pub quiz. However, as soon as the quiz begins, the signifiers take wing.

We usually associate what goes on at the bar and around the tables of the Vic with problems, with personal and family conflicts, open or supressed. However, the *intent* of the commercial is to stress togetherness. Everyone in the Vic, physically, and in terms of purpose, is facing in the same direction. That *signifies* something different from what we are accustomed to, but the shock, and the entertainment value, take hold when the cast breaks out into foreign languages, extolling the virtues of the BBC and *Eastenders* as the Corporation's most popular export.

The nature of *Eastenders* has been imaginatively subverted, turned on its head, for the 'real' soap, if I might put it that way, derives its strength and fascination from its convincing portrayal of a localised sub-culture and community. It is a slice-of-life drama characterised by its closed, or semi-closed cultural context. The commercial, however, converts the cast of cockneys into multilinguists and by doing so transforms *Eastenders* from a tale about Walford, London, into a story about TV texts as *commodity*.

Indeed, this is largely what intertextuality does, even if that is not always evident either to producers or consumers: it sells itself by replication and in turn it sells the idea of itself and those things, cultural and consumerist, with which it comes in contact. If the Egyptian pharaoh Tutankhamen could have profited from his exploitation by generations of publicity-minded archeologists, museum curators, fine art publishers, magazine editors, poster makers, directors of resurrected Mummy movies and TV documentarists he would have had wealth enough to build himself a pyramid higher than the Empire State Building.

Discourse: the macro-text

We have seen that signs are assembled according to codes (fixed or flexible) into texts (open or closed). In turn, texts contribute to, are part of, broader 'canvases' of communication called *discourses*. The News is a discourse; that is, a way of telling us things and in the telling also explains them. In terms of public awareness and esteem, the News has the status of a *dominant* discourse.

In *Social Semiotics*[18] Robert Hodge and Gunther Kress define discourse as 'the site where social forms of organisation engage with systems of signs in the production of texts, thus reproducing the sets of meanings and values which make up a text'. Kress, in an earlier book, *Linguistic Processes in Sociocultural Practices*,[19] refers to the institutional nature of discourse which gives expression to institutional meanings and values. In this sense discourse is the 'talk' of the powerful – the power elite – in the community; the means by which they impose, or seek to impose, their definitions:

> Beyond that, they [discourses] define, describe, delimit what is possible to say (and by extension what is possible to do or not to do) with respect to the area of concern of that institution, whether marginally or centrally.

Discourse, then, is not only a means of communicative exchange, it implies a set of rules concerning the nature of that exchange. If the institution is a media corporation, like the BBC, public and private discourses will be framed by institutional rules but also by rules governing the institution as a whole. The corporation's Charter constitutes one aspect of the BBC's permitted discourse but so do external pressures such as the part played in broadcasting legislation by government.

Texts, then, are the 'micro-data' of 'macro-exchanges' called discourses; and just as the text is embedded in the discourse, so the discourse is embedded in the system. That system is an arena of debate and conflict. Some discourses dominate, others are subordinate but in a pluralist society no discourse has a natural monopoly.

We have arrived at a confluence, a meeting, of theoretical perspectives, for the nature of discourse as a terrain of struggle brings us back to the notions of *hegemony* and *ideology* discussed in Chapter 1.

The semiological approach to textual analysis

The reading of signs is as old as mankind: farmers and sailors read the weather signs, physicians read the signs of illness and disease, attempting to discriminate between symptoms and their causes. Sherlock Holmes, Charlie Chan, Maigret and Hercule Poirot snapped up their criminals by reading the signs and deciphering their configurations.

We associate the 'cultural detective' Roland Barthes with a system of analysis that has had far-reaching influence in the study of texts as well as being a useful analytical device. Barthes[14] posed two *orders of signification*. These are *denotation* and *connotation*. The first order of meaning, denotation, is the stage of identification and recognition. It is the level of description: all the prime characters of *Eastenders* are sitting in the Vic. They are taking part in a pub quiz and they are answering in foreign languages. At the level of connotation, or the second order of meaning, we begin to ask the question Why? – why are they assembled in such a way; why are they speaking in tongues? At one level we read what is going on; at the other, we read *in* to it, interpret it.

It is at this, the level of connotation, that value judgments are made and where what we value may clash with the value expressed in the text. For Barthes the same orders apply whether a text is being read or created: we take a photograph; denotation is the basic process, the mechanical reproduction on film of the image that the camera has been pointed at. The connotational component involves the decisions made by the person taking the photograph, the selection he or she has made from available paradigmatic choices.

Contrary perceptions, competing values

The clue to how we operate at the connotational level may be found in the language we use, the terms we select to describe things or situations. We may refer to 'freedom fighters' who 'risk their lives for a cause'. Others may describe the same persons doing the same things as 'terrorists' who 'wreak mindless violence upon the public'. At the connotational level we are saying as much about ourselves – our perceptions, our mindset, our mental script – as the subject we are analysing.

Yet this is not to mark out the denotational as the terrain of objectivity in comparison with connotation as the terrain of subjectivity. The denotational is not value-free, untinged by ideology. The apparent objectivity of fact-prior-to-analysis may disguise a degree of selectivity which is ideologically motivated. In a sense the denotational may be more ideology-prone because that ideology is disguised as fact.

Barthes sees in public communication a number of features working towards meaning, or signification, at the level of connotation. There are our feelings, emotions and values; the cultural contexts which influence our perceptions and expectations; and these include our place in society, high, low, prestigious, ignored or neutral. At the same time we are influenced by an intertextual carousel of signifiers – flags, fashions, uniforms, brand names, logos; each, Barthes believes, supporting and reinforcing dominant discourses.

Barthes would have rejected Baudrillard's metaphor of the blizzard of signifiers. His descriptor was 'myth'. In *Introducing Communication Studies*[10] John Fiske wishes Barthes 'had not used this term because normally it refers to ideas that are false'. We use the expression 'It is a myth that... ', meaning there is little or no truth in an assertion.

'Myth' used in its general sense refers to the distant past when ancient peoples invented stories to illustrate truths, about the origins of life, for instance. Barthes' definition of myth is not entirely different from this because he sees society constantly 'inventing' stories which seek to explain socio-cultural-political truths. In perhaps his best-known book, *Mythologies,* Barthes begins by defining myth as 'a type of speech', 'a system of communication', but also 'a type of speech chosen by history'. Myths have power but they are characterised, like metaphors (which in a sense they are) by imprecision:

> Myth does not deny things, on the contrary, its function is to talk about them; simply it purifies them, it makes them innocent, it gives them a natural and eternal justification, it gives them a clarity which is not that of an explanation but that of statement of fact.

Barthes links myth with the ideology of the bourgeois society that reflects a social ordering which myth renders 'natural', a 'statement of fact', seemingly incontrovertible:

> In passing from history to nature, myth acts economically: it abolishes the complexity of human acts, it gives them the simplicity of essences...it organises a world which is without contradictions because it is without depth, a world wide open and wallowing in the evident, it establishes a blissful clarity: things appear to mean something by themselves.

The Nazi party in 1930s Germany promoted the myth of Arian superiority. In the hands of the state propaganda machine, the myth helped forge the unity of the German nation: it restored national pride following Germany's defeat in the First World War and subsequent economic recession. Myths need only to be believed in, and acted upon, to become real. It took another world war to resist that myth and force it into retreat.

To carry conviction myth requires to be constantly *expressed* through public means of communication – the press, broadcasting, cinema, literature, art and architecture. Like everlasting life, myth is short on proof but not its power to win converts. Much has been made since the 1970s of Barthes' myth-theme. For our purposes here we need to acknowledge the role in myth-making of mass communication, while at the same time noting that myths change and are challenged by counter-myths.

Audience: the language of reception

At the beginning of this chapter I argued that the terminology of study has been fed by a number of tributaries. The 'semiological tributary' has been outlined here, joining the mainstream via a different route from transmission models attempting to explain communicative processes. With Roland Barthes we sense a transition. He works the territory of signs and codes but he relates the texts assembled out of signs to cultural and political contexts. If de Saussure was essentially a linguistic animal, Barthes is a cultural creature; and, as his interest in myth as a dominant mode of explaining contemporary society exemplifies, very much a *political* being.

The convergence of these streams of terminology is largely the result of the impact of cultural studies scholarship and its interest in the relationship between mass communication, audience and the exercise of power. Professor Stuart Hall, now of the Open University and Goldsmith's College, London, but then working from the University of Birmingham Centre for Culture Studies, assisted by a number of scholars whose research has contributed to our knowledge of media-audience exchange, has been prominent among those who have championed a multiple focus on media production, texts and reception.

In his article 'The determination of news photographs' in an important book of the 1970s, *The Manufacture of News*, edited by Stanley Cohen and Jock Young,[20] Hall introduces us to the term *preferred reading*. This duly acknowledges that a text is *read*, scrutinised, rather than merely glanced at. It also reminds us that a text may be visual (and aural) as well as verbal, and that many texts are combinations of what is seen and heard. In the case of photographs, captions add to the clues which direct our understanding.

The preferred reading springs from the intent of the transmitter of the work. In the case of a news photograph, the preferred reading is how the paper would like its audience to accept, or interpret its message; and the meaning of that reading, Hall believes, will rest largely with the traditional social and political values of the time. They will signal a degree of hegemonic influence if not of control; and that preferred reading will directly or indirectly connect with the interests of the power elite, prominent among whom are the media institutions.

Hall defines three modes of response to texts which audiences can take up – *dominant, negotiated* and *oppositional*. In the first, audiences respond to the discourse approvingly. They take on board the preferred reading more or less in its entirety. The negotiated response suggests a more questioning attitude. Perhaps the main parameters of the discourse are accepted but parts of it are greeted with queries and doubts. The oppositional response rejects the message altogether. We can see the various responses at work in relation to a party political broadcast on TV. Supporters of Party X are likely to nod with approval; floating voters may be partly persuaded, but are tempted to say, 'Yes, but… ' while supporters of Party Y may switch off, shout at the screen or go and open a can of lager.

Hall's definition of codes of response is a fine-tuning of those suggested by Frank Parkin in *Inequality and Political Order*.[21] Parkin refers to *dominant, subordinate* and *radical*. Later commentators have been of the opinion that these categorisations oversimplify the complex responses of audience. What has been termed a *popular* response describes inattention on the part of audience, where the preferred reading is not even glanced at, never mind read.

A useful term to link with preferred reading is that originating from the Italian scholar Umberto Eco. In a paper entitled 'Towards a semiotic inquiry into the television message',[22] Eco refers to *aberrant decoding*. This means a 'wrong' or aberrant reading of the *work*, that is according to the preferred reading of the communicator or communicators. Deliberately, out of principle, partiality or cussedness; or by misperception, misunderstanding or accident the *work* has been misread.

Yet it is only an aberrant decoding in that it runs counter to the communicator's purpose (unless, of course, the encoder – an artist, for instance – seeks deliberately to prompt multiple readings). When we, as audience, read texts we approach them with our life history in tow – what we agree with, what we disagree with, what we find acceptable and what we don't, and what we are used to. Accompanying us are our own values, our own stories.

This is what makes meaning so elusive and so volatile. The student of communication must cope with such uncertainty while at the same time sharpening the skills of analysis. There are plenty of answers, but no *right* answers, only some which carry more conviction (at a given time, among certain people in specific circumstances).

Our reading of texts confirms that meanings are not only elusive and volatile, they are multi-layered. Surface meanings may undergo modifications as we dig beyond the surface to deeper ones, while manifest meanings – those made clear and prominent – may conceal the latent meanings which are either hidden or have not yet taken shape.

As we shall see in the next chapter, reception has been of central interest to those scholars we associate with investigating the *uses* to which audiences put media products, and the *gratifications* audiences gain from those products. Their research findings are referred to as Uses and Gratifications Theory.

Of course the codes of response suggested by Hall and Parkin are really only ratings of approval/disapproval, acceptance/rejection. Our responses as audience are more complex than that. They are *cognitive*, *affective* and *connative* in nature. In the cognitive mode we operate rationally, intellectually. We seek information, we analyse, we search for understanding. In our affective mode our feelings are at work, our senses, emotions and imaginations stimulated.

In the connative mode we are stimulated into behavioural responses, even if it is only feeling an echo in our limbs of the athletes' actions as we watch them on TV in the comfort of our armchair. Our responses are subconscious as well as conscious, are interactive, sometimes instant, sometimes delayed, indicating that research into audience response must be as interested in long-term as short-term media 'effects'.

The terminology of production and consumption is employed and examined in detail throughout the rest of this book. The identity and nature of audience is explored in Chapter 3, and in Chapter 5 the ever-expanding language of news theory is explained and discussed. In Chapter 8 we encounter the language of audience research and discover that the advertising industry has assembled a virtual dictionary of names for us, the consuming public.

SUMMARY

This chapter has set out to give an overview of the core language of communication and media study. It acknowledges the debt the subject owes to other disciplines and recognises that terminology has been, as communication studies have evolved, fed by different 'tributaries' which have flowed into a common estuary.

The propagandist or mass manipulative model dominant during the period immediately before and during the Second World War became, in the 1950s and 60s, matched and to a degree subsumed by the transmission model of message sending-receiving. This contributed terms stressing the instrumental nature of communication and indicating an essentially *linear* process.

Linguistics contributed a *structuralist* approach to analysis in which the structures and systems of language became a critical focus of attention. In a cultural studies sense these structures were viewed and examined within socio-cultural contexts. Semiology, an amalgam of theoretical perspectives, brought to the study of communication a vision of the nature of communication as an expression of culture and devices of analysis, encouraging us to penetrate the levels of meaning; warning us to note its complex and mercurial nature, constantly subject to contextual influences.

Terminology has followed scholarly preoccupations. Once meaning had been deemed the product of *negotiation*, between the creator of the text, the text itself and the consumer of the text, interest in the nature of that consumption process – what audience does with messages – became a prime interest of study.

Mass communication carries the dominant discourses of our time. Consequently there has been vigorous scrutiny of the operation of the mass media in relation to the exercise of power, by the powerful, over culture; and the actual or potential counter-power of audiences, nationally and globally, to negotiate meaning in the face of what Jean Baudrillard has termed a blizzard of signifiers.

We are at the point when we need to ask what 'sense' audience makes of the 'blizzard' of information, of signs loaded with preferred readings which daily greet the public. How aberrantly do we decode the messages of mass communication; how aberrantly *can* we decode them? Chapter 3 sets out to address such questions.

KEY TERMS

transmission, transaction, negotiated ■ source, sender, transmitter, receiver, destination ■ message ■ channel ■ medium feedback/cybernetics ■ noise: mechanical, semantic, psychological fields of experience ■ encoder, decoder ■ sign ■ code ■ text iconic, indexical, symbolic ■ paradigm, syntagm ■ metonym, metaphor orders of signification: denotation, connotation ■ myth ■ intertextuality discourse ■ codes of reception: dominant, negotiated (subordinate), oppositional (radical), popular ■ cognitive/affective/connative

========================= **SUGGESTED ACTIVITIES** =========================

1. There are many variables which influence the nature of encoding and decoding –
the education of the participants, for example. Make a list of IVs – Intervening
Variables – which may modify the individual's reading of a newspaper, magazine
or advertisement.

2. Try a simple analysis of the photograph in Figure 2.7, which comes from the
BBC Hulton Picture Library.

Analyse it according to Barthes' orders of signification. Note the signifiers –
those intended to be significant by the youth, but also the way the photograph
wishes us to 'read' the images. They say every picture tells a story: what kind
of story might this picture illustrate?

Finally, look out some pictures of modern youth, preferably from different
countries. How does the 'story' of contemporary youth differ from images of
the past?

Figure 2.7   British Youth, 1977. Photograph from Hulton
Getty Collection.

3. Magazine or TV advertisements provide fertile ground for the analysis of signs. Take two contrasting ads and examine how the elements, the signifiers, are encoded to elicit the desired response. Note the use of words to reinforce the message.

   Do the ads make references to other sets of signs, or imply a knowledge on the part of the decoder of such signs? Do the ads appropriate aspects of culture (like using a famous painting or evocative situation)? What do you consider are the reasons for using such points of reference?

4. To remind you of how some of the major terms mentioned in this chapter interlink and interact, see Figure 2.8. Without looking back at the chapter, ask yourself the following questions:

   ■ What is the difference between the signifier and the signified?

   ■ What is a code?

   ■ What does the term 'work' refer to?

   ■ What is meant by preferred reading?

   ■ What are denotation and connotation?

   ■ What are open/closed texts?

   ■ What do we mean by dominant, negotiated and oppositional reading?

   ■ If you had to insert the term 'myth' into the diagram, where would you put it?

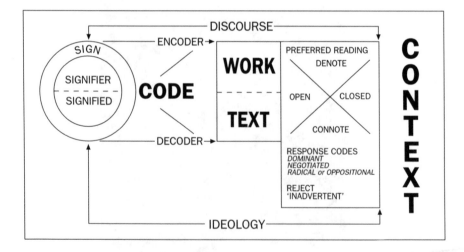

Figure 2.8   A semiological model

================ **NOW READ ON** ================

Diane McDonnell examines in depth the nature and nurture of discourse in *Theories of Discourse* (UK: Blackwood, 1986). Further exploration in this area would benefit from a reading of *Feminism and Discourse: Psychological Perspectives*, edited by Sue Wilkinson and Celia Kitzinger (UK: Sage, 1995). Also from Sage, published in 1996, is a two-volume work edited by Tuen A. van Dijk, *Discourse Studies: A Multidisciplinary Introduction* (Volume 1 entitled *Discourse as Structure and Process*, volume 2, *Discourse as Social Interaction*).

Other recommended texts are *A Theory of Semiotics* by Umberto Eco (US: Indiana University Press, 1979) and *Language, Context and Text: Aspects of Language in a Social Semiotic Perspective* by M.A.K. Halliday and Ruquiya Hasan (Australia: Deakin University Press, 1986).

3 Audience: the Uses We Make of Media

AIMS

- To examine the often conflicting perspectives on audience response to media communication.

- To relate the uses to which audiences put their experience of media to changing patterns of production and consumption.

- To provide a brief account of some of the most influential theories of audience response.

- By emphasising the significance of the structures – in particular those of corporate ownership and control of media – out of which the media operate, to assess the potential for audience resistance to the shaping power of mediated communication.

The increasingly central part which audience analysis plays in media studies is identified in this chapter and the differences of opinion over the relative power of media and audience examined. Reference to the pessimistic views held by the Frankfurt School about the apparent powerlessness of audience is followed by summaries of Uses and Gratifications Theory, Dependency Theory and Cultivation Theory. Mention is made of emancipatory/repressive uses of media prior to media performance being discussed in Chapter 4.

Non-media influences – IVs, Intervening Variables, Significant Others – are discussed and active audience theory related to enthnographic perspectives which recognise diverse responses to media on the part of audience. Finally the perceived dominance in all aspects of culture of the great corporations, and the implications for audience, are given due note before they are discussed more fully in Chapter 9.

Identifying the complexities of audience response to media

Proof of how and to what extent audience makes use of media is hard to pin down, but basically researchers are in the business of analysing audience use and response with a view to measuring the *power* of media. Do the media have the power to shape, modify or alter our attitudes? Do they teach us ways of thinking; create consensus amongst us; stir in us alarm; make us more anxious, more security-minded?

The trouble with seeking this Holy Grail of media studies is that our perceptions of audience response are difficult to disentangle from the actual facts of audience. Indeed, while 'audience' is a word constantly being employed in media practice and media study, arriving at a definition of what *it* is is not unlike defining what 'friends' are: you may be able to count them, but people can be 'friends' in many different ways and to different degrees.

A person may be unmistakably a member of an audience, in seat 10 of row G at the theatre. He or she may actually be seen to clap at the interval and the end of the play – but how can we be sure this member of the audience actually does appreciate, understand, enjoy the performance or is just relieved to have the thing come to an end so that there can be a timely retreat to the bar?

Having raised doubts about 'audience' as anything more than a general term for an infinite number of variations, we must nevertheless acknowledge that there have been plenty of people who consider they have a very good notion of what audiences are, what they 'do' with media and how media affect them, even to the point of predicting audience reaction.

In relation to 'effect' the pendulum of great effect/little effect has swung backwards and forwards over the years. What one might term the 'down-play' school of analysts have not been convinced that the media have very much power over us. In *Watching People Watching Television*[1] Peter Collett and Roger Lamb summarise their findings from experiments they conducted in which people watching television were filmed while doing so. It seems that we as audience do an amazing number of things while watching TV, from eating dinner to knitting jumpers, from listening to music or doing homework to kissing and vacuum cleaning. On the face of it this would seem to indicate that, because we are not concentrating hard – at least some of the time – we are not being strongly influenced.

The research findings are interesting and perhaps more surprising to media professionals than to ordinary viewers. But do you have to be concentrating all the time to be influenced? There may be moments, perhaps when the news comes on, or a programme which seems especially relevant or fascinating, and suddenly even the knit-one, pearl-one has to be interrupted.

At the other end of the spectrum are commentators who have believed that the media exert a considerable influence over audience and this belief is usually linked with a view that the influence is often a bad one. For example, there are the pessimistic visions of the Frankfurt School of theorists, early exponents of *critical theory*, that is, critical of the downside effects on audience of mass communication.

The Institute for Social Research, founded in Frankfurt in 1923, became the meeting point of young Marxist intellectuals such as Theodor Adorno, Max Horkheimer and Herbert Marcuse.[2] When in 1933 Hitler came to power in Germany, the Institute moved to New York (returning to Germany in 1949). Profoundly influenced by what they judged the successful brainwashing of the German people by Nazi propaganda, the Frankfurt scholars considered mass media a malevolent influence, a power against which the public was virtually defenceless.

They believed – and the belief continues to win adherents to this day – that modern culture, the ways we do things, our ways of expressing, recording, celebrating, perceiving the world, has been commandeered by the mass media, and therefore by the masters of the mass media, and adopted to the service of company profits. By being commercialised, culture has been somehow contaminated: the essential oppositional value of, for example, the arts, has been in the view of the Frankfurt School appropriated and transformed into a tame and toothless embellishment of commerce.

Uses and gratifications theory

Several writers on media in the 1960s and 70s, including Denis McQuail and Jay Blumler, countered the critical theory view that audiences were easily brainwashed, that they always believed what they were told and seemed, somehow, to have no mind of their own. What came to be termed Uses and Gratifications Theory shifted attention from the message-makers of the mass communication process to the message-receivers: the audience.

How, the dominant question became, did audiences *use* the media to *gratify* their needs? This gratifications approach worked from the premise that there is a plurality of responses to media messages; that people are capable of making their own minds up, accepting some messages, rejecting others, using the media for a variety of reasons and using them differently at different times. A crucial factor, given especial emphasis by Jay Blumler and Elihu Katz in *The Uses of Mass Communication*,[3] published in 1974, is the influence upon members of the audience of the cultural and social origins from which their needs arise.

The nature of these needs had been examined a couple of years earlier in 'The television audience: a revised perspective', published in *Sociology of the Mass Media*.[4] Blumler, Denis McQuail and J.R. Brown posed four major categories of need which the media serve to gratify:

- Diversion
- Personal relationships
- Personal identity
- Surveillance

■ Diversion

We use the media to escape from routines, to get out from under problems, to ease worries or tensions. Of course a programme does not have to be escapist for us to escape. Crime series such as *The Bill* or *NYPD Blue* strive after realism; they address serious problems, but thankfully they are other people's problems. The key, we might remind ourselves, is the safety of our own living-room.

If you are about to go to hospital *Casualty* might be worth giving a miss; while enjoyment of *Pulp Fiction* or *Natural Born Killers* will be somewhat muted if the cinema is just around the corner from where muggings are an everyday occurrence.

■ Personal relationships

We often begin to know characters on TV as much as we know people in real life; in some cases more intimately. To watch soaps regularly is to enter worlds as closely detailed and as fully documented as our own. We observe many lives as they unfold and interact; we are granted knowledge of characters and situations which even the most gregarious individual in real life could scarcely match. We are even permitted to know what is going to happen to characters before they know themselves, and before it happens. We are privileged – through the magic of editing – to observe developments which occur simultaneously. In short, we know more about *Neighbours* than we do about our own neighbours. This process of identification is given the term *parasocial interaction*.

As we watch, we may take note. These people have become our friends and neighbours. If not friends, they are our companions. What is more, they are our friends' and companions' friends and companions. We go to college or to work, and the topic of conversation may well be what has happened in last night's soap. If you are not a fan you may find yourself an outsider to the dominant social communication of the day.

■ Personal identity

We may be safe from the turbulences that buffet the lives of soap characters, but we may also share some of those troubles. We accept the convention that, in soaps, crises come thick and fast. We may look to soaps to help resolve our own crises: how do the characters resolve life's struggles – unemployment, illness, disappointment, loss of loved ones, rejection, falling out?

We explore life, test it out, via characters in 'real life' fictional situations. We may look to reinforce our confidence about something: 'Yes, that's right, it's what I'd do' or 'Is that the sort of thing that I should be doing?' We may seek reassurance about our own lifestyle, our own decisions, even our own values. And we can be sure that despite all these speculative responses, they are being shared by millions of other people across the world.

IDENTIFICATION AS ADULATION

In India, an estimated 650 million people watched the 78 instalments of *Ramayana*, a tale of gods and goddess, and such was the adulation bestowed by the population on the writer-director, Sagar, and the cast, that people touched the floor in reverence when the soap came on; turned up in thousands to greet Sagar when he made a public appearance, and elected to Congress in 1991 the actress who played the goddess Sita.

■ Surveillance

Blumler, McQuail and Brown quote a viewer as saying, 'Television helps us make up our minds about things'. We use the media to gain information, to keep an eye on the world and to clarify what we think about it. At election times we may be in doubt as to who to vote for. Politicians come under public surveillance. In turn the public comes under the surveillance of researchers into audience intentions – in particular the pollsters eager to gauge the intentions of voters.

Along with other campaigns of persuasion, elections highlight both media performance and audience reaction. Which party is winning, getting its message over; how is this occurring? Elections are focal points for asking questions such as, which particular medium is most persuasive; which medium do people rely on for objectivity; do people believe what they are told?

Yet the very coherence of uses and gratifications theory, its neat tabulation of response following stimulus, raises queries concerning its tendency towards prescriptiveness. True, it liberates audience from being classified as a lumpen mass, and it offers us structures on which to base our investigations into audience reaction. Its problem is that it perceives *use* as largely a matter of individual rather than interactive or communal experience – not in the sense that it ignores interaction between individual and text, but in the interaction which goes on *outside* of the text.

For example, in a family of five watching TV each one may be 'using' the programme for a different purpose, to gratify a different need. Uses and gratifications theory can cope with that situation; but the crucial extra dimension is the influence of the interaction *between* members of the family and how this affects media use; for each interaction has its antecedent as each family has its own history.

With hindsight we can fault a number of theories of effect because of their over-concentration on one aspect of the communicative process to the neglect of others. The matter is well summarised by Tamar Liebes amd Elihu Katz in *The Export of Meaning: Cross-cultural Readings of Dallas,*[5] a work we shall return to when we deal with research methodology (Chapter 8) and media effects (Chapter 10):

As critical theorists became aware that they were studying texts without readers, gratifications researchers came to realise that they were studying readers without texts. The idea that readers, listeners, and viewers can bend the mass media to serve their own needs had gone so far [with the gratificationists] that almost any text – or indeed, no text at all – was found to serve functions such as social learning, reinforcing identity, lubricating interaction, providing escape etc. But it gradually became clear that these functions were too unspecified: these studies did not specify *what* was learned, which aspect of identity was reinforced, what was talked about, where one went to escape etc.

Nevertheless, the convergence on reader decodings of media places audience at the centre of interest as never before, clearly implying as Liebes and Katz confirm 'an active reader – selecting, negotiating, intepreting, discussing or, in short, being involved'.

Issues of dependency

Observers of audience reaction to the mass media during the 1950s brooded over the power of the media to create in the public mind a degree of dependency; and Dependency Theory has had considerable influence on attitudes since that time. If we are truly in the age of mass-produced information, well into Marshall McLuhan's definition of the world as an electronic 'global village', becoming *Netizens* as well as citizens, media analysts will be constantly attempting to measure the degree to which we, as audience, are dependent upon media for the information, and possibly guidance – clarification – with which to form our concepts of the world.

In an article 'A dependency model of mass media effects' in *Inter-Media: Interpersonal Communication in the Media*[6] published in 1979, two American researchers, Sandra J. Ball-Rokeach and Melvyn De Fleur cite the following media role functions in relation to audience dependency:

The resolution of ambiguity or uncertainty – but in the direction of closing down the range of interpretations of situations which audiences are able to make.

Attitude formation

Agenda setting

Expansion of people's system of beliefs

Clarification of values – but through the expression of value conficts.

The media, the authors argue, are capable of activating audiences but they are also capable of *de*activating them. They believe that the fewer the *diverse* sources of information there are in the media world, the more likely the media will affect our thoughts, attitudes and how we behave. The authors are also of the view that media influence will increase 'when there is a high degree of structural instability in the society due to conflict and change'.

It is for this reason that such concern is expressed about the ownership and control of mass media. The British Campaign for Press and Broadcasting

Freedom sees restricted ownership as a root cause of bias, inaccuracy and irresponsibility in the press. In the autumn of 1992, the Campaign's newsletter *Free Press* worries that:

> the concentration of power in the hands of a few companies leaves them free to ride roughshod... over basic ethical standards. In doing so they often spread damaging untruths and mess up the lives of ordinary people who have no means of redress.

PAPER TIGERS OF THE SAME STRIPE

This was the title of a *Washington Post* article by Richard Harwood, reprinted in the *Guardian* (28 July 1994). The author, as the subhead explained, 'bemoans the loss of diversity and vitality in today's homogenised domestic press'. Harwood writes that although the population in the USA has quadrupled this century, there are a thousand fewer newspapers than in the period up to 1930. 'As their numbers decline, conformity and standardisation increase: standard formats and designs, standard sections, standard comics, standard ads, standard columnists and, increasingly standard ownership by the chains – those large media conglomerates that have bought up most of our surviving newspapers.'

The emancipatory use of media

Linked also with ownership and control and consequently audience's potential to chose and make the best for themselves of that choice, is a classification of use posed by Hans Magnus Enzensburger.[7] In this case the *use* refers to how the media operate, or are permitted to operate, with regard to their perception of audience. The emancipatory use of media is contrasted with its *repressive* use. In Enzensburger's view the nature of media output conditions the nature of reception.

The emancipatory mode is characterised by decentralisation of programme control. Each receiver is conceived of as a potential transmitter as well as receiver. Audiences are mobilised as individual members of communities rather than treated as isolated individuals making up a mass. Emphasis is placed on feedback from audience and interaction through participation.

A process of political and cultural discourse is encouraged, of sharing as contrasted with indoctrination or depoliticisation. Production rests in the hands of the community rather than being confined to specialists. Control resides in the public sphere rather than with property owners, bureaucracies, media barons or multinational corporations.

Quite clearly if the freedom of audience to use media in the way it wishes depended on the full exercise of the principles of emancipation, a glance at the way

Repressive versus Emancipatory Use of Media

Repressive	Emancipatory
Centrally controlled programme	Decentralised programme
Single transmitter, various receivers	Each receiver a potential transmitter
Immobilisation of isolated individuals	Interaction from participants through feedback
Inactive behaviour of consumers	Politicising (a learning process)
Production by specialists	Collective production
Control by owners or bureaucrats	Societal control through self-organisation

mass communication is organised, controlled and transmitted today might induce less than optimistic conclusions.

Cultivation theory

The fear that dependency on media makes for dependent people emerges from the large-scale researches conducted by scholars at the Annenburg School of Communication at the University of Pennsylvania into the ways that media, television in particular, influence our visions of reality – the world out there; the way TV *cultivates* those visions in certain directions.

For example, research has been directed at audience perceptions of the connection between the portrayal of violence on the screen and people's visualisation of violence – the amount of it – in the real world. During the Annenberg researches stretching over three decades from the early 1970s, Professor George Gerbner and his team explored the links between heavy viewing of TV and perception-cultivation.

They detected a process occurring which they term *mainstreaming*, whereby television creates a confluence, a coming-together, of attitudes. According to Gerbner, audiences use TV to confirm fears and prejudices about the 'way things are'. In their article 'The "mainstreaming" of America: violence profile number 11', published in the Summer 1980 edition of the *Journal of Communication*, Gerbner, Larry Cross, Michael Morgan and Nancy Signorielli write, 'in particular heavy viewing may serve to cultivate beliefs of otherwise disparate and divergent groups towards a more homogeneous "mainstream" view'; and this view tends to shift, politically, towards the right.

TV's images 'cultivate the dominant tendencies of our culture's beliefs, ideologies and world views'. What occurs, according to the Annenburg research, is a convergence of people's concepts of reality to that which is portrayed on TV.

Blurred, blended and bent?

In an article entitled 'Television's Populist Brew: The Three Bs', published in the Spring of 1987 in the American periodical *Etcetera*, Gerbner follows up the notion of convergence by identifying three things which happen to audiences for TV. The three Bs are the stages through which mainstreaming occurs. First, television *blurs* traditional social distinctions; second, it *blends* otherwise divergent groups into the mainstream and thirdly it *bends* 'the mainstream in the direction of the medium's interests in profit, populist politics, and power'.

These are worrying conclusions and are in tune with Bad News forecasters generally. The findings of the Annenburg School give some credence to the more sensationalist views of writers such as Neil Postman who, as the title of his best-known book suggests, believes that audiences are – by the ill-graces of TV – amusing themselves to death, brain-softened by too much mindless entertainment.[8]

In the Age of Showbusiness, writes Postman, focusing on the TV diet as served up in the United States, all discourses are rewritten in terms of entertainment. Substance, he believes, is translated into visual image to the detriment of political perspectives and the capacity of audience to seriously address the issues of our time.

The resistive audience

Audiences can be a nuisance. They are prone to doing things which the communicators do not wish them to do; or, to be more precise, what the communicators wish audiences to do with their publications or their programmes is not always what audiences actually do with them. The editorial team of a newspaper would clearly wish readers to follow the paper's agenda, that is take note of the major stories of the day as signalled by the front-page headlines.

However, many readers may have their own agendas – their own priorities. They may turn straight to the sports page or the TV schedules. They ignore the *preferred reading* and by ignorance, cussedness or inadvertence, *aberrantly decode* the messages aimed at them.

Television has been better able to impose its own agenda on audiences because of its unavoidable sequencing in time: there is no turning to the sports report till the sports report is broadcast. The audience is obliged to toe the agenda-line of the programme; or is it? Once again, we experience the phenomenon in audiences of selectivity.

'When the news comes on,' some viewers might say, 'I go out and make the tea.' How many more, one might ask, do this when party political broadcasts are screened, leaving the only 'observers' in the room a couple of cushions, the cat and a standard lamp?

No recall, no use?

The temptation is to dismiss 'effect' but this would be as risky as opting for the scenario which casts the mass media in the role of Orwell's Big Brother. Admittedly, in a court of law, very little of the 'evidence' for the effects of media on audiences would be considered as proof. Perhaps we ought to be thankful about this. What is clear is that effect is complex.

Let us for a moment concentrate on the information retention of audience.

Various studies indicate that audiences by and large do not retain very much even shortly after a broadcast. Media researcher Colin Berry in an article 'Message misunderstood' in the *Listener* (27 November 1986) writes:

> The evidence from both laboratory research and studies of audiences for live broadcasts, is sobering. People seem to be failing to grasp much of what it has been assumed is getting across… My colleagues and I found, in work supported by the IBA [Independent Broadcasting Authority], that knowledgeable, well-motivated grammar school sixth-formers retained little more than 60 per cent of news information they were tested on minutes after viewing.

The finding seems to be in tune with those who subscribe to the so-called three-minute culture hunch theory, the one which fears that the attention span of the average member of audience is only three minutes (or less). My own response as a teacher to Berry's 60 per cent finding is that if this were achieved in class it would be pretty marvellous: my problem would be to discover which 60 per cent that was (the beginning, middle or end) and whether that 60 per cent was destined to last an hour, a day or for ever.

Plainly not all items of information have the same significance or salience. A news bulletin which carries items such as a major rail strike, the latest GATT talks in Venezuela and a skateboarding duck would probably have me scoring two out of three on a retention scale, particularly if I had to get to work by rail in the morning. As for the duck, I would probably remember its exploit for the rest of my life, without it having any significance for me other than its oddity.

Another researcher, Greg Philo, in *Seeing and Believing: The Influence of Television*[9] takes an opposing view to Berry. Referring to his own researches into people's responses to media coverage of the miners' strike in Britain (March 1984 to March 1985), Philo writes, 'I found that many details of news coverage (times, dates, places etc.) were not retained by the audience groups. But they could reproduce some of the key explanatory themes'. Once more, complexity: plainly audiences pay selective attention. Some researches indicate that we retain more about people and places than causes and consequences.[10]

Domains: cognitive and affective

Media texts can be put to many uses; often, as we have seen, unpredictably: solace, identification, surveillance, escape, clarification, problem-resolution or just plain routine. Emphasis has been placed in analysis upon how these uses arise from cognitive and affective needs. The *cognitive* domain involves matters relating to the mind, to the intellect – knowledge, learning, finding out, problem-solving; while the *affective* domain concerns feelings and emotions. We turn to the media for the satisfaction of both.

Sometimes we read, hear or watch things which upset or contradict our expectations. Our attitudes, beliefs and values might be suddenly given a jolt and we experience *cognitive dissonance*, a sense of uneasiness, of discomfort. How this operates in our responses to messages is analysed by Leon Festinger in *A Theory of Dissonance*.[11]

He argues that people will seek out information which confirms existing attitudes and views of the world. In other words, they will select *in* those elements of information which are congruent, that is, in line with, existing attitudes, beliefs and values, while at the same time selecting *out* those elements likely to increase dissonance. What is happening is a process of reinforcement or confirmation.

If people are (cognitively and affectively) against blood sports, they are likely to derive strength for their standpoint – reinforcement – from seeing an anti-blood sports documentary on television. They may pay less attention to those speakers on the programme who might be in favour of blood sports. In examining the nature and quality of the attention that audiences pay to the media we must realise such attention has to be won in the first place: no stimulus, no coverage – no attention and therefore no response, affirmative or otherwise.

We remember things by association; by establishing connections we 'figure things out'. As audiences we are well aware that the media are constantly making connections for us. In the news, stories on similar themes are made to connect; in advertising we are coaxed into making associations between products and pleasures. Enticing images of association are dropped into our minds in the hope that such images will activate themselves over time.

In *Seeing and Believing*, Greg Philo reports on how he presented groups with a series of 12 pictures from the miners' strike. Picture 1 showed a shotgun on a table, its double barrels facing camera. When asked to write a news bulletin based on the pictures, the groups persistently opted to associate the gun with the striking miners. In fact, the gun belonged to a non-striking miner concerned to defend his family.

Philo's point, to which his experiments seem to add weight, is that media coverage of the strike had implanted in the minds of many a link between strikers and violence, a pairing which he considered had become a stereotype. Now it is true that the strike involved many scenes of violence, but this was meted out quite as much by the police as the striking miners.

In other words the miners could have been visualised according to an alternative paradigm or classification, as *victims* of violence rather than its perpetrators. Philo discovered that even people sympathetic to the strike were identifying the gun as the possession of a striking miner.

According to Philo's research the media, by their own selectivity and emphasis, have the potential to translate that take-up position to audience perceptions of reality; of what 'really happened'. By a process of closure, of limiting audience access to a particular paradigm, the reading by audience of the event has been syntagmatically defined: a story has been imposed through a particular arrangement of the 'facts'.

'Reality', the 'truth' of what happened, has been affirmed through the reiteration of certain patterns of interpretation (and not other patterns of interpretation), by a constant focus on some aspects of physical conflict (as opposed to others, not made explicit). The media create pictures in the head – streams of signifiers linked by various forms of explanation, by newsreaders or reporters – which prompt expectations of similar pictures and explanations in the same mode.

In this sense media can be said to act as agents of consonance. Having created a set of expectations, the media have then, by the *nature* of their coverage, induced a *self-fulfilling prophecy*:[12] striking miners are liable to violence. The pictures prove it and predict it.

Frames of reference

In *The Export of Meaning*,[5] Liebes and Katz refer to two basic types of framing used by audiences for TV, the *referential* and the *critical*. The first connects media with reality: 'Viewers relate to characters as real people and in turn relate these real people to their own real worlds'. The second, the critical reading, goes beyond assessing the way TV reflects reality and examines how this is done:

> Referential readings are probably more emotionally involving; critical readings are more cognitive, dealing as they do with genres, dynamics of plot, thematics of the story, and so on.

The authors affirm that the status of audience 'has been upgraded regularly during the course of communications research':

> In short, the reader/listener/viewer... has been granted critical ability. The legendary mental age of twelve, which American broadcasters are said to have attributed to their viewers, may, in fact, be wrong. Dumb genres may not necessarily imply dumb viewers.

From their research findings Liebes and Katz identify two main types of readers, those who remain almost exclusively in the referential frame and those who commute between the referential and the critical.

Significant others

It is useful to remind ourselves that audiences have their own *lived experience* to connect with the *mediated experience* derived from reading the papers, listening to radio, watching TV or going to the cinema; and an important part of that lived experience is other people who make up a context of influences equal to and often more powerful than those of the media themselves.

We use media referentially and critically in our everyday exchanges with others and in those exchanges media messages, media 'truths', media influences undergo modification and reshaping at a personal or group level. The media are forces for social mediation but in turn they are themselves socially mediated.

When we are in doubt about something, in need of clarifying our views or our feelings, of sorting things in our minds, we turn to *significant others* – parents, teachers, friends. Even if such influentials share the opinions conveyed by media there is always the process of scrutiny, of checking, of saying Yes – but; of taking a negotiated stance, if not a radical or oppositional one.

Indeed as early as the 1940s research findings concerning the crucial role of significant others in the formation of opinion was proving influential. In *The*

People's Choice published in 1944,[13] Paul Lazarsfeld and his colleagues describe their study of public reaction to media coverage of the 1940 election in the United States.

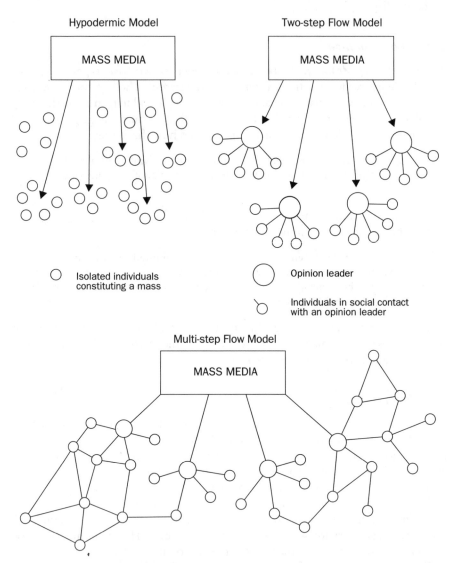

Figure 3.1   One-step, two-step, multi-step flow models of communication. From McQuail and Windahl. The one-step model suggests the hypodermic needle view of media's connection with audience – linear, one-way, powerful, each member of the audience perceived as an isolated individual. The two-step model acknowledges the role of significant others, opinion leaders as mediating factors between transmission and reception. The multi-step flow version acknowledges that once a media message has been received it may, at an interpersonal level, pass through any number of phases of summary, interpretation, re-formation and onward transmission.

They found little evidence of the direct influence of the media; rather people seemed to be more influenced by face-to-face contact with others. Opinion leaders, the authors found, tend to be more interested in media, better informed, more up with events than average. Lazarsfeld identified a two-stage, or two-step process of influence (see Figure 3.1). Step one took the message from media to audience; step two involved opinion leaders. The model was eventually developed into a *multi-step* process, in which interaction, and reprocessing of the messages of media, undergo further mediation. The reader may wish to consider what adjustments might have to be made to the multi-step model in the light of the sheer volume and extent of mediated experience available today.

In times of peril

Of course there are occasions when even the opinions of the most independent significant other are dimmed or silenced. Wartime is a case in point. Those who argue against war are usually drowned out by the cacophony of pro-war enthusiasm, when most media are likely to speak as one voice. On the national or world stage, opinion leaders may cease to count if their views run against dominant media opinion. Their words of caution or remonstrance may no longer be published or broadcast. Protest itself, and those who protest at war, are soon labelled by terms of insult designed to neutralise their message – 'pacifist', 'enemy within' and 'traitor'.

Individual opinion can rarely avoid being influenced by public opinion, the opinions which are dominant, which are asserted and which at least appear to represent a consensus. When public opinion is running in one direction it takes nerve and sometimes valour to express contrary opinions in public.

Yet however dangerous speaking out becomes, someone, somewhere, some time will risk it; not alone, perhaps, but given strength by the support of others, with a voice which may turn silence into voluble protest. In such circumstances, power often lies in groups, in the bonds that unite them, in their commonality of values. The group's solidarity provides individuals with the courage to resist, and sometimes against all odds.

The 'project of self'

This is an appropriate moment to ask the question who 'we-as-audience' are and what 'we-as-audience-within-contexts' hope for ourselves as we encounter media communication. John B. Thompson in *The Media and Modernity: A Social Theory of Media*[14] perceives individuals as being involved in a constant process of *self-formulation*. We are creating, as it were, the *project of self* and in this process we negotiate a route between our lived experience and mediated experience. It is a process which calls for, and stimulates, a condition of *reflexivity* that is, constant scrutiny and adjustment of self in relation to experience, lived and mediated. Thompson writes:

Individuals increasingly draw on mediated experience to inform and refashion the project of self... . The growing availability of mediated experience thus creates new opportunities, new options, new arenas for self-experimentation.

With new mediated experience 'we find ourselves drawn into issues and social relations which extend well beyond the locales of our day-to-day lives'. Potentially our concerns as well as our horizons are extended; and – to an extent – what happens to others outside of our spatial zones ceases to be 'none of our business'.

From being localites we are encouraged to become cosmopolites. Thompson says, 'We find ourselves not only to be observers of distant others and events, but also to be involved with them in some way'. Not infrequently, having been 'released from the locales of our daily lives' we 'find ourselves thrown into a world of baffling complexity'. In consequence, living in a mediated world 'carries with it a new burden of responsibility which weights heavily on the shoulders of some'.

In working at the project of self, Thompson argues, we have choices:

Some individuals turn away from [the 'claims and responsibilities stemming from mediated experience'] and seek to maintain their distance from events which are, in any case, distant from the pressing demands of their day-to-day lives. Others, stirred by media images and reports, throw themselves into campaigns on behalf of distant groups or causes.

Thompson sees this as 'relatively new as a widespread phenomenon'. Clearly it is of considerable significance in examining the active-audience paradigm.

Ethnographic perspectives

An approach to the exploration of audience use of media which has had considerable influence upon the way we decipher response comes under the heading of ethnographic research. Ethnography, according to dictionary definition, is the scientific description of the races of the earth; that is, it investigates the history, customs and lifestyles of people in their social, cultural and environmental contexts; and with express regard for the native point of view.

Ethnography seeks to understand the particular meaning-making processes of those it studies and it is characterised by its acknowledgement of the complexities of these processes. Research methods vary but generally favour *participant observation*, that is investigating cultural interaction from the inside, the researcher becoming a part of the activities he or she is studying.

I discuss ethnographic research in more detail in Chapter 8 but for a moment let us look at aspects of cultural resistance which ethnographic research has highlighted. There is general agreement amongst the observers of culture, society and politics that in most societies there is an eternal conflict between dominance and resistance. Only the degree of that conflict varies, for dominance never entirely dominates as resistance is never entirely extinguished.

We are familiar enough with such conflict in the work situation where dominance is typified by a company sacking its staff and its staff protesting by going on strike. Such resistance, being dramatic, is newsworthy, but ethnography reveals significant and often fascinating patterns of resistance in what has been termed the 'politics of pleasure'.

While critical theorists might view the Consumer Age as one in which dominant economic forces tantalise the public with consumer goodies, and by doing so ensure a docile population, other commentators have actually seen in consumption a potential area of resistance.

At first sight, the public flocking to a sparkling new shopping mall is a clear indicator of corporate influence at work; an indexical sign of consumerism. However, John Fiske has argued in his chapter 'Shopping for pleasure' in *Reading the Popular*[15] that 'the department store was the first public space legitimately available to women' and the 'fashionable commodities it offers provide a legitimated public identity and a means of participating in the ideology of progress'.

His point is that 'the meanings of commodities do not lie in themselves as objects, and are not determined by their conditions of production and distribution, but are produced finally by the way they are consumed'. Style and fashion have long had the potential for subversion of their 'preferred reading' as two seminal works of the 1970s explained – *Resistance Through Rituals: Youth Subcultures in Post-war Britain* edited by Stuart Hall and Tony Jefferson in 1975[16] and Dick Hebdige's *Subculture: The Meaning of Style* first published in 1979.[17] Hebdige examines punk culture and its expression in dress, body ornament and music and perceives them as forms of self-empowerment:

> The punks wore clothes which were sartorial equivalents of swear words, and they swore as they dressed – with calculated effect, lacing obscenities into record notes and publicity releases, interviews and love songs. Clothed in chaos, they produced Noise in the calmly orchestrated Crisis of everyday life in the 1970s.

True, the cynical might say, 'But where are the punks now? And what difference did they make?' It has to be admitted, as Fiske[15] readily agrees, that resistance from the bottom up is difficult and rarely likely to be effective beyond the micro-level of everyday life; that is, it does not alter the structures through which dominance is organised.

This is not, however, a reason to deny its existence as resistance or its potency. As Fiske cautions, 'Scholarship that neglects or devalues these practices seems to me to be guilty of a disrespect for the weak that is politically reprehensible'. In his chapter 'Madonna' in *Reading the Popular* Fiske writes of the 'process of wrenching of the products of capitalism from their original context and recycling them into a new style' – something which Madonna set out to do, taking on patriarchy not by rejecting it but by parodying it; and in doing so providing a role model for girls worldwide in search of a language – a semiology – to use in the various frames of patriarchy they found themselves in, and in the process of furthering the project of self.

Madonna used her body – her sexuality – as a signifier of resistance; and 'body-talk' is part of that pattern of resistance which seeks to define and project identity. Today's ring through the nose (or the tongue) far from signifies what it might have done once upon a time, a sign of subservience. Rather it signifies the position, 'I am me, and I will do what I like with the appearance of me'.

Fiske says:

> Women, despite the wide variety of social formations to which they belong, all share the experience of subordination under patriarchy and have evolved a variety of tactical responses that enable them to deal with it on a day-to-day level. So, too, other subordinated groups, however defined – by class, race, age, religion, or whatever – have evolved everyday practices that enable them to live within and against the forces that subordinate them.

Such tactical responses may not be radical but, Fiske argues, they are resistive to the 'conspiracy' which some commentators perceive in the nature of mediated experience.

In Chapter 1 of *Reading the Popular*, 'Understanding popular culture', Fiske responds to the argument that resistive activity operates only at the micro-level by stating that such practices (what he calls *semiotic power*, of people forging their own meanings out of the signifiers available to them) 'may well act as a constant erosive force upon the macro, weakening the system from within so that it is more amenable to change at the structural level'. We return to this point in Chapter 10.

Shades of heresy

It is no coincidence that the title of a film starring Madonna – *Desperately Seeking Susan*, directed by Susan Seidelman in 1985, has been adapted as the title of one of the key texts of audience research – *Desperately Seeking the Audience*[18] by Ien Ang. In the film, the heroine played by Rosanna Arquette searches for an identity as a women free of dependence upon the man-made world that surrounds her.

The character played by Madonna – outrageous in dress, decorum and behaviour – proves a role model for Arquette who transforms herself from neglected housewife into 'new woman', rewriting the project of self which to date had largely been written by others. It is a feminist film of great charm and entertainment value and it is about self-formulation through resistance.

Ien Ang's book is also about resistance – the resistance of audience to being categorised, pinned down, subjugated to segmentation by those agents of dominance who dream of an age when audience, its composition and its tastes, is cut and dried. Ang details the work of the ethnographic investigator working in micro-situations where attention is trained upon family habits and interactions of which television viewing is a part – an interdependent part.

As Ang points out, such close (qualitative) scrutiny by ethnographic analysis often produces findings at odds with the (quantitative) findings of the media industry itself. The hunger for certainty about audience – about what produces healthy ratings – rarely derives much sustenance or help from ethnographers, some of whose conclusions border on heresy. Such is the singularity of findings concerning use and response that ethnography raises the ultimate (and to the media industry the ultimately unacceptable) question – is there such a thing as a television audience?

In *Desperately Seeking the Audience* Ang states that 'watching television is always behaviour-in-context'. If this is the case, there is a 'fundamental undecidability' about reliable audience measurement. Where the media industry is desperately in search of consistency and therefore of predictability, the true condition is variability.

Audience as consumers, audience as citizens

Ang believes that in the process of audience measurement two kinds of knowledge are in operation. The first she defines as *institutional*. This is based upon the desired goals of prediction and control. The more the media institutions can predict audience response, the more they can control it; and the more they can control it, the more successful media production becomes.

Appearing under the heading institutional knowledge is the classification *audience as consumers* and the dominant discourse is that of the marketplace. In constrast, *ethnographic knowledge* is concerned with what Ang terms 'actual audience' contrasted with the 'television audience' as defined under institutional knowledge. Ethnographic knowledge is anchored in the understanding of the infinite variability of uses and responses within contexts which are less representative of the marketplace than of the community. The ethnographic paradigm gives priority to audience as citizens.

These 'twin peaks' of knowledge – institutional and ethnographic – also represent different philosophies of communication, the one treating knowledge as a commodity, essentially a process of transmission, the other as a public service, a process of cultural exchange. The transmission model accentuates the role of sender; the exchange model the role of receiver.

Let us pause for a moment to focus on the competing paradigms of classifications of public service and private profit. We may usefully draw a parallel with education or health, paid for through taxes but free at the point of use (the public service paradigm) or paid for direct, as in 'public' school education and private health (the market paradigm). The one works towards equality of distribution, to the point where access and use become 'rights' of the citizen. The other is a segmental or selective process in which privileges go only to those who can afford them.

The fragmentation of audience

Ien Ang argues that TV viewing is 'a complex and dynamic cultural process, fully integrated into the messiness of everyday life, and always specific in its meanings and impacts'. Consequently, she believes '"television audience" is a nonsensical category'. This conclusion could well provoke a crisis in audience measurement if it were to be taken to heart outside academic cloisters.

If there was no more categorisation of audiences, no more measurement of this segment or that, there would be no more ratings, no more ratings wars and the industry would plunge into chaos and quandary as to who was watching, when, how and to what effect. Fortunately for the industry, it takes more than facts to destroy a myth.

The audience measurement industry has enough problems on its hands currently at operational levels for worries about philosophical justification to be seriously engaged. These problems arise from audience fragmentation brought about by new technology. The title of Ien Ang's book says it all – *Desperately Seeking the Audience*: as video, cable and satellite have segmented audiences; as the use of the remote control has facilitated zipping, zapping and grazing, as digitalisation makes channel scarcity a thing of the past, it has become increasingly difficult to define what 'watching television' actually means.

The ratings people brought in the Setmeter, a device which recorded when a TV was on, for how long and to which programmes it was tuned. That proved an inadequate measurement device because a TV set could be on yet with no-one in the room. Then came the People Meter which viewers operated as and when they viewed TV. This was a small improvement, but people are unreliable. They forget to switch the meter on; or neglect to switch it off if they are not watching TV but doing something else. What a headache! The faster the agencies of measurement run, the more elusive is the prize. This will not, of course, prevent them from running – ever faster, ever more ingeniously.

Ien Ang writes:

> We are living in turbulent times: the television industries and the governments that support them are taking aggressive worldwide initiatives to turn people into ever more comprehensive members of 'television audience'. At the same time, television audiencehood is becoming an ever-more multifaceted, fragmented and diversified repertoire of practices and experiences.
>
> In short, within the global structural frameworks of television provisions that the institutions are in the business to impose upon us, actual audiences are constantly negotiating to appropriate those provisions in ways amenable to their concrete social worlds and historical situations.

Couch potatoes may be alive and well in the Age of Television, ethnographic researchers believe, but they are by no means necessarily turnips; entertaining themselves they may be, but not necessarily to death.

Corporate intrusions

An author who takes issue with the optimistic view of the resistive audience is Herbert Schiller. In *Culture Inc.*[19] Schiller launches a frontal assault upon the way big corporations have colonised culture in the USA and with it the communications industry. From that base, of cultural sponsorship and media control, direct and indirect, they have set out to further their transnational interests by enculturalisation on a global scale.

According to Schiller, 'the Corporate voice, not surprisingly, is the loudest in the land' and it also rings around the world. He believes that consumerism 'as it is propagated by the transnational corporate system and carried to the four corners of the world by new information age technologies, now seems triumphant'.

Schiller talks of 'corporate pillaging of the national information supply' and the 'proprietory control of information'. Even the museum has 'been enlisted as a corporate instrument': history is adopted for corporate use through sponsorship. Thus eventually museums become reliant on corporate 'approval' of the past. The pressure upon them is to choose to record the kind of history that suits the corporate purpose.

Corporate power in the field of communication is so great, Schiller argues, that the active-audience paradigm is called into question:

> A great emphasis is given to the 'resistance', 'subversion', and 'empowerment' of the viewer. Where this resistance and subversion of the audience lead and what effects they have on the existing structure of power remain a mystery.

What Schiller is saying, in contrast to Fiske's more optimistic view, is that if resistance does not make inroads upon that which it is resisting then it cannot really be said to be resistance at all. It is not his intention to demean the notion of an active audience, rather to question just how – in the face of massive competition from the transnational Media Masters – people can hold on to and project their own agendas:

> It is not a matter of people being dupes, informational or cultural. It is that human beings are not equipped to deal with a pervasive disinformational system – administered from the command posts of social order – that assails the senses through all cultural forms and channels.

Schiller asserts that the ethnographic position tends to overlook *power-value*: if information is the central commodity of the modern age, then its 'possession' will be struggled over.

Who dominates, counts:

> Theories that ignore the structure and locus of representational and definitional power and emphasise instead the individual's message transformational capacity present little threat to the maintenance of the established order.

With this position, Ien Ang concurs. In her chapter 'Global village and capitalist postmodernity' in *Communication Theory Today*,[20] she recognises that 'the negotiations and resistances of the subordinate, confined as they are *within* the boundaries of the system, unsettle (but do not destroy) those boundaries'. What resistance does exist is inevitably fragmented. It would seem to be a matter, as Michel de Certeau has put it in *The Practice of Everyday Life*,[21] of 'escaping without leaving'. De Certeau does, however, believe that audiences 'resignify' the meanings which are presented to them.

Before we give too much ground to Herbert Schiller's pessimistic views concerning empowerment and the resistive audience it needs to be pointed out that his arguments have been challenged by a number of authors, of whom John B. Thompson, already quoted in this chapter, is one. In *The Media and Modernity*,[14] Thompson says that 'even if one sympathises with Schiller's broad theoretical view and his critical perspectives, there are many respects in which the argument is deeply unsatisfactory'.

In particular, Thompson (in Chapter 5, 'The globalisation of communication') counters Schiller's view that American cultural imperialism has wreaked havoc with indigenous cultures throughout the world, and that it is a seemingly unstoppable force. Thompson is of the opinion that 'Schiller... presents too uniform a view of American media culture... and of its global dominance'.

SUMMARY

This chapter has focused on two aspects of audience: uncertainty about defining it meaningfully and contrary opinions about the extent of influence the media have over audiences. Scholarly opinion has resembled the swing of a pendulum and continues to do so: media power is great and becoming greater; media power is limited, or even negligible. Each 'school of thought' says as much about itself, the situation in which its perceptions are formed and its knowledge assembled, as it does about audience. The Frankfurt School were influenced by the propaganda of Nazi Germany which so successfully won the hearts and minds of the German nation.

In America where it is a seemingly unchallenged maxim that the population turns to TV and not the press for its information, and for guidance in one form or another, researchers have acknowedged audience dependency, but further, an enculturalising process – Gerbner's notion of *mainstreaming* for example. The emancipatory use of media, in contrast to the repressive use, is referred to here, anticipating further discussion about media performance in Chapter 4.

Researchers of the ethnographic school, penetrating the contexts – in particular, of the family – in which media are consumed, have expressed optimistic views concerning the active audience and have produced convincing evidence that *negotiated* responses, if not radical ones, are commonplace. Cultural resistance is possible, at least at the micro-level and sustained resistance at this level could influence the macro-domain.

Other commentators, particularly American scholars, have raised their eyes from the micro-level of consumption to the macro-level of production and control, and they are less sanguine about the ability of audiences to 'hold their own' in the face of corporate influence over and extensive ownership of the means of mass communication nationally and globally.

KEY TERMS

uses and gratifications theory ▪ cognitive and affective
dependency theory ▪ emancipatory/repressive use of media
cultivation theory ▪ mainstreaming ▪ referential, critical reading
significant others ▪ ethnographic analysis ▪ semiotic power
audience-as-consumers, audience-as-citizens ▪ active-audience paradigm
empowerment ▪ power value ▪ corporate intrusion

SUGGESTED ACTIVITIES

1. For discussion:

   (a) What do you consider people get out of watching horror films, westerns, TV chat shows, game shows, cult movies and costume dramas?

   (b) How do the media confirm personal identity?

   (c) To what extent are newspaper reading, TV watching and cinema going classifiable as *rituals*?

   (d) At the micro-level, how do young people these days, in their dress, body language and leisure activities signal resistance to dominance?

2. Conduct a brief survey into user habits within group contexts — in a family, for example, or a group of students/workers living together.

   You are interested in *how* a newspaper or TV set is used rather than what is read or watched. Who gains first access; who scans the paper but does not read it fully; who hogs the paper? What are the patterns of TV viewing and what activities continue while the set is on? Is there a gender/age/class difference in the ways papers or programmes are used?

3. Ask permission to do some spot-research at a video-hire shop. Choose a busy period and note who borrows what (in terms of age and gender). Which are the most popular films in each of the categories of viewer you have selected? Supplement your findings with an interview with a counter assistant: do customers pick and chose or are they influenced by recent publicity?

4. Count and classify the appearance of members of the public in TV programmes, from providers of canned laughter to more proactive involvement, for example in chat shows. What are the 'rules of appearance'; how manipulative is TV of public presence and what new possibilities might there be for public involvement?

5. Take two advertisements from magazines or tape them from TV. Select a small sample of the kind of consumers you consider the ads are aimed at. Conduct a discussion with the members of the sample, watching out for the way original perceptions and attitudes are modified as opinions are exchanged.

NOW READ ON

For readability as well as good sense and enlightenment Ien Ang's *Desperately Seeking the Audience*[18] is a priority, but there are many fascinating volumes investigating different aspects of audience in its consumption of media.

Titles provide useful signposting, such as *Audience making: How the Media Create the Audience* edited by James S. Ettema and D. Charles Whitney (US: Sage, 1994) and *Remote Control: Television, Audiences & Cultural Power* edited by Eilen Seiter *et al.* (UK: Routledge, 1989).

Because of its dominance over other mass media, TV inevitably takes prime focus in volumes on audience response and participation. A good example is *Talk on Television: Audience Participation and Public* edited by Sonia Livingstone and Peter Lunt (UK: Routledge, 1994). Family viewing has attracted particular attention – see David Morley's *Family Television: Cultural Power and Domestic Leisure* (UK: British Film Institute, 1980); see also his later work, *Television, Audience and Cultural Studies* (UK: Routledge, 1992).

Video Playtime: The Gendering of Leisure Technology by Ann Gray (UK: Routledge, 1992) explores the ways in which gender finds definition in the use of technology. The uses to which young people put TV is investigated by Tannis M. MacBeth in *Tuning In to Young Viewers: Social Science Perspectives on Television* (US: Sage, 1996).

4 Media in Society: Purpose and Performance

AIMS

■ To familiarise the reader with three key models relating to purposes or functions of media in society.

■ To emphasise the fast-changing contexts, nationally and globally, in which modern media operate.

■ To outline a number of traditional normative theories of media and to focus on crucial roles played by media in society.

■ To examine principles of media performance.

The more prominently the media have featured in the life of a people the sharper has been the debate on what purposes the media ought to serve in society. In the 19th century the press were sufficiently influential to earn the title Fourth Estate, a part of the power structure alongside government, the church and the law. This chapter attempts a survey of a number of definitions of the purpose and role of the media, starting with three broad models of media function – *propagandist*, *commercial laissez-faire* and *public service*. The shift from public to private, aided and abetted by imperatives brought about by new technology, is sketched in to remind us of the rapidity of change and the volatility of definitions. Then six normative theories arising out of specific cultural/political contexts are discussed. A core feature common to all media, their relationship with centres of political and economic power, leads us to examine the part media play in reality-definition and as agents of social control. Ultimately how the media are constituted – as private or public enterprises – governs how they perform and what principles inspire practice.

Macro-level issues such as diversity, access and plurality are examined, and micro-level criteria such as objectivity, impartiality and balance. The notion of equality as a basic value guiding performance is broached. Finally perspectives are offered on the roles mass media might play in a future where global matters will increasingly affect our lives.

Propaganda, profit, power

Lord Beaverbrook (1879–1964), born in Canada but one of the most successful British media barons, owner of the *Daily Express* and founder of the *Sunday Express*, claimed that he ran his newspapers 'purely for propaganda, and with no other purpose'. That was honest, but not wholly correct. For his propaganda to be influential Beaverbrook needed to make his newspapers a success; and to be successful, newspapers have to provide more than propaganda. Beaverbrook was too good an entrepreneur, and too good a journalist, ever to forget that readers seek to be entertained as well as informed. The best pills come sugar-coated, though they are no less 'medicinal' for that. Beaverbrook's idea of the purpose of mass media has been classified as the *Propaganda* or Mass Manipulative model.

We generally associate the term propaganda with brazen stategies of persuasion, with information which is distorted, partisan or untrue. The noun (propaganda) has, then, got a bad name; but the verb (to propagate) is something no society can do without. The spread of opinions, attitudes, beliefs, and the advocacy of change or reform, have been key elements of communication throughout history.

Radical newspapers of the 19th century, in demanding economic, industrial and parliamentary reform, were functioning in the propagandist mode. The *Poor Man's Guardian* (1831–35) carried on its title head the logo of a printing press framed by the words 'KNOWLEDGE IS POWER' (Figure 4.1). Governments, the power elite of society and those with interests or causes to advocate have concurred with that view, recognising that knowledge is only power if it can be controlled, diffused or restricted as considered appropriate. In this sense, *not* telling is as significant as telling.

Figure 4.1 'KNOWLEDGE IS POWER.' Edited by James Bronterre O'Brien and published by Henry Hetherington, the *Poor Man's Guardian* was one of many radical 19th-century newspapers, most of them equally short lived, which defied authority's attempts to supress them. Stamp duty was levied on every paper printed and those who evaded this and other taxes on knowledge were liable to lengthy prison sentences. The police gave a sovereign for every vendor of unstamped papers convicted.

The taste of power

The Radicals were rarely able to sustain their crusade for causes unpopular with government because rival newspapers were concentrating on an alternative, *populist-profit* mode. Press barons such as Lord Northcliffe (1865–1922) in Britain and William Randolph Hearst (1863–1951) in America were no less propagandist in approach, but they were also businessmen, each with a flair for exploiting popular taste. As one of Hearst's editors said, 'What we're after is the "Gee-Whizz" effect'.

What came to be known in the States as the Yellow Press focused on sensationalism – scandals, corruption, murders. Serious news and comment were downsized if not excluded altogether. And with most of the press barons the lure of power – the power to influence society and those who governed it – was a decisive factor in the content and style of their publications.

Newspapers were weapons of influence with which the press barons could attempt to impose their views on the widest possible readership. Such barons also delighted in the prestige their newspapers gained for them along the corridors of power. Yet prestige was not always forthcoming and when it was, not always sufficient for men in whom meglomania – power-hungriness – was a common trait.

Advertising revenue from the late 19th century onwards gave press ownership a degree of independence which saw papers attacking government as much as supporting it, and in doing so invariably calling upon the reading public to exert their own power to influence.

With few exceptions, political power rather than political influence remained a dream for the press barons, Lord Beaverbrook being an exception. In 1911, then simply Max Aitken, he was knighted for services to the Conservative Party. In 1916 he received a peerage from George V. In 1918 Prime Minister Lloyd George appointed him Minister of Information. During the Second World War (1939–45) Beaverbrook became a member of the war cabinet of Winston Churchill, a close friend. He actually took up residence for a while in Number 12 Downing Street.

The most notable recent exception to the rule that media barons influence the powerful rather than join them in office is Silvio Berlusconi: his newly formed political party was propelled into power in Italy by the support of his own media empire. In fiction, the dream of political office eluded John Foster Kane, the larger-than-life press baron modelled on William Randolph Hearst, in Orson Welles' classic film *Citizen Kane*.[1] In the stranger world of fact, Berlusconi became prime minister of his country in 1994.

What did not prove an exception to the rule was his rightist politics: Berlusconi (nicknamed in Italy, 'Sua Emittenza', His Broadcastingship) took power with the support of neo-fascists; and he lost it again within the year because he found pleasing a nation more difficult than gratifying readers and viewers. The fact remains that the supportive, uncritical voices of Berlusconi's media empire had given him the influence to reach high political office at a pace which was breathtaking and seemingly unstoppable.[2]

Purely for profit?

The *Commercial laissez-faire* model has been cited as a rival to the propagandist model. This theory defines media ownership and production as being simply a financial enterprise with no other goal than to make profit; that is, there are no ideological axes to grind. Readers or viewers are simply consumers whose custom has to be won and sustained.

A case might be made that the media empire of Rupert Murdoch works to this principle. Indeed, it would be impossible to deny that profit now or profit in the future is the primary, bottom-line purpose of News Corp, BSkyB, Fox Broadcasting Company or the Papua and New Guinea *Post Courier* – all 'power properties' in the Murdoch empire.

Yet if we recognise that profit-making not only empowers those who are successful at it, but also requires empowerment, then we can readily identify the ideology from which profit-acquisition springs. By this I mean that, from the business angle, the making of profit should be as free (hence, '*laissez-faire*' – leave alone), as unrestricted by regulation as possible. Whichever socio-political conditions favour profits will be reinforced by the arguments and moral support of those best able to benefit from those conditions.

Trade unionism stood in the way of Murdoch's vision of a viable and profitable media business: he took on, and defeated, the print unions. Where there are rivals, including other media moguls or competing corporations, News Corp turns its firepower upon them. In a *Guardian* article 'The keeper of the global gate',[3] Henry Porter quotes the *New York Times* which states that 'Mr. Murdoch does a disservice to journalism by using his media outlets to carry out personal vendettas for financial gain'. The paper accuses him of using his papers in America, Britain and Australia, 'to advance a political agenda'.

It would seem that the propaganda model and the commercial *laissez-faire* model can be seen, together with the personal drive, ambition and vision of the individual or corporate entrepreneur, to merge into a straightforward *power* model. Further, we might classify it as a model of *control* because ultimately that is what power is about – *having* control, over self, others, situations, over knowledge itself (or at least access to it).

The media barons have notoriously exercised high levels of control over their properties. They hire and they fire. They take a direct interest in content and approach. They decide the political hue of their newspapers and broadcasting companies. Essentially, though, they are pragmatic and opportunist. Unlike many politicians they are the controllers of ideology not its slaves. If supporting Party X is seen as good for business, Party X will receive support; yet just occasionally Party Y may seem a better bet. Practical necessities temper the fervour of ideology.

The public service model: technology and competition

It is useful at this point to differentiate between the functions of media, the purposes to which they are directed, and their performance. The one I will term *normative*, the other, *performative*; a version, if you like, of the proposition that people should be judged not by what they say they do but by what they do do.

In exploring the question, 'What are the media for?', we are immediately confronted by a number of other questions which need to be answered before we can progress. For example, *who* says what the media are for – a nation's citizens or its power elite; consumers or producers; public sector media or private sector media? In some countries, totalitarian in nature, government decides what the media are for. In democracies there is a *plurality* of definitions.

Clearly the dominant voices of the time assert their definitions over others; and if the dominant voices are the media themselves then those who control the media have something of a monopoly over who says what to whom and why. In countries where media are divided betweeen public and private ownership conflicts over purpose and performance are ongoing, often bitterly fought; and each contestant has one eye on government and the other on the public.

The newspaper barons in Britain during the 1920s greeted the arrival of public service broadcasting as represented by the BBC with suspicion and later, hostility, for they saw radio as a serious threat to their media hegemony. They feared a rival paradigm of media purpose – the *Public Service* model. A committee chaired by Sir Frederick Sykes, set the task of making recommendations for the future of broadcasting in Britain, established a principle which was to influence the broadcasting policies of many countries throughout the world.

The Sykes Committee report declared:

> ... we consider that the control of such a potential power [of broadcasting] over public opinion and the life of the nation ought to remain with the State, and that the operation of so important a national service ought not to be allowed to become an unrestricted commercial monopoly.

The BBC became the first broadcasting service in the world to be financed through an annual licence fee and it became a model for similar national broadcasting systems. In contrast, of course, the American broadcasting system was, from the start, privately owned, funded by advertising. Yet here too the principle of public service was recognised with the foundation of the Federal Radio Commission formed in 1927 to regulate excesses and to encourage quality broadcasting. Today the Federal Communications Commission (FCC) serves a similar, if cautiously modest function.

An end to control through scarcity

What protected state broadcasting systems down the years, and what ensured that PSB (Public Service Broadcasting) continued as a central feature of cultural life was in part the desire of governments to exert control over such a powerful means of communication. Perhaps more importantly, the limitations of existing technology restricted the number of possible broadcasting channels and therefore the number of broadcasting licences available.

Today, hostility to PSB among media moguls such as Rupert Murdoch is undiminished, and it is aided by a loss of faith in the public service ethic among power elites. New technology has transformed channel 'dearth' into channel 'plenty'; and that technology has come increasingly under the control of operators in the private sector.

Terrestrial broadcasting is being outflanked by satellite transmission, undermined by cable, evaded by video. At the same time, public sector media are becoming increasingly marginalised: programmes traditionally broadcast nationally such as the coverage of national and international sporting events, are fast becoming available to us only through subscription.

With the transfer from analogue to digital technology and the subsequent convergence of data systems, competition for control of the means of delivery is intense, ruthless and inescapable. The public sector has to compete on three fronts – against the predatory ambitions of the private entrepreneurs; against governments, themselves subject to intense pressure from the moguls of the private sector; and the truly daunting challenge of how to control the whirlwind of change brought about by new technology.

In the words of the BBC's Director General, John Birt, delivering the 1996 MacTaggart Lecture at the Edinburgh Festival, 'The impact [of new technology] will be seismic'. Birt was of the opinion that 'the digital age will be marked not by openness and diversity but by dominance'.

A world 'born of spectrum scarcity, a handful of channels and of regulation' is swiftly being superseded and the new age will witness competition 'to rival the 19th-century battle for the railroad or the 20th-century battle for office software systems'. For Birt the 'hallmark of the digital age must be full cultural and economic freedom'.

Media moguls might be expected to clap their hands in agreement: after all, the freer they are to expand, the fewer regulations impeding their national and global ambitions, the better – so why was Birt so eloquently advocating their case?

What he was certainly doing, he might assert, is acknowledging inevitable realities and in consequence shifting the basis on which PSB has operated in the past; one typified by *regulation*, that is rules – codes of conduct – which guide expenditure, programming, programme content and the nature of presentation.

Birt's shift of ground may be unavoidable: digital technology, and with it the unifying of electronic services of all kinds, will make regulation more difficult if not impossible. His position seems to be – if you can't beat them (the private sector operators) then join them (in the marketplace) and attempt to beat them. The risks are high; and the 'solution' precarious, for Birt's MacTaggart speech was a fervent plea to government to permit a substantial increase in the licence fee – something the British Tory government had not done since 1985, and refused to do again in 1996.

Any survey of the principles and practices of media must be conducted with these seismic shifts in mind. Indeed, it is because of such fundamental changes in the nature of 20th- and 21st-century media that we need to examine the roles media play in society and the success (or lack of it) with which they perform those roles.

Private advances, public retreats

The temptation to see the media world in terms of a struggle between public and private should be firmly resisted if we are then expected to take sides, classifying one or the other as preferable. The private sector does not have a monopoly of entrepreneurialism and adventure; and the public sector does not have a monopoly of public 'virtues'. What we should worry about is one disabling the other or displacing it altogether.

It is no exaggeration to say that PSB, wherever it exists, is in mortal danger. As audiences fragment, the justification for a universal licence fee becomes harder to defend. As transmission traverses national frontiers, the relevance of national systems becomes open to question. As global communication on the Internet threatens to overtake sex as a pastime, the very future of 'mass media' itself, and of the profession of journalism, might be perceived to be in jeopardy. In cyberspace, everyone is his or her own reporter; or so the argument goes.

Students of media will respond with caution to such heady predictions. A glance at the media scene will fail to spot the end of print media. Supplements to our newspapers proliferate and get fatter. Despite the onslaught of TV, multi-screen cinemas survive and sometimes prosper. Regardless of the near perfect sound reproduction of the CD, orchestras and bands still command audiences. Though radio has long since been driven to the margins of media use, it continues to attract listeners nationally and locally.

The structures, too, remain substantially in place, or to be more exact, the *networks* of control. In 1996 British Telecom joined with the MCI company of America to form the world's second largest telecommunications giant, vying with a network formed of Time-Warner, the largest media company in the world, Tele-Communications Inc., the largest cable company in the USA, and Microsoft Corporation, the world's largest manufacturer of computer sofware.

BT's new partner, MCI, also has business links with Microsoft and with Murdoch's News International. Telecommunications, the pessimist might fear, is being sewn up. Simultaneously other alliances carve up the map of world entertainment provision. The names of the players are not unfamiliar – Disney, Viacom – Oh!, and Microsoft and Murdoch!

Classifications of purpose revisited

We may not hear the clash of battle but we can be sure it is raging; and we may need to be wary of whatever 'peace treaty' emerges from the struggle, for the signatories to it, the beneficiaries, will be corporate, not individual, with the public functioning largely as spectators. This is a timely moment to conduct an overview of contrasting theories of purpose and to examine a number of principles of media performance which may or may not survive into the new Digital Age.

All parties to the definition of the functions or purposes of media find little difficulty agreeing that the task of media is to *inform*, to *educate* and to *entertain*. Yet for the student of communication, such a trio of media goals resembles a set of holograms, appearing to have substance and meaning but reaching out to them only locates thin air. Information, yes – but what information; education, yes – but what do we mean by education; entertainment, certainly – but does its separate classification mean that it cannot also be informative and educational or that information and education cannot be entertaining? Several commentators, best known among them Denis McQuail, have sought to create a more complex taxonomy of purposes as they operate in varying contexts.

They are referred to as *normative* theories. By this we mean functions as they *should* be according to dominant criteria; in some cases an ideal, in others a necessity; and they constitute guidelines to performance. In *Mass Communication Theory: An Introduction*,[4] McQuail posits six normative theories of media purposes:

- Authoritarian theory
- Free Press theory
- Social Responsibility theory
- Soviet theory
- Development theory
- Democratic-participant theory

In each case the theory relates the performance of media to the position taken up by the state towards the transmission of information, comment and expression.

Authoritarian theory

The Authoritarian theory describes a situation where government, in the hands of a tyrant or a ruling elite who exercise repressive power over the people, lays down the law as to what the media can communicate. In this context the media are servants of state, the mouthpiece of government. If they are perceived to fail in that capacity, by showing a degree of editorial independence, they are censored or shut down.

Some media thrive in these conditions. *El Mercurio* had no difficulty getting published in Chile during the tyranny of the generals following the assassination of the Marxist President Allende in 1973. The editorial board of the newspaper would no doubt have justified their position by saying that the paper was dedicated to upholding authority (in face of Marxist chaos); that they were a force for cohesion in times when discipline – control – not liberty was the prescription for national survival.

Free Press theory

On the face of it Free Press theory, sometimes referred to as Libertarian theory, is the exact opposite of Authoritarian theory: its first principle is that the free press is servant to none but its readership in its task of informing, educating and entertaining. The press of the Western world would place itself in this category.

Free expression, unchecked by censorship – external or internal – is what media are about. The 'free' claim fearlessness in the pursuit of truth. They take a pride in being the conscience and watchdog over the rights of the people.

It is with the Free Press theory – so the theory goes – that error is exposed and the truth arrived at; and, in the USA, this principle is duly enshrined in the First Amendment to the Constitution. This states that 'Congress shall make no law... abridging the freedom of speech of the press'. McQuail asks, as perhaps we all must, exactly *whose* freedom the media are expressing; and how free is free in situations dominated by competition, reliance on advertising and deeply affected by patterns of ownership, all operating in wider contexts in which there are conflicting interests and competing definitions of freedom.

Social Responsibility theory

Social Responsibility theory works according to the notion that the media have a number of obligations to the public; what one might term a public stewardship. Public Service Broadcasting would come under this heading, for regulation by law or self-imposition, is seen as necessary in order to operate socially responsible checks and balances upon freedoms.

The liberty which Free Press theory demands might result in attacks in print or on air upon minorities. This would be freedom unchecked by responsibility: the right of free speech takes priority over the social – the public – damage that can be caused by such free expression. In party political matters Free Press theory insists on the right to be biased in favour of one party against another, to flatter the one and disparage the other, whereas the Social Responsibility theory would urge that, in the public interest, and in the interests of true representation (or an aspiration to it), both sides of a case should be put.

For such a theory to work successfully, there are implications for ownership and control, not just of one newspaper or broadcasting company, but across the whole spectrum of media. The theory would demand a pluralist media in a pluralist society and this would only be possible through multiple ownership. Under such criteria a newspaper owner would not be permitted to move into TV, especially if the owner's paper published in the same city as the TV company he/she was interested in controlling.

Soviet theory

The Soviet system has passed away and, with it – for the time being at least – Soviet theory. It is still worth outlining its principles, if only to explain how it differed from Authoritarian theory. In practice, of course, it didn't: the press, broadcasting, cinema, book publishing – indeed all message systems – were in the service of the state. But they were not privately run, as was the case with *El Mercurio* of Santiago. The media in Soviet Russia were the voice of the state, yes, but theoretically they were also the voice of the people.

They had the task of informing and educating the people in socialism because this was viewed as unquestionably in the people's interest. The role of the media was to mobilise and to sustain the socialist revolution, to defend it against counter-revolution and to protect it from the 'evil' influence of capitalism. Censorship was acceptable if it meant that the people were shielded from ideas and information which might contradict, and therefore undermine, the ruling ideology of communism.

Development theory

As the name implies this theory relates to media operating in developing, or so-termed Third World nations. It has parallels with the Soviet theory because media are seen to serve a particular social and political function. It favours journalism which seeks out good news, in contrast to the Free Press position where journalists respond most readily to stories of disaster, and for whom 'bad news is good news' because it commands bigger headlines.

Development theory requires that bad news stories are treated with caution, for such stories can be economically damaging to a nation in the delicate throes of growth and change. Grim headlines can put off investors, even persuade them to pull out their investments. As an antidote to the bad news syndrome, Development theory seeks to accentuate the positive; it nurtures the autonomy of the developing nation and gives special emphasis to indigenous cultures. It is both a theory of state support and one of resistance – resistance that is to the norms of competing nations and competing theories of media.

This is the reason why the actors in the Free Press system are often unhappy with and rejective of Development theory attitudes and practices. They attack these as censorship. The wealthy capitalist nations, and their media advocates, see the world as their backyard. Supported by the technology with which few developing nations can compete, the West recognises no frontiers to free enterprise; and what frontiers are set against it are simply bought away, evaded by satellite or crushed by the software of information, education and entertainment which has more power than the colonising armies of the past (see note 5 for a comment on the New World Information Order, associated with Development theory).

Democratic-participant theory

This represents the sort of media purpose the idealist dreams up in the bath. It is an aspiration rather than a phenomenon which can be recognised anywhere in practice, yet it is surely one which any healthy democracy should regard as a goal. Denis McQuail, having queried whether the Democratic-participant theory warrants a separate normative classification, concludes that it deserves its identity because it challenges reigning theories and offers a positive strategy towards the achievement of new forms of media institution.

This theory places particular value upon horizontal rather than vertical modes of authority and communication. It stands for defence against commercialisation and monopoly while at the same time being resistant to the centrism and bureaucracy so characteristic of public media institutions. The model emphasises the importance of the role of receiver in the communication process and incorporates what might be termed Receiver Rights – to relevant information; to be heard as well as to hear and be shown.

MCQUAIL'S FIVE BASIC FUNCTIONS OF MEDIA

Having analysed the six normative functions of media, Denis McQuail provides the reader with a useful summary of his own, under five headings – Information, Correlation, Continuity, Entertainment and Mobilisation.

Information

- providing information about events and conditions in society and the world
- indicating relations of power
- facilitating innovation, adaptation and progress

Correlation

- explaining, interpreting and commenting on the meaning of events and information
- providing support for established authority and norms
- socialising
- coordinating separate activities
- consensus building
- setting orders of priority and signalling relative status

Continuity

- expressing the dominant culture and recognising sub-cultures and new cultural developments
- forging and maintaining commonality of values

Entertainment

- providing amusement, diversion, the means of relaxation
- reducing social tension

Mobilisation

- campaigning for societal objectives in the sphere of politics, war, economic development, work and sometimes religion

---

From *Mass Communication: An Introduction* (UK: Sage, 1983)

A Right of Reply would be a basic element of the model as would be the right, on the part of sections of the community, special interest groups or sub-cultures, to use the means of communication available. As McQuail puts it, there is in the model 'a mixture of theoretical elements, including libertarianism, utopianism, socialism, egalitarianism, localism'. In short, people power.

Functioning according to roles

If, in a first-stage analysis, we can identify a number of normative functions of media, some of them overlapping, we can further approach the task of understanding purpose by examining the roles the media play in society and how they perform those roles. Three such *roles* are of a 'canine' nature: the watchdog, the guard dog and the lapdog.

In their capacity as watchdog the media are the eyes and ears of the public, its defender against possible abuses by the state. As guard dogs they sit sentinel at the house of the masters. Obviously they do not recognise themselves in the role of the lapdog: such a description is left for critics of media performance.

The guard dog role is arguably most recognisable in the normative practices of Authoriarian and Soviet theory but few commentators would deny its activity in democracies. The watchdog role *ought* to prevail in systems of a pluralist nature and often does but it is hedged about by forces whose interests demand dogs that bark only when they are commanded to do so.

We can identify many roles relative to normative requirements. A newspaper wishing to perform in accordance with Democratic-participant theory will act as *advocate* of public participation in all walks of life. It will support such ideas as the representation of workers on boards of management and it will perform as *documentarist* in revealing managements that deny such representation.

Yet while this paper altruistically defends public interest it cannot ignore the fact that it is in competition with players of other roles, such as purveyors of scandal, titillation, sensation or just plain fun. It would be a mistake, however, to dismiss such roles as merely decorative, for while some observers might see the tabloid press as *court jesters*, the papers cast themselves among the world's most earnest *preachers*. Their sensationalism almost invariably has a moral if not political purpose; and if it has such a purpose, then it has an ideological intent.

In this sense a prominent role of media is that of *definer*. John Hartley argues in *The Politics of Pictures: The Creation of the Public in the Age of Popular Media*[6] that the media define what is right by describing what is wrong. He calls this *photographic negativisation* 'where the image of order is actually recorded as its own negative, in stories of disorder'. 'Good grief,' one might exclaim, 'so all these stories of scandals are actually parables about how to behave properly!'

Agents of order

A primary role played by media in society is that of *representatives of order*. This view is argued by Richard V. Ericson, Patricia M. Barnak and Janet B. L. Chan in *Representing Order: Crime, Law And Justice in the News Media*.[7] We shall be discussing news in the next chapter but it is worth quoting here points made by Ericson and his colleagues.

First, like the law, the media are agencies of policing. They produce stories 'that help to make sense of, and express sensibilities about, social order'. Things are represented in terms of correctness or incorrectness rather than in terms of truth or falsehood. The authors of *Representing Order* believe the media work towards 'legal control through compliance'. Second, it is the custom and practice of media, overtly or covertly, to define control as *institutionally* grounded within the structures of government 'and particularly its law enforcement apparatus'.

We need not confine our attention to the news to realise how deeply conscious-ness of law and order penetrates everyday life – thanks in large part to the media. At national or local level we can be forgiven for thinking sometimes that here is not the News but the Police News. Yet this penetration extends well into newspaper columns and TV schedules marked 'Entertainment'.

How many cop series are on TV at the moment? In cynical moments we might wish to ask how many series are *not* about cops and criminals. Programmers might respond that audiences enjoy crime stories, that such series have high ratings, but the fascination runs deeper, perhaps feeding our own profound needs for order which are rarely so neatly fulfilled as by a crime story that solves the mystery and brings wrongdoers to book.

Essentially crime stories are about deviance, that is deviance from acceptable norms, of codes of conduct within the community. In their capacity as guard dogs, the media keep a close watch on the boundaries which divide conformity from deviance. By their reporting, they locate that dividing line and in doing so become the definers of deviance. They patrol that boundary, aware of course that the boundary is built of ideology not bricks. Thanks to the media, it might be said, Western governments have had no need of a Berlin Wall.

Media in the role of mobilisers

Mobilisation of public opinion in support of a cause is at its most dramatic in times of war when the overriding principle of performance as far as the media are concerned is to be absolutely clear which side 'we' are on. Again, this position comes under the heading of representing order. Media which attempt to give fair coverage to the enemy's point of view are soon accused of being unpatriotic.

When, during the Falklands War between Britain and Argentina in 1982, the *Daily Mirror* raised questions about the wisdom of fighting such a war, her rival, the *Sun*, mobiliser-in-chief of the war effort with its ardent support of 'our boys', was outraged and accused the *Mirror* of treason. Generally in times of crisis – which the media will have also been instrumental in defining (hence the term *crisis definition*) – the media take on the duty of uniting public opinion in support of the government, the 'war' effort and the nation.

Particularly in times of conflict 'nationhood' is subject to especially robust definition: our eyes and ears are blitzed with images which reinforce patriotism – flags, uniforms, weapons, library pictures of our past victories on land, sea and in the air. What is occurring is a process in which *consent* to state action is being nurtured; or as Edward Herman and Noam Chomsky have famously termed it, the *manufacture of consent*.[8] The public is desperate for information, for reassurance, for guidance, for leadership. Consensus, the feeling of togetherness, means something: differences tend to be forgotten or minimised. We become dependent upon the media who, in their turn, are dependent upon the authorities as to how much information is to be made public.

If there is a scarcity of information there are still pages to fill; the TV news has still to go out. What rushes to the aid of performance is conjecture, or guesswork. Experts are wheeled in by the busload to clarify, to predict; and the less hard news there is – for in wartime censorship is usually at its most rigorous – the more *human stories* have to be produced. Personalisation, always a key principle of media performance, sweeps to the top of the agenda, and the cast of characters is divided between heroes (us) and villains (them).

Hartley in *The Politics of Pictures* calls this *Wedom/Theydom* and it quickly succumbs to the darker practices of *demonisation*. With such performances in such times we recognise most vividly the role of media within the cultural apparatus of the state. We see that the bottom line, in terms of value, is *power*.

Principles of media performance: possibilities and problems

Let us now examine a number of principles which define normative, or 'best' media performance. At the macro-level these can be identified as *diversity* of sources and outlets and *accessibility* on the part of the whole public to information, both of these contributing to a *plurality* of opinions in society.

To diversify is to make different, to give variety to. Relatedly, to *diverge* is to tend from a common point in different directions; to vary from the standard. Media provision should, then, as commentators such as Denis McQuail believe, be both diverse and capable of divergence. In our use of media we should have the option of the serious and the amusing, the challenging and the relaxing and we should be able to experience through the media a diversity of viewpoint.

At the same time we as audience should be able to access information and comment without always having to have recourse to the Murdochs and the Berlusconis of the world. Consequently, diversity applies to channel as well as content and style; and that would mean a diversity of channels as well as a diversity of ownership and control. To ensure diversity of channel there must be regulation. Who controls the airwaves, the print works, the distribution networks, the telecommunications systems, who commands the fibre-optic cables and the satellites, exerts power over choice.

In addition to the benefits of channel diversity, 'best' performance would be to require diversity of *source* – that is, where information originates; where newspapers, radio and TV get their information from. Much raw material for news emerges from sources which are essentially in the business of *news management* aimed at putting over the source's position in a favourable light.

Governments are the most substantial suppliers of information in any society, followed by transnational corporations among whose portfolios are news agencies. The American, Herbert Gans, has pointed out that 'Journalists get most of their news from regular sources which, as study after study has shown, are usually speaking for political, economic and other establishments'.[9]

Diversity and the free market

The case is often put that deregulation and privatisation encourage diversity: where there are more channels, more programmes to choose from, diversity inevitably follows. In an article 'Deregulation and the dream of diversity' published in the *Journal of Communication*,[10] D.R. LeDuc is less than impressed by this argument. He comments, in reference to claims of increased over-air channel choice, 'it resembles the degree of diversity in dining opportunities experienced when a McDonalds restaurant begins business in a town already served by Burger King'. We need to assess both *vertical* and *horizontal* diversity, the one being the number of options offered by a single channel, the other, options available at any time across the range of channels. We might conclude that more sometimes means less.

We might be equally hesitant in concluding that diversity where it exists ensures plurality of opinions. One of the legislative glories of history, the First Amendment to the American Constitution, guarantees the freedom of the press (and consequently of broadcasting and other forms of media communication). We can sit back and admire, but before we rejoice and uncritically recommend the American approach to the liberties of expression, we should recognise that the First Amendment awards the media a mighty power over which neither individuals nor the community has much influence.

Indivisible or unlimited freedom, as some commentators have pointed out, does have its drawbacks, for the First Amendment also protects the 'voice' of the great corporations who, in law, are deemed to have the rights of individuals. Hence media barons and corporate media empires have the freedom – indeed the *right* – as well as the capacity to dominate the public discourses of the time. The American scholar, Harold Innis, writing in the 1950s, in works such as *The Bias of Communication*,[11] was of the view that the First Amendment to the American Constitution, so lauded as a human right, actually served as an obstacle to free speech.

Golden triangle or lead weight?

At the micro-level of operations three related and interconnecting goals can be identified. These are *objectivity*, *impartiality* and *balance* (see Figure 4.3). They comprise what we might, initially, call a golden triangle of public service principles, and would apply as much to the press as to regulated broadcasting. In each

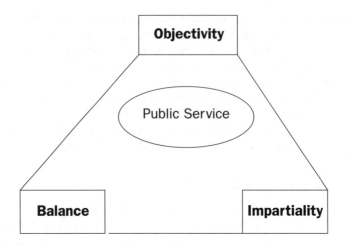

Figure 4.3   Criteria of public service communication

case there are problems of definition, just as there are problems when communicators are accused of bias.

John Fiske, in his chapter on 'Popular News' in *Reading the Popular*[12] rejects objectivity as a goal in decisive manner:

> Objectivity is authority in disguise: 'objective' facts always support particular points of view and their 'objectivity' can exist only as part of the play of power. But, more important, objective facts cannot be challenged: objectivity discourages audience activity and participation.

Fiske implies a significant criterion of performance – that it should stimulate audience activity and participation.

Fiske's position suggests that at best there are only 'objectivities'; in which case they are for all intents and purposes 'subjectivities'. However, efforts have been and will continue to be made both to define objectivity and to insist on it. A fair shot at definition has been made by J.H. Boyer. Writing in the *American Journalism Quarterly*[13] on 'How editors view objectivity', Boyer suggests the following criteria:

1. Balance and evenhandedness in presenting different sides of an issue.
2. Accuracy and realism in reporting.
3. Presenting all main relevant points.
4. Separating facts from opinion, but treating opinion as relevant.
5. Minimising the influence of the writer's own attitude, opinion or involvement.
6. Avoiding slant, rancour or devious purposes.

After citing these in *Media Performance: Mass Communication and the Public Interest*,[14] Denis McQuail poses a number of queries as to the possibility of attaining all or any of the Boyer Six. He lists the difficulties: first, in news, items have to be selected; all reported events have to be presented in wider frames of reference; omissions, gaps and silences are unavoidable and may reflect implicit judgments about relevance and assumptions about society and its values; and news is always produced within a context of numerous powerful internal and external pressures.

The most telling argument – one taken up later in Chapter 5 – is that underpinning the notion of objectivity is an assumption that out there is an identifiable reality about which to report. 'No account of reality,' says McQuail, 'can be uniquely correct or complete, except in the most trivial instance.' He goes on to question the desirability of objectivity as a governing principle, arguing that it is misleading to offer something which cannot be delivered.

All accounts are *versions*; thus the dominant power to express will generally if not always have the advantage, for this power is better placed, better resourced and quickest at getting over its 'version' to the public. A pedantic insistence on objectivity would, in any event, impede some of the media's most important performances – in the reporting of human interest stories, the occasionally stirring partisanship and in investigative journalism where subjectivity can be so trenchant and revealing.

It will have already struck the reader that objectivity, impartiality and balance are not very different ways of saying the same thing, each springing from the idea that communicators can step out of the contexts in which they find themselves. To do this they would also have to step out of their skin, shed a lifetime's 'project of self' – a striptease which public sector communication often demands of its reporters and presenters, insisting on them playing the 'golden triangle' game.

This would be a reasonably acceptable scenario if all communicators played by the rules of objectivity, impartiality and balance. The press patently do not, which arguably gives them an advantage in terms of influence if TV and radio are committed through regulation to strict neutrality. Rules of engagement that apply to some media and not others makes for an uneven playing field.

Media performance and human rights

As we have seen, in modern society the media may be regarded as a contemporary equivalent of the ancient Greek *agora*, usually the city or town square in which the population gathered to discuss the affairs of state. This 'public space' or sphere has been, down the centuries, fought over and latterly built over. In some circumstances, that space was a physical one. In Britain, there was a time when the common people possessed by tradition rights of access and use of open spaces: a greater part of these was 'privatised' by acts of enclosure. The power elite made the rules and the rules were forged in their interest and to the cost of the dispossessed.

Without the power of the vote, without a collective voice, the unpropertied classes were condemned to a fate from which there was little escape via the law or government. Yet during the 19th century in Britain the dispossessed did find a voice in the Pauper or Radical Press. The public space which had been curtailed by enclosure was gradually reborn through the pages of newspapers.

It was sustained and enlarged by radical speechmakers and pamphleteers, by political action groups such as the Chartists, each assembling piece by piece a philosophy which would enunciate human rights, the centrepiece of which was the notion of *equality*. This was not arguing that all men and women are equal; rather that they should be treated equally; that they should have equal rights, equal access to information; an equal voice in the *agora* or forum in whatever form it existed. Today, we remain a long way from that ideal, but the principle holds good, shaping and influencing all the other human rights which have been drawn up, debated, installed, overthrown, restored – in short, fought over, down the years.

Human rights are always worth listing and worth repeating, particularly so if we set a condition of media performance that it honour those rights by supporting them, arguing for them, defending them against their abuse. That, at least in my view, would be the chief performance criterion of a media seeking to contribute to the public good.

Let us list the freedoms which many consider essential in a fair and democratic society:

- Freedom of speech and expression
- Freedom of access to information
- Freedom of belief and worship
- Freedom of movement
- Freedom of assembly

Key to the five principles is the overarching criterion of *equality* – equal opportunity to speak and express; equal opportunity of access, and so on. McQuail, in an article entitled 'Mass media in the public interest' and published in *Mass Media and Society*,[15] talks of Public Communication Values. Equality he subdivides into Access, Diversity and – yes – Objectivity as exemplified by neutrality, fairness and truth. He makes the vital point that equality supports policies of universal provision; that is, information is seen as a right not a privilege.

In the same volume, James Curran in 'Rethinking the role of media' sees that in an age where the power giants of government and the corporations have shared the spoils of the Communication Age, the media have ceased to be an agency of empowerment and become an accomplice by which the public has been sidelined.

It is the job of media, says Curran, to facilitate and protect the public sphere. One of its roles must be defender of public rights against encroachment by state and corporate powers: that is, performing the role of watchdog, not guard dog. Curran writes, 'The media should be seen as a source of redress against the abuse of power over others'.

Models of performance

Ultimately, the practice of media ethics begins, even though it does not rest with, the practitioner. What model of behaviour should inspire the would-be journalist, photographer, cameraperson or editor? In 'The crisis of the sovereign state' published in *Media, Crisis and Democracy: Mass Communication and the Disruption of Social Order*,[16] John Keane offers a cogent and inspiring definition, first by way of contrast:

> Quality journalism rejects tabloid newspaper tactics, whose golden rules are: please the news desk; get front page coverage and stay in front of everyone else; reflect the prejudices of readers; defend nationalist hype and page three pin-ups; fight for 'the scandal of the gay vicar' and other sensational exclusives with as little legal comeback as possible; remain emotionally uninvolved in any and every story; if necessary, invade privacy on a scale that would impress a burglar; all the while explaining to the interviewees that their willingness to cooperate will help others in similar plight.

The honest journalist need not stoop to such tactics. Keane goes on:

> High quality investigative journalism lives by different rules. It seeks to counteract the secretive and noisy arrogance of the democratic Leviathan.[17] It involves the patient investigation and exposure of political corruption, misconduct and mismanagement. It clings to the old maxim of American muck-rakers – 'the news is what someone, somewhere, *doesn't* want to see printed'.

> It aims to sting political power, to tame its arrogance by extending the limits of public controversy and widening citizens' informed involvement in the public spheres of civil society.

As the world changes, so do the purposes, roles and performance of media. Today the issues the public needs to address, through the mediation of mass communication, are global as never before. In *Understanding Media Cultures: Social Theory and Mass Communication*,[18] Nick Stevenson speaks of 'citizenship entitlements' and the concept of citizenship 'has to be applied to local, national and more transnational levels'. Appropriately at each level the public needs to be served – by its governments as well as its mass media – in four major ways:

1. By being informed about 'the operation of expert cultures'.
2. By being helped towards an understanding of 'the desires, demands and need interpretations of others who are distant in time and space'.
3. By being nurtured into an understanding of ourselves 'as a social community'.
4. By being participants in 'aesthetic and non-instrumentally defined cultural experiences'.

Stevenson writes:

> Modernity has witnessed the increasing specialisation of certain forms of expert knowledge. Most citizens do not understand the workings of complex global economies, are perplexed by the scientific debates on global warming and are unsure of the exact precautions they should take in order to prevent themselves becoming infected with the HIV virus.

The media have a role to play in explaining such matters to publics worldwide 'within a decommodified zone and outside the control of state power', providing 'a space where irrational prejudices could be challenged and an informed and genuinely democratic debate could take place'.

Functions 2 and 3 are especially crucial in conditions 'of cultural and psychic fragmentation'. The first relates to our obligations to others, not only to those within our own cultures but to those beyond our cultural and geographical boundaries whose lives, nevertheless, are impinged upon by our own behaviour. Stevenson says:

> Given the global risks of ozone depletion, global warming, toxic dumping and the long-term effects of nuclear power, local decisions would have to be tied into an appreciation of global frameworks.

The media, because of their capacity to 'shift information spatially, are uniquely positioned to make such information available to us'. In Stevenson's view, the systems best able to provide such a service are public media because they are likely to 'put the communicative needs of citizens before the interests of powerful economic and administrative structures that maintain the *status quo*'.

Communities also need to be reminded of who they are, of their need to 'form identities in common with others' while at the same time guaranteeing tolerance of alternative identities and cultures. This does not mean unquestioningly honouring 'timeless forms of myth, ceremony and ritual'. Rather, a mature public and a mature media should be concerned to identify needs 'based upon reflexivity, ambivalence and cultural questioning': we reflect upon ourselves, our cultural condition (and conditioning) and we seek to live with, and tolerate, differences and contradictions. It is all part of the process of self-formulation referred to in Chapter 3.

Stevenson's fourth criterion also relates to the upholding of public interest in the face of private invasion. The aesthetic dimension is that part which exceeds the instrumental. The look, feel or sound of a thing is a criterion separate from its function or its market value. It works cognitively and affectively; it is about feelings, emotion and sensation and as such we can recognise it, enjoy it but rarely quantify it.

Stevenson quotes the British TV playwright Dennis Potter who, in his last interview before his death in 1994, said that without the backing of a public broadcasting system his work – challenging, unnerving and often difficult – might never have flourished. A system whose first principle was profit and therefore demanded optimum-size audiences for its programmes would draw back from the risk of broadcasting Potter's ground-breaking work. That would have been a loss to the canon of TV drama but also a loss to the community in terms of cultural richness.

Stevenson argues that 'Cultural forms of communication that challenge mass entertainment agendas should be given access to the media'. At the same time acknowledgment must be made of 'wider sets of responsibilities and obligations', for 'freedom of expression is never absolute'. Such recommendations as Stevenson makes have a special urgency at a time when 'public service is being undermined by more globally orientated commercial networks'.

===================================== SUMMARY =====================================

This chapter set out to examine the propaganda, the commercial *laissez-faire* and the public service models of media purpose, going on to discuss a number of normative functions arising out of social and political structures. The picture is broadened out by identifying some key roles which media play in society, as definers of reality, agents of control, mobilisers of public opinion and manufacturers of consent.

Media performance is viewed in relation to such guiding principles as diversity and access and operational level goals such as objectivity, impartiality and balance. Equality is seen as key to the media's capacity to advocate and support public rights within a fair and democratic society. Finally, markers are laid down concerning the responsibilities of the media within changing global situations.

KEY TERMS

propaganda/commercial *laissez-faire*/public service models ■ plurality
normative theories ■ diversity, access ■ objectivity, impartiality, balance
watchdog/guard dog ■ crisis definition ■ photographic negativisation
mobilisation ■ personalisation ■ demonisation ■ equality
citizenship entitlements

================================ SUGGESTED ACTIVITIES ================================

1. For discussion:
   (a) As new technology increasingly fragments the provision of media what future can there be for systems of public service in broadcasting?
   (b) How might Democratic-participant modes of mass communication be developed in the face of dominant Free Press modes?
   (c) What defensive strategies might developing nations adopt to counteract the 'cultural invasion' by core nations such as the United States?
   (d) In what ways might the media help mobilise moves towards equality in society?

2. Examine copies of the tabloid/popular press with a view to identifying how they see their functions in society, what duties and responsibilities they seem to have with regard to readership.

3. Scrutinise TV programmes for a week in search of evidence of 'global commitment' to the understanding of others.

4. Work out the percentage of broadcast programmes available to all compared to the proportion of programmes which are restricted through encryption (for example, cable/satellite transmissions).

NOW READ ON

Media Performance: Mass Communication and the Public Interest by Denis McQuail (UK: Sage, 1992) referred to in this chapter is the text to go for. It is immensely thorough and readable. The citizenship theme is admirably dealt with by Peter Dahlgren and Colin Sparks in *Communication and Citizenship: Journalism and the Public Sphere* (UK: Routledge, 1993). The role of media in a democracy, and their duties to serve it can be explored in John Keane's *Media and Democracy* (UK: Polity Press, 1991). Nicholas Garnham's *Capitalism and Communication* (UK: Sage, 1990) examines media in relation to the power-value of capitalism.

The media's role as rooter-out of deviance is vividly illustrated in *The Enemy Within: MI5, Maxwell and the Scargill Affair* by Seamus Milne (UK: Verso, 1994). *Don't Mention The War: Northern Ireland, Propaganda and the Media* by David Miller (UK: Pluto, 1994) and *The 'Uncensored' War: the Media and Vietnam* by Daniel Hallin (US: Oxford University Press, 1986) also offer fruitful insights.

One of the most readable books on the theme of the risks public service media take when, performing the role of public watchdog, they challenge the activities of government is Roger Bolton's *Death on the Rock, and Other Stories* (UK: W.H. Allen, 1990), an account of Thames TV's *This Week* investigation into the shooting in Gibraltar by the SAS (Special Air Service) of three members of the IRA in March 1988.

5
The News: Gates, Agendas and Values

AIMS

- To present the case that by its nature and practice the news is the product of the cultural contexts in which it operates: and rather than mirroring reality, constructs ritual formulations of it.
- To explain with reference to landmark theories three core features of news production – gatekeeping, agenda setting and news values and to examine their interactivity.
- To reflect on the role of ideology in the process of news production.

Sooner or later in every study of media communication we must descend from the high ground which offers us an overview of the terrain to examine texts and practices – the specifics which provide evidence to substantiate theories. So far attention has been trained on generalities such as the nature of audience and audience response and the purpose, within context, of mass communication. More than any other message form, the news provides us with documentation that illustrates and illuminates key connections – between public communication and the exercise of power, between freedom and control, between reality and representation. It is, by its content and its shaping, a discourse which purports both to present reality and to explain it.

This chapter puts the case that the news is inevitably *slanted* because a culture's views of the world at large are coloured by a primary interest in 'its own kind'. This we call ethnocentrism, manifesting itself substantially, though not entirely, in nearness, or proximity. We note also that 'slant' is demonstrated by a preference for featuring Knowns as against Unknowns: the elite are visualised as not only being in the news but making it.

Strategies of news construction – gatekeeping and agenda setting – are examined in relation to the underpinning criteria of news selection, which we call news values or newsworthiness. Acknowledgement is made of the powerfully competing agendas in contemporary society which strive to attract and manipulate public attention and in doing so affect the nature of news production.

The cultural orientation of news

An old adage has often been cited as a definer of what makes news. It asserts that a fly in the eye is worse than an earthquake in China. Though ethically indefensible, the adage nevertheless pinpoints two crucial factors in the selection of events to be reported – the *ethnocentric* nature of news coverage (its culture-centredness); and the significance of *proximity*, or nearness.

What happens to 'us' is considered the prime principle of newsworthiness; and if a number of us are killed in that earthquake in faraway China reports of it will guarantee that the tragedy will be more fully reported.

Geographical proximity does not automatically qualify as a value demanding news attention. Events in the United States are more readily and substantially reported in Britain than events in Europe, despite the ties that bind the British to Europe; and the difference is more than one of language. Australia and India share with the British and Americans the English language but command far less media attention in Britain. The difference is one of *power-value* arising from key economic, political and cultural interactions, in which America has been the dominant partner. The high profile granted to the USA in the British media is at best only modestly reciprocated in American media.

The news is as much about the perceived *importance* of self and other as it is about 'reality'. As perceptions of importance – significant events, occasions, developments – change, so does reality definition. At a primitive level we might envisage news as the view a sentry has at the mouth of our communal cave: who or what out there is for us or against us, and what threat might they pose? The purpose here is one of *surveillance*.

From the beginning, then, news as a version of reality is skewed by a cultural bias and conditioned by the specifics of situation: the guard dog barks, the sentinel geese cackle and we take action to protect ourselves, whether the 'invader' is a foe from across the water or a scare about salmonella in pre-cooked meals.

Cultural ritual

The surveillance function affirms the *tribal* nature of news; that it is part of the rituals which dominate our lives. As our ancestors took guard when dusk fell and watched the night hours for signs of danger, so the Eye of News reports to us daily in the papers, on the hour on radio and several times daily on TV. It is as ritualistic as changing the guard; and in the nature and ordering of its content the news resembles a ceremony. Indeed, we are so familiar with content and style that it might be said that the news is actually *olds*: what has by precedent been counted as news continues to be classified and used as news.

The *conventions* of news production are often so formulaic that they hint at a rightness born of hallowed tradition which in turn, when queried, is righteously defended. In this sense, the news is not in the business of telling us about reality; rather it is privileged to inform us about what is *important* or salient about reality. And importance is key: people or institutions featuring regularly in the news do so because they are important to society. They are primary actors in the ritual of cultural reinforcement and renewal, lords and ladies of the dance. Thus a media bias towards reporting their doings and sayings is, convention decrees, only natural and proper.

Herbert Gans in *Deciding What's News*,[1] says that 'knowns' are four times more likely to be in the news than 'unknowns'. He gauged that fewer than 50 individuals, mostly high-placed federal officials, regularly appear on American TV news.

The ritual of news is characterised both by its ethnocentric nature (its 'us-centredness') and what might be called its 'power-centredness'. Both aspects of the ritual demand a considerable degree of selection, of inclusion and exclusion. The same criteria for selection seem to apply to news *sources*. According to Allan Bell in *The Language of News Media*,[2] 'News is what an authoritative source tells a journalist... . The more elite the source, the more newsworthy the story'.

In contrast, says Bell, 'alternative sources tend to be ignored: individuals, opposition parties, unions, minorities, fringe groups, the disadvantaged'. As far as our opening adage is concerned – about the fly in the eye – selection depends on which fly and in which eye.

News as construct

We are seeing, then, that the news is culturally positioned, and we view reality through a cultural prism. That the rendition of reality is so convincing is explained partly because the news, framed for us by the media, is usually all that we have to go on as a portrait of realities beyond our known environment; and partly because the news is constructed with such professional skill.

Television news suggests that what we see is what there is, that we are being presented with mirror images of reality. One of the best books on 'life seen through a media prism' is edited by Stanley Cohen and Jock Young. It captures the point being made here in its title: *The Manufacture of News*.[3] Contributors to this volume examine the reporting of events and issues in terms of a process of assembly, of construction according to dominant cultural-political criteria. Among subscribers to *The Manufacture of News* are Johan Galtung and Mari Ruge, and Professor Stuart Hall whose work is referred to later in this chapter.

As audience our attention is not, however, drawn to the 'constructed' nature of news. Rather we have grown so accustomed to the modes of news presentation that we are, unless especially cautioned, likely to judge that it is at least a close encounter with reality. Yet journalists provide us with a clue to their trade as 'assembly-workers' when they refer to news reports as 'stories', thus implying a process of invention. As Allan Bell puts it, 'Journalists do not write articles. They write stories' (a theme taken up in the next chapter).

We begin to recognise the artifice of news only when we come face to face with the real thing through lived experience: disasters, riots, protest marches, strikes, demonstrations – news media have filled our heads with visions of how these things 'look'. Just occasionally we encounter such events personally and the shock of the real to our mediated experience can be devastating.

Selecting the news: gatekeeping

In studying the news we need to explore three linked features of production – *gatekeeping*, *agenda setting* and *news values*. The operation of the first two depends upon the demands of the third, which in turn regulates the *conventions* of news presentation. Gatekeeping is about opening or closing the channels of communication. It is about *accessing* or refusing access. In an article 'The "Gatekeepers": a case study in the selection of news', published in *Journalism Quarterly*, 27, 1950, David M. White presents a simple model of the gatekeeping process (Figure 5.1).

White had spent a period of research observing the activities of a 'Mr. Gate', a telegraph wire editor on an American non-metropolitan newspaper. The notion of 'gate areas' had been posed three years earlier by Kurt Lewin in 'Channels of group life' in *Human Relations* 1, 1947. Lewin's particular attention was focused upon decisions about household food purchases but he drew a comparison with the flow of mass media news.

While the term gatekeeping originates at this time, the practice of it is as old as history and it is an identifiable practice in many areas of communication. Students who have done any research will have already experienced gatekeeping: you want some information or you would like to talk to someone, perhaps to interview them for a project you are preparing. Some gates open, some are ajar and need pushing and some are firmly closed against you: why?

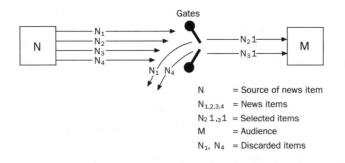

N   = Source of news item
$N_{1,2,3,4}$ = News items
$N_2 1_{,3}1$ = Selected items
M   = Audience
N_1, N_4 = Discarded items

Figure 5.1   White's simple gatekeeping model (1950). From D.M. White, 'The "Gatekeepers": a case study in the selection of news' published in *Journalism Quarterly*, 27 (1950) and latterly reproduced in *Communication Models for the Study of Mass Communications* (UK: Longman, 2nd edn, 1993) by Denis McQuail and Sven Windahl.

Students doing projects or dissertations know why. Those whose say-so rules the opening and closing of gates may be too busy. They are more likely to open the gate – like the news – to Knowns rather than Unknowns. As one of my own students put it in a project log, 'The people I wanted information from didn't think I was important enough to bother with, being a mere student. And I had nothing to exchange with them for their advice and their time'.

At a personal level, gates can sometimes be prised open through sheer determination and persistence, but ultimately the gate swings on hinges of reward; of purpose – of worthwhileness. White's model features a number of competing news items (N). At the gate, the sub-editor – 'Mr. Gate' – selects those items considered of sufficient interest and importance to be passed through to the next stage of news production. Thus N_2 and N_3 have been selected and have undergone the first stage of transformation, hence White's use of the 'to-the-power 1' at this point (indicating that the 'assembly' process – of shaping and selection – has already begun).

$N_2 1$ and $N_3 1$ are no longer raw information: they are *mediated* information. White's model does not give the criteria for selection and rejection of news items, nor does it acknowledge the fact that in the general process of mediation there are many gates and that gatekeeping in one form or another is taking place at all levels and at each stage of the news manufacturing process.

In 1959 J.T. McNelly produced a model of news flow which reflects the many-gated reality of news processing. It also indicates that modifications take place to the story as it passes through each gate (Figure 5.2). At every stage in the mediation process, decisions are taken, not only about what events to cover, but how these might be covered and by whom; and gatekeeping is far from being the monopoly of media operators: audience too exercises the powers of selecting and rejecting.

We are all gatekeepers: we self-censor. We decide to say something to another person – the comment passes through the gate. But we may decide *not* to say anything; or we might need to summarise, modify, spruce up, distort that which passes through our communicative gate. Yet again, we see the importance in the process of communication of *intent*.

Reporters with leftish political leanings, working on a rightish newspaper will, if they wish to stay on the payroll, gatekeep pre-emptively; that is, they will be selective about the stories they submit for publication, knowing that certain stories (sympathetic to the left, for example) would simply not be published – so why waste time and effort in submitting them?

Self-regulation of this kind is essential if the gates of access to sources of information are to be kept open. In most countries the chief supplier of information is government, and most governments regularise (even ritualise) the provision of information to the media, in particular to what are termed 'lobby correspondents'. Here, a degree of reciprocal gatekeeping is often a condition of access. Government will provide a certain amount of information in return for the journalist using that information 'properly'. 'Improper' use of that information may lead to the exclusion of a newspaper's lobby correspondent from the privileges of daily access to government news sources.

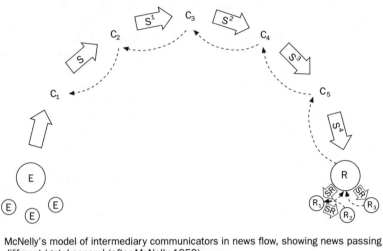

McNelly's model of intermediary communicators in news flow, showing news passing different 'gatekeepers' (after McNelly 1959)
Key to symbols in diagram:
E = Newsworthy event
C_1 = Foreign agency correspondent
C_2 = Regional bureau editor
C_3 = Agency central bureau or deskman
C_4 = National or regional home bureau editor
C_5 = Telegraph editor or radio or TV news editor
S, S^1, S^2, etc = The report in a succession of altered (shortened) forms
R = Receiver
R_1, R_2, etc. = Family members, friends, associates, etc.
SR = Story as modified by word of mouth transmission
Dotted line = feedback

Figure 5.2   McNelly's model of news flow (1959). Taken from McQuail and Windahl (see Figure 5.1). An important feature of the McNelly model is the SR feature which recognises the part audience itself plays in the mediation of news. The model originates in J.T. McNelly's article, 'Intermediary communicators in the international news', published in *Journalism Quarterly,* 36 (1959).

News gathering, news editing

As we have seen, selection operates at every stage of the news production process. It varies, however, in its nature and concentration. A.Z. Bass, writing in *Journalism Quarterly*, 46 (1969) poses a 'double action' model of internal news flow (Figure 5.3). This identifies two stages of production: Stage 1, *news gathering* and Stage 2, *news processing*. In Stage 1, reporters and photographers encounter raw news directly, or at least more directly than editors and sub-editors back at the newspaper, radio station or TV company. They are usually employed on one news story at a time. By the very fact that they are 'at the scene', they have a degree of choice on what features of an event they will select, and how they will report on them.

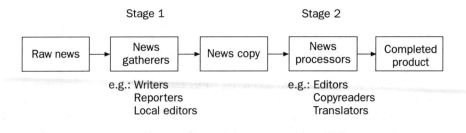

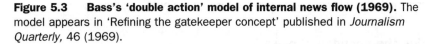

Figure 5.3   Bass's 'double action' model of internal news flow (1969). The model appears in 'Refining the gatekeeper concept' published in *Journalism Quarterly,* 46 (1969).

Once their report reaches the news organisation pressures of selection mount. The editorial team has many stories to deal with. They have to balance the demands of one story against another and, as Bass points out, they have to work in accordance with the organisation's norms and values. Far more than are reporters in the field, the editorial team is influenced in its decision-making by the cultural climate of the institution which in turn operates more centrally in the eye of government and the public.

Gates in times of crisis

The sound of gates slamming to, in times of crisis such as war, can be as loud as the enemy's artillery. During the Falklands War of 1982, between Britain and Argentina, it became difficult if not impossible to breach the walls of Fortress Information. Press and television were obliged to queue up at a drawbridge manned by the Ministry of Defence. During the Gulf War of 1991 the situation was different, though arguably no better for the free flow of news. The Allied forces kept the gates of information wide open, but they controlled the nature of that information, permitting the positive, closing off the negative. In *War and the Media: Propaganda and Persuasion in the Gulf War,*[4] Philip M. Taylor writes:

> Television is often regarded as a window on the world and in some respects it is. But in wartime, its potential to become a window onto the actual battle front is limited, not just by the nature of the medium itself but also by the curtain of darkness which military censorship attempts to draw over it.

Many commentators have pinpointed the inadequacies of Gulf War coverage as a result of its being gatekept by the military authorities. What TV could show of the war was what the military authorities granted them to show. For example, library footage (provided by the military) appeared to demonstrate the 'cleanness' of the war rendered possible by the technological wizardry of modern armaments. The resultant 'reality' had more in common with a video wargame than any resemblance to what was actually happening in Iraq as Operation Desert Storm settled the 'mother of all battles'.

Gates operate for and against media personnel. It is significant that Don McCullin, one of the world's best photographers of war, was gatekept throughout the Falklands War. While other reporters and photographers were permitted at least into the outer courtyard of Fortress Information, McCullin was not even allowed to cross the moat.

The Ministry of Defence was, according to its own lights, making the correct decision: McCullin's pictures would not have differentiated between Britons and Argentinians in portraying them as victims of war. His imaging of war as hell would not have sustained the war effort, nurtured consensus about its necessity; rather his pictures might have been instrumental in turning the public against the war.

Setting the agendas of news

An agenda is a list of items, usually in descending order of importance. Meetings have agendas which have to be worked to. If an item is not on the agenda prior to the meeting there is only one place that it can be raised during the meeting – under Any Other Business. The agenda for a meeting is normally drawn up by the secretary to the meeting in consultation with the meeting's chairperson. This gives them some power – to decide what will or will not be discussed at the meeting.

At the meeting itself, the chairperson has certain powers over the agenda. He or she may extend or curtail discussion on topics. The skilful chairperson will usually rule by consent, without the need to resort to voting. In Japan it is a tradition that decisions must already have been tacitly settled prior to the meeting. This is to avoid loss of face resulting from disagreement in public. Meetings conducted in Western countries may seem to be different, open rather than closed texts, as it were. Yet appearances can beguile. For every overt or public agenda there is a covert or hidden one.

As far as the media are concerned one might say that the overt agenda is synony-mous with the public agenda; that is, what is of most importance to the public appears top of the media agenda. Yet it has to be acknowledged that wherever there are competing interests, rival ideologies or conflicting priorities, agendas are arenas of struggle. Those whose discourse dominates also choose the agenda and order its items. In the media industry reporters may wish to pursue certain agendas, but their activity will be reined in by agendas of ownership and control.

The link between media agendas and public perception of what constitutes news is a vital one to explore. If the public look to the media for news, what the media decides is news is what the public recognise as news. What is emphasised by the media is given emphasis in public perception; what is amplified by media is enlarged in public perception.

This is illustrated by Donald McCombs and Malcolm Shaw's agenda-setting model of media effects (Figure 5.4). The authors of the model state in 'Structuring the "unseen environment"' in the *Journal of Communication*, Spring 1976:

> Audiences not only learn about public issues and other matters through the media, they also learn how much importance to attach to an issue or topic from the

emphasis the mass media place upon it. For example, in reflecting what people say during a campaign, the mass media apparently determine the important issues. In other words, the mass media set the 'agenda' of the campaign.

Amplification of issues

McCombs and Shaw argue that the agenda-setting capacity of the media makes them highly influential in shaping public perceptions of the world: 'This ability to affect cognitive change among individuals is one of the most important aspects of the power of mass communication'. The model is an oversimplification, of course. It assumes one agenda – that purveyed by the media – which then becomes the agenda of the public. It can be argued that members of the public have their own agendas, shaped by their own personal circumstances.

There are plenty of *intervening variables* which influence our perceptions and our judgments other than media coverage, though it has to be said that none may be quite as powerful as the full force of media definitions – especially if the media are promoting the same definitions in similar ways. A single newspaper claiming that Party Z at an election will put up taxes may not sway public opinion, but ten newspapers saying the same thing, and TV channels reporting what ten newspapers are claiming, may well – through a process of amplification and reinforcement – drive the tax issue to the top of the public agenda.

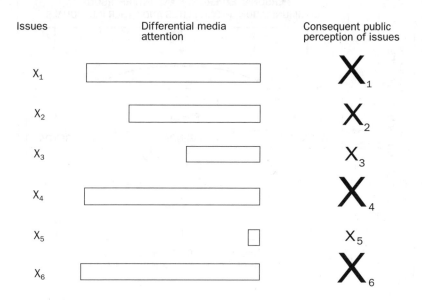

Figure 5.4   McCombs and Shaw's agenda-setting model of media effects (1976). From McQuail and Windahl (see Figure 5.1). Once again X represents an issue whose importance is amplified by coverage in the media. Even issues of considerable importance may remain of modest or negligible importance in public perception if they suffer media neglect.

The McCombs and Shaw model does not tell us whether effects are direct, or, from the point of view of media, intentional. Also, as Denis McQuail and Sven Windahl point out in *Communication Models for the Study of Mass Communication*,[5] the model leaves us uncertain 'whether agenda setting is initiated by the media or by members of the public and their needs, or, we might add, by institutional elites who act as sources for the media'.

A later model of agenda setting is posed by E.M. Rogers and J.W. Dearing (Figure 5.5). This identifies three interactive agendas. The *policy* agenda is that propagated by government and politicians. It is one often riven by counter-agendas – the right of the party, the left of the party. Appropriate emphasis is placed in this model on contextual factors: influences pressing in from national and world events.

The Rogers and Dearing model is a useful update of McCombs and Shaw, but one might ask why the three agendas are presented as being of equal size and presumably equal power. Because the model is still a linear one, it does not sufficiently indicate the dynamic relationship between the agendas or the potential for conflict. The policy and media agendas seem to be operating as *balancers* with the public agenda as being central (which of course is what it should be but rarely is). The model conveys balance, thus it is normative.

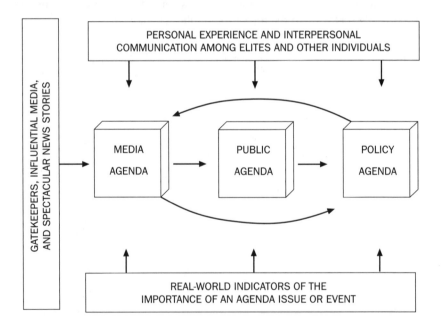

Figure 5.5   Rogers and Dearing's model of the agenda-setting process (1988).
From McQuail and Windahl (see Figure 5.1). This model, first published in an article 'Agenda-setting: where it has been, where is it going?' in *Communication Yearbook* 11 (US: Sage, 1987) serves very usefully as a basis for examining the whole contextual scene of news making.

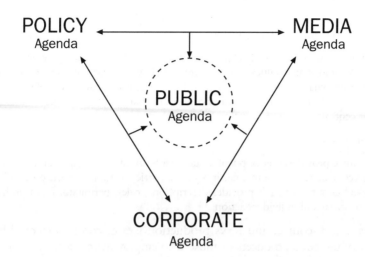

Figure 5.6   Tripolar model of agendas: policy, corporate and media. The public agenda is the only one which does not arise from consciously formed and articulated aims and objectives. Government, corporations and media largely know what they want from the public and how to go about getting it. The first two are also aware that in order to create and influence public opinion they have to do it through cultural apparatuses of which the media is arguably the most important. On the other hand, pressure groups in society are instrumental in influencing public opinion with a view to using the force of that opinion to influence government or the corporations.

To focus on the actual distribution of influence one would have to add an extra agenda – that of the corporations which dominate contemporary life (Figure 5.6). Corporate agendas often work in alliance with, and occasionally in competition with, the policy agendas of government, aiming to influence if not order public agendas. The reader may be justifiably tempted to add further arrows to this model to emphasise the interactive nature of the agendas.

Agenda, discourse and climate of opinion

We have seen that just as there are many gates there are several agendas; so any analysis of agenda setting must start with the question – *Whose* agenda, and articulated through which *discourse*? What is obvious is that there is much more to the agenda-setting process than merely listing what is important and what is less important.

Having been placed in a hierarchy of importance, stories are shaped into a discourse – a way of defining and presenting information and ideas; of creating preferred meanings out of which will hopefully arise preferred readings. Let us remind ourselves of the nature and importance of discourse by recalling a definition offered by Gunther Kress in *Linguistic Processes in Sociocultural Practice*:[6]

> Discourses are systematically-organised sets of statements which give expression to the meanings and values of an institution. Beyond that they define, describe and delimit what is possible to say (and by extension – what is possible to do or not to do) with respect to the area of concern of that institution, whether marginally or centrally.

Kress continues:

> A discourse provides a set of possible statements about a given area, and organises and gives structure to the manner in which a particular topic, object, process is to be talked about. In that it provides descriptions, rules, permissions and prohibitions of social and individual action.

News is a discourse, and news production is a discourse anchored by the ideology of the news producers or those who employ them, particularly if we are talking about the press. No news production, however, is independent of the values which shape and drive the players at all levels. The degree to which the media agenda is also that of the public, its discourse an influential part of public discourse, depends in large part upon the *standing* of the media in public perception – its credibility as a source of information.

In an article 'The future of political communication research: a Japanese perspective' in the *Journal of Communication*,[7] Ito Youichi discusses the relationship between media, government and public in Japan. He speaks of *extracted* information – that which the public draws from sources other than the mass media, from personal experience and observation, for example, and talking to others. Youichi introduces the Western reader to a concept shared by the Chinese and Koreans as well as the Japanese – *kuuki*. This can be translated as a *climate of opinion requiring compliance*. It may be nurtured by the media or by those in government or be the product of extracted information on the part of the public. In other words, it becomes the force of public opinion.

The tripolar model of agendas illustrated in Figure 5.6 helps us keep in mind the potential for *alliances* of influence in the public arena. Media revelations about government corruption, for example, might create an alliance between media and public. Government, now the odd one out in the threesome, will have to move into line – respond to the climate of opinion requiring compliance – by taking action over that corruption. Similarly, gross intrusions into privacy on the part of the media might lead to an alliance between government and public and pressure upon media to put its house in order. Youichi writes:

> Mass media have effects only when they stand on the majority side or the mainstream in a triadic relationship that creates and supports the kuuki that functions as a social pressure on the minority side.

He is of the opinion that 'Scholars should pay more attention to the conditions under which mass media credibility is or is not maintained'.

News values

The complexities of gatekeeping and agenda setting may at this point seem to be sending us every which way. We sense, however, that somewhere in the scrummage there is at least a vague set of rules of combat as far as media performance is concerned. Such rules we refer to as *news values*.

The names of two Norwegian scholars, Johan Galtung and Mari Ruge, have become as associated with news value analysis as Hoover with the vacuum cleaner. Their model of selective gatekeeping of 1965, while not carrying quite the romance of the apple that fell on Newton's head, is nevertheless a landmark in the scholarship of media (Figure 5.7).

They were not the first to assemble a list of criteria for news selection. As early as 1695 a German writer, Kaspar Steiler, wrote about news values in his book *Zeitungs Lust und Nutz*, roughly translatable as *Uses and Gratifications of Newspapers*. Steiler discusses *importance* as a news value and the *proximity* – nearness to home – of events. Also, he identifies events which are *dramatic* and *negative*. The American Walter Lippman produced his own analysis of news values in 1922, in *Public Opinion*.[8]

Galtung and Ruge first proposed their now-famous taxonomy or classification of news values or factors in an article in the *Journal of International Peace Research*.[9] This was reprinted in *The Manufacture of News*[3] and elsewhere. Of equal note when news values are being discussed is another contribution printed in *The Manufacture of News* – Stuart Hall's seminal article, 'The determinations of news photographs', a must-read for any student of media.

In the Galtung and Ruge model potential items of news resemble guests arriving at a hotel. Standing sentinel is the doorman, Media Perception, who lets some visitors pass through the revolving door of news values while others end up back

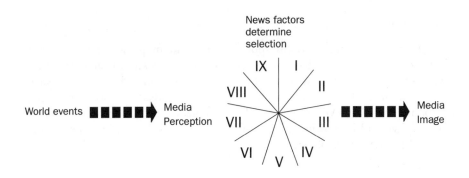

Figure 5.7   Galtung and Ruge's model of selective gatekeeping (1965). From McQuail and Windahl (see Figure 5.1). The model suggests that until a world event is *perceived* as being newsworthy by the media, it will not qualify for consideration for transformation into a media *image* of that event.

in the street. As the privileged guests emerge from the revolving doors they do so with the shape and gloss of media images. They have been processed as well as selected.

A number of values the authors define as being culture-free, others culture-linked, though it has to be said that attempting to describe any activity as being unaffected by the culture that surrounds it is a knotty problem and one which may not really warrant the effort. Indeed, the authors acknowledge that 'what we choose to consider an "event" is culturally determined'.

Events, argue Galtung and Ruge, will be more likely to be reported if they fulfil any one or more of a number of conditions, particularly if they fulfil these conditions in combination. Below, I have listed and enlarged upon the 12 news factors which Galtung and Ruge identify.

- Frequency
- Amplitude
- Unambiguity
- Familiarity
- Predictability
- Surprise
- Correspondence
- Composition
- Eliteness – of people
- Eliteness – of nations
- Personification
- Negativity

Frequency

If the event takes a time to occur approximate to the frequency of the medium's output of news – hourly, four times daily, daily or weekly – it at least initially qualifies for inclusion in news rather than if it has an 'awkward' timescale (usually, long). A murder, for example, is more newsworthy than the slow progress to prosperity of a Third World country. The completion over months or years of a dam that will aid irrigation and thus improve crops is less likely to be reported than if the same dam is blown up by terrorists.

Amplitude

The bigger, the better, the more dramatic, the more likely the event is to achieve what the authors call 'threshold value', meaning poised to pass through the gate; and 'the more violent the murder the bigger the headlines it will make'. Amplitude alone may not necessarily constitute a news value. In order to qualify it will be subject to regulation by geographical or cultural proximity. Three hundred people can die in a plane crash in Nepal and this *may* warrant an inside story in the Western press. However the presence of 'our own' people on board, however small in number, is likely to drive the story up the agenda.

Unambiguity

Galtung and Ruge speak of *clarity*. The more uncomplicated the events, the more they will be noticed and reported. A number of qualifications attach to this value. Some events are of sufficient amplitude to warrant coverage even though they may be complicated. Industrial disputes often fall into this category. What may happen is that the dispute is reported but freed from the complexities which surround it. We are seeing here the link between value and the process of news construction.

Finding an event complicated or ambiguous, the media will generally work towards simplification; and one approach is to single out those items within a complex story which actually are unambiguous, such as actions, which may be direct and clear-cut, whereas the causes of those actions are more complicated.

Recent commentators, Marc Raboy and Bernard Dagenais, speak of a 'tendency to flatten a complex and multi-textured phenomenon into simple formulations'and such a tendency they see as value-loaded. In their introduction to *Media, Crisis and Democracy*,[10] the authors cite the case of the Gulf War (1991) in which Iraq, having occupied neighbouring Kuwait, was invaded by a military coalition of 28 countries, spearheaded by America, and including Britain and France. Raboy and Dagenais are of the opinion that the Western media:

> blackened Saddam Hussein (the Iraqi president) and his regime, obscuring all possible consideration of the real meaning of the war, of US designs and motives, of the manipulation of public opinion and disinformation.

Oversimplification on the part of the media has less to do with the pressures of time (deadline meeting) than with value-judgments, manifested by the collusion which occurs between authority and media in times of crisis. Indeed Raboy and Dagenais see *crisis* as a news value in its own right because it provides dramatic stories.

Familiarity

Emphasis has already been placed upon ethnocentrism as a news value: that which is familiar to us, about which we know something, whether it involves neighbours, neighbouring communities or neighbouring nations, is considered important because events affecting them could also be events affecting us. We are more 'at home' with what is familiar to us, generally more interested in people and places we know than those strange to us.

Galtung and Ruge state that while 'the culturally distant will be passed by more easily and not be noticed' an exception to normal practice will come about through *relevance*: a 'remote country may may be brought in [to the news] via a pattern of conflict with one's own group'.

▪ Predictability

Drawing upon a work by B. Berelson and G.A. Steiner, *Human Behaviour: An Inventory of Scientific Findings*,[11] Galtung and Ruge refer to a 'hypothesis of consonance' where news is what is expected to happen, a fulfilment of predictions. News operators 'know' what news is: when events conform to this expectation, they are reported, largely in set, or routine ways, reflecting routine thinking. Galtung and Ruge contend:

> A person *predicts* that something will happen and this creates a mental matrix for easy reception and registration of the event if it does finally take place. Or he *wants* it to happen and the matrix is even more prepared, so much so that he may distort perceptions he receives and provide himself with images consonant with what he has wanted. In the sense mentioned here 'news' are actually 'olds', because they correspond to what one expects to happen... .

In short, this is a version of wish-fulfilment. It is a practice seen by a number of commentators to result in stereotyping of people and situations. Reporting of race often stands accused of allowing expectations to become predictions, and predictions in turn to become self-fulfilling prophecies. If black youths are associated in the minds of the media operators with violence, then, the hypothesis of consonance would suggest, those operators will actively look for violence to occur. This theme is analysed by Christopher P. Campbell in *Race, Myth and the News*.[12] The author writes of 'a kind of tunnel vision' which contributes to contemporary racist attitudes in the media.

▪ Surprise

News values compete with one another and the value of surprise runs counter to that of predictability. That which is unexpected may well prove a vital news value. Thus dog biting man (especially if he is a postman) is scarcely news; but man biting dog, that is newsworthy. As Galtung and Ruge say, 'Events have to be unexpected or rare, or preferably both, to become good news'.

Skinhead youths crashing heads is news because the action might be deemed to be predictable. Equally, skinheads might qualify as news if their behaviour contradicts the stereotype: if they surprise media expectations by, for example, campaigning on behalf of multiracial neighbourhoods.

▪ Correspondence

Once a story is up and running it will often continue to be covered even past its sell-by date in terms of its headline potential. Galtung and Ruge say:

> The channel has been opened and stays partly open to justify it being opened in the first place, partly because of inertia in the system and partly because what was unexpected has now become familiar.

It is in the interest of the media to keep stories simmering because there is always the potential to give an old tale a new twist. For example, it is common practice to link stories on similar themes, for such links strengthen news value. Old stories are regularly dusted down and given new life where they are perceived to clarify or reinforce – and amplify – the significance of new stories.

Composition

This value arises from what Galtung and Ruge term a 'desire to present a "balanced" whole'. A diet of really bad news cries out for some balancing good news: the grim needs to be matched with the cheerful, the horrific with the heart-warming. Television news often rounds off with a human interest story – light, humourous, oddball.

The cynic might see even in this practice a degree of manipulation: let people go to bed thinking the world is an entirely horrible place and in future they may switch off the news altogether. The danger is of distraction or *deflection*, where what we remember of a news bulletin may not be the headline story about government corruption but the end-of-bulletin 'filler' about a yodelling parrot or a baseball team which has won its first game in 25 years.

Eliteness

The term 'eliteness' is actually used by Allan Bell in *The Language of News Media*[2] in offering his own variation on Galtung and Ruge; but the authors count as a primary value the importance of elite people, elite institutions and elite nations in the news. The elite are Knowns. They have titles, positions – they are easily referenced; enabling stories to be *personified*, to be shifted from the theoretical and the general to the specific, the focused and the colourful. And of course having qualified for coverage the elite increase their public profile by being featured in the media.

Galtung and Ruge believe that 'Elite people are available to serve as objects of general identification, not only because of their intrinsic importance'. Being the influentials in society, its leaders and leader-makers, the power elite have symbolic value. Hence their words as well as their actions are reported. Their opinions are more sought after and recorded. The most banal utterances of presidents and prime ministers will be reported even though they do not qualify under any criterion other than that they issue from 'top' people.

Personification

The *potential* for personalising a story, by emphasising its human interest, is a critically important factor of news, one invariably operated by the popular press. For every issue or event there has to be a person to associate with it, to encapsulate it, to symbolise it. Personality becomes a metonym for the story and its theme, and the characteristics of both become interchangeable.

There seems to be the need for somebody to blame, to shoulder responsibility, to be answerable: after all, you can't take a picture of an issue. Matters of political, economic, industrial or environmental importance; issues concerning gender, race, crime and punishment may involve thousands or millions, but they are swiftly re-presented in person-form: a general becomes the epitome of the war effort; the complexities of an industrial dispute are boiled down to the features of the leading protagonists.

Negativity

The only good news, it has often been said as far as news gatherers are concerned, is bad news. If immigrant workers in Germany are being terrorised by fascist gangs; if their houses are being fired with petrol bombs; if they are beaten to death on the streets of Breman or Stuttgart, then Germany will feature on the agenda of British or American news media more readily than that nation's generous hospitality to refugees from Bosnia.

What Anthony Smith has termed 'aberrant news values'[13] are especially assertive in a Free Press system. This point hardly needs stressing, but the effects of bad news reporting are of critical and ongoing importance in our analysis of media performance. Bad news creates bad impressions. We carry images of people, groups, communities and nations in our heads which have been placed there by the media.

What is treated negatively risks being thought about negatively. Because the media are preoccupied with outcomes, we, as audience, rarely acquire information beyond the bad news. We are told WHAT but rarely HOW or WHY. Explanation and analysis, the tracing of effects back to causes do of course feature in media coverage; but the media operator might argue that sensation rather than analysis sells newspapers and boosts TV ratings.

Operational factors

Having produced their list of news factors which set the agenda that controls the media gates; having provided advice which might enable us to at least know how lived events become mediated events in the news, Galtung and Ruge suggest three hypotheses under the headings *selection*, *distortion* and *replication*.

The more an event satisfies news values, the more it is likely to be selected. Once an item has been selected what makes it newsworthy will be accentuated. This the authors call the distortion stage; and the process will recur at each phase of production as the item passes to audience. Replication is what happens when a 'version' reaches a new step in the process.

It is the *version*, not the reality, which is being worked upon: the 'longer the chain [of processing activities], the more selection and distortion will take place... every link in the chain reacts to what it receives... according to the same principles'. In other words, once the features of a story have been assembled, once the construction is under way, the subsequent phases of the operation build on the construction, not on 'reality'.

TELEVISION'S NEWS VALUES

Galtung and Ruge base their taxonomy of news factors on criteria operated by the press. In *Journalists at Work* ,[14] Jeremy Tunstall applies Galtung and Ruge to news values which govern TV news selection, suggesting four points of difference:

1. In TV the visual is given pre-eminence
2. News items which include film of 'our own reporters' interviewing or commentating on a story are preferred
3. TV makes use of a smaller fraction of the *number* of stories the newspapers carry, and even major items are short compared with newspaper coverage
4. There is preference for *actuality* stories which film of actual events makes possible for TV.

The status of source

In *The Language of News Media*[2] Allan Bell, making some useful additions to Galtung and Ruge, writes of *attribution* as a value. The reliability or status of the source of information is crucial, and this is closely linked with elite choice: organisations are more 'reliable' sources than individuals, unless of course those individuals are elite persons. 'The more elite the source,' says Bell, 'the more newsworthy the story.' He puts it bluntly: 'News is what an authoritative source tells a journalist.'

He refers to those who 'wear a general mantle of authority and are part of the institutional network where journalists expect to get information'. This value applies not only to what people do, but to who is saying what: 'Talk is news only if the right person is talking'. In this sense, the elite not only *are* the news, they *make* it. Bell is voicing similar sentiments to those of the American analyst David Barsamian who refers to journalists as 'stenographers to power'.[15]

The exception that proves the rule

If what Allan Bell says is true, that some sources of information – like trade unions – suffer from media neglect; and if proximity – cultural, geographical or commercial – is a prime value for news selection, why is it that in the 1980s Poland hit the headlines in the British press and was regularly reported on TV?

After all, Poland is classifiable as a faraway country of which we know little. And yet in the early 1980s the activities of the Polish trade union Solidarity sprang into British headlines. British trade unionists must have looked on in amazement as a Conservative government and a Conservative press turned the Polish workers into heroes and not demons.

What was going on? Had news values suffered a rush of blood to the head? Was the world of values being suddenly inverted? These questions had extra pertinence in the light of what was happening to trade unions in Britain. Worker rights were being drastically restricted by new legislation. There is a plausible answer:

This is not exactly the missing piece from the news values jigsaw because the assumption is obvious enough that the power elite come with their values, their ideology, attached. Nevertheless, any taxonomy that does not include reference to ideology is failing to offer a basis for explaining the 'Poland conundrum'.

The explanation for Solidarity suddenly becoming the headline flavour-of-the month in Britain lies not in the fact that here was a trade union fighting for the good of its workers; rather it was because its struggle was seen to be part of a grander conflict between Western nations and the Iron Curtain countries, between capitalism and communism.

Any force – even a trade union – standing out against the ideology of communism, for that is what Solidarity was perceived to be doing, would stimulate Western interest, Western support and media coverage. In this case, the news values of importance and proximity were secondary to ideology.

Ideology and the news

Stuart Hall in 'The determinations of news photographs' (in *The Manufacture of News*[3]) perceives two levels of news value. The first he describes as *formal*, the other *ideological*. Formal news values belong to 'the world and discourse of the newspaper, to newsmen as a professional group, to the institutional apparatus of news-making'. Ideological news values 'belong to the realm of moral-political discourse' in society.

This 'double articulation' as Hall terms it 'binds the inner discourse of the newspaper to the ideological universe of the society'. In practice 'there is probably little or no distinction between these two aspects of news production,' believes Hall. Ideology is essentially hidden, representing a ' "deep structure" whose function as a selective device is un-transparent even to those who professionally most know how to operate it'. Hall believes 'Events enter the domain of ideology as soon as they become visible to the news-making process'.

It would seem appropriate, then, that the model of news values suggested by Jörgen Westerståhl and Folke Johansson in the *European Journal of Communication*, 1994[16] places ideology in the centre of the news-making process (Figure 5.8).

Figure 5.8   Westerståhl and Johansson's model of news factors in foreign news (1994). Ideology, put where it belongs, in the centre of the news-making process.

Though the model relates specifically to foreign news, it has a general application. *Drama* enters the picture and, as with news stories as well as fictional ones, the drama is bad news for someone. Stuart Hall is more specific. For him, in the domain of political news, the most salient news value is *violence*.

In the Westersthål and Johansson model recognition is given to *access*, as much a circumstance as a value. If journalists have easy access to events – as they had during the Vietnam War (1959–75) – they are are obviously more able to use the evidence of their own eyes, their own direct experience, than if they are herded together far from the war zone and fed information by officials – as they were during the Gulf War.

Sometimes all routes to information are blocked to reporters. They are denied physical access to events and they are refused even official information. This was the case with the Chechen civil war in the Soviet Union between 1995 and 1996, a largely unreported conflict resulting from hazards of access to the Chechen capital, Grozny, and other parts of the country. The McCombs and Shaw model (Figure 5.4) is apposite here, for minimal media coverage of the Chechen war meant that public interest in or knowledge of the fate of the Chechen people was modest where it existed at all.[17]

Very often, at home as well as abroad, the only information available is from official sources. Westerståhl and Johansson speak in their article of 'reporting coloured by national interest'. As far as Western nations are concerned, that interest is coloured by a 'common Western ideology'; in short, capitalism; in particular, in the decades of the 1980s and 90s, of the 'free market' variety, characterised by policies of privatisation, deregulation and commoditisation.

Where ideology appears to have no particular purchase, nations and the media that report them tend to take no sides. An example given by Westerståhl and Johansson is the Iran-Iraq war of the 1980s which 'represented a case where the readiness in the Western world to identify with either side was at its lowest level'.

For this reason, few news values were activated: 'in terms of news coverage, the death of, let us say, one Israeli soldier counted as much as the death of hundreds of Iranian or Iraqi soldiers'.

The Gulf Crisis of 1990–91 featured hundreds of Iraqi soldiers; but also among the players of that exhaustively covered drama was a 'presence' few of the media seemed to mention much, but which made the ideological difference – oil; an 'untransparent' feature of Gulf War coverage.

Ideology and the pressures of time

A further criterion of newsworthiness which begs a mention here is one posed by Philip Schlesinger in the 1970s and which seems to be even more relevant now: *immediacy*. The emphasis on the importance of time in industrial societies, discussed in Chapter 1, has embedded itself in Western news values: the world is in a rush; time is ideological.

In an article entitled 'Newsmen and their time machine' in the *British Journal of Sociology*,[18] Schlesinger defines immediacy as the time which has elapsed between the occurrence of an event and its public reporting as news. It refers to the speed with which coverage can be mounted; and the model example would be a 'live' broadcast: 'News is "hot" when it is most immediate. It is "cold", and old, when it can no longer be used in the newsday in question.'

Immediacy is embodied in every newsperson's mental script. It shapes and structures his or her practices. It structures the news presentation, the running order and the time slots for each piece of news. Related to this is *pacing*: 'Each news bulletin is structured according to a concept of the right pace'; and this pace is dictated by the need to 'move things along' in order to keep the audience's attention.

The news value of immediacy can be linked to an addition Allan Bell makes to the Galtung and Ruge taxonomy – that of *competition*. What dictates choice and treatment is the competition from other newspapers, from other broadcasting channels. If, as Herbert Gans says in *Deciding What's News*,[1] the chief criteria for news presentation are clarity, brevity and colour then news producers will compete to be clear (unambigous), brief (so as not to lose audience interest) and colourful (in order to capture and hold attention).

In short, the news has to be entertaining, and immediacy is perceived to be an essential ingredient of entertainment. Yet Schlesinger argues that immediacy creates situations in which news is all foreground and too little background; where the emphasis on *now* obscures the *historical* sequence of events. He speaks of 'bias in the news against the long-term, and it is plausible to argue that the more we take note of news, the less we can be aware of what lies behind it'.

Figure 5.9 Cartoon published in *Index on Censorship*, **3**, 1994.

SUMMARY

Stress has been placed here on the cultural orientation of news, its ethnocentric nature and its resemblance to ritual. However effectively, through professional skill, the news convinces us that it replicates reality we have to keep in mind that it is only a *version* of reality; and that it is highly constructed.

The process by which an event is transformed into news has been examined here. News values govern decisions about the selection of events and these manifest themselves in agenda setting – giving priority to some events or issues rather than others. Every potential news item passes through a number of media 'gates' and at each gate further selection – and *mediation* – takes place.

News values classified by Galtung and Ruge have been explained and linked to Stuart Hall's two *levels* of news value, formal and ideological. Selection, distortion and replication are seen to confirm the notion of news as a *construct* and a number of other values, such as crisis, immediacy and access are discussed.

Ideology is viewed as a key feature of news production. It operates within cultural and institutional contexts, influencing the ways in which news represents reality. News as a composite of 'stories' is touched upon, a theme taken up in the next chapter when the forms and features of *narrative* are explored.

KEY TERMS

ethnocentric ■ proximity ■ knowns, unknowns ■ discourse

mediation ■ gatekeeping ■ agenda setting ■ news values

extracted information ■ kuuki ■ hypothesis of consonance

formal and ideological news values ■ attribution ■ immediacy

SUGGESTED ACTIVITIES

1. Discussion:
   (a) What strategies might non-elite persons or groups devise to improve their chances of having their voice heard on local and national news agendas?
   (b) Consider the view that the news is an agency of social control.
   (c) Compare their effectiveness as news media of newspapers, television and radio.

2. Study a TV news bulletin (or bulletins) and gauge the number of stories involving elite and non-elite persons. Document the time devoted to such stories and indicate the particular news value/news values which have 'opened the gate' to such stories. How much attention has been paid to what the actors in the story say compared to what they *do*?

3. Examine tabloid newspapers in search of examples of Wedom/Theydom – references to minorities, foreign nationals, other countries. How are they described, categorised? What difference is there in coverage of stories of 'other' between the tabloids and the so-called quality press?

4. Video record a TV news broadcast and play it to a group of viewers, half of whom you blindfold (or have sitting with their backs to the screen). When the bulletin is over, conduct a test on how much non-visual information the

participants can remember. Who scores best, those who could see the on-screen images or those who couldn't?

5. Do a gender count of a day's news, in the papers and in broadcast news. Do women feature as prominently as men; and with what kind of stories are women/men most familiarly identifiable?

NOW READ ON

It is risky to fall into the trap of believing that the latest books render earlier ones out of date. Roger Fowler's *Language in the News: Discourse and Ideology in the Press* (UK: Routledge, 1991) still provides an invaluable read concerning the way news is assembled into discourses through language.

Also warmly recommended are the following: *Understanding News* by John Hartley (UK: Methuen, 1982); *The Known World of Broadcasting News: International News and the Electronic Media* by Roger Wallis and Stanley Baron (UK: Routledge, 1990); *Journalism and Popular Culture* edited by Peter Dahlgren and Colin Sparks (UK: Sage, 1992) and *Whose News? The Media and Women's Issues* edited by Ammu Joseph and Kalpana Sharma (UK: Sage, 1994).

For readers fascinated with what it is like to work as a top journalist, see an entertaining States-side volume, *Breaking the News* by James Fallowes (US: Pantheon, 1996). Lastly for an analysis of news as global practice see Mark D. Alleyne's *News Revolution: Political and Economic Decisions about Global Information* (UK: Macmillan, 1997).

6 Narrative: the Media as Storytellers

AIMS

- To highlight the role played by narrative in human discourse.
- To examine the process of framing in the creation of narratives.
- To discuss genre, narrative codes and character.
- By comparing news and fiction narratives to explore how they interact in contemporary modes of media storytelling.

Although Charles Dickens' highly opinionated schoolmaster in *Hard Times*, Mr Gradgrind, insisted that the most important thing in life as in education are 'facts! facts! and more facts!' stories are what we remember the most. They arise out of our historical and cultural contexts. They are signifiers of it but they are also modes of explanation: by our stories, as it were, shall we be known; and sometimes such stories have the power of myths to leave all facts – and often reality itself – behind.

This chapter works from the premise that humans are storytelling animals and that the story, the narrative, is central to the recounting of facts (in the news) as well as in fiction. The information mode in message communication is compared to the story, or ritual mode and the two are seen to be overlapping and interactive.

Elements of stories – rhetoric, metaphor, symbol, for example, are illustrated; and processes of storytelling examined, the way narrative is used to frame content and meaning. The purposes of framing suggested by Robert Entman, Roland Barthes' five narrative codes, Vladimir Propp's archetypical story features and Milly Buonanno's criteria for fictionworthiness are briefly described. The 'newsness' of fiction, the role of facts, is touched upon in relation to popular TV drama such as soaps, while the fictional qualities of news are highlighted.

Throughout, news as narrative is kept in steady focus, as are those factors external to the storytelling process which powerfully influence it – pressures to win and retain audiences, conventions of production and the possibilities opened up by new technology.

Homo narrens: the storytelling animal

The more we examine news production the more it resembles the process which produces fiction; that is, the creative process. Drama? It's what the news is about. Fascinating characters? – watch the news. Slice of life? The unfolding of meanings? Humour, pathos, tribulation, revenge, madness, lust, sacrifice? Saw it on the box last night!

A colleague I once worked with on teacher training courses always used to query matters of educational import with the words, 'What's the story?' He was a philosopher and the word 'story' had a number of meanings. On occasion, the word might mean 'angle' – what's the angle? Or it could suggest something that was not apparent, that needed rooting out, as in a murder mystery – a hidden agenda. But most of all the word seemed to be used in relation to the significance of the matter in hand – okay, these are the facts, but what do they amount to?

Storytelling – narrative – has always been an entertaining way of exploring and communicating meaning. One might say that, along with music which is itself so closely associated with stories through song, the story is both the oldest and the most universal form of interactive expression. It is almost as natural and familiar to us as breathing. Arthur Asa Berger writes in *Narratives in Popular Culture, Media, and Everyday Life*:[1]

> We seldom think about it, but we spend our lives immersed in narratives. Every day, we swim in a sea of stories and tales that we hear or read or listen to or see (or some combination of all these) from our earliest days to our deaths.

The Autumn 1985 issue of the *Journal of Communication* looked in depth at the notion of *Homo narrens*, humankind, the storytelling animal. The theme, addressed by a number of authors, was that storytelling is a key human discourse. Frequently in these *Journal* articles it is acknowledged that while telling a story the narrator is also communicating a story about him or herself in terms of attitudes, beliefs and values. For example, the resistance among many researchers, particularly in America, to hard-line theories on the power of media to manipulate audiences can be interpreted as a 'story' about humane people – democrats – determined to see in their fellows similar traits of principle and independence.

In 'The narrative paradigm: in the beginning', Walter Fisher[2] believes that rationality – the capacity to work things out from a standpoint of experience – is determined by the nature of persons as narrative beings, by:

> their inherent awareness of *narrative probability*, and their constant habit of testing *narrative fidelity*, whether the stories they experience ring true with stories they know in their lives.

Probability here suggests that a story is 'likely', that it answers real experience. Fidelity suggests that there is sufficient truth in the tale to be convincing.

We look to stories for verification, and we relate them to our personal stories. In news terms, we ask ourselves, do the stories in the papers or on TV ring true? 'Storyness', or the story format, can be seen as an alternative mode of communicating experience to that which claims essentially to transmit information.

Transmission mode, story mode

In 1926 George Herbert Mead defined two models of journalism, the *information* model and the *story* model, stating that 'the reporter is generally sent out to get a story not the facts'.[3] What Mead poses as models of journalism, Jerome Bruner sees as ways of thinking, the one the *analytical* mode, the other the *story* mode.[4] Both are deeply inscribed in our mental script as individuals and as communities. The storyness theme is taken up by Peter Dahlgren in his Introduction to *Journalism and Popular Culture*.[5] He writes that 'Storytelling.... is a key link which unites journalism and popular culture... narrative is a way of knowing the world'.

Few journalists like to be reminded that they are operating in the story mode. The job of the serious reporter is to provide information and analysis not to turn news into entertainment. John Langer in his own contribution to *Journalism and Popular Culture*, 'Truly awful news on television', calls this position into question and asserts that 'serious news is also based around a story model'. However, 'it pretends that it is not – it declares that its major concern is with imparting the important information of the day'. The assumption is that fact (evidence of realities) and fiction (that which has been invented) are separate, that there is no blurring between them. Langer believes that 'the world of fact and the world of fiction are bound more closely together than broadcasters are prepared to have us believe'.

Peter Dahlgren agrees, saying 'Journalism officially aims to inform about events in the world – analytical mode – and does this most often in the story mode'. On the one hand, then, we have the goal of information transmission underpinned with such guiding principles as objectivity, impartiality and balance; on the other we have the much more *subjective*, ritualistic nature of the story, which, as Dahlgren notes, both 'enhances and delimits the likely range of meanings'; and above all, like social rituals generally, has the power to bring about a sense of shared experience and of shared values. This, it might be said, is the 'story' of news: it is about cohesion making as much as it is about information transmission.

Symbol, rhetoric, myth

Stories are built around protagonists who are archetypal, with character traits that are readily recognised – heroes, heroines, villains and victims. Something happens, an event producing a state of *disequilibrium*, of imbalance, which has to be corrected or resolved. In the resolution we may read a message, a moral – about valour or self-sacrifice. A parable creates out of the specific (a story about a good

Samaritan, for example) a message of universal significance. A case could be put that most stories are parables, however much they disguise their 'message'.

As consumers of stories we like both novelty and familiarity, for after all there is a limited number of story formats. These are recycled to our profound gratification, especially the old tale given a new twist. We like to be teased, scared, taken down a cul-de-sac of narrative yet we are content to retrace our steps knowing that by doing so we will eventually reach the climax, the resolution – the one part of narrative which news stories cannot always, or even often, deliver.

Fantasies exist side by side with realism. In stories we meet our dreams and nightmares and often these have symbolic significance for the community at large. American professor Ernest Bormann, also writing in the *Journal of Communication* of Autumn 1985 refers in 'Symbolic convergence theory: a communication formulation' to *rhetorical fantasies* which 'fulfil a group psychological or rhetorical need'.

By rhetorical we mean the use of language – spoken, written, visual; of sign systems – in order to persuade; and rhetoric presumes the use of rhetorical devices, among them symbolism and metaphor. The more skilfully, the more artfully, these are employed, the more likely they are to achieve their goals. When members of a mass audience share a fantasy, writes Bormann, 'they jointly experience the same emotions, develop common heroes and villains, celebrate certain actions as laudible, and interpret some aspect of their common experience in the same way'. The story-within-discourse is essentially a conveyor of value, articulating meaning symbolically – most vividly through metaphor.

As the French philosopher Roland Barthes (1915–80) argued, such stories possess power through simplicity (and often simplification), which amounts to *myth*; and myth, according to Barthes, renders truths *natural* and therefore too 'commonsensical' to challenge. Myths are stories about community: they are stories writ large, usually on a macro- rather than micro-scale. The mythical element is not so much the *action* of the story but the meaning behind it.

In news stories a number of mythical properties receives a regular airing. Barthes, in *Mythologies*[6] says:

> Myth does not deny things, on the contrary its function is to talk about them; simply, it purifies them, it makes them innocent, it gives them a clarity which is not that of an explanation but that of a statement of fact.

If unambiguity is a news value then the power of myth to make the complicated clear and accessible might be deemed a production value. This power, Barthes believes, can mislead as it simplifies, for myth 'abolishes the compelexity of human acts' – in Galtung and Ruge's terms distorts through selection (see Chapter 5, Note 9) – and 'establishes,' Barthes believes, 'a blissful clarity: things appear to mean something by themselves'.

In answer to my colleague's question, 'But what's the story (behind the story)?' Barthes would say – *order*. Once again we are seeing communication functioning as control. By making things 'appear to mean something by themselves' myth enables 'explanations' to stand alone, released from historical and cultural contexts, and thus protected against contrary or alternative meanings. After all, this is what rhetoric sets out to do. By artifice in one form or another, it distorts by selection. To the informed critic, it defines itself by what it leaves out – its *absences*. Yet if its preferred reading is to succeed, what is left out of its message has also to be 'out' of the public's mind.

We need to acknowledge that the world Barthes analysed has moved on. Cultural contexts of the late 20th century have become so replete with doubts, so peppered with postmodernist cynicism, that it is difficult to believe in the survival of any grand order of truth (like the story about the inevitable progress of human kind) capable of aspiring to the status of myth.

Narrative frames

Every story has its narrative format or frame. In some stories the narrator, the storyteller, is evident: he or she refers to 'I'. First-person narrative is admitting that the story is to be told from a single point of view. It is a subjective account. Third-person narrative distances the author from what goes on in the story. The author is like the Holy Spirit, intangible but ever present. We are aware that this is a contrivance. Yet if our disbelief is suspended by artful storytelling we forget authorship and find ourselves adopting the 'real' world of characters and action 'free' of authorial strings. In fact, that is one of the criteria of effective narrative, to make the strings invisible.

Writing in *Channels of Discourse: Television and Contemporary Criticism,*[7] Robert C. Allen differentiates between what he calls the *Hollywood narrative mode* and the *rhetorical mode*. The first hides the means by which the text is created. It invites audience to believe that what they are seeing is real: one is absorbed into the text without being, as it were, addressed by it. In contrast, the rhetorical mode directly addresses the viewer. Allen sees the news presented in this way – the newsreader looks directly out at us. Similar formats can be recognised in cooking, sports and gardening programmes on TV: 'The texts are not only presented for us, but directed out at us'.

The approaches can, of course, be combined. The rhetorical mode at least in terms of a voice-over is a regular framing device. For one thing, this can be instrumentally useful by providing us with vital information which might waste time being communicated in any other way than through a narrator. For example, in the opening sequence of Michael Curtiz' *Casablanca* (1942) a voice-over sets the scene. Little is left to guesswork on the part of audience. *Closure* has occurred. That is, we are told exactly how to read what we are seeing. There is a preferred reading – very much the Hollwood mode.

In contrast, *Paris, Texas* made by German director Wim Wenders in 1984 offers us, at least in its initial stages, a more open text. During the first few moments of the film we see, in longshot, a man emerging from a rocky desert. We watch him take a desperate last swig from his water bottle. An eagle gazes down on him from the foreground and an atmosphere of mystery tinged with menace is created in our minds by a single guitar accompaniment.

In a sense, the guitar replaces the voice-over, yet we as audience are given the space to muse on who this man might be, where he has come from and what circumstances have brought him to this sorry pass. Curtiz is essentially mediating communication in terms of a model of transmission; indeed he employs newsreel in the opening of the film, along with traditional newsreel-format graphics. In the Wenders film there is an emphasis on *symbol*, an attempt to reach, obliquely, beyond explanation to meaning.

Though different in their use of narrative form, both of the films mentioned here subscribe to the classic *structure* of stories: something occurs which creates disequilibrium which prompts actions and reactions which work towards resolution and the restoration of equilibrium. We see this occurring in some TV narratives and not in others.

Soaps: resolution delayed

A television sitcom concurs with the disequilibrium-equilibrium process. Generally each 'upset' has to be 're-set' by the end of the programme. With soaps, however, disequilibrium is a constant. Though some storylines are resolved, the 'whole' story of the soap remains in a permanent state of disequilibrium – of new dramas, new crises, new twists of fate.

For a soap opera *time* is a key element in the framing process. There are 30-minute slots to be filled, each to conclude with unfinished business, preferably dramatic and suspenseful, while not being so dramatically 'final' that the series cannot continue into an endless blue yonder. Soaps need time, to bed down, unfold, and in their own time they reflect the timescales of audience. In some cases, the time-frame *of* the soap is as important as the timeframes *within* it. The soap 'frame', thus presented with time in largesse, requires many characters and many plots. Soaps are full of talk, of gossip. We generally learn of action by report rather than see it occur. The action is largely in the cutting, the quick-bite scenes which frame both the story and the time in which it takes place. Soaps move through time but they also suspend it to suggest simultaneity, of actions taking place at exactly the same time.

One suspects that the template or mould out of which soaps emerge is not all that different from the one which produces popular narratives of all kinds, including the news. They must attract and hold attention. They must gratify both *cognitive* (intellectual) and *affective* (emotional) needs. They must facilitate *identification* and *personal reference* as well as *diversion* (see reference to Uses and Gratifications Theory in Chapter 3).

On commercial channels, soaps are 'framed' by advertisements; and on all channels the nature of the product is influenced by competition for the loyalty of audience and an awareness that soaps are far and away the media world's most popular entertainment. As Bryan Appleyard, writing on soaps in the UK *Independent*[8] neatly puts it, 'Television is foaming with soaps as never before'.

For Appleyard the essence of soap narrative is language and character, not action or incident. He is critical of the apparently increasing dependence of soaps on realities portrayed in news narratives: 'the deluge of incident is taken from the headlines. Lesbianism is talked about in the newspapers and suddenly there are lesbians in *Brookside*.'

This, believes Appleyard, is confusing relevance with reality and soaps are in danger of becoming 'closed worlds, feeding off every passing sensation'. Here, excessive ratings consciousness 'warps' the frame until both content and style are disengaged from the aesthetic criteria which give soaps their value as stories. Transmission, as it were, has triumphed over ritual.

Purposes and locations of framing

Writing in a *Journal of Communication* article, 'Framing: toward clarification of a fractured paradigm',[9] Robert Entman believes that a crucial task of analysis is to show 'exactly how framing influences thinking...' for 'the concept of framing consistently offers a way to describe the power of a communicating text'. Essentially, framing constitutes *selection* and *salience* – what is most meaningful.

Entman suggests that framing serves four main purposes, to:

1. Define problems
2. Diagnose causes
3. Make moral judgments
4. Suggest remedies

These, he argues, will function varyingly according to the text, but they operate in four locations in the communication process:

1. The communicator
2. The text
3. The receiver
4. The culture

Communicators 'make conscious or unconscious framing judgments in deciding what to say, guided by frames (often called schemata) that organise their belief systems'. Before we frame, we are *in* a frame. The text will not only be framed by the framer within a frame it will be shaped by a number of factors – requirements concerning format and presentation, aesthetic considerations, notions of professionalism and pressures to meet the expectations of convention.

When the text comes to be 'read', the frames as presented may be at variance with the frames which guide the receiver's thinking. For Entman the culture is 'the stock of commonly invoked frames... exhibited in the discourse and thinking of most people in a social grouping':

> Framing in all four locations includes similar functions: selection and highlighting, and use of the highlighting elements to construct an argument about problems and their causation, evaluation and/or solution.

This approach is useful in the study of the encoding of messages and gauging their effectiveness. It emphasises the subjective nature of encoding by recognising the 'invisible' schemata – psychological templates – which, however hard we are trying to be objective and impartial, deeply influence our responses.

For successful communication – that is, winning the interest and attention of audience, and perhaps even going beyond that in terms of gaining the audience's assent or approval – there seems to be a need for a meeting of schemata; a common ground (or to refer to Wilbur Schramm's model illustrated in Chapter 2, an overlap in *fields of experience*). The communicator selects, then attempts to give salience (special importance) to those parts of the story which may fit with the existing schemata in a receiver's belief system.

The power of the frame lies both in its capacity to exclude and to structure the 'storyworld' in terms of dramatic contrasts, what may be termed *binary framing*. Things are defined in relation to their opposite – heroes-villains; good-evil; kind-cruel; tolerant-intolerant; beautiful-ugly. In *Narratives* Berger talks of 'central oppositions'.[10] The parallel with news narratives is strong here. Binary differences are a prevalent characteristic of news formats, as we have seen; and they reflect in the main the viewpoints of the dominant.

Genre, codes and character

More than ever before, narratives interact and overlap but for convenience they continue to be classified under the term *genre*. The word originates from the French, meaning a style, a form. Westerns comprise a film genre. There are horror movies, road movies, musicals, sci-fi movies and crime thrillers – all genres. Still-life paintings, historical novels, romances and who-dunnits constitute genres. In TV we are familiar with genres such as soaps, sitcoms, chat shows, quiz shows and wildlife documentaries. Genres share common characteristics and are governed by codes which regulate content and style.

Variety works within a frame of sameness. In some genres the frame is tight, highly restrictive to the point of being ritualistic. Other genres have 'flexible' framing and offer the potential for change and development. Soaps have this potential, sitcoms less so, contends Jasper Rees reviewing the second festival of sitcoms run by the UK's Channel 4 in the *Independent*:[11]

> In a play, events take place which irrepressibly alter the relationship between the characters. Whatever happens in a sitcom, you always go back to square one at the start of a fresh episode; the idea of stasis is built into the design.

No doubt sooner or later a writer will come along and create a sitcom which breaks new ground, though this will depend as much upon external framing mechanisms such as programming and popularity as the nature of the genre itself.

Each genre contains a range of signifiers, of conventions which audiences recognise and come to expect while at the same time readily accepting experiment with those conventions. Knowledge of the conventions on the part of audience, and recognition when convention is flouted, suggests an active 'union' between the schemata of the encoder and that of the decoder.

Audience, as it were, is 'let in on the act' and this 'knowingness' is an important part of the enjoyment of narrative genres. When the hero in a Western chooses not to wear a gun (a great rarity), audience (because we are familiar with tradition) recognises the salience of this decision. Such recognition could be said to constitute a form of participation.

We use our familiarity with old 'routines' as a frame for reading this new twist of narrative. We wonder whether convention will be flouted altogether as the story proceeds or whether the rules of the genre will be reasserted by the hero taking up the gun to bring about a resolution to the story.

BARTHES'S NARRATIVE CODES

We can explore the difference between narrative forms and we can assess their similarities. In his book *S/Z* Roland Barthes[12] writes of a number of codes, or sets of rules, which operate in concert in the production of both 'real' and fictional stories. He argues that all stories operate according to these five codes 'under which all textual signifiers can be grouped' in a narrative.

Students are recommended to read *S/Z* for it is a most singular volume. It takes the form of a detailed deconstruction of a 23-page story, *Sarrasine,* written by Honoré de Balzac (1799–1850) in 1830. Each line in the story is linked to one or more of the five codes of narrative.

■ Action (or Prioretic) code

This portrays the events which take place in a story. It is the code of 'what happens', detailing occurrences in their sequence.

■ Semantic code

Barthes talks of the code of the *seme* which Richard Howard in the Preface to *S/Z* calls the Semantic code. It refers to character; to characterisation. Barthes refers to this code as the Voice of the Person. Actions are *explained* by character. Essentially the semantic function is to make clear, to explain, to bring about understanding. Thus in a story it can be instrumental in bringing about relevation. A character may reveal features about him/herself which carry the story forward, creating new events or new developments.

■ Enigma (or Hermeneutic) code

Under this code, termed by Barthes the Voice of Truth, 'we list the various (formal) terms by which an enigma [a mystery] can be distinguished, suggested, formulated, held in suspense and finally disclosed'. This code involves the setting up of mystery, its development and finally its resolution. A good detective story usually contains many enigmas, some of them

continued

deliberately placed there by the author to mislead – clues which take Monsieur Poirot or Inspector Morse on a wild goose chase, enjoyable to the audience, before further clues bring them back into the 'frame' of discovery (of who committed the murder) and resolution.

■ Referential (or Cultural) code

This, the Voice of Science, as Barthes terms it, functions to inform or explain. Such codes 'are references to a science or a body of knowledge' – physiological, medical, psychological, literary, historical and so on. In a historical drama the referential code operates to explain to us how people dressed, what their homes looked like, how they travelled from place to place. The French film term, *mise en scène,* meaning 'placed in scene', detailing the 'staging' of the story, is an equivalent of the referential code.

■ Symbolic code

As the term suggests, this code works at the connotative level of imagery where elements of the story – character, incident – are transformed into symbolic representations such as justice, reward, love fulfilled, good triumphant. Symbol works at every level of the story. In a Hollywood-style gangster movie of the 1940s and 50s, the gangster's (invariably blonde) moll symbolises in her dress, speech, body language, not only her own relationship to a patriarchical world, but that of all women 'under the thumb' of males. In Westerns (almost invariably) the dress, hair and demeanour of women, and the context (bar or chapel) in which we encounter them, will symbolise what their ranking order is in the social milieu of the story.

They will also signify the woman's fate: in George Marshall's *Destry Rides Again* (1939) the saloon-bar singer Frenchie, played by Marlene Dietrich, falls in love with the hero, played by James Stewart (who doesn't wear a gun). Love is not permitted to overcome her dubious past and her criminal present except by sacrifice. Frenchie is shot in the back while protecting Destry/Stewart. She fulfils destiny and at the same time opens the way for the hero to marry the 'nice' girl in the story.

Symbols employing metaphoric forms illuminate and enrich the texts of stories and they work in unison with semantic codes. The TV Inspector Morse drives an old red Jaguar. This symbolises the kind of person Morse is – cultured, somewhat olde-worlde, resistant to the more traditional brashness of police-ness. It also helps to explain how such a detective, from whose car stereo emerge the strains of opera, never pop or jazz, goes about his profession.

Symbolic coding not only fills out our view of character, it pushes on the action. In a Western, when the hero buckles on his gunbelt, we know that the villains have pushed their luck one notch too far. Confrontation lies ahead: resolution will be brought about by violence exercised in the name of justice.

continued

The gun may additionally serve a referential function. In an age when women have ostensibly proved parity of treatment with men it can be seen as symbolically apt for women to be as ready to aim straight and pull the trigger as their male counterparts; officially, as cops, or out of self-defence.

How we decode such a story is another matter, and this will obviously depend, among other things, on who we are – male or female – what our attitude is to the use of guns and the degree of openness or closure that the text of the story permits us: are we intended to cheer when the heroine blows away the villain, or are we to be left with the nagging doubt that there might have been another way to arrive at a resolution of the situation?

Gender coding

Tracing the links between encoding, decoding and the context in which the interaction takes place is as essential to the student of communication as searching for the motive for a crime is to classic detectives. In fact the detective and his task provide a useful metaphor for study: for the student/detective, the goal is to find out who did it and why. This will involve examining 'the ground' – cultural, social – for clues as well as probing the cognitive and affective signs given off by the 'murderer' who will no doubt have left traces of his or her 'style', or way of going about things.

In the study of texts, awareness of different codes helps us know what we are looking for. The action code in a number of genres (and in real life too) is traditionally associated with male characters. Maleness equals action which suggests decisiveness that may further indicate dominance. Enigma codes relate more to women: femaleness is associated with mystery; often suggestive of a secret, victimised past. The obvious alternative for a novelist, playwright, film maker, creator of a comic strip, TV commercial or story for children is to switch the conventions so that females appropriate 'male' codes.

This also usually means breaking with social conventions, shaking a subversive finger at the rules. The outcome may underline cautionary messages as happens in Ridley Scott's movie *Thelma and Louise* (1991) where the women's rebellion against a world dominated by men's demands, men's expectations and men's abuses is resolved only by their suicide: cold comfort for such a spirited lunge for personal freedom.

It is important to note that in posing his five codes Barthes is not claiming to fix narratives within prescriptive rules. On the contrary; he writes in *S/Z*, 'The code is a perspective of quotations, a mirage of structures; we know only its departures and returns'. Just when we think we understand the symbolism of 'blondeness' in narratives, we find that it has been extended or transformed by new encoding. In Alfred Hitchcock's *To Catch a Thief* (1995), the blonde Grace Kelly is the epitome of refinement, sophistication and distinction.

Indeed, attempts to link blondeness with dumbness have often turned out to be witness to the opposite. Marilyn Monroe was often cast 'dumb' and often *played* dumb, but we know she was an altogether more complex personality, and an altogether more talented actress than the stereotype allowed. Madonna took the stereotype and reshaped it into a story about the liberated woman.

Even when we encounter (to quote Bryan Appleyard) 'that epically wide-eyed sex bomb Raquel' in *Coronation Street* we recognise a re-energising of character-story features brought about in this case by a strand of northern toughness, of emancipatedness, and a degree of wit and self-parody. Like Ena Sharples and Bet Lynch, Raquel is (or was, for she departed the Street in November 1996) larger than life, but, Appleyard believes, 'not alien to it'.

The same can be said of the characters and situations in the best of the soaps. They are far from 'real life' yet nor are they alien to it, a fantasy. Barthes writes of 'a galaxy of signifiers, not a structure of signifieds'. He could be referring to soaps and, as far as a 'structure of signifieds' is concerned, he could also be talking about news narrative.

Propp's people

In a study of Russian folk tales, Vladimir Propp classified a range of stock characters identifiable in most stories. These may be individualised by being given distinguishing character traits but they are essentially *functionaries* enabling the story to unfold. In *Morphology of the Folk Tale*[13] Propp writes of the following archetypal story features:

- the *hero/subject* whose function is to seek
- the *object* that is sought
- the *donor* of the object
- the *receiver*, where it is sent
- the *helper* who aids the action
- the *villain* who blocks the action

Thus in one of the world's best-known folk tales, Red Riding Hood (heroine) is sent by her mother (donor) with a basket of provisions (object) to her sick granny (receiver) who lives in the forest. She encounters the wolf (villain) and is rescued from his clutches – and his teeth – by the woodman (helper). This formula can be added to and manipulated in line with the requirements of the genre, but it does allow us to differentiate between *story level* and *meaning level*, between the *denotive* and the *connotative*, between the so-termed *mimetic plain* (the plain of representation) and the *semiotic plain* (the plain of meaning production).

The tale of Little Red Riding Hood, examined at the connotative level, is rich in oblique meanings and in order to tease these out we begin to examine the characters and events as symbols. We may perceive the story as a parable, that is a tale with a moral: little girls should not be allowed in the forest unprotected, however great their granny's needs. But then we begin to ask more questions – why did Red Riding Hood's mother send her on such a perilous journey in the first place; does the wolf stand for more than a wolf, granny more than a granny; and what is the significance of the stones which in some versions of the story end up in the wolf's stomach?

We are seeing that even the simplest of stories, long part of the cultural heritage of many countries, is a moveable feast, its connotative richness varying from reader to reader and context to context; and stories produced in contexts are significantly modified by new contexts. The chilling lines of *Ring-a-Ring-a-Roses*, describing the onset of the plague – the Black Death – became over time a 'harmless' children's nursery rhyme; in this case the horror of the real being subsumed by the rhythmic charm of language itself.

It would be instructive for students to select a number of popular narrative forms to see how far they conform to Propp's formula. Then they might turn to the primary folklorists of our age – the advertisers. In a commercial, the *subject* is the character who stands in for the consumer. The *object* is what the product being advertised can *do* for the subject/hero/heroine, such as bringing happiness, satisfaction, fulfilment, glamour, enviability. The *donor* or giver, is the originator of the advertisement. And the *villain*? – any factor which deprives the subject of his/her desires (like dandruff, bad skin, overweight, thirst, hunger or irritable bowel syndrome).

Newsworthiness: fictionworthiness

Certain parallels can be discerned between the narrative approaches of news and folktale; and also, of their function. The Cold War of the 1950s onwards was often reported, particularly in the popular press, as a cautionary folktale in which heroes (us) were on guard against the villains (the Russians): Wedom/Theydom was the dominant narrative structure. In our Red Riding Hood basket were nuclear weapons and granny in the forest might varyingly have symbolised democracy or the free world in peril.

We recognise once more how narrative can be used to bring about socio-cultural cohesion, uniting audiences. In *Visualising Deviance: A Study of News Organisation*[14] Richard Ericson, Patricia Baranak and Janet Chan speak of news journalists as a 'deviance-defining elite' who 'provide an ongoing articulation of the proper bounds to behaviour in all organised spheres of life'. In stories, order is disrupted: things happen and then there is usually resolution.

For John Hartley, *disorder* is a news value. Writing in *The Politics of Pictures: The Creation of the Public in the Age of Popular Media*,[15] he says that the 'fundamental test of newsworthiness is disorder – deviation from any supposed steady state...' A first principle of news media performance is to alert the public mind to *visions of order* – by portraying the opposite: binary framing in action. Hartley's view, already touched upon in Chapter 4, is that visions of order are 'photo-negativised into stories of disorder'. The sequence is predictable and seems inevitable:

Vision/Perception → Selection → Distortion → Fiction

Hartley says, 'Journalism, in short, makes sense by inventing the real in the image of vision'.

If, then, 'the fact of fiction', as Ericson, Baranak and Chan put it, can be seen as central to the news, it comes as no surprise to learn that this mode of 'fact-fiction' has proved an influential model for 'fiction-fiction'. In a paper published in the *European Journal of Communication*,[16] Milly Buonanno links newsworthiness with what she terms *fictionworthiness*. She examines the ways in which Italian TV fiction has increasingly used the news as a model for its own themes and approaches.

BUONANNO'S CRITERIA FOR FICTIONWORTHINESS

1. *Substantive* criteria, that is, factors concerning 'the prerequisites likely to confer importance and interest on a story'. These could be major issues of the day.

2. Criteria relevant to the *product*, that is factors 'concerned with specific elements of story content, in particular aspects that are considered more interesting and appealing and which maintain viewing enjoyment'.

   Buonanno believes that 'In the same way that one says of journalism: "bad news is good news", one could say of fiction that a "bad" story – that is to say a sad and tearful, violent and criminal story – is a good story'.

3. Criteria relevant to the *media*. The *kind* of news stories which have always fascinated the press – tales of crime and misdemeanours – have long proved fictionworthy and are a staple diet of TV drama.

4. Criteria relevant to *audience*.

5. Criteria relevant to the *competition*.

The attraction of the news is obvious: it is dramatic, contemporary, relevant and familiar. Also, it is often stranger than fiction. As Buonanno puts it, 'we live today in a reality which surpasses and challenges every fantasy... '. Noting the mutual reinforcement one text gives another, she speaks of:

> a circle of intertextual references substantially self-referential, that is to say, within the very media system: just as television seemingly becomes ever more a highly 'newsworthy' subject for the press, equally news becomes ever more 'fiction-worthy' for television.

Shared values

On the casting couch for fictionworthiness are some old favourites from Galtung and Ruge. At least on Italian TV those characters of high social status – the elite –

find themselves fictionworthy. Buonanno cites *Dallas* as an American parallel while confessing that 'the exceptions are mainly to be found in British productions, where more often working-class environments are presented'. Proximity is a fiction value as it is a news value. A story is 'considered to be much more interesting if it possesses accessibility – geographically, temporally and culturally'.

Perhaps the dominant fiction value arising out of news practices is *topicality*. Buonanno writes:

> A story of topical interest is not simply a story set in the present, but a story which aspires to recount and testify to the reality of the present in its most relevant and significant form.

The image of TV as a mirror of society, a true reflector of realities, also appears to prevail in fiction values. As audience, we have an appetite to know 'how things are now', either by revelation or confirmation while a dominant aim of those assembling 'realities', in fictional or news form, is one of legitimising one definition of 'truths' against another. Crime series often provide us, in addition to dramatic stories, with visualisations of contemporary urban society driven by poverty, unemployment and the loss of community values. Cops often have the role thrust upon them of social workers and social psychologists as well as law-keepers.

What such series draw back from doing is offering any formula for solutions, an *institutional* remedy for the socially rooted crimes they so effectively highlight. The producers will honestly and justifiably say – that is not our job. Yet whose job is it? We seem to be witnessing an uneasiness with the social *status quo* but no determination to alter it; and, of course, it has to be acknowledged that if the causes of the crimes dealt with in crime series were energetically addressed there might be no series to dramatise them.

In his chapter on narrative in *The Media Studies Book: A Guide for Teachers*,[17] edited by David Lusted, Adrian Tilley remarks that:

> narratives are about the survival of *particular* social orders rather than their transformation. They suggest that certain systems of values can transcend social unrest and instability by making a particular notion of 'order out of chaos'. This may be regarded as the ideological work of narrative.

The implication here is that narrative is about rendering things 'natural' – Barthes' myth-making. What happens on screen is 'the ways things are'; natural, and therefore to be expected, put up with, coped with: *c'est la vie*! Such a standpoint deserves to be analysed and challenged – hence, in Tilley's view, the importance of *narrative analysis* which 'can make the "natural" relations between narratives and social orders not only less natural but possibly even open to change'.

Fiction and public debate

This is a moment to remind ourselves that the 'work' as Barthes defines it only becomes 'text' when it is 'read' by audience. The mere fact that drama or documentary raises issues by means of narrative is enough to stir audience response. Soaps in particular prompt individual, group and public responses which modify or alter attitudes and certainly raise issues higher on public agendas.

Few stories have so alerted public interest in Britain during the late 1990s as the 'Jordache Story' which featured in the British soap *Brookside* between February 1993 and May 1995. This brought incest to public attention perhaps more dramatically than ever before. After serving in prison for domestic violence, Trevor Jordache persuades his family to take him back. Once more he is violent towards his wife Mandy. He has in the past already sexually abused his elder daughter, Beth. Now it is 14-year-old Rachel's turn. Mandy and Beth plot his death. They bury his body in the garden. Prison follows for both of them. Beth takes her own life. Rachel gives evidence of how Trevor raped her. Mandy is released from prison.

Such was the interest, controversy and serious debate which the Jordache Story provoked that Channel 4 Television commissioned Lesley Henderson of the Glasgow University Media Group to investigate public responses. Her approach to this task is mentioned later in Chapter 8 but the conclusion of her report *Incest in Brookside: Audience Responses to the Jordache Story*,[18] is relevant here. She affirms the significance of contemporary popular storytelling in relation to issues of social importance:

> This study reveals that *Brookside*'s child sexual abuse storyline communicated complex and important messages about the issue… [it] increased knowledge and understandings about the language, reality and effects of abuse… By addressing the difficult topic of child abuse *Brookside* illustrates how a traditionally 'entertainment' genre can be used to enhance knowledge and understandings about a social problem.

Lesley Henderson's research also identifies important areas of audience resistance, to the way the events were handled, to the way characters responded to those events; and also to the way other media – in particular the press – attempted to 'get in' on the story. By announcing beforehand what was going to happen next in the story, the press provided an additional 'frame' around the actual drama as it appeared on screen.

This served as a *secondary text* to the *primary text* of the programme itself and inevitably influenced the 'reading' of the story. The *Daily Mirror* (23 June 1995) reported that Beth would commit suicide. Under the headline BETH US DO PART, the *Mirror* declared:

> Beth, jailed in the body-under-the-patio cliffhanger, can't face another five year sentence. Although an appeal is pending, she decides to end it all.

The *Mirror* became part of the story, and its sensationalist announcement, Henderson points out, 'provoked distress and anger' particularly among those groups tested in research who themselves were 'survivors' of child abuse. That Beth should not face things out, and thus fail to prove an inspiring example, was bad enough, but to be told so bluntly in the press made matters worse. Indeed the reports in the press, Henderson says, 'sparked protests and demonstrations'.

The interaction between primary and secondary texts and the audience must be a constant focus of media study because the ideological thrust of secondary texts may well rework the ideology of the primary one in the minds of audience: we have, then, yet another *intervening variable* between encoding and response. In the case of the reporting of the Jordache Story, the negative news values of the press intruded between the *Brookside* story and its audience.

Not only did newspapers 'give the game away' by telling readers what was going to happen, they imposed their own judgmental attitude. *TV Quick* (22–28 July, 1995) announced – BETH: A WASTED LIFE. 'Such coverage,' believes Henderson, 'presented "Beth's" death in a way which undermined all the positive strengths of the character and placed her firmly in the category of "victim scarred for life".'

News as narrative

If much TV fiction takes its lead, at least in terms of content, from the news, we have to recognise that news as narrative breaks the golden rule of fiction by surrendering the *code of mystery* at the very beginning. In the Jordache Story, as we have seen, press announcements proved a 'spoiler' and dismayed many in the audience. The decision to put the ending first is plainly based upon the precept that news is information, fact not fiction; that news is about transmission, not ritual: news is *not* a story and it is definitely not an invention. It is for real.

Understandable though it is, this insistence on departing from sequential narrative of traditional story modes, or what is termed *diachronic structure* (A comes before B and B leads on to C) poses problems. Justin Lewis in *The Ideological Octopus: An Exploration of Television and Its Audience*[19] argues that news is a 'form that, by abandoning narrative, abandons substantial sections of the viewer's consciousness':

> If we study this narrative structure in more detail, we can see just how strange news 'stories' are. The hermeneutic code is not only ignored, it is turned inside-out. History inevitably has an enigmatic quality – we do not know how the future will unfold. Television takes this history and squeezes the sense of mystery right out of it. The main point of the story does not come at the end, but at the beginning. It is like being told the punchline before the joke, or knowing the result before watching the game, or being told 'who-dunnit' at the beginning of the murder mystery.

As audience, we do not 'have our interest awakened by enigma and gratified by a solution' as in traditional stories. In researching the capacity of audience to recall the gist of news programmes, Lewis found that:

> most respondents had great difficulty recalling 'stories': their discussion tended to revolve around discrete moments in each item. If they did not already know details of events leading up to the item (which applied to most of the audience most of the time) they were extremely unlikely to remember anything the item told them about the historical context.

Lewis is of the opinion that the format of news narrative relies on viewers making links, relating item to item, comprehending references which have a history that is rarely explained, largely assumed. In short, to make sense of the news a viewer has to be highly *news literate*. Any student of media can test this by scrutinising news bulletins for their capacity to make sense of the news process itself, never mind what the news contains.

Swarming signifiers

The jump-cutting, the contortions with time; the inserts of related materials to other stories; the joining of one story to another because 'it connects' in some way, all require a combination of prior knowledge and skill in reading the news text which only the most sophisticated news addict is likely to possess. What happens when the average viewer loses track or concentration and then attempts to make sense of a shot where the Australian prime minister is talking about relations with Indonesia while attending a world leaders' conference in Washington at which a delegation of Aborigines have interrupted his address with questions about ancient land rights can only be guessed at. Lewis argues that the narrative structure of news:

> for most viewers, cannot sustain the links and development necessary to go beyond crude association. TV news does not necessarily ignore historical details, it simply fails to persuade the viewer to fit these details together.

It is difficult for the reader or the viewer to resist what Lewis terms 'associative logics' unless we, as audience, have an alternative mindset – of knowledge, reference points, personal experience and ideological framework. Lewis believes that 'in the absence of any other information, it is the media's framework or nothing' for most viewers. If this framework is communicated in the disjointed narrative style characteristic of news presentation, problems of comprehension on the part of audience are compounded:

> The consequences of this are profound. It suggests that many viewers find it difficult to place those views of the world that are repeatedly put forward on the news, in any critical or qualifying context.

Technology and news narrative

In news narratives, and indeed in most story narratives on TV and in the cinema, a do-or-die function is to attract and retain audience attention. Increasingly the wonders of technology are employed to fulfil this function. What seems to have become a key narrative feature is the *sound-bite*, serving what communicators perceive to be a fickle, inattentive audience, with a high dosage of JPMs (jolts per minute).

Daniel Hallin in an article 'Sound-bite news: television coverage of elections, 1968–1988', published in the *Journal of Communication*[20] and summarising his researches into American news reportage, says that the length of the average sound-bite shrunk from 40 seconds in 1968 to less than 10 seconds in 1988. Readers are invited to check out tonight's offering: is 10 seconds beginning to look like slow-motion?

There was a time when a political advocate could expect to string a number of coherent and uninterrupted sentences together before being quick-cut to someone else talking or to inserts of action film. Hallin argues that this trend, driven by technogical possibilities, has made the news more *mediated*. If the narrative rule has become – After 10 seconds, cut! then the description of news as an assemblage, a *construct*, is all the more apt: content is manipulated by style which in turn is technology-driven.

Hallin writes:

> Today's television journalist displays a sharply different attitude towards the words of candidates and other newsmakers. Today, those words, rather than simply being reproduced and transmitted to audience, are treated as raw material to be taken apart, combined with other sounds and images, and integrated into a new narrative.

In this manner technology and ideology are working in partnership. Like Justin Lewis, Hallin expresses unease about sound-bite treatment of the news, and concern whether audience possesses the capacity to keep up with the pace demanded of it. We may recall the 'highlights', the nuggets of information conveyed in dramatic pictures – but do we grasp the whole story?

A victim of sound-bite journalism, Hallin believes, is analysis: the explanation of causes is sidelined by the presentation of pictures which record the drama of outcomes. Also, personality dominates over argument. Hallin points out in his article that sound-bites favour elite persons over ordinary voters. In American election coverage the words and opinions of non-elite people dropped from over 20 per cent of sound-bites in 1972 to between three and four per cent in 1980 and 1988.

The trend has been, writes Hallin, towards an increasing dominance of election campaigns by insiders. Along with this has occurred an emphasis on competition between election hopefuls – who's ahead, who's trailing? Hallin calls this 'horse-race journalism' and the casualty is policy analysis. The author's research confirms a correlation between sound-bite length and horse-race emphasis. With the increasing stress on dramatic narrative, Hallin believes, there has been a loss – since 1968 – of seriousness in the treatment of news.

Soaps as a model for news narratives?

Considering that news, by its resolute breaking of the rules of sequence which govern most stories, is seen to confuse audiences, why not, asks John Fiske, take a leaf out of the book of soaps narrative? In his chapter 'Popular news' in *Reading the Popular*,[21] Fiske argues that '"objective" facts always support particular points of view and their "objectivity" can exist only as part of the play of power'.

News, he is implying, the way it is framed, structured and presented for audience consumption is a story about power.

Fiske contends:

Rather than being 'objective' therefore, TV news should present multiple perspectives that, like those of soap opera, have as unclear a hierarchy as possible: the more complex the events it describes, the more the contradictions among the different social positions from which to make sense of them should be left open and raw.

The author believes that news narrative should be 'less concerned about telling the final truth of what has happened, and should present, instead, different ways of understanding it and the different positions of view inscribed in those different ways'. By seeking to emulate popular narratives, news would be acknowledging that 'people cope well with contradictions'. Of course Fiske duly admits such moves would prove 'a risky business, for the meanings that people will make will often evade social control'.

Fiske also argues that news should resist its currently all-pervading tendency towards *narrative closure*. News should, 'like soap opera, leave its multiple narratives open, unresolved... for that is television's equivalent of the oral narratives through which we make sense of our daily lives'.

SUMMARY

Whether information is factual or fictional it has, as this chapter suggests, to be assembled into a narrative; and in the telling of stories, whatever their format or genre, meanings are made and communicated.

This chapter has stressed the importance of stories, and their symbolic significance, to society. Narratives are examined in relation to the frames which give them structure and direction. Robert Allen's differentiation between the Hollywood narrative mode and the rhetorical narrative mode, and Robert Entman's analysis of the purposes of framing are noted.

Genre and the codes which govern the construction of differing genres such as sit-coms and soaps are discussed prior to focusing on Roland Barthes' five Narrative Codes – Action (or Prioretic), Semantic, Enigma (or Hermeneutic), Referential (or Cultural) and Symbolic. Vladimir Propp's taxonomy of archetypal characters in narratives and Molly Buonanno's study of the way modern popular fictional narratives borrow from news modes and news content are outlined.

Reference is made to Justin Lewis' critique of news narratives and the concern expressed by Daniel Hallin that the 'sound-bite' approach to news narrative, facilitated by new technology and driven by the need to win and sustain audience attention, has made the news more mediated than ever before.

The importance of narrative arises from the notion that ultimately all stories are framed by ideologies prevalent in the cultural contexts in which they are told. As the Greek philosopher Plato (*c.* 428–347 BC) believed, those who tell stories also rule society.

KEY TERMS

Homo narrens ■ storyness ■ information model, story model

social cohesiveness ■ myth, closure ■ frames, schemata

binary framing ■ genre ■ codes of narrative

primary, secondary texts ■ diachronic structure

fictionworthiness ■ sound-bites ■ horse-race journalism

SUGGESTED ACTIVITIES

1. Discussion

   (a) Taking into account both media texts and media audiences, discuss the extent to which reception itself is ritualistic.

   (b) Consider the argument that soaps are a 'woman's genre'.

   (c) Breaking the basic rules of a genre may stretch it creatively; but what are the dangers?

   (d) What might be the effects of reformulating the news (as John Fiske suggests) along the lines of the first principle of storytelling, namely keeping the audience in suspense concerning what happens next?

2. Select a single episode of a TV soap, sitcom, cop series and so on and attempt a detailed deconstruction according to Roland Barthes' five codes of narrative.

3. Attempt a similar exercise using Propp's archetypical story features:

   ■ the *hero/subject* whose function is to seek

   ■ the *object* that is sought

   ■ the *donor* of the object

   ■ the *receiver*, where it is sent

   ■ the *helper* who aids the action

   ■ the *villain* who blocks the action

4. You may wish to investigate sport as storytelling, using Propp as a starter. Sports' coverage, in the press or on TV provides us with fascinating insights into stories about heroes and heroines, victories and defeats.

A glance at the film/media/sociology/television shelves of the best bookshops will indicate a steady stream of new volumes on the media as storytellers and myth-makers. *Mass-Mediated Culture* (US: Prentice-Hall, 1977) by Michael R. Real and *Story and discourse: Narrative structure in fiction and film* (US: Cornell University Press, 1978) by Seymour Chatman are unlikely to be among them but will reward patience in waiting for your librarian to obtain them on loan. Also be sure to try *Myths, Media and Narratives: Television and the Press* (UK: Sage, 1988) edited by James W. Carey, John Ellis' *Visible Fictions: Cinema,Television, Video* (UK: revised edition, 1992) and for a specific focus on film narrative, David Borwell's *Narration in the Fiction Film* (UK: Routledge, 1986). On sports narrative and ideology, John Hargreaves' *Sport, Power and Culture* (UK: Polity Press, 1986) is a leader in its field; but also look out for *Women, Media and Sport: Challenging Gender Values* edited by Pamela Creedon (UK: Sage, 1994).

Also recommended are *Disney Discourse* edited by Eric Smoodin (UK: Routledge, 1994) and Arthur Asa Berger's book, mentioned in this chapter – *Narratives in Popular Culture, Media and Everyday Life* (US: Sage, 1997).

7 Pressures and Constraints in Media Production

AIMS

- To survey the personal, social and institutional pressures which media practitioners have to cope with in their working lives.

- To examine the principles and practice of media professionalism in the light of rapidly changing circumstances.

- By focusing on information sources, to address the problem faced by news practitioners of attempts by influentials in society wishing to 'manage the news'.

- To outline briefly the position of women and of ethnic minorities in media professions.

The first part of this chapter uses Maletzke's model of the constituents of media production to examine the pressures and constraints upon media practitioners, focusing on the communicator as an individual within a production team which in turn operates in a media organisation. Idealism is seen to be unavoidably modified by the necessities of circumstance and context – by the law, by institutional norms, values and practices and by market forces.

A key theme of much research into media practices is the heavy reliance of media upon drawing information from official sources, thus opening practitioners to the accusation of compliance. Problems concerning the under-representation of women and of ethnic minorities are linked to habits of exclusion and stereotyping which have proved to be deeply ingrained at all levels of media.

Media communication and the 'project of self'

In Chapter 3 I quoted from John B. Thompson's *The Media and Modernity: A Social Theory of the Media*,[1] in which he refers to 'the project of self'. He is speaking specifically of how members of audience seek to connect up personal development with both *lived* and *mediated* experience. The media practitioner – journalist, broadcaster, photographer, advertising copywriter or film-maker – is even more directly involved in this process of self-formulation; in the 'project of self', negotiating a passage between personal needs and aspirations, the demands of the media world he or she is active in, and the realities of the lived experience of social, cultural, political and economic life.

Many of the students I interview express an ambition to become journalists, for the perception they have of the profession seems relevant to their personal vision: it is congruent with their developing project of self. The attractions are obvious: you are out and about rather than stuck at a desk; you rarely know what reporting job you will be on from day to day. There is the possibility of travel, of danger, of meeting interesting people; and journalism is widely held by young people to be a service to the community.

I usually ask applicants to tell me what in particular they see themselves doing as journalists and, more importantly, what evidence they can produce of commitment. Many have already fixed up for themselves work experience or work shadowing in newspapers or local radio, usually by sheer persistence. What is most noticeable among such applicants, apart from enthusiasm, is idealism: they see news-gathering and presentation as central features in a country's mental and physical health. Though they may not put it exactly this way, journalism is the eyes, ears and voice of the public in a democracy.

Well, perhaps it would be if it could be. In the West, where Free Press criteria are the norm, informing and speaking up for democracy have a number of barriers to overcome. The young idealist will encounter some of these barriers soon enough: the pressures of time and competition; the need to expand circulation and oblige the advertisers; the compulsion to indulge in 'horse-race' journalism as Daniel Hallin describes it (see Chapter 6, Note 20); the insistence on personalising issues; the temptation to put entertainment rather than information on top of the daily agenda; and not the least, the sensationalisation which so often obliterates the truth.

A useful model highlighting the features of producers, production and consumers of mass communication is that of G. Maletzke published in *The Psychology of Mass Communications*.[2] A selection of the elements of the Maletzke model will be discussed beginning with the 'communicator arm' of the model shown in Figure 7.1. Here Maletzke identifies a range of pressures and constraints affecting the journalist's communicative behaviour.

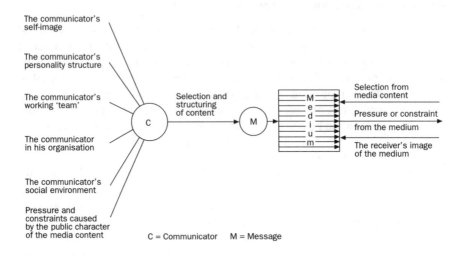

The communicator's
self-image

The communicator's
personality structure

The communicator's
working 'team'

The communicator
in his organisation

The communicator's
social environment

Pressure and
constraints caused
by the public character
of the media content

Selection and
structuring
of content

C

M

M
e
d
i
u
m

Selection from
media content

Pressure or constraint

from the medium

The receiver's image
of the medium

C = Communicator   M = Message

Figure 7.1   The 'communicator arm' of Maletzke's model of the mass communication process (1963). Six major factors have exerted influence on the communicator and therefore affect the way he/she selects and structures messages for media consumption.

■ The communicator's self-image

Let us imagine that you, the reader, have been taken on to a regional newspaper as a trainee reporter. Your self-esteem, as a result of the appointment, may well be high. You have a clear idea of your self-image as a result of the way people treat you; their respect for you. You will have produced some efficient and interesting reports in order to have gained your place. Much will depend, in the new environment, on how others recognise your abilities and demonstrate that they recognise them by for example giving you increasingly challenging tasks to do.

You will be moving to a clearer appraisal of your role as a *professional*, part of which will be the notion of 'doing a good job'. Sooner or later there will come a time when you are asked to do something you consider *un*professional if not unethical. It may simply be a request that is not so much unprofessional or unethical as simply distasteful, like intruding upon the grief of a bereaved family in order to get a story.

You may feel varyingly acute degrees of dissonance, of unease. You ask yourself, conscious of the image you hold of yourself, 'Is this the sort of thing *I* ought to be doing?' To refuse the particular task is to put your job on the line. Either way, you will attempt to shift your feelings from those of dissonance to consonance. If you are to stay in the job this dilemma will recur: will you attempt to 're-educate' self or should you try some other profession?

▪ The communicator's personality structure

Some psychiatrists hold that the 'script' of an individual's personality is written in the early years of childhood. Socialisation and experience shape attitudes and values and these will continue to affect behaviour throughout life. If, for you, kindness and compassion are values which dominate over competition and acquisition the work you produce as a journalist will, if permitted, reflect these values.

Equally you may be a person of commitment who wishes to act – get involved – rather than as a reporter must do, observe and record. The values of a journalist like the Australian, John Pilger, determined warrior against injustices worldwide, expresses with eloquence and passion his personal vision. Getting angry, turning that anger into the communication of analysis and protest is the hallmark of Pilger as a crusading journalist; key to his personality.

A young reporter might say, 'Yes, but Pilger is famous. He has more freedom to express his views and therefore himself than the rest of us'. The 'rest of us' have, the argument might continue, to strive after objectivity, balance, impartiality (professional values) even though we may not believe any of them to be really possible.

As Pilger says in the preface to *Heroes*,[3] a collection of his journalistic writing, neutrality is a 'non-existent nirvana'. Attempting something you do not believe in will prove an intolerable strain unless the inner voice of self – conscience – can be squared by argument or rationalisation.

▪ The communicator's working 'team'

Objectivity and neutrality may or may not be crucial norms for a media work team, but whatever norms have been engendered by people working together will be the ones most difficult to ignore. The dynamics of groups tend to demand a measure of conformity to group rules and practices and the reward for this conformity is the satisfaction and pride of belonging.

Students of communication will be familiar with teamwork and will recognise that individual initiative and group norms often come into conflict and have to be resolved, usually in the group's favour. Either that, or the group's performance will be impeded. In a successful group what counts for the team member is the respect and admiration he or she is held in by other members of the group. The more habitual the work of the group and the more its efforts are given status and recognition by those in important positions outside of the group, the tighter will be the bonding.

Some commentators argue that media people are performing to impress other media people, with audience response a secondary consideration. As Allan Bell puts it in *The Language of News Media*,[4] 'Mass communicators are interested in their peers not their public'.

▪ The communicator in his/her organisation

The independence of a working group survives only as long as the organisation to which it belongs tolerates that independence and only as long as the working group fulfils the greater aims and objectives of the organisation. The bigger the media organisation the more likely it is to be hierarchically structured; a bureaucracy. There will be normative ways of doing things; procedures and regulations; and communication between the levels of the hierarchy will be tightly controlled.

Joining a major national newspaper group, a young reporter would have to attune to the political, social, economic and cultural standpoints of the organisation. You would be unlikely to succeed in your new job if you submitted stories which regularly ran counter to the ideology of your employers.

The communicator's social environment

A person's education, upbringing, social class and social expectations will all affect communicative behaviour within the work context. The media workforce is predominantly middle class; and its collective script is influenced by middle-class expectations and values. Many commentators have argued that a substantially middle-class workforce will, consciously or unconsciously, report the world according to middle-class assumptions and perceptions.

Pressures and constraints caused by the public character of the media

Your ambition may always have been to move on from a local reporting job into public broadcasting. You will discover that being employed by a corporation answerable to government is to experience constraints arising from the organisation being one which itself is under public scrutiny. You may decide that working for state-linked media is too inhibiting: you want to throw caution to the winds, so you opt to switch to the private sector. In all probability the local commercial station's output is livelier, probably a lot more fun. Yet once more there is a 'regulatory' body ever prepared to exert influence over content and style – the advertiser.

A constant pressure upon media operating in the public domain is the law. Should you intentionally or inadvertently write or broadcast something defamatory about a member of the public or a company or institution proof of slander (spoken defamation) or libel (written defamation) could result in enormous fines for you or your employer. You could be landed in court for obscenity, for breach of commercial confidentiality and perhaps most seriously – in the UK – for divulging information covered by the Official Secrets Act.

The dangers are not confined to punishment after the event. Perhaps the worst form of censorship for a journalist is what is termed *prior restraint*. The subject of a proposed report or programme hears that it is about to go out. In certain circumstances a decision in court may ban or at least postpone the broadcast or the publication.

Let us look at the Maletzke model in full (Figure 7.2). It is complex but helpfully comprehensive. It acknowledges a structure of response on the part of the receiver which corresponds to that of media performers and media performance. We might read into it an indicator that successful media communication requires both axes of the model to take into consideration the pressures and constraints each experiences and each expects. The basic formula would seem to be that the news values held by the communicator produce the news that the receiver/public values.

■ The communicator's image of the audience

The popular press (in particular) claims to have its finger on the public pulse: it knows its readership and considers the factors on the right-hand side of the Maletzke model. It therefore speaks for its reading public in discourses likely to be understood and appreciated; and in language – *tabloidese* – which is as accessible as it is lively.

Colin Sparks in his chapter 'Popular journalism: theories and practice' in *Journalism and Popular Culture*[5] says that it is not 'a particular mystery as to what the nature of the news values of this "popular journalism" is' and thus how it is designed to fulfil the perceived needs of readership:

> Relatively speaking these newspapers will tend to give more space to sport than to politics, stress more that extraordinary category 'human interest' than economic life, concentrate heavily upon individuals rather than institutions, upon the local and the immediate rather than the international and the long-term and so on.

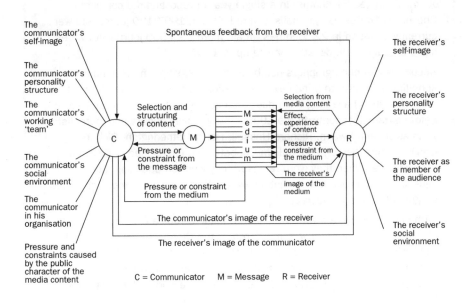

Figure 7.2   Maletzke's full model of the mass communication process (1963). It is, at first glance, rather formidable but careful examination of its parts will indicate how useful it can be as a reminder of the complexity of the encoding-decoding process.

Above all, Sparks believes, the 'structure of the "popular" in modern journalism is... one which is massively and systematically "depoliticised"', presumably because the communicator's image of audience in this case is of readers uninterested in, and turned off by politics.

Of course 'depoliticised' certainly does not mean ideology-free. On the contrary, believes Colin Sparks, there is 'a conception of politics which concentrates on the everyday at the expense of the historical' and avoids generating 'a picture of the world in which social classes are capable of transforming the fundamental structures of social life through their own self-activity'.

The young journalist coming from media education in which the purposes, roles and performance of media have been closely scrutinised is unlikely to be surprised by the expectations of popular journalism and its vision of audience. Yet the pressure to conform to institutional norms, values and practices will constitute an ongoing challenge.

RISKING LIFE AND LIMB

In 1993 at least 63 journalists were killed, worldwide, according to figures issued by *Reporters Sans Frontières*[6] and this compared with 72 in 1991 and 61 in 1992. In 1995, the New York-based Committee to Protect Journalists cited 51 deaths. In a single year of reporting the conflict in Chechnya, 14 Russian journalists were killed. In 1997 180 journalists were currently in prison in 22 countries. In all, more than 500 journalists were killed on duty in the decade running up to 1997.

Reporters and photographers risk bullets, beatings-up, imprisonment, sometimes torture, to bring news to a nation's breakfast table. Respect and admiration have long been due to those who put the quest for a story before personal security. In the 19th century radical editors and journalists such as Joseph Swann, Richard Hassell, Henry Hetherington, Richard Carlile, James Watson and William Cobbett were imprisoned in Britain for their writings. When they were released they went on attacking the injustices, inequality and corruption around them. Above all they demanded progress towards democracy.

With similar courage award-winning journalist Veronica Guerin, pursuing a drugs trafficking story was murdered at the Clondalkin traffic lights in Dublin in 1996. Leading editors in Britain and Ireland issued, in anger and sympathy, a joint statement which read: 'Veronica Guerin was murdered for being a journalist. She was a brave and brilliant reporter who was gunned down for being too tenacious in her investigation of organised crime in Ireland. We view this assassination as a fundamental attack on the free press which is essential to the democratic process.

continued

Journalism will not be intimidated. We hereby commit our news organisations to continue the investigation of the stories which cost Veronica Geurin her life.'

A journalist of equal standing in the the courage stakes, Maggie O'Kane, in an article about Guerin, 'The tragedy is there are no rules any more' published in the *Guardian* (28 June 1996) poignantly sums up the nature of the investigative journalist: 'She [Veronica] was driven by what drives most of us – a mixture of deep insecurity, a need to keep shining in the job, ego, and a notion that maybe sometimes it did some good.'

■ The receiver's image of the communicator

We do well to bear in mind statistics such as those printed above when 'journos' come in for public criticism in, say, intrusion cases. Sadly, examples of intrusions into privacy, muck-raking and sexational titillation tend to give all the press a bad name. It is in the nature of news coverage that reporters appear, with notebooks and a headful of questions, at times of disaster and distress. They probe and they harry. Sometimes they will not let a matter alone. They become despised.

That, of course, is at the immediate location of disaster and distress. Elsewhere, out of earshot and out of sight, the 'public' wants to know; is hungry for information, for tittle-tattle as much as for hard news. Disapproval there may be, but there is also a degree of public dependency: the audience needs news but it also *wants* stories – dramatic, stirring, exemplary, reaffirming.

In an article 'Has communication explained journalism?' in the *Journal of Communication*,[7] Barbie Zelizer writes of the way 'publics let reporters present themselves as cultural authorities for events of the "real world"'. Journalists do what they do, good or bad, because they are confident of public acceptance; and this constitutes, says Zelizer, 'one of the outstanding condundrums of contemporary public discourse'.

We, as public, are accepting of journalism's claim to be the key mediator of reality: 'Audiences tend to question journalistic authority only when journalists' versions of events conflict with the audiences's view of the same events.' Just occasionally the journalistic view is so at odds with the public's perception of reality that general acquiescence turns to positive and determined resistance.

The tasteless and sensationalist coverage by the *Sun* newspaper in Britain, of the tragedy of spectators crushed to death during the Football Association Cup semi-final between Liverpool and Nottingham Forest (15 April 1989) at Sheffield's Hillsborough stadium, created such outrage among the people of Liverpool that the newspaper was banned throughout the city – not by the city council but by the people themselves who arguably felt affronted in relation to every feature of the receiver arm of Maletzke's model.

Pressures and constraints of message and medium

Journalists are generally perceived to be the first gatekeepers. The decision as to who to send on a story lies with the news editor but from that point on the journalist is at the front line of mediation, deciding what information to include and what to leave aside; which points to emphasise and which to minimise. First, there is pressure to find an angle – a key notion (or message) to hang the story on. Second, the pressure is likely to be one related to the news value of amplitude.

No reporter wishes to cover a story when little of significance seems to have occurred. If storylines are not evident the reporter's *instinct* for a story will resemble the detective's hunt for clues. There is a particular satisfaction the journalist experiences when his or her story hits the front page; and the pressure to 'make the front page' is as much personally driven as institutionally required.

In fact the determination to write a highly newsworthy story may well conflict with institutional constraints. If you are working as a reporter on a local newspaper you may stumble on a case of local government corruption or serious pollution caused by a local firm. The adrenalin flows. Your notebook bulges with damning information. It is full of juicy quotes given you by members of the public – then why are you suddenly greeted back at the office with blank stares and shakes of the head?

Your story, or at least most of it, is on the 'spike': 'This,' you might be told, 'isn't the sort of paper that prints that sort of story. We have our advertisers to think of. Are you aware that Company X takes a full-page spread twice a month?' This is a constraint brought about by the perceived role of the paper within its community. On a broader canvas, media must take heed of commercial or political giants – companies or states, home or away – whose interests may impact on editorial policy. Stories about human rights abuses in nations such as China, Indonesia or Saudi Arabia, for example, have to be weighed in the balance against their commercial goodwill as important trading nations; and the temptation to trade silence for lucrative business contracts is ever present.

It can be argued that we are not talking here about the constraints of the medium as a mode of communication; rather the point is that while the medium shapes the message it is the constraints upon message itself which limit the possibilities of the medium. Equally it might be said that the *possibilities* of the medium are both a challenge and a constraint.

Today, technology not only makes for speed of output, it is a driving force to the point when speed becomes a principle of operation. As Jo Bardoel describes the situation in a *European Journal of Communication* article, 'Beyond journalism: a profession between information society and civil society',[8] journalists have to cope with 'a whirling communication carousel of immediate action and reaction'.

Indeed, as Bardoel recognises, digitalisation is scarcely destined to slow down the 'communication carousel', for it threatens to rewrite the 'story' of mass communication in that each member of the public will have the capacity to be his or her own journalist, his or her own programme planner. Bardoel does, however, see a future for serious, analytical journalism, in *making sense* of the whirling carousel of information. In future, the journalist's task may be to help unload the overload.

◾ The receiver's self-image and personality

All their lives students of media have also been receivers of media. Self-image will in part have been affected by exposure to media in its many forms and this experience is reflected in comments such as 'I wouldn't be seen dead reading – watching – wearing – listening to' and so on. What we read, watch, wear, listen to and so on is what we are, or like to think we are. The advertiser concentrates in particular on the self-image of the prospective consumer.

An advertising campaign many years ago for the UK *Times* called it the paper for Top People. The covert message was that by reading the *Times* you could rank yourself among the Top People even if you weren't one. The problem was that if successful advertising boosted sales of the paper beyond the constituency of Top People, Top People would stop subscribing to it.

Self-image is essentially about individuality; and individuality is a cherished and highly marketable personality trait. Tailoring messages which address the individual-in-the-mass is a prime challenge for the communicator. A key strategy is *segmentation* according to a number of personal, social and cultural criteria, as we shall see in the next chapter when approaches to audience research are discussed. Such a strategy depends for its success on communicators *knowing* their audience, its doubts and anxieties as well as its dreams and aspirations; its tastes and its preferred lifestyle.

◾ The receiver's social environment

The receiver as member of readership/audience has been documented in Chapter 3, and is a recurring theme throughout the book, so this tracing of the Maletzke model concludes with brief observations on the social environment in which reception takes place.

The producers of mass communication messages are part of the context in which audiences use those messages. They are themselves audience in the sense that they are subject to the pressures and constraints placed upon society generally. Recession, social or cultural fragmentation, racial strife, conflict between management and workers, the rise and rise of crime, the pollution of the environment, the nation's health, morale, spirituality, these all influence the nature of message production.

Sitcoms of the 1990s have contained a duly proportionate share of unemployed characters and, in Britain, financial hardship resulting from free market policies and the rolling back of the welfare state, has never been far away from the families that have populated long-running soaps such as *Eastenders* or *Brookside*.

Such powerful narratives dramatise problems. Solutions to those problems are left for audiences to conjecture upon; which is perhaps as well, for solutions on screen, unless matched by solutions in real life situations, only diminish audience trust in the integrity of media communication.

Of course in countries where normative practices can be analysed in terms of the Authoritarian Theory of media (as discussed in Chapter 4), the power of media communicators to reveal to a community the nature of its own social environment is strictly censored if not forbidden altogether. All that is permitted are visualisations that conform to the requirements of those in total authority. For example in Saudi Arabia the audience for media is denied any public reference to politics, religions other than Islam, pork or pigs, alcohol or sexual innuendo (*US State Report, 1995*, quoted in *Index on Censorship* **4** (1996). To defy such constraints is to invite arrest, trial and imprisonment.

The dilemmas of professionalism

Framing all the aspects of Maletzke's model as far as the media communicator is concerned is the notion of professionalism and the principles and operational conventions which shape that professionalism. We encounter once more that important trio – objectivity, impartiality and balance. A feature common to these, however precisely we define their differences, is that journalists must not take sides; must not reveal their personal bias, show favour, sympathy or antipathy.

In other words, journalists must position themselves outside the action. They are observers, not participants. This is a convention hardened by tradition, and occasionally regulation. To breach it is to commit the worst of crimes – to be unprofessional. The dilemma is real, profound and largely unexamined. Just occasionally the role of impartial observer is rejected for a 'higher good'. This painful but arguably enobling choice is well illustrated in one of the best feature films about journalism, *Under Fire* (1983) directed by Roger Spottiswoode and set in Nicaragua, when a news photographer played by Nick Nolte puts aside professionalism and involves himself in political events.

The People's Army, struggling against the repressive machinery of state, suffers a terrible blow – their charismatic leader is shot dead on the verge of sweeping the tyrants out of office. Nolte is asked by the revolutionaries to fake a picture of the leader to make him appear to be still alive. By every rule in the professional book, Nolte must refuse. On the other hand, the situation cries out that he bend the rules in the name of the people's struggle against oppression. As audience for *Under Fire* we are expected to respond affirmatively to this potential act of 'professional suicide' and to celebrate its successful outcome for the revolutionaries.

Here the journalist has taken the side of the underdog rather than stayed aloof; and Spottiswoode's message seems to be that where issues of right or wrong, democracy or repression are involved, the power of the word or of the image should be wielded by journalists as 'part' of life rather than their behaving as though they are somehow disengaged from it.

'Bystander journalism'

This point was given heartfelt support by a 'real' journalist, Martin Bell of the BBC, in the autumn of 1996. The veteran foreign correspondent's speech to News World '96, a conference in Berlin of 500 news broadcasters from all over the world, called for an end to '"bystander journalism" based on the old tradition of detached, cool and neutral reporting'.

Bell had been badly wounded four years previously while covering the civil war in Bosnia. While acknowledging the need to honour fairness and the meticulous concern for facts, Bell declared in his Berlin speech:

> I do not believe we should stand neutrally between good and evil, right and wrong, aggressor and victim... It is a real problem we should address: my answer is what I call journalism of attachment, journalism which cares as well as knows.

Not surprisingly Bell's employer, the BBC, was unimpressed. Lucien Hudson, a senior editor on the 24-hour international news channel, BBC World, was of the opinion that the 'journalism of attachment' was very risky.

Bell's speech prompted interesting responses. From Eason Jordan, executive vice-president, CNN International – 'If you are a real human being you have compassion and feelings. As long as you are accurate and fair, to be compassionate is acceptable for a reporter'; from Tim Gardam, Channel 5 (UK) controller of news – 'That kind of journalism is always far easier in foreign affairs than reporting Britain or British politics', and finally from the *Guardian*'s foreign correspondent, Martin Woollacott:

> Objectivity is critical, but pretending that both sides or different sides in a war are equal or equally wrong is foolish. There is usually a side which is preferable and sometimes which is enormously preferable.

Martin Bell proved he was no bystander by agreeing to be put forward as the anti-corruption candidate at Tatton, Cheshire, in the British General Election of May 1997. He became the first Independent MP in over 50 years, gaining an 11,000 majority over his Tory rival, Neil Hamilton.

Professionalism at the level of myth

A fascinating and exhaustive study of the institutional norms, values and practices of the British Broadcasting Corporation was conducted by Philip Schlesinger. In his book *Putting 'Reality' Together: BBC News*,[9] he explores what he terms myths of professionalism which held sway in the corporation. First, Schlesinger identifies the *micro-myth*. Here, the *autonomy* of the production staff is held to be self-evident, responsibility being fully delegated downwards from the Director General.

Second is the *macro-myth* which enthrones the view that the BBC is socially unattached. In spite of the myth of independence, Schlesinger found that an 'invisible framework of guidance is omnipresent' – the institutional *ethos*. Of the newsroom, Schlesinger writes:

> The style of control is one which relies upon responsible editors, who have been thoroughly socialised by long exposure to the mores [essentially, norms and values] of the Corporation that they will 'instinctively' make the right decision.

Claims to independence, Schlesinger argues, have validity only within the notion that the 'value framework... has already, largely been developed at higher levels of control, to which most newsmen have no access'. Most journalists, whether working in broadcasting or for newspapers, will probably recognise this state of affairs. They will have at least a nodding acquaintance with the *control features* listed by Schlesinger such as the hierarchy of positions and (not least, or to be belittled) the attraction of a secure, well-remunerated job; features which 'tend to ensure conformity in the newsrooms'.

Perhaps the most familiar control feature, and the one by which careers rise or fall, is the senior editor's power to assign news staff to stories. Few pressures can be greater for the journalist than the one which starts everything off – being chosen to cover one story rather than another; being favoured (or not favoured) in what Schlesinger calls a 'pecking order'. Much depends on track record: how well did you manage last time?

Schlesinger cites *reliability* as a prime criterion for selection. This does not simply mean reliability to come back with a good story, fully documented and well told. People tend to be chosen for their proven record for saying 'what one wanted in an acceptable (that is, inconspicuous way)'. In other words, what counts is a safe pair of hands; or to supplement one useful cliché for another – horses for courses.

This situation is illustrated in another thought-provoking movie about media people, Karl Francis' *Giro City* (1982). Glenda Jackson as film director and Jon Finch as reporter are scheduled to cover two stories, financial corruption in Wales and the conflict in Northern Ireland for a commercial TV station. Finch is a top-class reporter, independent but suspect, likely to put his pursuit of the truth ahead of his responsibility to appear 'evenhanded'.

He is about to crown a fine investigative story about Ireland with an interview with a British cabinet minister. At the last moment, he is substituted as interviewer. A 'safer pair of hands' is put in his place to give the minister an 'easier ride'. As for the Welsh story, the truth is struck silent as the law renders the 'case' *sub judice*. Few films better illustrate the pressures and constraints upon journalists than *Giro City*.

Schlesinger explodes the micro-myth of autonomy, of independence, believing that the news, with its 'flagship' – highly prestigious, high-profile – function, is 'the home of the conformist'. True, official ideology stresses autonomy, but this 'does less than justice to the substantive controls which actually constrain production'. Part of the myth is that some 'controls' are inevitable: within the parameters of the possible, the near-impossible is achieved.

Emerging out of this, along with team spirit, is a sense of pride in upholding the principles that guide and are required of broadcasters – balance, objectivity, fairness, freedom from bias and impartiality. Schlesinger points out that these terms are, in the 'ordinary discourse of newsmen', for the most part 'interchangeable'.

Ideological keynote

'Impartiality,' believes Schlesinger, 'is the linchpin of the BBC's ideology: it is a notion saturated with political and philosophical implications'. Yet impartiality can have meaning only 'in the context of an existing set of values, and in the case of the BBC the relevant complex of values is that of the "consensus"'. To be impartial, it is necessary to be uninvolved in that which is being reported. The BBC and most other news producing organisations, however, are not floating islands above the fray. They are actors in the drama of social, cultural, political and economic events; influenced and influencing.

Schlesinger says that what the BBC produces as news is 'structurally limited by the organisation's place in Britain's social order'. The main consequence of that position is that 'the outputs of broadcasting are, in general, supportive of the existing social order'.

Pressures to conform to dominant norms and practices exist in every organisation, media or otherwise. As far as the BBC is concerned, Schlesinger states:

> I was faced with a mass of conformists. Their conformity lay not in their personal style, dress or lack of sexual peccadillos, but rather in their adoption of the model of corporate professionalism provided for them by the BBC by degrees varying from unreflecting acquiescence to the most full-blown commitment.

Schlesinger quotes a senior news and current affairs editor as saying, 'Every time a man reveals a personal commitment he reduces his professional usefulness, until the moment arrives when he may be said to have used up all his credit-worthiness'. For personal 'commitment' we can also read personal *value*. It seeems that survival in the institution would depend upon a practitioner being value-*free*. Schlesinger calls this the 'myth of value-freedom'. The bottom line of the institutional message might be – either subscribe to the myth or get out. The myth is 'essential for public consumption' and thus it must be 'believed by those who propagate it' as 'a condition of employment'. Such beliefs, argues Schlesinger, 'anchor news production in the *status quo*'.

News management and the hazards of source

Maletzke's model offers us a comprehensive framework for investigating the variables working at the stages of message formulation and reception. The audience's perception of the communicator as message-producer is recognised, but in our survey of pressures and restraints we need to pay critical attention to the journalists' own sources, for it is an old axiom that a story is only as reliable as its source.

The central criticism levelled at the reporting fraternity is that they rely too heavily upon official sources, that is, briefings in one form or another by those in authority. In Chapter 3, I quoted Allan Bell as saying in *The Language of News*

Media that news 'is what an authoratitive source tells a journalist'. He refers to those who 'wear a general mantle of authority and are part of the institutional network where journalists expect to get their information'.

Obtaining information that does not come from official sources is a genuine problem even for the journalist determined to cut through the protective cordon of those 'authoritative sources' whose purpose is the *management* of news. Philip M. Taylor in *War and the Media: Propaganda and Persuasion in the Gulf War*[10] writes:

> Despite the existence of well over a thousand journalists in the Gulf from a wide variety of news-gathering organisations with differing editorial styles and journal-istic practices, they were all essentially dependent upon the coalition military for their principle source of information about the progress of the war. It was monopoly in the guise of pluralism.

The pressure to 'get a story' in such situations means that the official account is considered better than no account. In an ideal world journalists would resist attempts by official sources to write their stories for them. In practice, perceived necessities can often serve as an alibi for merely reworking official briefings.

Journalists are rarely short of information – provided by all the agencies in a society who wish their story to be told. What they are always short of and desper-ately in need of is the kind of information people in authority do not want them to print or broadcast. There are occasions when a reporter looks out on the world and sees plenty of news management, but pitifully little news.

Spin-doctoring

Let us be clear about the meaning of *news management*. This does not refer to news teams involved in news production; rather it describes the myriad forces in society which want to get a story about themselves, preferably favourable, into the news. The term 'spin-doctors' describes the public relations personnel – usually former journalists (indeed *current* journalists) – who, working for political parties, corporations or pressure groups, strive to get their patrons' message across via the mass media, with one hand pressing the 'good' news, with the other, suppressing the bad. They are there to ensure that preferred readings are greeted by dominant responses.

In the Glasgow University Media Group's 1993 publication, *Getting the Message: News, Truth and Power*,[11] David Miller reports on the way that the Northern Ireland Information Service controlled – news managed – the informa-tion coming out of Northern Ireland and how it did this by exercising what Miller terms a 'hierarchy of access'.

Working under the direction of the Northern Ireland Office (NIO), the Northern Ireland Information Service, according to Hansard of 7 May 1991, spent £7.2 million in the year 1989–90 on press and public relations in a

campaign to define the situation in Northern Ireland according to the requirements of the Westminster government.

Specifically the strategy was to emphasise two themes: terrorism as an assault
on democracy and the fact that Northern Ireland's commercial and industrial
progress ('carrying on regardless') was making terrorism irrelevant. Miller writes:

> Because of the perceived difficulty of getting good news into the media [about
> Northern Ireland], the information service itself has two staff who produce 'good
> news' stories for the international market... They attempt to 'place' these stories in
> suspecting and unsuspecting magazines and newspapers.

We are witnessing here an example of practices exercised worldwide, which
might be described as *disinformation*. Of course journalists are themselves guilty of
this but they are often as much victims of disinformation as perpetrators (and
perpetuators) of it. More usually, journalists and their editors 'let through' official
information either without checking it out or challenging it.

Miller quotes an unpublished disssertation by Eamon Hardy for Queen's
University, Belfast, on the Northern Ireland Information Service and its link with
the Northern Ireland press.[12] In a three-month period Hardy discovered that
Belfast's three daily papers used between 57 per cent and 68 per cent of Northern
Ireland Office press releases as the basis for news stories. Channel 4's *Hard News*
picked up on the fact that very little of the original briefing was altered, Hardy
telling them that:

> Attached to each press release there are things called Notes to Editors, which are
> supposed to be a government analysis of its own facts and figures and quite often I
> found that, in fact very often, you have journalists using these Notes to Editors as
> their own analysis.[13]

According to Miller, the Northern Ireland Office operated selectivity as to how
much information reporters would receive. There seemed to be a pecking order:
the more *influential* reporters were (that is, the more important their paper or
country of origin), and the more likely they were to use NIO information
favourably (that is favourable to the arguments of the government), the more they
would get the red-carpet treatment. London-based media outlets, particularly
television, featured high up in the hierarchy of access.

Miller says:

> Journalists from Western countries are seen as more important than journalists
> from what was the eastern bloc or the Third World... Even among Western
> journalists degrees of access can depend on the importance to the British govern-
> ment of the country they are from. French and German journalists, for example,
> are higher up the priority list than their counterparts from Norway, Denmark,
> Sweden or Finland... But the main target for information efforts overseas has long
> been the United States of America.

Competing for control

News management is about two things, controlling the content of news which reaches the public and perhaps even more important, influencing public and media agendas. In *Journalism in the 21st Century: Online Information, Electronic Databases and the News*,[14] American media commentator Tom Koch challenges the view that the media set public agendas, or even their own. First, he reminds us of the general situation journalists find themselves in; that is, employees of corporate institutions:

> Mainstream reporters and editors directly serve not the public at large but, rather, the economic necessities of those corporations that hire and pay them. [In turn] Those news corporations... exist to provide advertising space for the advertisements whose sale may guarantee sustaining financial returns.

Profitabliity, then, exerts a tight grip over agenda setting.

Immediately the principle of objectivity (what Koch calls 'journalism's instrumental myth') meets the obstacle of business bias. Koch believes that 'journalists do not set the agenda they publish and broadcast. Instead they affirm and reflect the decisions of others':

> The traditional assumption has been that reporters, or at least their editors, determine what events will be covered, and, therefore, are conscious contributors to any bias in the news. In reality, news professionals are almost totally dependent on press releases and the public statements of sanctioned 'experts' and officials.

Koch sees journalists not so much as producers of misinformation as casualties of it, condemned to reproduce elite messages for want of other sources of information. In an earlier work, *The News as Myth: Fact and Content in Journalism*[15] he defines two forms of event, the *boundary event,* that is, the actual occurrence – accident, death, disaster – and the *journalistic event* which follows it, in which a report is based upon what journalists glean from officials. In *Journalism in the 21st Century* Koch writes, 'Editors assign reporters to follow publicly sanctioned, journalistic events and not investigate their antecedent boundary occurrences'.

They will, for example, report a presidential speech on the dangers of drug dependency, and by reporting it they will turn presidential opinion into fact, rather than investigate the reality of what is claimed:

> Reporters rarely question independently the legitimacy of the speakers' statements, and truth is reduced to the reasonably accurate reportage of what an official says in press conference or a similarly public forum.

The result, Koch believes – and this goes some way to explaining the ingrainedness of stereotypical images – 'is a compliant press whose job is to report and relay what officials tell them to write' and the power of these officials to set the news agenda and control the media 'is increasingly evident the higher one goes on the political or economic ladder'.

Bucking officialdom: an online route

If the 'middleman' intrudes so assertively in the production of news narratives, then – Koch suggests – cut out the middleman. Modern technology, in the form of the modem, computer and telephone line makes this direct link with boundary event information a possibility as never before. The Internet, with its scores of browser services permitting fast access to vast stores of information, promises to radically alter the information-seeking process. Koch believes:

> Online technologies – usually called 'databases' or, less frequently, 'online libraries' – efficiently place an enormous amount of information at the command of the reporter or the writer. Further they do so with incredible specificity. Data available from online sources are so vast that it would take an expert months or years to search through them manually for the pertinent fact or the seminal article.

Any field can be narrowed 'to the appropriate and crucial information within minutes by a competent data researcher'. Koch sees in electronic databases the possibility of greater objectivity and less bias in reporting because more fundamentally '"complete" information may enter the public forum on a regular basis'.

This liberation of journalism (and consequently of the public it serves) from traditional information sources and therefore from the ideologies which those sources protect and project may not be welcome to power elites, but, Koch concludes:

> it is a lesson of the printing revolution that officials find it difficult or impossible to prevent the resulting flow of information when technology and economies combine to make a new level of dissemination both possible and profitable.

All this, of course, relies on the continuing independence of online services from the control of the great corporations.

Uneven playing fields 1: gender imbalance

What constitutes both a contraint and an issue in the world of media communication is the treatment of women and of ethnic minorities *by* media and their under-representation in terms of media employment. If my experience of the quality, drive and commitment of the women applying for media studies degrees is anything to go by, the future may demand the exercise of positive discrimination – in favour of men. This impression is given weight by surveys in the United States, Britain and the Netherlands which record substantial increases in the number of women entering schools of journalism or enrolling for other communications courses, to the extent that reference has been made to a 'gender-switch'. Yet this trend is unevenly reflected in the media profession itself.

Public relations, advertising, magazine production and publishing appear to offer better opportunities for women than other specialist media fields. In *Feminist Media Studies*,[16] Liesbet van Zoonen writes that 'One of the factors explaining why some areas of communication provide more opportunities for women than others is the status of the medium'.

Where the status of the medium is low, she argues, opportunities for women increase. She cites the example of radio where it has been displaced in importance and status by television: 'The resulting loss of prestige may have decreased male competition for job openings enabling women to fill the gaps.' On the other hand, 'in many developing countries radio is still the mass electronic medium and dominated by men'. Van Zoonen adds that 'local (low prestige) media almost invariably employ more women than national (high prestige) media'.

Once employed, women have further problems to deal with, in particular the attitudes of male colleagues and decision makers:

> Gruesome anecdotes of women encountering blatant sexism abound, and can be found in any number of popular press cuttings, biographies and research reports…Whatever particular cultural form they may take, discriminatory attitudes towards women on the workfloor seem to be common practice in media production world wide.

Women's domestic and parental responsibilities constitute the toughest hurdle of all to their careers in the media. As van Zoonen points out, 'media work and motherhood have been made notoriously difficult to combine due to a lack of provision at the work place and to social values and beliefs'. Women journalists are often expected, by male colleagues and by the organisations which employ them, to perform professionally in a manner different from men; to subscribe to expectations of 'femininity'. Van Zoonen says:

> Women are confronted by social and cultural expectations of femininity and at the same time are expected to meet criteria of professionalism. In the Netherlands, for instance, many female journalists feel that they are judged primarily as women being subjected to continual comment on their appearance and 'invitations' from male colleagues.

There is no evidence, van Zoonen argues, that women constitute a different group of professionals from their male colleagues. She refers to her own research in the Netherlands: two-thirds of the women journalists she talked to did believe that 'women journalists pay more attention to background information and are more willing to look for spokeswomen instead of spokesmen' than their male counterparts yet there was no difference 'in the actual selection of topics or issues'.[17]

The chief problem facing women is that they generally enter an organisational culture whose *mores* and discourses are male-orientated. To survive, women must adapt, become socialised into the ways of the institution – what van Zoonen believes 'tends to reaffirm a conservative *status quo*' which she discerns already having begun at the stage of journalist training.

The 'maleness' of news

According to Sue Curry Jansen conditions and prospects for women are equally disadvantaged in the United States. In 'Beaches without bases: the gender order' published in *Invisible Crises*,[18] Jansen states that the news generally, and international news in particular, needs to be viewed through the 'prism of gender'.

When it is, we come to realise that news content and news gathering are 'gendered' with a profound, and institutionalised bias towards maleness:

In the United States men write most of the front-page newspaper stories. They are the subject of most of those stories – 85 per cent of the references and 66 per cent of the photos in 1993. They also dominate electronic media, accounting for 86 per cent of the correspondents and 75 per cent of the sources for US network television evening programmes.

Women, women's issues and problems are not newsworthy unless they can be labelled according to traditional female roles – wife, mother, daughter. 'Men are typically assigned to *hard* news, news that has significant public implications. Women, in contrast, cover *soft* news stories and stories related to topics traditionally associated with female responsibilities'. In international news coverage, 'women not only are marginal but also normally absent'.

Jansen quotes a term used by Robert W. Connell in *Gender and Power* [19] when he talks of 'hegemonic masculinity' which dominates political and economic life as well as media. Hegemonic masculinity describes masculine relationships characterised by dominance and subservience, men to men, and men to all females; and this situation is replicated, Connell argues, in the global ordering of relationships between nations. Jansen continues:

Under the present global gender order, policymakers and journalists find it more *manly* to deal with guns, missiles, and violent conflicts than with matters like female infanticide in China, the increased trade in children in the sex markets of Manila and Bangkok in the wake of the AIDS epidemic, the impact of the intifada on Palestinian women, or the political activism of groups such as Women in Black, Israeli women who support the intifada.

The author is angry but not without optimism for the prospect of gender-shifts in the emphasis of news content and production. Women are seeking empowerment in all sorts of ways but such actions do not get into the news. Jansen asks:

How many readers of this book know that women have established a feminist radio station, Radio Tierra, in Chile? How many know that they are producing and distributing feminist videos throughout the Americas? How many know that women in Sri Lanka have formed underground media collectives to produce videos documenting human rights violations?... How many know that the Manushi collective in India has published a successful magazine that confronts the oppression of women in that society?

Media scholars are then asked whether they are aware of the resistance among traditional media operators to such attempts to assert women's rights; for example in Kenya when similar efforts by the editorial staff of *Viva* magazine were halted by transnational advertising agencies:

These agencies threatened to withdraw advertisements if the advertising-dependent magazine continued to address issues like prostitition, birth control, female circumcision, polygamy and sex education.

Such stories, says Jansen, 'have low or no news value within the framing conventions of mainstream objective media'. They will be found only 'at the margins of journalism'. However, 'a new journalism dedicated to breaking this code of silence is emerging in the wake of global feminism,' believes Jansen. 'As a result, the old Western journalistic establishment may be approaching the eleventh hour in its crisis of credibility if not survival.'

MALE BIAS IN TV ELECTION COVERAGE

The UK Fawcett Society published in April 1997 the findings of a week's monitoring of election coverage during the main news bulletins on the BBC, ITN and Channel 4. Eighty per cent of this was carried out by male journalists; and the number of women featured as spokespersons in the news was similarly in a minority. Of 26 government officials asked for their views, none was a woman. It was encouraging news, then, that the number of women MPs returned to parliament in New Labour's landslide election victory on 1 May 1997, significantly increased from 62 under the Tories to 120, 100 of whom were Labour, including journalist Sally Keeble and former *Guardian* journalist Ruth Kelly. Five women – a record – were appointed to the first Cabinet of Prime Minister Tony Blair.

Uneven playing fields 2: ethnic imbalance

If women have to struggle to make their professional way in face of 'hegemonic maleness', a similar state of imbalance exists in terms of ethnic representation. All too often in the West, the media is a 'white person's' world. In an overview of this kind there is insufficient space to do more than touch upon the issue of under-representation of ethnic minorities in all areas of media production, or to examine the implications this has for a multicultural society. It ought, however, to be considered by students of media a vital topic for enquiry.

Such an inquiry needs to reach back into examining traditional ways of *representing* minorities in print, broadcast and film media which have in large and distressing part been covertly (and often overtly) racist. Tuen van Dijk in *Racism and the Press*[20] writes:

> From the point of view of a 'white man's world', minorities and other Third World Peoples are generally categorised as 'them', and opposed to 'us' and, especially in western Europe, as not belonging, if not as an aberration, in white society.

According to van Dijk the media do not address the problems of minorities; rather they define minorities *as* the problem (see Figure 7.3). In the reproduction of current realities, by word and image, the tendency at least in some media, especially the tabloid press, is that ethnic minorities exist only in the sense that they seem to pose problems to the white majority. When they speak out, or take action, their message is *re*-presented stereotypically; and when such representation is objected to by advocates of anti-racism they too receive a 'bad press'.

Figure 7.3   Another example of police prejudice. This illustration from an advertisement for the Metropolitan Police effectively illustrates the point Tuen van Dijk makes on the negative stereotyping that affects public perceptions of race. The viewer of the advertisement is led to assume that a black criminal is being pursued by a uniformed policeman. In fact, the 'criminal' is a plain-clothes detective and the real criminal is out of the picture. Perceptions of police prejudice against black members of the community are turned back on the spectator. We are invited to reflect on our own prejudices.

Invisibility as an issue

Every member of such minorities, and this will include a goodly proportion of the student fraternity, many of them aspirants to careers in the media, will recognise, be sensitive to (and often deeply offended by) this situation. Van Dijk's book is a study of racism in press headlines, the choice and treatment of topics related to ethnic minorities in the 1980s. His research findings showed:

> that minorities continue to be associated with a restricted number of stereotypical topics, such as immigration problems, crime, violence (especially 'riots'), and ethnic relations (especially discrimination), whereas other topics, such as those in the realm of politics, social affairs and culture are under-reported.

Whether a member of an ethnic minority is a student, a practitioner of media or simply a media-aware citizen he or she will be alert to van Dijk's assertion, arising from an empirical study among readers that:

> the reproduction of racism by the Press, is largely effective, not so much because all readers always adopt the opinions of the Press, which they often do and sometimes do not, but because the Press manages to manufacture an ethnic consensus in which the very latitude of opinions and attitudes is quite strictly constrained.

The dominant discourse, van Dijk is saying, is ethnocentric in a very specific sense. It works through highly selective perceptions in combination with omission or absence, and this applies as much to the *absence* of substantial ethnic representation in media professions as it does to the absence of 'good news' stories relating to ethnic minorities. The ethnocentric paradigm counts ethnic minorities as largely invisible; until, that is, they catch public attention by doing something which permits them to be defined as a 'problem'.

On the face of it, the achievement of fairer, non-racist treatment of ethnic minorities will come about by substantially more representation among those who report and present events in the press and in broadcasting. This is, it has to be admitted, a simplistic view. Racism is structurally ingrained in cultural practices. Until representatives of ethnic minorities become media moguls themselves; until they are seen to be vice-chancellors of universities, directors of banks, chairpersons of advertising agencies; until, as it were, they feature prominently around about the peak of the hierarchical triangle of power and privilege, they will continue to suffer disadvantage at both the macro- and the micro-levels of society.

It is useful to recall what has been discussed in this book on the purposes, roles and performance of media. By and large, serving the dominant elite takes priority in media practice, if not in theory, over the principle of 'full and fair coverage' for all; and *of* all. In *Racism and the Press* van Dijk draws a very clear connection between the racist attitudes often expressed in Britain's right-wing press and the view of minorities held by the general public.

Referring to the particular attention paid by the press to Vietnam boat people and Tamil refugees, the author states that 'once defined as positive or negative by the Press (and dominant politicians), such groups are generally confronted with similar attitudes from the population at large'.

Though the cases of press racism examined by van Dijk might today be considered history, the response mechanisms which produced them have not changed. Any positive attempt – through argument, protest or research findings – to counter the prevailing marginalisation of ethnic minorities in dominant culture continues to receive either a cold shoulder or a fiery rebuke; and often by the so-called liberal papers as well as the right-wing tabloids. Van Dijk states:

> There is evidence that anti-racist research (especially about the Press itself) is often ignored or ridiculed by the liberal newspapers too, whereas research findings that can be seen as confirming prevalent stereotypes tend to be given more attention, as is the case for research about problematic cultural differences or deviant behaviour of some segments of minority groups.

Van Dijk's most telling conclusion, based on earlier researches as well as his own, is that the 'reproduction processes involved [in Press racism] are essentially controlled by elites' and that 'the main direction of influence is top down', for 'Racist ideologies are not innate, but learnt'. In other words, a racist press is only part of a wider problem.

Middling progress

In a more recent study, *Black and White Media: Black Images in Popular Film and Television*,[21] Karen Ross identifies good news and bad. On both sides of the Atlantic, in American and Britain:

> The success of a number of black filmmakers has meant that mainstream black and white audiences can now enjoy a greater range of black-originated work showing a greater diversity of black images than has been possible hitherto.

Yet such progress has so far failed to dislodge dominant white perspectives and practices. In her final chapter, entitled 'Twenty-first century blues', Ross is forced to concede that the picture 'is still one of strict colour-coding'. Her views echo those of van Dijk. She acknowledges that a key feature of Western media industries is their 'dominance by white people and many of the problems of black (mis)-representation are a consequence of this fundamental fact'. It is the 'poverty of black images,' writes Ross, 'rather than their frequency that constitutes the real problem'.

We can no longer examine matters such as this within the boundaries of nation states. Globalisation means the transmission of images with at least a potential 'white world' bias to every corner of the earth; and this bias may, considering the narrowing basis of media ownership, be at risk of becoming as structural a part of cultural communication as it has been in the past.

The idea of global culture brought about by mass communication might at first glance seem to promise the opportunity of equality across peoples and nations. Karen Ross reminds the reader that 'the major problem with globalisation is its imperialist tendencies and its potential to displace indigenous cultures in favour of poor imitations of the West'.

engaging the otherness of Other... can we ever escape our provincial islands and navigate between two worlds?

Paul B. Armstrong, 'Play and Cultural Differences' in *Kenyon Review* No. 13 (1991) and cited in *Representing Others: White Views of Indigenous Peoples* (UK: University of Exeter Press, 1992), edited by Mick Gidley.

4. Look up references on Law and the Journalist: what legal constraints limit a journalist's access to and use of information? Compare the situation in different countries.

5. Prepare a treatment/synopsis for a radio or TV programme to be entitled 'Gender and the media'. Focus on issues such as pressures to conform to stereotypes, with particular reference to differences between images (what happens in the story on screen) and realities (what really happens). For example, is advertising progressive or regressive with regard to gender portrayal?

6. Carry out a survey of the representation on TV – of actors, news presenters, talk-show hosts/hostesses drawn from ethnic minorities and examine the nature of that representation.

7. Study an issue of a newspaper or a TV news edition with a view to locating the source of the information used. How often is source acknowledged? Are some sources apparently given more credence than others? How often are ordinary members of the public used as source and how is their information handled?

NOW READ ON

For a perspective on 'how things used to be' for editors and journalists who pushed the cause of alternative media in the face of traditional values, see Tony Palmer's *The Trials of Oz* (UK: Blond and Briggs, 1971), a sharp reminder that the Swinging Sixties were also an age of repressive censorship. For substantial research material on the profession of journalism and the contexts of journalistic activity in Britain, see Jeremy Tunstall's *Journalists at Work* (UK: Constable, 1971 and subsequent editions) and his *Newspaper Power: The National Press in Britain* (US: Oxford University Press, 1996).

Philip Knightley's *The First Casualty – From the Crimea to Vietnam: The War Correspondent as Hero, Propagandist and Myth Maker* (UK: Quartet Books, 1978) is one of the best-known accounts of journalists involved in and reporting war and perhaps ought to be read alongside Martha Gellhorn's powerful *The Face of War* (UK; Virago, 1986).

For work on the ethics of journalism, see *The Politics of World Communication: A Human Rights Point of View* by Cees J. Hamelink (UK: Sage, 1994).

More and more women are playing prominent roles in news gathering and presentation. Try *Women in Mass Communication* edited by Pamela J. Creedon (US: Sage, 1993), *Battling for News: The Rise of the Woman Reporter* by Anne Sebba (UK: Sceptre, 1995) and *Women Transforming Communications: Global Perspectives* edited by Donna Allen, Ramona R. Rush and Susan J. Kaufman (US/UK: Sage, 1996).

8 In the Wake of Magellan: Research as Exploration

AIMS

- To make the case that research is a key feature in the study and understanding of the media.
- To examine approaches to academic research and summarise the work of important contributors to the field.
- To give a brief overview of the aims and strategies of the media industry's own market research.

Most of the activities students of media will be involved in will include research. Research is the prelude to traditional essays and reports, but it is equally vital in the preparation of media artefacts such as radio and TV programmes, marketing assignments, the creation of advertisements or the production of newspapers and magazines.

Research is exploration. It gives practice in skills such as the design of questionnaires and interviewing techniques. It nurtures persistence, risk-taking, problem-solving and it has relevance for the future – the key to successful journalism is good research; knowing where to look and how to look.

This chapter discusses a variety of research approaches – content analysis, ethnography and investigation through focus groups and introduces some of the work of the best media researchers in the field. Their findings are landmarks in the development of our knowledge about media production and audience reception. They are stepping-stones in the evolution of a discipline.

All forms of mass communication, from advertising to broadcasting, from periodical or newspaper publication to the movies, rely on research findings either to continue the way they are or to change to cater for new expectations and tastes. In America, a blip in the ratings for a TV show can spell the end of its run. Market research, then, is big business because it is so crucial and a number of major 'commercial' research enterprises is discussed here.

Engaging the truth: research perspectives

In the early 1980s a small advertisement appeared in the Dutch women's magazine, *Viva*:

> I like watching the TV serial *Dallas* but often get odd reactions to it. Would anyone like to write and tell me you like watching it too, or dislike it? I should like to assimilate these reactions in my university thesis. Please write to…

The researcher, Ien Ang, chose a novel approach to finding out by eliciting women's written comments on one of their favourite programmes. From the 42 letters she received, Ang produced an analysis in book form, *Watching 'Dallas': Soap Opera and the Melodramatic Imagination*.[1] Though she worked only on the comments provided by her correspondents, knew nothing of their background and did not at any time follow up the comments by interviewing the writers, she nevertheless produced a notable piece of qualitative research.

Another researcher, working on the same material – a man, for instance – might well have placed differing emphases upon the material, drawn differing inferences; even come up with differing conclusions. Thus in scrutinising the research process we have to address the problem of objectivity. We can do this fairly swiftly by declaring that while fairness to source is imperative, objectivity could well be classified a luxury reserved only for the gods.

What Ang does in *Watching 'Dallas'*, and what all constructors of meaning must do, is 'engage' with the truth rather than promise its definition: mediation is unavoidable. Research is about information-gathering just as a journalist gathers information for a story. It involves selection and emphasis. It involves the previous experience, knowledge, interests and values of the researcher, however open-minded he or she plans to be.

The collation of data is a process of deconstruction – examining the parts – and reconstruction; and this involves turning one set, or many sets of clues into a specialist form, usually sentences in print. Putting anything observed, spoken about or experienced into words transforms it. Raw data has to be studied, collated, compared, analysed, synthesised and finally interpreted. That is what is so fascinating about doing it.

The rewards of research

Research can be enormously fulfilling. It can also be profitable in a number of ways. Research may obtain a researcher a PhD; it may lead to a job or a further research commission and in some academic institutions people's competence is judged according to the quantity and quality of their research. Little, or nothing, then is selfless. Where research is of direct interest to the making of profits, in industry, commerce and medicine, for example, or where research helps define audience needs, tastes and habits in the consumption of media products, it is in demand and can often be remunerative.

We can discern two strands of research here – the commercial and the academic. The results of such research enterprise often fuse, academic research being used for commercial purposes, commercial research offering data and reference points for academic directions and preoccupations. Ultimately all media research is about *content* – its nature, assembly, presentation and purpose; and *response* – the way audiences react to, deal with, and are affected by that content.

In the wider field of communication research, studies seek to explore patterns of behaviour, of speech and attitude, of customs and practices within cultural contexts. As students of communication, our interests will range, say, from the experience of the handshake in interpersonal greeting to the experiencing of, or role played by, television soap operas in family households. We may adopt the role of textual analyst, of observer or actual participator in the activities under observation. We may never actually meet the people we are investigating or we might spend our days and nights with them.

The commercial researcher would wish to know how people 'use' a TV soap opera for instrumental reasons: is it gaining or losing popularity; what features of the programme serve to command and sustain audience attention; and what does such a programme 'do' for people which can be replicated in future programming?

The academic approach differs in that there is less pressure to come up with answers, particularly the sort of hard-and-fast answers which those who employ researchers wish them to come up with. The academic researcher primarily wishes to arrive at a state of understanding and to communicate that understanding to others.

The rewards for this may be publication, the respect of the researcher's peers, even fame, not to mention being studied by generations of students of communication and media; but the most significant goal is discovery: the academic researcher is a modest emulator of Magellan with an *alter ego* of Galileo or Newton. Each of these did more than discover; they affected their world by their discoveries and influenced the course of history.

Research as an agent of change

The fruits of research also have the power to influence and in some cases, to change. For example, research into gender definitions and the treatment of gender may work towards attitudinal change with regard to the portrayal of women in media.

Feminist research not only wishes to uncover evidence about the continuing male-dominatedness – the patriarchy – of contemporary society, it also aims to use that evidence to bring about attitudinal and behavioural changes. In a 1987 *Journal of Communication* article, 'The potential contribution of feminist scholarship in the field of communication',[2] Brenda Dervin argues that research is enabling and *empowering*, that it gives women a voice in a world that generally renders them voiceless. Such research, says Dervin, 'is transformative in that it is concerned with helping the silent speak and is involved in consciousness raising'.

Research can be militant, subversive and, of course, it can be used against those whom it is intended to benefit, through selective use of the evidence offered, or simplifications (or distortions) of complicated findings – offences most often committed by the media when they, in their turn, mediate between the researcher's detailed findings and the media's audience.

What is considered newsworthy in a researcher's text is highlighted, amplified and the highlights replicated. Those original dependent clauses, the crucial academic cautions about not reading too much into limited results, tend to be marginalised or omitted altogether as eye-catching headlines and 'in-a-nutshell' summaries distort as they diffuse.

If researchers have to recognise that they can exert little or no control over the ways their research findings are used, once these enter the public sphere, they need also to remind themselves not to lose sight of their own interpretative role in drawing up and presenting research findings.

The saying that there are 'lies, damned lies and statistics' suggests that even if the researcher relies entirely upon questionnaire data, total objectivity remains a dream – for who wrote the questions in the first place, and who will compose the sentences which summarise and generalise the findings?

Approaches to research 1: content analysis

In 1982 Angela McRobbie published an intriguing content analysis of the British teenage magazine, *Jackie*. In an article ' "Jackie": an ideology of adolescent femininity', published in *Popular Culture: Past and Present*[3] the author charted the covert ideology that is intended to influence the reader of *Jackie*. She did not merely look at the content, she examined the source from which that content emerged – the publishing house of D.C. Thompson of Dundee, whose history had been characterised by 'a vigorous anti-unionism' and 'a strict code of censorship of content'.

From such a source arises material which McRobbie sees as the 'story' of *Jackie*, 'an implicit attempt to win consent to the dominant order – in terms of femininity, leisure and consumption, i.e. at all levels of culture'. Using a semiological approach to her analysis of the magazine, McRobbie identifies in *Jackie* discourses which are relentlessly encoded towards inculcating in the reader traditional attitudes and behaviour.

The view from Glasgow

Some of the most controversial – and readable – content analysis has been produced by the Glasgow University Media Group. Their chief research target has been television news in Britain; and the questions they have asked as they studied the news bulletin by bulletin, story by story has been – is the news biased, and if so, biased in favour of what or whom and against what or whom?

The GUMG concluded that broadcast news *is* biased, is *not* impartial and that bias and partiality favour those in authority against those who challenge it, in particular government and employers against workers and their unions.

Bad News,[4] the first in the Glasgow University Media Group series, challenges the traditional view that broadcasters are substantially more objective than their counterpart in the press. 'Our study,' write the eight authors, 'does not support a received view that television news is "the news that happens".' The Group's monitoring of news bulletins over a six-month period found a bias in TV against the activities of organised labour and a preoccupation with effects rather than causes.

Understandably broadcasters have reacted sceptically to the Glasgow Media Group's conclusions, accusing them of bias in their own perception of news production. Did they not realise the pressures journalists and programme makers work under? Undeterred, the GUMG produced *More Bad News* in 1980, *Really Bad News* in 1982 and *War and Peace News* on broadcast coverage of the 1982 Falklands War, the 1984 miners' strike and Northern Ireland, in 1985. The Group's conclusions reflect what McRobbie had been saying about *Jackie*. News, the authors declare in *More Bad News*, 'is not neutral and not a natural phenomenon: it is rather the manufactured production of ideology'.

Pennsylvania perspectives

On a grand scale perhaps the best-known research expedition has been that led by Professor George Gerbner from his home port at the University of Pennsylvania's Annenberg School of Communication. There are several references to Gerbner's work in this book and acknowledgement of the influence of his findings on the perceived impact of TV on audience.

The Cultural Indicators programme of research based at the Annenburg School has been tracking violence on TV for 30 years, using content analysis and extensive surveys of audience reaction. The CI has accumulated in a massive computer database observations on over 3000 programmes and some 35,000 characters coded according to many thematic, demographic and action categories.[5] We return to discuss the Annenberg findings in Chapter 10.

Gerbner and his team constitute a good example of how researchers not only add to our knowledge, they also extend our vocabulary by encapsulating hypotheses in new terminology. Once enshrined in language, once put to use and re-use, the hypotheses take on the substance of truth – until, that is, they are challenged by new research enshrining new terminology.

It was Gerbner and colleagues who introduced the notion of *Mainstreaming* in which a perceived effect of heavy TV viewing is the *convergence* of political attitudes into a centre position between Right and Left but ultimately with a skew towards the Right. Cultivation theory, with which Gerbner is chiefly associated, sees TV's images as cultivating and nurturing in the audience 'our culture's beliefs, ideologies and world views'.[6]

The size of this effect, cultivation research indicates, is less critical 'than the direction of its steady contribution'. Subsequent research has challenged Gerbner's extrapolations, arguing, basically, that people are actually less influenceable than the Annenberg findings seem to indicate.

PRESSED INTO BATTLE

When night fell the family gathered around the camp fire, and when the early part of the evening passed without incident, the young adults drifted beyond the limits of the fire. The older Boyash [gypsies] continued to trade stories over the remaining wine and coffee. Then, just as they were dispersing, a small hail of stones landed around the main courtyard of the camp.

Within seconds the family was readying itself for bloody battle. Most of those who had lingered around the fire were women and, incensed at the resumption of hostilities, they ran from wagon to wagon summoning the men and gathering all available weapons. I had retired to my *roulette* [wagon] and was about to undress for bed when Persa burst into the wagon.

She shouted that the Serbians were throwing stones again; we were going out to stop them. I would have hesitated, flattered that the family felt so comfortable with me that they would ask me to fight on their behalf. I was also worried about getting hurt.

But Persa had no sympathy for the distinction between participant and observer. She thrust a heavy stick in my hand and shoved me towards the door.

William Kornblum, Introduction to *In the Field: Readings on the Field Research Experience*[7]

Approaches to research 2: ethnography

The experience of William Kornblum, quoted above, arose out of perhaps the most challenging and certainly the most fascinating approach to research – what has been termed *participant observation*, a method of information-gathering which is usually associated with *ethnography*, the study of people interacting within domestic and communal contexts.

It exemplifies the mode of research referred to as *qualitative* as contrasted with *quantatitive* research typified by the Cultural Indicators project; and public opinion research generally. The differences are not actually of 'quality', for quantative research, dealing with hundreds or even thousands of respondents, rather than a handful, is obviously as anxious to come up with reliable, objective data as those researchers working in the ethnographic mode.

The differences are that quantative research is generally less personal;

researcher-respondent encounters take place in the questionnaire rather than face to face. Qualitative research is in-depth enquiry, its tools observation and interview; and it is a costly and often immensely time-consuming exercise. This is not to say that quantative data is necessarily cheaper to assemble or that it takes less time, though computer-reading of questionnaire responses has speeded things up.

The ethnographic researcher is concerned with more subjective understandings, involved with perceptions and interpretations. The focus is on interactions, 'namely,' as Liesbet van Zoonen puts it in *Feminist Media Studies*,[8] 'the implicit and explicit rules people employ to make sense of their everyday surroundings and experiences'.

Studying the ways – the 'lifestyle' – of the Boyash, William Kornblum lived with them to the point where they counted him one of them, which meant that they had come to trust him. That trust was the doorway into their true lives and, as the passage quoted here indicates, brought with it responsibilities and risks. Kornblum's experience was a far cry from the ivory towers where research is usually pieced together.

The hazards do not stop at the occasional hail of stones. To participate is to risk becoming partisan; to be, as it were, 'taken over', drawn away from being the objective and critical observer. New friendships may get in the way of the researcher's critical faculties. Yet the benefits – the unique insights, the richness of data arising from working within the field rather than witnessing it from the outside – can be enormous.

In the Introduction to *In the Field* Kornblum admits that there are experiences other than the adventurous:

> Usually the most trying aspect of this kind of research is the effort to obtain permission to spend time with the people one wishes to get to know. Once this is accomplished (and it is never entirely achieved), the work of observation and description can become, on the surface, quite routine and even boring...one's very presence can become a drag. From the standpoint of those being observed, the observer is ignorant of the most obvious truths and constantly exposes that ignorance by questioning behaviour that everyone else takes for granted.

A further point which Kornblum makes and which students of communication preparing research projects will readily identify with, concerns reciprocation, that is, having something to offer in exchange for the information required:

> In short, our respondents often find us tiresome unless we have something to offer them other than just our goodwill. Thus, it occurred to Persa that my size would be an asset to the gypsies, so she pushed me to the front line.

In the Preface to the same book, Kornblum and his co-editor Carolyn Smith describe how the experience of qualitative field research can have a 'profound effect on the researcher, who often must re-examine his or her values and attitudes and may be forced to make choices that would not be required in the ordinary course of events'.

Responding to Rocky

This aspect of participant observation is well illustrated by the field research experience of Valerie Walkerdine. In 'Video replay: families, films and fantasy', a 1986 account of her work published in *Formations of Fantasy*,[9] Walkerdine records an image of herself as observer and intruder:

> I am seated in the living room of a council house in the centre of a large English city. I am here to make an audio-recording as part of a study of six year old girls and their education. While I am here, the family watches a film, *Rocky II*, on the video. I sit, in my armchair, watching them watching television. How to make sense of this situation?

The family, called 'Coles' by Walkerdine, see the researcher's role as one of surveillance. 'Joanne,' Mr Coles announced to his daughter when Valerie Walkerdine arrived, 'here's your psychiatrist!'

The nature of this intrusion caused in Walkerdine strong feelings of dissonance and in her report she wonders whether 'this activity of research' is not a 'perverse voyeurism'. Here was a sophisticated academic subjecting a working-class family to a scrutiny which ran the risk of being judgmental. Walkerdine confesses reacting with a degree of abhorrence to the relish with which Mr Coles cheered Rocky's last-round victory, bloody and brutal.

She felt worse as he replayed the video again and again, dwelling on every detail of Rocky's triumph. She found such pleasure shameful and disgusting. However, back at the university Walkerdine replayed *Rocky II* in order to find reasons why Mr Coles might have derived the satisfaction he did from the movie. She began to look at things in a different light:

> I recognised something that took me far beyond the pseudo-sophistication of condemning its macho sexism... The film brought me up against such memories of pain and struggle and class that it made me cry... No longer did I stand outside the pleasures of engagement with the film. I too wanted Rocky to win. Indeed I was Rocky – struggling, fighting, crying to get out... Rocky's struggle to become bourgeoise is what reminded me of the pain of my own.

Like Rocky, Mr Coles was fighting 'against the system and for his children' and that struggle reminded Walkerdine of her own – academic – struggles as a working-class child to use education 'to get out'. The difference is that one struggle is seen in physical terms, the other intellectual, but all at once, the subject of the research and the researcher find themselves in the same 'ring'.

In *Interpreting Audiences: The Ethnography of Media Consumption*[10] Shaun Moores commends Valerie Walkerdine's 'conversion' as good ethnography:

> She makes a genuine effort to see things 'from the point of view' of her subjects, paying careful attention to the interdiscursive ties that bind Mr Coles into the film fantasy. Crucial to her reconsideration of the Coles' viewing pleasures is the detour she takes into autobiography.

Another significant difference between quantative and qualitative research is illustrated here. By its nature, quantative research must be specific and targeted. The key to good questionnaire design is precision: any question, or any answer, ambiguously phrased, poses problems for the analysis of data. In ethnographic research this ambiguity is an opportunity – for further enquiry; for making imaginative connections between comments and situations which, on the face of it, have no relevance to the researcher's aims.

While recognising the value of the approach of Valerie Walkerdine, and a number of other notable field researchers, and commending it as a 'striking alternative to the traditionally neutral and "objective" stance of social scentists', Shaun Moores suggests that identification with the subjects of research must not be pushed to the point where the critical faculties of the researcher are suspended. Some measure of distance between observer and observed needs to be preserved:

> Over the coming years, I believe that the continuing task for reception ethnographers will be to examine sympathetically the 'meaning systems' of others – whilst retaining a crucial space for ideological evaluation and critique.

RESEARCHING IS ALSO ABOUT WASHING UP THE POTS

Over a three-year period James Lull and his team of researchers studied the viewing habits of over 200 households in California and Wisconsin.

The researchers visited homes on a number of occasions and, in true ethnographic tradition, 'ate with the families, performed chores with them, played with the children and took part in group entertainment, particularly television watching'.[11] Such participant observation was essential, Lull believed, to reduce the danger of responses being influenced by the fact of watching: after a relatively short time 'the presence of the investigator in the habitat of his subjects...need not severely disrupt the natural behaviour of the family unit'.

Crucial contacts

Ethnographic research need not, of course, be participant. Indeed, there are many strategies of information-gathering aimed at finding out how people 'make sense of their everyday surroundings and experiences', though the most important of these is traditionally the interview in one form or another. The best research employs a number of information-gathering tools – observation, questionnaires, in-depth interviews, group discussions, role-play and the examination of documents, from letters to family photo albums, all seen as offering clues to the pursuit of greater understanding; and sometimes revelation.

The American researcher Janice Radway took a fascinating journey into the realm of women's reading of romance novels. She wished to find out the role such reading played in the lives of women, to what extent the romances provided antidotes to the 'real' world of marriage and families. In *Reading the Romance: Women, Patriarchy and Popular Literature*,[12] Radway used in her research structured questionnaires, open-ended group discussion and in-depth, extended, interviews.

In addition she focused on a *contact*, whom she called Dot, the woman behind the bookshop counter. Dot was able to cast the light of long-term experience on the choices women made of the books they read, and their reactions to them. The more participant is research, the more it needs a 'Dot', an insider-contact. Where the researcher wishes to gain entry into cultural communities access may rely upon this kind of sponsor, someone known in the community, trusted and whose 'friendship' can be the passport to acceptance.

Equally desirable is the chance to create *networks* of friendship, a key strategy for Edmundo Morales when he was researching peasant dependency on cocaine production in Peru.[13] In talking to villagers Morales would attempt a novel approach to establishing such networks. He would tell the women he was interviewing that he was in search of a girl to marry:

> This approach worked much better than just knocking on doors with a long questionnaire in hand and saying 'Hi, I am doing research on peasant economy and would like you to answer some questions'.

Morales says that while his intention 'was always to produce networks of friendship' he 'never went anywhere without actually knowing the setting and the host families'. Morales saw patience and good humour as essential characteristics of the successful ethnographer.

Public and popular

Research during the 1980s and 90s generally targeted two areas of media consumption. First, what John Corner has classified as *public knowledge*.[14] This involves news and other programmes such as documentaries, dealing with information as a public commodity and thus concerning itself with such issues as persuasion, the manipulation of information, audience comprehension and retention of messages. The other research area concerns *popular culture*.

An example of research work spanning both areas is that of Justin Lewis. In 1985 he interviewed 50 members of an audience for an ITN *News at Ten* bulletin. His findings were summarised in 'Decoding television news' in a book edited by Phillip Drummond and Richard Paterson, *Television in Transition: Papers from the First International Studies Conference*.[15] Lewis found a surprisingly large gap between the news stories as they were presented and the way audience members re-told those stories.

Having scrutinised, through empirical study, the responses to public discourse of a cross-section of people living in or near Sheffield, Lewis turned to the 'popular brief'. He conducted a study in the United States of responses to the *Cosby Show*. Much of Lewis's *The Ideological Octopus: An Exploration of Television and its Audience*,[16] draws upon the insights provided by these research probes. His findings confirm the unpredictability of people and the problem research faces in understanding the workings of the human mind: for example, the apparent ease with which a person can hold contradictory visions and opinions without suffering cognitive dissonance.

True, we recognise that what might be normal in the TV world 'is [Lewis observes] rather different from the normality of the world beyond it: but since we spend so much time watching TV, we are liable to lose our grip on distinctions between the two'. Lewis believes it would help if we as analysts dispensed with 'the notion that human consciousness is a rational and coherent place for thoughts to dwell'.

This is not to say that TV has less power to cultivate responses; quite the contrary, in Lewis' view. He writes of his study of the news and of *The Cosby Show* (whose dominant characteristic seems to have been its ambiguity):

> Both studies dispel two related notions. The first is the idea that television's ideological power rests upon the ability of its authors to infuse programmes with preferred meanings. The second is the notion that ambiguity reduces a programmes's ideological power, passing control, instead, to the audience.

The author believes that 'To comprehend the power of television...we must appreciate its influence regardless of intention and in the face of polysemy'. In other words, TV news is powerful in ways often unintended by those who produce and present it, and popular programmes, in their *apparent* unambiguity, are more influential than they might seem.

BLUMER'S FIVE PRINCIPLES OF RESEARCH

1. Audience studies should be carried out in the direct empirical context of media use.

2. Reception should be understood against the background of individual and collective life histories which render current events and meanings intelligible.

3. Uses and effects should be seen in relationship to other influences, not as isolated phenomena.

4. The process of interpretation of meaning by audience precedes and modifies media effect.

5. Media use should be related to the use of other communication technologies.

Herbert Blumer, *Symbolic Interactionism. Perspective and Method* (US: Prentice Hall, 1969)

'Empirical' refers to knowledge obtained through experience and Blumer is recommending that it is preferable to scrutinise audience response in the normal situation in which respondents experience media; rather, that is, than placing respondents in laboratory situations. By 'collective histories' Blumer acknowledges the importance of shared experiences derived from the group or community to which respondents belong, and these are a product of the past as much as an indication of the present. The author stresses that attempts to separate mediated from lived experience must be avoided by the researcher.

Approaches to research 3: focus groups

In British reception research the name of David Morley is deservedly one of the most familiar and respected. No chapter on research and research methods should fail to mention Morley's seminal work published in 1980, *The 'Nationwide' Audience*.[17] The research arose (as much of the best research and most of the most challenging ideas about media have done) from the Birmingham University's Centre for Contemporary Cultural Studies (CCCS).

The media group of the CCCS set out to measure audience responses to the BBC's *Nationwide* evening news-magazine programme which ran during the 1970s. The study was summarised in a 1978 monograph by Charlotte Brunsdon and Morley in *Everyday Television: 'Nationwide'*.[18] It examined the ideological connotations of the programme and its ways of addressing audience.

Stage two of the research project followed up textual analysis with a qualitative survey of readers' intepretations. Morley showed a video recording of a *Nationwide* programme to 29 groups made up of people with a range of educational and professional backgrounds; following up the screening with in-depth interviewing. *The 'Nationwide' Audience* examines how members of the survey groups decoded the messages they received, how they accepted, modified or rejected the programmes's preferred reading of events and issues.

Morley has this to say about his approach to interviewing group members:

> The initial stages of the interview were non-directive; only in subsequent stages of an interview, having attempted to establish the 'frames of reference' and 'functioning vocabulary' with which the respondents defined the situation, did I introduce questions about the programme material based on earlier analysis of it.

Non-directive questions are those which avoid giving a hint as to what answers the researcher might be expecting or wanting. They are the opposite of *leading* questions. By 'functioning vocabulary' Morley means that the terms that will be used in the research exercise will have been made clear to respondents, to ensure that everyone is, as it were, 'talking the same language'; and to help structure proceedings.

Morley's findings rejected traditional perceptions of the passivity of audiences. The indication was that audiences make up their own minds, that there is resistance to dominant discourses both between groups with common characteristics and between people within those groups. Generalising about the response of 'professional people' or trades unionists is unreliable and hazardous. Even when the dominant discourse was accepted, read according to communicator preference, members of the audiences did not come to that position without knowing why; without relating the message to personal knowledge and experience.

Shaun Moores[10] writes of Morley:

> Despite all its shortcomings... *The 'Nationwide' Audience* has justifiably come to be regarded as a landmark in the development of critical media theory and research...[and] an important turning point at which attention began to be switched from the narrow examination of textual forms towards an empirical examination of audience engagement with texts.

Morley draws the conclusion from his findings that the TV message is:

> a complex sign, in which a preferred meaning has been inscribed, but which retains the potential, if decoded in a manner different from the way it has been encoded, of communicating a different meaning.

In later work Morley unpicked some of the oversimplifications which characterise *The 'Nationwide' Audience*. For example in *Family Television* published in 1986,[19] he writes:

> There is a tendency in the *Nationwide* book to think of deep structures (for instance, class positions) as generating direct effects at the level of cultural practice. This is a tendency I would want to qualify now, to examine in detail the different ways in which a given 'deep structure' works itself out in particular contexts, and reinstate the notion of persons actively engaged in cultural practice.

Morley also says in *Family Television*, affirming Herbert Blumer's First Principle of Research, that the decision to interview groups outside their cultural or domestic contexts was something he would have changed: the response of audience to media messages should be conducted where audience normally receives those messages, usually in the home with their family or friends around them. Later research has taken this lesson to heart.

Now researchers observe response in context. They look at the geography and politics of reception – who sits where, in what relation to each other and to the TV set, and who (usually the man) is master of the remote control. Of course with the reduction in price of TV sets and the availability of portables, viewing has in recent years become less of a family-together activity; a trend which somewhat complicates the researcher's task.

The gun on the table

In Chapter 3, reference was made to research conducted by Greg Philo based on audience reaction to the coverage of the miners' strike in Britain between November 1984 and February 1985. A member of the Glasgow University Media Group, Philo used photographs of the strike as a stimulus, asking small groups of respondents to write up news stories from what they had seen. In particular there was a photograph of a shotgun lying on a table.

This proved an arresting focus, eliciting from groups attitudes which, in the main, put the miners in a bad light (one in tune with, and obviously influenced by, media coverage of the strike). Philo, in *Seeing & Believing: The Influence of Television*,[20] writes:

> The actual news story which it [the gun] was taken from concerned a miner, who was breaking the strike. He stated on the news that he was prepared to use the gun to defend himself. But it was apparent that in the imaginary news stories that were written, the gun was persistently being put into the hands of *striking* miners.

Philo's research findings challenge the position that Morley and other researchers take up concerning the capacity of audiences to assert their own against the preferred reading of the communicators. Philo's own students in a pilot study to the actual research project, which began a year after the strike was over, opted for the dominant response concerning the gun on the table. Even students of media, ever wary of preferred readings, nevertheless seemed all too ready to associate strikers and violence.

Philo worked with groups of on average nine respondents. These were drawn from four areas of experience, groups with a special knowledge or experience of the strike, such as senior police officers and miners' and women's support group members from Yorkshire; occupational groups – solicitors' offices in London and Glasgow and electronics employees in Harlow; special interest groups – mothers' and toddlers' groups in Glasgow, London and Kent; and residential groups – from southwest England, Bromley and Beckenham in Kent and Shenfield in Essex.

The groups were first asked to write a typical BBC news bulletin based upon 12 pictures of the strike, including the gun on the table; and then they were asked a series of questions, such as (Question 1): 'When you first saw the picture of the gun, who did you think it belonged to?' Question 2 raised the matter of audience perception of the objectivity of BBC News: 'Does the BBC news have a point of view? Does it, for example, favour one political party over another, or is it neutral? Is it biased, unbiased, pro-establishment, anti-establishment, accurate, impartial? How would you describe it?'

As with most research, especially of the imaginatively and innovatively designed sort, this project came up with a number of unexpected findings, not the least the quality of the news reports which groups produced and the clarity of recall of the incidents of the strike.

Philo's conclusions give weight to the case that television has powerful effects; for example, its power to instil in viewers patterns of association:

> There was remarkable unanimity of belief amongst the groups in this sample about what had actually been shown. In the general sample, 98 per cent believed that most picketing which they had seen on television news was violent... most remark-

able is the number of people who believed that these television images represented the everyday life of picketing.

The source for these beliefs says Philo 'was overwhelmingly given as television and the press, with the emphasis on TV, because of its immediate and more dramatic quality'.

The degree of acceptance of the television image, the degree to which associations, between shotguns and striking miners, between picket lines and violence nevertheless 'depends very much on what beliefs, experience, and information' the audience 'bring to what they are shown'. Equally important was whether, as Philo puts it, people have a 'critique of television latent in their beliefs'.

It is a revealing point, for in some cases it was only when respondents were pressed on an issue that the latent critique emerged. Without being pressed, respondents were in danger of taking images at their face value; a case of a message 'being absorbed in spite of other beliefs which were held'. Philo contends, following a stronger line over effects than David Morley, that 'where no critical view of television exists, the likelihood of accepting its account may be very great'.

Measuring response to TV's portrayal of incest

Another member of the Glasgow University Media Group, Lesley Henderson, was given the task by Channel 4 Television of gauging audience response to the portrayal of incest on the British soap opera, *Brookside*. For a brief summary of her findings, see Chapter 6. Here it is necessary only to commend to readers her research methodology, reported in *Incest in Brookside: Audience Responses to the Jordache Story*.[21]

Twelve discussion groups made up of 69 participants aged between 13 and 66 were selected from people living in the west of Scotland. The groups were pre-existing, that is the 'participants knew each other prior to the research sessions'. Henderson writes:

> This facilitated a relaxed session which was crucial given the sensitivity of the topic. It also allowed for the preservation of some of the elements of the social culture within which people discuss television, that is, with their work colleagues and friends.

Three of the groups were formed according to 'special interest' – social workers, representatives from women's organisations and teenage sexual abuse survivors. The remaining nine groups were drawn from the 'general population':

> Each session included approximately eight people, although the size of the groups ranged between three and ten. Sessions were moderated by the author and took place in schools, youth club centres, work places and participants' homes. The sessions lasted up to two hours and were all tape-recorded and then transcribed and analysed.

Each session of enquiry began with a general questionnaire about TV viewing habits, with the key question, 'Should child sexual abuse be portrayed in fictional television?'

> The group then divided into two or more subgroups and was invited to engage in a script-writing exercise. This involved giving them a set of still photographs taken from a key scene in *Brookside*'s storyline and [inviting them] to write matching dialogue. The group returned to discuss these scripts, the handling of specific characters and to debate the inclusion of such an issue in TV drama.

Students might wish to try a similar research exercise on specific issues such as screen violence, sound-bite reporting, aggressive TV interview techniques or shock-tactic advertisements.

Difference in audience decodings

Focus groups were used to particularly interesting effect by Tamar Liebes and Elihu Katz who summarise their findings in *The Export of Meaning: Cross-cultural Readings of Dallas*.[22] Their remit was to survey differences in reading *Dallas* between cultural sub-groups in Israel and also viewer groups in the United States and Japan (where *Dallas* had met with unexpected failure with audiences).

Forty groups of three married couples, of similar age, education and ethnicity were selected from Israel Arabs, newly arrived Russian Jews, veteran Moroccan settlers and members of kibbutzim. These were matched by ten groups of second-generation Americans in the Los Angeles area.

Later, eleven Japanese groups were selected and interviewed. The authors' findings give strength to the theory that an audience's cultural experience and expectations deeply influence the way texts are read and interpreted. The divergences of reading, of critical focus on varying aspects of the soap – of 'variations in decodings, involvements, uses and effects' – seemed to indicate that media texts are seen through the prism of cultural context. Their meanings are the result of negotiation arising from interactive responses. In unison with Greg Philo, Liebes and Katz speak of the 'fruitfulness of asking viewers to be critics'.

The recognition of pleasure

Throughout the 1980s and 90s the importance of the relationship between fictions and audiences has been fully recognised by researchers. Do soaps, for example, reach those parts, like Heineken lager, not reached by other message-carriers? Considering also that soaps are watched more substantially by women than men, how do women react; how are they affected; do such programmes empower or do they ensnare by stereotyping?

As we have seen, at the core of the study of media is the process of *representation* and the ways in which the media represent the world provide fertile grounds for investigation. Programmes which at one time were classified as 'mere entertainment' are now given serious research attention. How, researchers in the

1980s and 90s have asked, is social class represented in popular TV fare such as soaps; to what extent are feminist issues addressed?

Richard Dyer in the Introduction to a monograph, *Coronation Street*,[23] sees in soaps both class and gender given a prominence 'conspicuous for their rarity on British television'. An early but long-defunct rival to the queen of all British soaps, *Coronation Street* was *Crossroads*. A doctoral thesis by Dorothy Hobson was published in 1982 under the title *'Crossroads': The Drama of a Soap Opera*.[24] Hobson highlighted the situation in which a series was immensely popular, particularly among female viewers, yet derided by critics in the popular press. She found *Crossroads* to be a 'progressive' text, raising – as do most other soaps – problems and issues seen by women to be part of their everyday lives.

No soap has received more attention from media critics and researchers than *Dallas*, dealing as it does with a panorama of representations – class, strong female characters, big business, family life (most of it made up of feuding) and 'American-ness'. Mention of *Dallas* brings us back to Ien Ang's little advertisement in a Dutch magazine. Like Dorothy Hobson, Ang reads women's responses to the soap as a potential source of liberation – 'from the chafing bonds' of the pressures of everyday life. She found from analysing the written replies to her ad a phenomenon which had rarely been given due recognition in research writings – the role of *pleasure*.

That this was deemed almost a discovery might seem surprising. Yet until this time soaps had largely been dismissed *because* they appeared to aspire to nothing beyond entertainment. In *Watching 'Dallas'*[1] Ang identifies two contrasting ideological standpoints. The *ideology of mass culture* perceives that which is popular as being somehow harmful; brain-rotting perhaps; standards-sagging maybe.

In contrast, the *ideology of populism* recognises the importance of pleasure and that it is a personal thing. It can be a stimulus to self-and-other awareness. It is perceived by those who experience it as something to be relished because it has been earned. What researchers need to clarify is what degree of *reprocessing* of popular messages goes on in the minds of audience.

Researching audience use of media technology

Considerable interest has been shown by researchers in the use, within the home, of media technology. This interest accelerated with the introduction of the video recorder. All at once we as audience were no longer dependent upon the schedules of the TV companies: we could even ignore these altogether and play recordings; and if we possessed a video camera we could entertain ourselves with our own creations.

Not only can we schedule our own viewing through the VCR's recording facility, we also have a measure of control over time itself: we can fast-forward (skip the 'boring' bits or the adverts) and we can better negotiate viewing habits with those around us: you watch your programme while I record mine on another channel.

British researcher Ann Gray conducted in-depth conversations with 30 Yorkshire women about their use of the VCR during the mid-1980s and her findings were published in *Video Playtime*.[25] Like David Morley, Gray is interested in issues such as gender, the division of labour in the home, the role of leisure and the power relations exercised in family units; her theme – technology as being *socially situated*.

As so often occurs with interviews, Gray found her subjects talking about more than their use of VCRs. Initially she wondered whether chit-chat which had nothing to do with video use had anything to contribute to her research. In fact she realised, on listening to the recorded tapes of her interviews, that the prevalent 'storytelling' which characterised the women's responses to and divergences from her questions proved to be a means in which those questions were reinterpreted in a meaningful sense for the subjects themselves.

Ann Gray borrowed a colour-coding device employed by Cynthia Cockburn in research for her book *Machinery of Dominance: Women, Men and Technical Know-How*.[26] Gray ascribed the colour blue to items of technology, from kitchen to tool shed, perceived to be 'masculine', and pink to items thought to be 'feminine'. This approach, she writes:

> produces almost uniformly pink irons and blue electric drills, with many interesting mixtures along the spectrum... my research has shown that we must break down the VCR into its different modes in our colour-coding. The 'record' 'rewind' and 'play' modes are usually lilac, but the timer switch is nearly always blue, with the women having to depend on their male partners or their children to set the timer for them.

Gray found in many of her respondents a sense of inadequacy concerning their use of equipment and this was linked to self-deprecation, of respondents running themselves down. She quotes Edna as saying, 'Oh no, I haven't a clue, no. If there's anything I want recording I ask one of the boys to do it for me. This is sheer laziness, I must admit, because I don't read the instructions'.

The sense of inadequacy Gray found among her sample of respondents links with one of Dorothy Hobson's findings with regard to women watching *Crossroads*: they seemed to feel they had to apologise for the pleasure they gained from watching the soap. This is not to say that Ann Gray found her respondents naïve as well as apologetic. Rather she identified a strategy among her respondents which she called 'calculated ignorance'.

Edna, asked about working the VCR timer in future, says:

> I'm not going to try, no. Once I learnt how to put a plug on, now there's nobody else puts a plug on in this house but me... so [*laughs*] there's method in my madness, Oh yes.

Ignorance, then, is a defence strategy against exploitation. What Edna seems to be doing is resisting having 'blue' objects turned into 'pink' ones. It would appear that the colour to aim for in the use of the VCR, is lilac: that is, equality.

The HICT Project

The 1990s have seen increased research interest in the notion of 'technology-as-text' or as British researcher Roger Silverstone puts it, 'There is meaning in the texts of both hardware and software'.[27] Silverstone, along with several other well-known contributors to the field – David Morley, Sonia Livingstone, Andrea Dahlberg and Eric Hirsch – has been involved in a major and ongoing enquiry into 'The Household Uses of Information and Communication Technologies'.

This investigation receives a warm commendation from Shaun Moores in *Interpreting Audiences*[10] 'because of its commitment to looking at a collection of objects in the household media environment, its efforts to elaborate an overall conceptual model for exploring the role of information and communication technologies in home life' and for its 'concern to develop a "methodological raft" for empirical research on domestic cultures'.

Such is the enormity of the data collected that the results of the enquiry have only partially been published. However, out of data collection have emerged theoretical perspectives. For example, Silverstone along with Morley and Hirsch, speaks of a 'moral economy' which operates within the culture of the family. In a chapter, 'Information and communication technologies and the moral economy of the household' in *Consuming Technologies: Media and Information in Domestic Spaces*,[28] the authors identify four constituents of the 'moral economy'.

WATCHING THE WATCHERS

In 1985 British researcher Peter Collett conducted a study in which video cameras were fitted inside the TV sets of a number of households. Families watching TV became TV-watched families. Collet and Roger Lamb, in their report 'Watching Families Watching TV' for the Independent Broadcasting Authority, 1986, say that the dominant impression suggested by their filming was not of neat rows of attentive watchers giving TV their undivided attention. Rather, the picture was of a wide range of non-viewing activities – of watchers with their backs to the TV, chattering, children being dressed, meals being eaten, arguments occurring. For broadcasters, sobering findings.

First there is the process of *appropriation*: technology, once it crosses the threshold from shop to home, becomes a belonging (even part of the family) whose use soon reflects the relationships of those who use it, not the least the power bases for use (who, for example, is or is not allowed to 'touch it'). At the same time, the next two constituents are in place: *objectification* and *incorporation*.

Objectification refers to display in the home, where and how the items of communication technology are arranged in relationship to other domestic objects (pride of place or tucked away in a corner). Incorporation involves the actual use of the technology – the patterns of use and the part the technology plays in the family's day-to-day activities.

So far what has happened is that the technology has been absorbed into an environment whose perspectives are essentially domestic, inward-gazing. The fourth constituent of use is *conversion*, where the actors in this techno-drama turn from their private world to the world beyond the household. That which is cultivated in the private domain – knowledge or experiences derived from TV for example – is 'traded in' beyond the front door as 'coin of exchange' in social interactions at the workplace, the club or pub or even in the polling booth. The authors give the example of a teenager employing his skill at computer games, developed in the home environment, as a 'ticket' of entry into peer culture.

Segmentation: the marketplace approach to consumer research

While academic researchers and commentators have been slow to acknowledge the significance of pleasure-taking in media consumption, market researchers have always had this at the forefront of their enquiries. Seeking to please is the goal; knowing how to please is half the problem: the other half is to know how to go on pleasing. In order to do this, market research must above all things seek to know its audience.

A primary strategy is segmentation, that is, dividing up the consumer population into those most likely, those potentially likely and those unlikely to consume what has been produced for them. Once segmented into groups, defined by class, age, gender or according to our purchasing power and lifestyle, we are treated as segments, encouraged to think and behave in the ways we have been defined as thinking and behaving. What we are perceived to be, we are intended to become. The more this happens, the more, arguably, Gerbner's cultivation theory has relevance.

After all, the advertising industry is the giant among the pygmies in terms of investment in audience research; and the last thing the industry does with its research findings is publish them in research journals, and leave it at that. Research is used to shape and influence. If consumerism has its way, we will come to recognise ourselves by identifying with the images the spin-doctors have created to reflect and entice us. We are Mainstreamers perhaps, governed by a need for security; Aspirers (seeking status); Succeeders (desiring control); or even Reformers (dedicated to the quality of life).[29]

In the United States, subject to the segmentation strategies of, for example, PRIZM (Potential Rating Index by Zip Market), we might find ourselves classified under 'Pools and patios' or 'Bohemian mix'. If we were being segmented according to 'Needham Harper Worldwide', a classification which in America divided over 3,000 respondents into ten lifestyle groups, men might find themselves labelled as Herman the retiring homebody or Dale the devoted family man. Women can look to be classified as Eleanor the elegant socialite or Mildred the militant mother. If you do not see yourself in the categories, you may suspect there is something wrong – with yourself; so you must try harder. There seems to be no category for Debbie or Derek, the debt-ridden students.

Segmenting by VALS

Perhaps the best-known classification of communities-as-consumers is VALS – Values and Lifestyles. Arnold Mitchell and a team of researcher colleagues, sponsored by SRI International, published in 1983 the findings of large-scale, quantatitive research in *The Nine American Lifestyles*.[30] For the researchers, lifestyle was a 'unique way of life defined by its distinctive array of values, drives, beliefs, needs, dreams, and special points of view'.

The VALS scheme links values and lifestyles to choices, tastes and patterns of consumer spending. It examines the interaction between person, context and ideology. Each works on the others and is influenceable by the others in a process subject to fluctuation and change. What is fashionable today, what boosts self-image, what impresses society and sells in the marketplace is, for tomorrow, fit only for car boot sales.

Of the nine segments of the consumerist population examined by Mitchell, the largest – 35 per cent of the whole – and consequently the one which matters most to the adworld, is that of the Belonger. The equivalent of the British categorisation of the Mainstreamer, the Belonger is generally middle class, middle aged and concerned with security. While VALS' chief aim has been to assist in the process of 'matching product to producer' it has obviously played a significant part in matching voters to policies, electorates to presidents and prime ministers.

Keeping up with the Satos

Researching differences in order to categorise is not just a commanding force in the West. The Hakuhodo Institute of Life and Living in Japan produced its own six-segment market typology of consumers:[31]

Crystal Tribe (attracted to famous brands)
My Home Tribe (family-orientated)
Leisure Life Tribe
Gourmandism Tribe (tempted by gluttony)
Ordinary People Tribe
Impulse Buyer Tribe

The Hakuhodo Institute shares with VALS, and indeed with the advertising industry wherever it operates, the belief that what is sold is not products but *self*. What is purchased is not hardware or services but *image*. Indeed in the Introduction to its research the Hakuhodo Institute speaks of 'life designer' as being a preferable term to 'consumer'.

Reference is made to 'hitonami consciousness', *hitonami* meaning 'aligning oneself with other people' which, rendered in consumerist terms, indicates a desire to 'keep up with the Satos'; in other words, social conformity. However, the Institute detected trends – similar to those manifested in the West – away from conformity towards the need to express individuality.

What research across the affluent regions of the world seems to indicate, at least tentatively, is a *convergence* of attitudes and lifetyles. In the light of such trends, Hakuhodo produced a new typology:

The Good Old Japanese
The Silent Majority
The Confident Middle Class
The Style-orientated Japanese
The Do-it-my-way Japanese
The Confident Theoreticians

The problem with market research is its selectivity. The VALS scheme identifies the Need-Driven (that is, the poorest in the community) as 11 per cent of the population of the United States in the 1980s. In global terms, however, the Need-Driven are arguably in a majority. While in the better-off countries consumerist values can find fulfilment, in the Third World all that is often permitted the Need-Driven population are images of affluence, of the Gourmandism Tribe, of lifestyles alluring yet out of reach. Information on how such people respond to the affluence of Other, what they make of such second-hand experiences, is thin on the ground; yet it ought to be an area of critical research for the future.

Convergence of research approaches

Let us briefly return to current trends in academic research. Over the years scholars have recognised that research needs to take in all aspects of production, texts and audience responses. To focus on only one feature is to risk forfeiting discoveries about the interaction between them and with forces outside the media production/media consumption process. Whether we are researching or analysing we need to recognise the *coorientational* nature of these, the 'big three' (see Figure 8.1).

Each element of the model acts in recognition of its relationship with the other elements, feeding forward and feeding back in a process of constant interaction. This was acknowledged by members of the Glasgow University Media Group, traditionally so closely associated with focusing on production and text to the exclusion of response. In 1993 the Group produced a reader edited by John Eldridge, *Getting the Message: News, Truth and Power*.[32]

Significantly, in the concluding chapter of this book, 'Whose illusion? whose reality? Some problems of theory and method in mass media research', Eldridge indicates that emphasis on media production, focusing on the communicator's

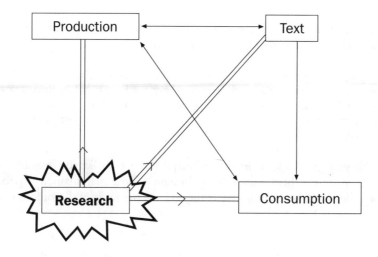

Figure 8.1   Research as coorientation

end of the process – what the Glasgow Group has been famous for – is not enough. Such research data needs to be analysed in relation to documentation concerning reception, which must be investigative, critical and educational; meaning pro-active, with a job to do.

It must be work which displays 'to viewers and readers and listeners the possibilities for highlighting perspectives, checking codes and interpreting messages' and which places an emphasis upon 'a coping strategy of resistance to mass media'. Yet again we see research as having goals beyond those of record, where discovery is an initial step towards the possibilities of change.

Somewhere in the middle of our model, shifting, turning, forming, reshaping according to dynamics influenced by culture, class, ecomomics, politics and new technology is *meaning*, or rather a space – an *agora* – in which meaning is asserted, negotiated or rejected. What the researcher is doing is attempting to go beyond common sense, to identify the ideologies which rule the dominant discourses and to measure the degree to which people absorb these, question, reject or re-form them to serve their own ends.

In particular, young researchers – readers of this book, perhaps – have much to do in terms of measuring the uneven access to TV of *minorities*, the often questionable textual representation of these minorities and the response of minorities within the audience to such representations.

Larry Gross, colleague of George Gerbner, points out in an article on sexual minorities in the mass media in *Remote Control: Television, Audiences & Cultural Power*,[33] that those elites in society who define the public agenda 'are (mostly) white, (mostly) middle aged, (mostly) male, (mostly) middle and upper class, and entirely heterosexual (at least in public)'.

The aim of empirical audience research, say Ellen Seiter and her co-editors in the Introduction to *Remote Control* should be to:

> incorporate the perspectives of people of colour, of the elderly, gays and lesbians, women and the poor – those whose voices have not been heard in media research so far, and who do not constitute the desirable demographic groups targeted by advertisers – into the study of the media in society and the development of alternative media.

In this way the work of the researcher promises to make the invisibles visible and help create for them a *constituency* in which those marginalised by labelling, stereotyping or demonisation may come to be more fairly and more understandingly represented.

RESEARCH AS AUTHENTICATION

An article in the Sunday Observer of 1 September 1996 (34) led off with the following headline:

THE NOTORIOUS WAR PHOTOGRAPH THEY SAID WAS A FAKE...

The authors of the article, Rita Grosvenor and Arnold Kemp were referring to perhaps the most famous and the most controversial war photograph in history – Robert Capa's Spain's Falling Soldier (so famous that it has proved too expensive to reproduce here).

Against a bare hillside and a featureless sky a republican soldier is hurled back by the force of the bullet which kills him. His right arm is flung outwards, his rifle slipping from his grasp. Legs buckle, neck jerks partially sideways: for him, the last moment of life, but for the photographer a supreme moment of truth.

So supreme, in fact, that critics have doubted the authenticity of Capa's picture, suggesting that the incident may have been staged for the benefit of the camera; thus casting a shadow over the reputation of one of the 20th

continued

century's foremost photographers. Capa was blown up by a mine in 1954 while covering the Vietnam War. Painstaking research may prove to extinguish the shadow from Capa's reputation.

Just as amateur archeologists have occasionally dug up pots of gold, so amateur researchers have 'excavated' vital evidence that challenges prevailing 'truths'. The story of the photograph that has come to encapsulate the poignance and tragedy of the Spanish Civil War (1936–39) has been given new clarity and resonance as a result of evidence painstakingly assembled over many years by an amateur sleuth. At the age of 14, Mario Brotons had fought in the Civil War. He was present at the same time as Capa on the Cerro Muriano front near Cordoba in September 1936.

Later in life, Brotons became haunted by Capa's picture. He felt sure he recognised the picture's terrain and the dress (not uniform) of the dying soldier – open-necked shirt and light-coloured trousers. Brotons was convinced that this soldier was a miner from Linares in Andalucia, in particular one of the 300 militiamen of the Alcoy contingent, recognisable from the cartridge belts and harnesses they wore, hand made by local leather craftsman to the garrison commander's special design.

Brotons identified the Falling Soldier as Federico Borrell Garcia, a 24-year-old millworker from the town of Alcoy (Brotons' home town), recorded dead on 5th September 1936.

Though archives in Madrid and Salamanca recorded that many militiamen had been wounded on the Cerro Muriano front that day, each registered only one death – that of Federico Borrell (maternal surname, Garcia). Questioned about the soldier in Capa's photograph, 78-year-old Maria, widow of Everisto, Federico's younger brother, confirmed that the man in Capa's picture was her dead brother-in-law: 'I knew him well'.

Sadly, Mario Brotons died in 1996 before he could publicise his discovery, though he left behind him copious documentation which was given headline treatment in the UK *Observer*,[34] As this chapter has argued, and as Brottons' painstaking investigation shows, research is exploration and detective work. It demands skill in reading the signs, both present and past. Just occasionally research resembles archeology which breaks the Code of Enigma, in Brottons' case going a long way towards authenticating a unique action in a unique moment which created a media text of timeless and universal significance.

======================= **SUMMARY** =======================

This chapter has presented an overview of landmarks in media research, detailing the differing perspectives and approaches of academic and of commercial enquiry. All research can be seen to be instrumental in purpose. Market research wishes to find out what audiences like now so that what is served up to them in future will prompt equal interest. Scholarly research has other aims, first to gain understanding, ideally to cast illumination on the path towards the unattainable – the whole truth; secondly to draw the attention of others to such illumination.

Three modes of academic research are discussed here – content analysis, participant observation or the ethnographic approach and enquiry based upon focus groups of respondents. Major contributions in these areas are described, trends of interest among researchers identified and current views on the necessity for the integration of methods noted.

The practice of segmentation of audience/consumers is considered the prime aim of commercial research, the emphasis of interest being on *large* segments, often to the neglect of other elements of the population. Critics see, in contrast, the importance of academic research in studying minorities both as part of mediated experience and in terms of their response to it.

KEY TERMS

mainstreaming ■ cultivation theory ■ insider contact
friendship networks ■ public knowledge, popular culture
ideology of mass culture/ideology of populism ■ moral economy
appropriation, objectification, incorporation, conversion ■ segmentation
VALS: values and lifestyles ■ life design
hitomani consciousness

======================= **SUGGESTED ACTIVITIES** =======================

1. Discussion
    (a) What problems are posed for the researcher by the fragmentation of audience resulting from diverse modes of media communication?
    (b) Do the advantages of audience segmentation outweigh the disadvantages?

(c) Review the strengths and drawbacks of participant observation, that is, being 'part of the activity' under investigation.

2. Research methodology is usually divided up between the *quantatitive* and the *qualitative*. Itemise the specific methods of research which fall into each category (for example, questionnaires, interviews, observation) and assess what might be the strengths and weaknesses of each one.

3. 'Young people are turned off by the coverage of politics in the media'. Design a questionnaire which probes *whether* this statement is true and discover how young people could be made more responsive to such coverage. Is it the word itself which is the turn-off, its narrow definition as describing the activities (and antics) of politicians?

   The aim of the questionnaire should be to ascertain whether, by using alternative descriptors (for example, *human rights*), a more encouraging picture of young people's attitudes might emerge.

   Ask no more than five questions, four of them closed (that is requiring an answer which can easily be turned into statistics – yes/no/don't know or a simple tick) and one open-ended question (allowing for free comment by the respondent). Remember to leave enough space on the questionnaire for this.

   Examples:

   (Closed)   Does politics bore you?

   (Open-ended)   How might the media make politics more interesting for young people?

4. You have been asked to prepare a five-minute piece for a magazine programme on local radio, your theme, *What do listeners think of the radio station's coverage of local issues?* Using a portable tape-recorder, conduct a street survey of the opinions of members of the public.

   Questioning should avoid yes/no answers and encourage the interviewees to speak their minds freely, therefore the more open-ended the questions the better.

5. You wish to gauge public response to a major issue in the news. Bring together two small groups and present each with a series of pictures illustrating the issue. Ask the groups to write a short news story: how much of the original do they remember; how much of the 'angle' of treatment, in the press or on TV, do they recall; what interpretation (of their own, or the media's) do they place on the story?

NOW READ ON

There are practically as many books on *how* to research as volumes on *what* research has been done. Readers wishing to take advice on research methodology are recommended the following:

A Manual for Writers of Research Papers, Theses and Dissertations by Kate T. Turabian (UK: Heinemann, 1982); *Speaking Ethnography* by Michael H. Agar (US: Sage, 1986); *Cultivation Analysis* edited by Nancy Signorielli and Michael Morgan (US: Sage, 1990) and *Measuring Media Audiences* edited by Raymond Kent (UK: Routledge, 1994).

Two volumes published by Sage in 1996 will reward careful attention – David L. Altheide's *Qualitative Media Analysis* (US) and *Qualitative Researching* (UK) by Jennifer Mason.

9 Ownership and Control: Ongoing Issues

AIMS

- To examine the notion that in a media-saturated world, information has increasingly been transformed into a commodity subject to market forces.
- To identify the factors threatening public service communication in the New Information Age.
- To consider the nature and extent of corporate influence in media communication worldwide.
- To draw attention to global imbalances both in the supply of information and its flow.

What makes the study of media communication such a contemporary activity is its concern for issues which affect our everyday lives as individuals within communities, as members of groups, as consumers, voters and citizens. Issues rise and fall in importance and new trends in media create new issues. Central to this chapter is the issue, touched upon frequently in the book so far, of ownership and control and the power this has over communication in the public domain. Here this issue is viewed in more depth and the implications for society at home and abroad of current modes of media control – of the management of information systems – are examined.

Information has proved to be the most vital 'product' of the late 20th century and stands to increase in 'commodity-value' in the 21st. It is therefore of maximum interest to the major players on the public stage – the state and transnational corporations. And key to our interest as media-watchers is how that information is used to shape public perceptions of reality.

The alliance – often uneasy, often conflicting – between the nation-state and big business, is explored in relation to public and private spheres of mass communication, trends in deregulation and privatisation, and fears by a number of critics of cultural encirclement of the public by the great corporations.

Although new technology has facilitated the growth of information and speed of access, development globally has been uneven, with core nations seen to be information-rich and periphery nations information-poor. Finally, the chapter acknowledges crucial power shifts which threaten traditional Western hegemony.

Information, disinformation, 'mythinformation'

Two cases drawn from recent media history illustrate the vulnerability to distortion of information made public by mass communication – from the United States, the Oliver North Story and from the UK, the Story of the Vanishing Scott Report.

In July 1987 a military adviser was summoned to give evidence in the United States to the Iran-Contra Hearings. These concerned secret arms sales to Iran, the proceeds of which were used to supply cash for arms to the Contras, right-wing rebels intent on the overthrow of the Marxist government of Nicaragua. The affair was widely seen as a government cover-up by a deeply embarrassed Reagan administration.

The accusatory spotlight fell not upon the President or his Vice-President, George Bush, but upon a minor player in the drama. In the dazzling glare of public attention Oliver North chose not to play the role of victim. Instead, he reached for stardom, declaring to the American nation on TV, 'I came to tell the truth... the good, the bad and the ugly'.

North's words, borrowed from the title of a Clint Eastwood movie,[1] were not casually chosen. He did not see himself as the villain of the piece but as someone to be admired. He presented himself on TV as a hero – the proud little man taking on the faceless power of state bureaucracy. He believed, rightly as it turned out, that his American audience would come to see him as a real-life Clint Eastwood character. In their minds, fact and Hollywood heroes of the silver screen would blur and merge.

The sufferer in this menage of media and myth-making was the truth, or at least any clear path towards public understanding of it – what had actually happened, who was really involved, who gave the orders in this attempt by a big nation to subvert the sovereignty of a tiny country such as Nicaragua?

A number of commentators on the North trial believed it to be a cleverly managed piece of disinformation or to be more exact, *distraction* on the part of the Reagan administration. North was groomed for, and achieved, stardom, in a story that obscured the true 'story' of events by creating in the public mind another one, more accessible, more consonant – at one with – popular expectations; a romance manufactured in Hollywood and wrapped in the Stars and Stripes.

Keep Ollie, dump congress

This New York graffito of 1989 is quoted at the head of his chapter 'Oliver North and the news' by Robin Anderson in *Journalism and Popular Culture*.[2]

Anderson argues that the whole Oliver North episode confirmed, or indeed created, in the public mind a preference for myth over truth in the sense that 'myth appeared more reasonable than the black world of covert policies, cynical motivations and the real lack of American values'.

Though some commentators referred to North's testimony as 'soap opera hearings' Anderson believes North 'hit the bedrock of fundamentally masculine mythologies quite removed from soap opera. He tapped into the various codes of action/adventures and war heroes deeply etched in the genres of popular culture'. In one sense North was the victim in that he was abandoned by authority to take personal blame for what had been a government conspiracy.

ABC news made this clear on the day before North gave evidence (6 July 1987):

> Almost from the opening gavel these hearings pounded home one point. In the Iran Arms sales and the efforts to arm the contras, all roads led to and from Oliver North.

By focusing on the activities of one individual, the 'story' exonerated by exclusion the guilt of those who had authorised North's behaviour.

We have already noted Roland Barthes' view, expressed in *Mythologies*,[3] that the significance of myth is its ability to transform the meaning of history; and therefore of truth. The process is as follows: first the 'story' is drained of its historical truth through the restriction or reinvention of information. The empty shell awaits an ideological re-creation – as Anderson puts it, 'repackaged via the "concept", in this case American hero mythologies'. Anderson believes that the 'human cost of the Contra war which was continually denied... can be formulated into a postmodern spectacle of American values', that is a preference for image over truth, of mediated over lived reality.

Plainly Hollywood myths – almost invariably asserting the gender dominance of the male – are not confined to the Wild West of long ago; and such myths underscore, and often fuel, visions of the world as a dangerous place, one perpetually in crisis and thus demanding that the nation's 'guard' must be kept up at all times.

In Chapter 7, reference was made to Robert W. Connell's term, *hegemonic masculinity*.[4] We can see in the Contra affair and arguably in American foreign policy generally a 'gendered' picture of the world situation, often uncritically affirmed by the mass media. Sue Curry Jansen in 'Beaches without bases: the gender order' in *Invisible Crises*[5] regards gender values as the basis of Cold War mythology:

> The Cold War may be over, but the dangerous worldviews of men in power show few signs of pacification or of imaginative reconstructions. The Persian Gulf War was, among many things, a *boy thing*, in which George Bush demonstrated – live and in colour – that his missiles were bigger, better, and much more potent than Saddam Hussein's.

Downsizing issues

Let us turn to a second case study relating to the vulnerability of information in the public domain, the tale of Sir Richard's Vanishing Report. Using mythologies of heroes and villains is one way of manipulating or obscuring evidence in public life. Another is to treat genuine issues as if they were of marginal importance; and, by downsizing them, strike them off the public agenda. This was the strategy of the British tabloid press concerning the Scott Inquiry report of 1996.

It was another case of secret government corruption, this time in Britain. The Conservative government, its ministers and its civil servants, repeatedly denied to parliament that a 'blind eye' had been turned to the export of weapon-making technology to Iraq's President, Saddam Hussein immediately prior to the Gulf War of 1991. Chaired by Sir Richard Scott, the enquiry set up to look in to the Arms for Iraq affair found that officialdom had been economising with the truth. This time government stood accused of undermining the sovereignty of its own people.

'It will be hairy for ten days,' believed William Waldegrave, Chief Secretary to the Treasury, when the Scott Report was published.[6] One broadsheet describing the findings as 'the most damning indictment of the behaviour of ministers and civil servants'. However, although the government survived a House of Commons debate on Scott by only one vote in February, it was soon to be 'greatly assisted', believed Richard Norton-Taylor in his *Guardian* article, 'Scott free?', 'by the short attention span of most MPs and most sections of the media'.[7]

CORRUPTION IN HIGH PLACES

An exchange between Labour MP Tony Wright and Sir Richard Scott, Commons Public Service Committee, 8 May, 1996.

WRIGHT (To Scott): Did something constitutionally improper happen?

SCOTT: Yes. I think it did and I said so.

WRIGHT: Did ministers behave in ways in which ministers ought constitutionally not to have behaved?

SCOTT: I have said so, yes.

WRIGHT: Was Parliament denied information that Parliament constitutionally ought to have been provided with?

SCOTT: I think so, yes.

No minister resigned from the British government following the Scott enquiry and Waldegrave's prediction was fulfilled. While acknowledging that the one-vote victory for the government was ONE HELLUVA CLOSE SHAVE FOR THE PM, the *Daily Star* (Tuesday, 27 February 1996) declared in its editorial, 'The rest of us are SICK TO DEATH of the Scott Report'. One of the most important issues of any time – corruption in government – had become a bore. The *Star* believed 'It's time now to move on to more important things' [the underline is theirs] 'and let the Government get on with the business of running Britain'.

The UK *Sun* of 16 February was no more willing to take on the role of watchdog, or protector, of Parliament and public, choosing not to snap abuse but to turn the whole business into a joke. Above their banner head, 'YOU'RE SCOTT FREE', the *Sun* chanted, 'IT'S ALL OVER • THANK SCOTT IT'S ALL OVER • THANK SCOTT IT'S ALL OVER'. Readers were treated to '10 THINGS YOU CAN DO WITH REPORT', including turning it into briquettes 'and letting them smoulder on the fire', or using it as the 'perfect cure for insomnia. Reading a page or two is guaranteed to put anybody to sleep'. Finally, 'File it away in a dusty vault and forget about it – just like the Government probably will'.

The cases of Oliver North and of the treatment of the Scott Report illustrate how momentous issues are also issues about media performance discussed in Chapter 4: the role of public watchdog is sidestepped; matters of critical importance in democracies are trivialised; the evidence is marginalised, dismissed even, by myth or ridicule. Personalisation rules.

The *Sun* (Tuesday, 27 February 1996) introduced what is termed a 'spoiler', that is, one story introduced in order to deflect public attention from another: beside a page 2 report on how the government was saved by a single vote, the paper printed a story by political editor Trevor Kavanagh, 'LABOUR SOLD ARGIES ARMS' in the 1970s. This was designed to neutralise concern about the current issue, ignoring the fact that Britain had not been in conflict with the Argentinians until 1982, three years into the Tory government of Margaret Thatcher.

Power games and spin-doctoring

It is not only the media who stir the pots of myth and guide us into what to think about (and what to put out of mind), but also the media-culture machines of government and other elite forces in society. We have seen from our examination of news values the tendency to personalise issues, sensationalise events and spectacularise presentation. Such lessons have been taken on board by advocates of all kinds.

These days we learn from the pages of the press that one of the giant agencies of the advertising world has won yet another election. We pause, we read on: they have not actually won the election, simply 'engineered' victory through sophisti-cated propaganda. Under a headline 'NORIEGA'S HEIR WINS PANAMA POLL' the UK's *Guardian* announced that 'Saatchi & Saatchi has notched up another election in Central America...' Phil Gunson, writer of the report,[8] notes:

> The victory of Ernesto 'the bull' Perez Balladares in the Panamanian presidential elections returns to power the party that backed Manuel Noriega's thuggish six-year rule. And it marks the second time in a fortnight that Saatchi & Saatchi has won an election in central America.

The first of the London-based advertising agency's triumphs was in El Salvador where they advised Armando Calderon Sol of the Arena party who, says Gunson, 'steam-rolled the leftwing opposition in last month's second-round presidential poll'. Arena 'is an extreme right neo-fascist party...the party of the death squads'.

Gunson quotes Alberto Conte of the rival public relations firm McCann Erikson. He considered Saatchi & Saatchi – in their Panama campaign – had 'a very disciplined client [in Balladares] who accepted all their recommendations'. It was a 'well-structured campaign with attention to detail. The experts did their job and the "product" followed instructions to the letter'.

Gunson then quotes radio commentator Fernando Nunez Fabrega who said that the 'making of the president' included advising Balladares to use his hands a lot:

> He has big hands, and apparently that has a sexual connotation. Also, they finished dyeing his grey hair white at the front to make him look more distinguished.

In public relations work the political 'hue' of clients' money counts for less than its substance. PR has always had a role to play in the commerce and the politics of developed nations. Now, thanks largely to TV, it operates more than ever transnationally, employing ever more imaginative strategies to mould images intended to prompt, shape and influence public reponses.

Struggles for dominance: private sector v. public sector

The issue of who controls the dominant means of communication, who speaks to the public – and how, can be said to be the frame within which all other issues can be seen to connect. Depending on the matters in hand, the prize is consensus – public interest, public support or merely public acquiescence.

We as the targeted public may sense the struggle for our allegiance and suspect that this struggle is at least as much in the interest of the communicator as in our own interest. The thoughtful community is uneasy about and seeks to resist the desire of governments, of authorities, to control message systems. We argue for rights of access and expression. We witness private sector enterprises also wishing to dominate message systems in the name of profit – and we call for protective regulation.

The struggle is often presented in stark terms – between public and private ownership and control. However, the issue is less about the *categorisation* of ownership and control, public or private, and more about the *degree* and *extent* of that control. The issue is monopolistic tendencies; the problem, the capacity of agencies representing the public to establish and sustain checks upon those tendencies. In an age characterised by the deregulation and privatisation of public ultilities of all kinds as well as telecommunications and broadcasting, we see traditional checks and balances – regulatory requirements – in retreat and at risk.

In Chapter 4, the principle and practice of public service in media production was briefly discussed. In particular, the future of PSB (public service broadcasting) will continue to be a key issue for study and debate. Indeed, it was fear of commercial appropriation of public channels of communication that created PSB in the first place.

Presented with with the task of recommending how a state broadcasting company should be run, the Sykes Committee (1923–24) in the UK put the case for public service very succinctly. Its report is worth quoting again here:

We consider that the control of such a potential power [of broadcasting] over public opinion and the life of the nation ought to remain with the State, and that the operation of so important a national service ought not to be allowed to become an unrestricted commercial monopoly.[9]

Such principles framed the growth and development of the BBC, and a number of other state broadcasting systems, over many decades.

The role of the State has always been controversial: authority and freedom of expression have rarely made for contented bedfellows. But then nor have public service and commercial values. Sykes' belief that there should be some counter-vailing power to that of market forces continues to command wide support – first, because it acknowledged the difference between the public and the private sphere in the life of a nation and second because it recognised the predatory nature of the private sphere.

The public arena is where audience is located. It is also the marketplace where consumption takes places. To win consumers, the private sphere needs audience. What it is not obliged to take into consideration is the public as citizens. Only in the public sphere, fenced off, albeit modestly, from commercialisation and consumerisation, so it has been believed, can certain values and practices be maintained (see the Social Responsibility theory of media outlined in Chapter 4).

Few would assert that public service broadcasting has fully replicated the *agora*, or fulfilled its ideal as being an example of public communication working in Democratic-participant mode. But it has arguably been the best *agora* available. Even so, its virtues may not be sufficient to ensure its future.

Three developments in the final decades of the 20th century have threatened the survival of PSB – first, the ambition in the Age of Information of the private sector to expand its interests; second, the ideology of many governments favouring the private over the public and their policies of privatisation of public utilities; third, and smoothing the way for the other two, the possibilities of diversification brought about by new technology.

All at once, channel scarcity (on which public service regulation has so much relied) ceased to be an obstacle to expansion. The potential availability of 500 or more TV channels poses a formidable threat to any system of public service because, as was explained in Chapter 3 on audience and audience reception, it has become increasingly difficult to identify and define what 'public' is being served.

The narrowing base of media ownership

While there are many more available channels for the transmission of information and entertainment than in the past, there are fewer controllers of those channels. In the United States in 1982 some 50 corporations controlled half or more of media business. In 1986 that number had dropped to 29. In Britain between 1969 and 1986 nine multinational corporations purchased between them over 200 newspapers and magazines with a total circulation of 46 million.

In Australia in 1989 two men – Rupert Murdoch and Kerry Packer – controlled 84 per cent of the sales of the 30 best-selling magazines. As the 1990s progressed, Murdoch came to control 63 per cent of metropolitan daily paper circulation, 59 per cent of Sunday papers and 55 per cent of surburban local circulation.

The trend has shown an even steeper upward curve in the mid and late 1990s with Murdoch's News Corporation spearheading satellite transmission, through Sky TV and Star TV, Hong Kong, at a pace which rivals marvel at and try to emulate and governments lack the will to influence or control.

Media moguls in the 1990s never had it so good: Murdoch in Australia, Britain and the US, Silvio Berlusconi in Italy, Reinhard Mohn in Germany, Ted Turner (of CNN), Henry Luce and the Warner Brothers – Harry and Jack – in America. These conquistadors have built global empires of news transmission and entertainment which some observers fear might become empires of the mind.

Murdoch has been called 'perhaps the most ruthless predator in the history of the world news media' by Christopher Browne in *The Prying Game: The Sex, Sleaze And Scandals of Fleet Street and the Media Mafia*.[10] Certainly, Murdoch has proved himself something of a regulation-buster, rolling back Federal Communications Commission controls in the US when he was permitted by the FFC, in contravention of its own regulatory code, to run a broadcasting station and a newspaper in the same city. With his acquisition of 20th-Century Fox, and the subsequent launching of Fox TV, Murdoch became a mogul of Mister Universe proportions.

In 1988 the merger of the giant media groups Time and Warner created the world's biggest media corporation, employing over 300 000 people. The company owns subsidiaries throughout the world. Its magazine readership is estimated to be some 120 million. All this – without even mentioning Disney, Disneyland, Euro-Disney (and doubtless in the future Russo-, Afro- Asia- and even China-Disney).

'The great myth about modern proprietors,' writes Nicholas Coleridge in *Paper Tigers: The Latest, Greatest Newspaper Tycoons and How They Won the World*[11] 'is that their power is less than it used to be. The fiefdoms of Beaverbrook, Northcliffe and Hearst, often invoked as the zenith of proprietorial omnipotence, were in fact smaller by every criteria than the enormous, geographically diffuse, multi-lingual empires of the latest newspaper tycoons.'

Coleridge claims:

> The great media empires spanning the world have subjugated more territory in a decade than Alexander the Great or Ghengis Khan in a lifetime and funnelled responsibility for the dissemination of news into fewer and fewer hands.

Whether or not we consider Nicholas Coleridge to be exaggerating we might pause to consider the advantages media moguls have over the moguls of old: today their territories are restricted by neither time nor space – the next conquest is only a fax away.

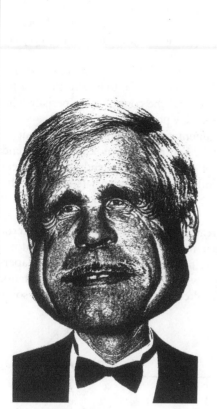

United States – Ted Turner

Europe – Silvio Berlusconi

The World – Rupert Murdoch

Figure 9.1 Global moguls

Corporate power and the media

We have seen throughout this book the possibilities of approaching communication from different points of the compass – from the perspective of producers and production, from the point of view of media content, via the semiological analysis of the text, and from the angle of audience perception and experience. Whichever approach we choose, we encounter the proposition that communication is *power* and that power is obtained and held through *control*.

Who controls the means of mass communication has the potential power to influence the ways in which society works. Therefore it has to be a constant task in the study of mass media to monitor control and the controllers, especially when the public domain of communication has so few powerful advocates.

In Chapter 5, I suggested an amendment to the agenda-setting model of Rogers and Dearing.[12] To the policy, public and media agendas a fourth agenda has been added (see Figure 9.2), that of the corporate agenda. Governments work with corporations, corporations influence governments (sometimes they have bigger incomes!) and the media are very often, and increasingly, part of corporate porfolios.

We underestimate the influence of great corporations nationally and internationally if we pay attention only to their media holdings, for the influence of transnational corporations is expressed not only through the newspapers, periodicals, radio and TV stations they own or in which they have substantial shareholdings: corporations are also 'into' culture, that is, all forms of social, communal expression.

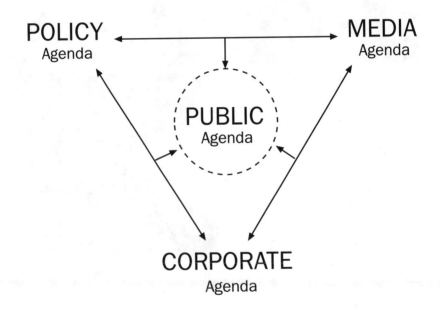

Figure 9.2   The dynamics of public agenda setting

They appropriate cultural services – such as museums, art galleries and libraries – by sponsorship or, as in America, by actually owning these 'public' services. From grand opera to Disneyland the mighty corporations are cultural benefactors: they are at one and the same time gamekeepers, preserving culture, and poachers, 'trapping' culture for private gain.

The key to corporate practices is public consumption. Marshall McLuhan's metaphor of a 'global village' to describe the effects worldwide of the advance of electronic communication is less apt now than the metaphor, referred to in Chapter 3, of a shopping mall: the public space has been roofed over. There are tinkling fountains, glittering glass chandeliers reflected in time-capsule elevators; there are boulevard-style cafés and play areas for the kids.

It is an ambience of leisure at the core of which is spending. In one sense the mall resembles the public parks created by community-spirited town councils but in another it is their antithesis. The 'public sphere' as represented by the shopping mall opens up no intended perspectives but one: consumption of goods and services for profit.

In the United States television has always been a shopping mall, a means of delivering audiences to producers of consumer goods. Fair enough one might say; after all, people need goods, enjoy luxuries and benefit from being informed. The danger – and the issue – is that people may be regarded as consumers first second and entirely; not voters, not citizens, not members of a community (unless community values and consumer values happen to be one and the same). They are viewed, as it were, one-dimensionally and consequently, critics believe, human needs other than consumerist ones are overlooked and neglected.

Caution: don't malign the mall (entirely)

The problem with employing metaphors such as that of the universal shopping mall is that they acquire a momentum which carries them beyond the power of evidence into the realms of generalisation. It is a temptation the media theorist must strive to resist.

At first sight, John Fiske seems to be subscribing to the 'myth of the mall' when, in his chapter, 'Shopping for pleasure' published in *Reading the Popular*,[13] he describes shopping malls as 'cathedrals of consumption'. Yet Fiske goes on to argue that members of the public make proactive use of malls for their own purposes, make their own running in terms of consumer choice and judgment, rather than tamely behaving according to the requirements of the manufacturers of goods:

> The pleasures and meanings offered by the plenitude of goods in shopping malls are multiple, and bear the dominant ideology while offering considerable scope for cultural manoeuvre within and against it.

What Fiske is describing is resistive, at least in a modest sense, but it is nevertheless significant for the individual:

> On the economic level such glittering excess [as is evident in the shopping mall] provides a daily demonstration that the capitalist system works, and on the ideological level that individualism can flourish within it... exercising choice is not just 'buying into' the system: choice also enhances the power of the subordinate to make their cultural uses of it.

Whether or not we go along with Fiske's views – which are all too briefly summarised here – the point to be made is that a 'yes but' clause has to be inserted into every assertive generalisation about the power of the overlords of culture and media to turn us into slaves of consumerism. The mall is not a cathedral. Customers are not worshippers. Goods are for sale but there is no obligation to buy; and there are many reasons why people assemble in shopping malls other than to spend money.

Such qualifying comments should not prevent the student of media seeking answers to a number of questions: how far, for example, can a community hold on to values other than consumerist ones in contexts where the corporate resources of consumerism are so vast, so intrusive, so pervasive and often so brilliantly calculated?

It would be difficult to prove how influential the marketing strategies of Saatchi & Saatchi were in Panama, El Salvador and elsewhere in setting the agendas for, and parameters of, political dabate; but it must be more than a happy coincidence that the politicians served by Saatchi & Saatchi won their respective elections. Our concern is whether marketing strategies can ever truly guarantee open, full and well-informed debate: does a free market further other freedoms or does it appropriate the *agora*, subject it to commercial imperatives and thus transform it into a corporate enclosure, global in extent?

Culture: corporatisation?

Looked at from one point of view, the technology of computers, cable, satellite and video has opened up wonderful opportunities for information access and transmission; opportunities which could potentially undermine or at least circumvent the hierarchical control of media systems. With a multimedia facility of computer, modem and telephone at our disposal, we can tune in to super highways of information exchange – and, on the face of it, there are no highway patrols in sight; and no Big Brother Corp.

In an article 'Critical communication research at the crossroads' published in the *Journal of Communication* Robert McChesney[14] enthuses over this new informational liberty: 'We stand on the threshold of an era in which society finally has the technology to democratise societies in a manner unfathomable only a few years ago.' Yet there is a catch: it seems there are highway patrols after all:

> The great barrier to the democratic application of these technologies is the corporate control of communication and the relative powerlessness of the public in capitalist societies.

Few authors have registered more acute concern about the 'corporatisation' of public expression than Herbert I. Schiller. In *Culture Inc.*[15] he examines the dangers, as he views them in an American context, that arise from the privatisation of information:

> Transforming information into a saleable good, available only to those with the ability to pay for it, changes the goal of information access from an egalitarian to a privileged condition.

Not only does information come at a price, the information itself is judged according to its potential commercial demand. Schiller quotes the president of an American database company, Dialog, as saying 'We cannot afford an investment in databases that are not going to earn their keep and pay back their development costs'. Asked which areas were currently failing to pay their way, the spokesman replied, 'Humanities'.

In 1987 Dialog showed discrimination of another kind, refusing to make available certain databases to trade unions who wished to use the data in their bargaining with management. Situations such as this one can be found throughout society, in matters of scientific, legal, forensic and technological data: information is for sale; and if it isn't saleable, it's not available. As Everette Dennis has neatly put it, 'What you don't know can hurt you'.[16]

Schiller writes of 'corporate envelopment of public expression' where the 'public information stockpile is transferred to corporate custody for private profit-making'. He talks of 'corporate pillaging of the national information supply', setting the scene of a power struggle where the corporations – especially in the United States – appear to be winning hands down: 'Who is in control determines the answer to the first question that faces any social order: who gets what?'

Schiller has little doubt that in the big match, Corp *v.* Public, Corp wins, even when it ought to be clear to the crowd that there has been some ball tampering:

> How to account in an age of intensive publicity for such reticence about such a remarkable public relations achievement – the transfer of wealth from the poor to the rich without a sign of public indignation?

Art: appropriated?

Schiller's concern does not stop at the ways information is 'corporatised' and held to ransom. He fears that cultures too have been appropriated: the corporate appetite is whetted by any cultural phenomenon – art, sport, music, festivals, parades, public celebrations of all kinds – which can serve corporate objectives. Even the museum in America 'has been enlisted as a corporate instrument'.

It is unquestionable that corporate sponsorship has provided massive and sometimes life-sustaining support for sport and the arts. The motive does not necessarily spring from a love of sport and the arts, or from altrusitic notions of enriching the social and recreational life of the people. Sponsorship does two things: it brings the name of the company to public attention and it associates that name with the occasion that draws people in through the turnstiles. The *image* of the one must be appropriate to the image – the desired reputation – of the other.

Art, Schiller argues, must fit the image of something timeless (like profits), detached from social and historical contexts. Looking at the *kinds* of art sponsored by the great corporations, Schiller observes that emphasis is placed upon 'the social neutrality of art and its alleged universalistic essence'. The art object is 'abstracted from its social and historical context... lovely, perhaps, but without meaning or connection'.

Of course there is nothing new about corporate sponsorship. We owe, over centuries, great architecture, music, painting and sculpture to the patronage of the church, the transnational corporation of the past. The church was circumspect about what art was created in its name and highly censorious of what it disapproved of. Schiller would doubtless argue that the difference is in scale and reach: Catholic art in Europe was dominant but escapable. Enculturalisation through media artefacts is less easy to evade.

In turn, John Fiske might retort – 'You are concentrating too much on the production of culture, and ignoring how people in manifold ways respond to that culture'. True; but the nagging question remains: what if art suddenly challenged everything corporations stands for – the ideology of consumption – would such institutions be any more tolerant of 'heresy' than the old Inquisition?

'Regulatory favours'

During the Thatcher years in Britain and the Reagan–Bush era in the United States the transnationals not only expanded their control over the information industry but were substantially aided by government policies of deregulation and privatisation.

In America the Federal Communications Commission, a national regulatory body created to nurture and protect public service broadcasting, spent the Reagan years doing just the opposite. Its officers were, in Schiller's words, 'deregulation obsessed'. One by one rules which protected the principle and practice of broadcasting in the interest of the public (rather than in the interests of consumerism) were withdrawn, largely at the behest of media owners.

In *Media Moguls*[17] Jeremy Tunstall and Michael Palmer refer to 'regulatory favours', that is, conglomerate deals with government in return, as the authors argue, for 'a good press'. For example, newspapers owned by a corporation will support government directly, mute criticism of it or withhold from the public information that could damage or embarrass it.

In turn government either abolishes or waives official media regulation. Such regulation may concern the nature and extent of ownership; it may stand in the way of cross-media ownership; it may be designed to exert control over programme content – such as insisting on a percentage of 'serious' programmes (documentaries, for example) being allocated prime-time rather than late-night slots. It may regulate the amount of imported material that can be shown in the interests of protecting home-produced programmes.

Tunstall and Palmer's choice of language concerning the activities of the great corporations is no less emotive than that of Herbert Schiller or Christopher Browne. 'By implication,' they say, 'media conglomerates are not independent watchdogs serving the public interest, but corporate mercenaries using their muscle to promote private interest'.

James Curran in 'Mass media and democracy: a reappraisal', published in *Mass Media and Society,*[18] echoes the concerns expressed by Schiller, Tunstall and Palmer and other scholars, declaring that the trend towards deregulation and privatisation has 'resulted in television becoming increasingly embedded into the corporate structure of big business'. Curran cites an example of corporate sensitivity to 'bad' news with the case of the conglomerate, Toshiba. A subsidiary of the company, Toshiba-EMI, had issued a record attacking Japan's nuclear programme, something the parent company was closely involved in. The record was withdrawn.

If transnational corporations own newspapers and broadcasting stations; if they sponsor the arts and control the music scene, the chances of their 'subsidiaries' criticising anything the parent corporation does are slim. Curran argues:

> The free market... compromises rather than guarantees the editorial integrity of commercial media, and impairs in particular its oversight of private corporate power.

He warns that corporate aspirations to global control have seriously reduced media diversity. He is supported in this view by Jay Blumler writing about the precarious position of public service broadcasting throughout Europe. Discussing the 'inexorable internationalisation of communication networks' in a *European Journal of Communication* article,[19] Blumler believes that 'the international marketplace is no supporter of programme range... In fact... it is structured *against* diversity'.

Limits to plurality

Convergence of ownership, then, seems to imply an intensification across the media terrain of the ideology of consumerism. Convergence is also manifested in the extraordinarily *intertextual* nature of modern mass communication. Every artefact seems to interlink with, live off, support, reinforce every other one. Denis McQuail in *Media Performance: Mass Communication and the Public Interest,*[20] picks up this point about the mutual reinforcement of media texts, speaking of:

> a worldwide 'intertextuality' of the main mass media of books, newspapers, phonography, film, television, radio, magazines. They overlap, reinforce and feed each other in content and commercial as well as technical arrangements.

Centre stage are advertising and public relations, owned by and working on behalf of corporations. Nicholas Garnham in *Capitalism and Communication: Global Culture and the Economics of Information*[21] believes the great corporations operate 'in the interest, not of rational discourse but of manipulation'.

They are no friends of the public sphere; rather it is in their interests to privatise it, own it and control it, hence the antipathy often seen in corporation-owned media, newspapers in particular, to the work of institutions which uphold the public service ethic. The BBC in Britain has incurred as much wrath from private sector voices as it has, over the years, from government.

In a free market for information exchange, and the free expression of opinion, institutions of all kinds, governmental, industrial or commercial show themselves sensitive to public criticism – or rather, criticism in public; and are ready to head it off wherever possible. Plurality of opinion is, like diversity of provision, to be encouraged on corporate terms or not at all.

NOT TONIGHT FOR *NEWSNIGHT*

The BBC found itself at the centre of controversy in the Autumn of 1996 when news broke that, having spent over £100 000 on two investigative programmes for the *Newsnight* programme, the Corporation had decided to axe them. Made by award-winning TV journalist Martyn Gregory, each film probed alleged 'dirty tricks' by one of Britain's biggest corporations, British Airways.

In an article, 'Flight from the Truth' published in the *Media Guardian* (30 September 1996), the aggrieved Gregory wrote, 'The BBC's decision to axe both of my films on new evidence of British Airways dirty tricks is a disgrace which betrays everything that BBC director-general John Birt claims that BBC journalism stands for... Press speculation on the role that his [Birt's] friendship with BA's chief executive, Robert Ayling, may have played is precisely that: speculation.

'I will deal with the facts; it is undeniable that Birt has created a craven culture in the BBC, and in the case of these two films the BBC has readily bowed down before corporate interests'. Gregory concedes that the material in the film 'was potentially dynamite'. Luckily, in a generally pluralist nation the 'truth' will out in some form or other.

A full account of the BBC's 'craven' submission to 'corporate interests' is to be found in Gregory's book, *Dirty Tricks: British Airways' Secret War Against Virgin Atlantic* (UK: Little, Brown, 1996). Ironically Gregory's publisher belongs to another corporate giant – Time-Warner.

Alongside the convergence of media control there has been an expansion of consumer choice in the sense that there is a wider range of 'cans' to select from the supermarket shelf. Yet it is the *nature* of that choice which causes concern, specifically the lack of choice between ideologies; between interpetations of reality and alternative strategies for social, economic and political change. Aspects of gender and ethnicity tend to remain in similar cans with similar labels.

Accountancy rules

The issues of corporate dominance discussed here have had an often far-reaching effect on the working lives of media people. Perhaps as never before broadcasting has become, in the free market economy, subject to the iron 'discipline' of the company accountant. Barbara Thomass in an article in the *European Journal of Communication*,[22] examines the impact of market forces on media employment in the European Community. She writes that:

> an explicit political intent to subjugate the UK broadcasting to the laws of the market and at the same time cripple the trade unions has led to the transformation of the broadcasting scene in the United Kingdom, leading critics to suggest that money, rather than programmes, is the main issue.

Companies seeking the commercial TV franchises in the UK in 1993 shed labour in order to finance their bids in a 'blind' auction. Faced with the uncertainty of knowing how much a successful bid for a franchise might be, companies cut their own costs to the bone in order to beat the competition (without ever knowing how much the competition was going to bid!). With fewer people of talent to work for them, and competition for an increasingly fragmented audience never more intense, commercial sector companies are confronted with the question – can quality be sustained or must it be sacrificed in pursuit of maximum-size audiences to satisfy the advertisers?

The BBC too has been forced into cost-cutting. Thomass estimates that there have been over 3000 job losses at the BBC since 1993. As in hospitals, competition has become an internal requirement. Thus the BBC is not only to compete with other broadcasting instututions, internal departments and personnel must compete with each other for available work.

The so-called system of Producer Choice (allowing programme makers to go outside the corporation for personnel) has created within the corporation a sense of uneasiness, distrust and trepidation. Throughout the broadcasting world, indeed throughout employment worldwide, secure jobs have gradually been replaced by the insecurity of short-term contracts.

The casualisation of labour linked with cost-cutting has been the policy of government as well as corporate practice. The ideology of 'the user pays' (in health as in supermarkets) represents in the words of Nicholas Garnham in a chapter entitled 'The media and the public sphere' published in *Communicating Politics: Mass communications and the political process*,[23] 'an unholy alliance between Western governments, desperate for growth, and multinational corporations in search of new world markets in electronic technology and information goods and services'.

Garnham states that the result has been to:

> shift the balance between the market and public service decisively in favour of market and to shift the dominant definition of public information from that of a public good to that of a privately appropriable community.

Corporatism and democracy

Because public discourses have been corporatised to such a considerable extent, few aspects of community life are free of corporate influence. As we have seen, the media play a crucial role in endorsing the discourses of capitalism. They appear to have been careful at all times to cut with the grain of 'approved' state ideology while at the same time using that ideology for their own benefit.

For example, pressure from the corporations eventually persuaded the American legislature to treat the corporate voice as having the same rights under the Constitution as an individual. Thus advertising copy, advertising discourses, are protected under the First Amendment; and so is pornographic 'communication'.

If, by the constant association of one practice with another, of one image with another, the two – corporate interest and civil rights – become blurred and merge imperceptibly, then one of the classic appropriations on the corporate record is what Herbert Schiller describes as the 'incessant identification of consumerism with democracy'.[15] The trick is to change the preposition 'with' to the verb 'is': consumerism *is* democracy: attack consumerism, pose alternative lifestyles to consumerism and you are in danger of 'subverting' democracy itself. Thus, as Schiller argues, 'any interference with private ownership and enterprise' might be classified as 'a perilous step toward concentration camps'.

The multinationals claim, through the many media voices they control, that global capitalism is good for peace, good for democracy and, in any event, there is no viable alternative. It is an issue of our time that the media voices that are capable of at least providing the space and time for alternatives to be posited and discussed, rarely do so; and the matter is urgent.

The case the global corporations put forward in their own defence is summarised by Richard Barnet and Ronald Müller in *Global Reach: The Power of the Multinational Corporations*:[24]

> Increasingly, the most powerful argument voiced in defence of the global corporation is precisely this lack of alternatives. Compared with avaricious local business, it is said, global firms are better. They pay more in taxes, they employ more people, and they cheat less.

> Compared with dictatorial and corrupt governments, the World Managers are relatively enlightened and honest. Compared with selfish local interests clutching at privilege, global corporations are less parochial. Compared with the Stalinist police state, a world run by the global corporation promises more freedom and less terror.

End of story? The authors, in a book which was written in 1975 but could have just been published, declare that the survival of the species itself depends upon the reining in and the restructuring of global business. Barnet and Müller apply a very simple criterion to the case for or against global domination by the corporations: if a social force is to be classified as *progressive*, it must prove that it is likely to benefit the bottom 60 per cent of the population worldwide.

On this score, Barnet and Müller contend, global companies have done little, are doing little and will continue to do little for the world's have-nots. Indeed, by making profit the lord and master of all their activities, by constantly shifting their operations from one – low-paid – labour force to another across national boundaries and by plundering the environment in the name of consumerism which must forge on ever upwards, ever onwards, [the global corporations aggravate problems of mass starvation and mass unemployment.]

Delicate balances

Three fundamental states of human need are, in fact or potentially, violated by the kind of world society the global corporations are creating. First, say Barnet and Müller, there is the threat to *social balance*:

> As owner, producer, and distributor of an ever greater share of the world's goods, the [global corporation is an instrument for accelerating concentration of wealth.] As a global distributor, it diverts resources from where they are most needed (poor countries and poor regions of rich countries) to where they are least needed (rich countries and rich regions).

Barnet and Müller believe that the 'ideology of infinite growth' has the force of a religious crusade. [Global corporations 'act as if they must grow or die, and in the process they have made thrift into a liability and waste into a virtue'. [This grow-or-die obsession conflicts with the *ecological balance* which the human race must sustain both for its own interests now and for future generations:

> The corporate vision depends upon converting ever-greater portions of the earth into throwaway societies: ever-greater quantities of unusable wasted produce with each ton of increasingly scarce mineral resources; ever-greater consumption of nondisposable and nonreturnable packaging; ever-greater consumption of energy to produce a unit of energy; and ever more heat in our water and our air – in short, ever more ecological imbalance.

The *psychological balance* though more difficult to identify and define is, believe Barnet and Müller, the most significant of all. To maximise profits, World Managers have 'based their strategy on the principles of global mobility, division of labour, and hierarchical organisation – all of which may be efficient, in the short run for producing profits but not for satisfying human beings'.

Standing full-square to amplify the concerns Barnet and Müller raise in *Global Reach* are the media. The issues could be said to cry out for informed debate in the media-*agora*. They demand to be placed high on the agenda of public concerns. That they are not is because the media belong to the corporations which, according to Barnet and Müller, have caused the problems in the first place. Yet again we encounter the media seemingly in their role as guard dogs, protecting their masters' 'property' rather than serving as watchdogs of public interest.

Scratched onto a surface in the ancient city of Pompeii was an early warning to consumers to be on their guard: BUYER BEWARE. The warning holds good not only for products and services but for ways of life and, critically, for our studies of the way media assist in defining reality, truth and meaning.

A case can be made that of all the notions which come at us via the pages of newspapers, through broadcasting, by cable or satellite; of all the images that massage our senses, the one to be most wary of is the impression that social change (except that engineered by the World Managers) is undesirable (things are best the way they are) and in any event beyond the power of ordinary people to bring about.

In the 1970s Richard Barnet and Ronald Müller already feared that:

> By marketing the myth that the pleasures of consumption can be the basis of community, the global corporation helps to destroy the possibilities of real community – the reaching out of one human being to another.

Faced with the barrage of messages which advocate the consumer-communal paradigm, the citizen is unlikely to rise up and demand the overthrow of the 'system'. We arrive at perhaps the most significant argument made in *Global Reach*:

> How much the pervasive sense of meaninglessness in modern life can be attributed to the organisational strategies and values of the huge corporation we are only beginning to understand, but for the longer run the psychological crises associated with the emerging socioeconomical system are potentially the most serious of all, for they undermine the spirit needed to reform that system.

'Semiotic resistance'

More recent commentators have been less pessimistic about the public's power to resist corporate influence; but it is a resistance which is individual, or group-orientated in nature – *negotiated* rather than *radical* or *oppositional* (see Chapter 3 for details on codes of response). John Fiske terms it 'semiotic resistance'.

PEOPLE POWER?

...what I like to call 'semiotic resistance' differs from politically active resistance... [and this resistance is not] an agent of incorporation, a sort of internal bread and circuses[24] that ends up by winning people's consent to the *status quo*.

...Semiotic resistance is the power of the people in their various social formations of subordination and disempowerment to resist the colonisation of their consciousness by the forces of social power...

Semiotic resistance stems from the fact that people use the discursive resources of a society quite differently from the way that the dominant forces do. They talk, they think, they joke, and all the time they are making *their* sense of their particular form of subordination, they are exploiting their power to use discourse differently, resistingly.

John Fiske, in discussion at a symposium 'Television and History', in the National Humanities Centre, North Carolina, March 1987 and printed in Fiske's *Reading the Popular* (US: Unwin Hyman, 1989)

Fiske acknowledges the subordination of ordinary people, that the dominant discourses of the time are not their discourses; and he does not claim that 'semiotic resistance' is the creator of discourses. The 'people at the top' are still doing the running: they are the encoders of mass communication messages, but their power to ensure a preferred reading is limited.

In any case, Fiske, in the same discussion in North Carolina, says:

> I would like to point out that organised resistance in the political domain is always the work of a tiny activist minority, but that in the long run, its effectiveness depends on millions of people thinking differently, people who have resisted the colonisation of their consciousness, people whose interior semiotic resistances provide a groundswell of support that prevents the activists from being marginalised as eccentric extremists, and makes them into spokespeople.

Fiske's is a liberal and a generous view and it will hold a strong appeal to students of media; indeed, such students might come to regard themselves as potential members of Fiske's tiny activist minorities. Most certainly students of media have a better-than-average chance to resist the colonisation of their consciousness because they are trained in their studies from day one in surveillance.

They analyse – unpack, deconstruct – media texts; they scrutinise the origins and sources of messages and much of their work centres around the ways audiences respond to the discourses aimed at them. They can not only be confident that their studies are relevant and meaningful, they should recognise such studies as a vital contribution to citizenship. On the other hand, they will readily appreciate the awesome power and influence of Barnet and Müller's World Managers.

Global imbalances in informational and cultural exchange

It is important for the student of media to be constantly aware of the interconnection of issues and of the interrelationship of the local and the global. An issue worthy of study and extended research is that of the uneven distribution of information in micro- and macro-contexts.

Equality of opportunity depends crucially upon an equal spread of information, for information is the hinge upon which decisions can be made to the benefit of the individual, the group or the nation. Without the necessary information – scientific, medical, technological, economic or political – protagonists in a competitive world are at a serious disadvantage.

For example, in Europe there is an average of 1400 free public libraries per country while in Africa the average is 18. America and Japan are respectively served by over 150 and over 120 daily newspapers while in 30 countries there is only one; in 30 more it is estimated there is no newspaper at all. These figures are quoted by Cees Hamelink in his chapter 'Information imbalance: core and periphery' in *Questioning the Media: A Critical Introduction*.[25]

Hamelink surveys the global communications scene, identifying *core* nations, the *information-rich* and *periphery* nations, the *information-poor*. This *information imbalance*, says Hamelink, puts a great proportion of the world's population at a serious disadvantage, rendering it susceptible to exploitation, manipulation and – unless the imbalance is rectified – destined for a future of continued deprivation.

Put together, all the countries in the periphery own a mere 4 per cent of the world's computers. Of the world's 700 million telephones, 75 per cent are located in the world's nine richest countries. Perhaps most significantly in an age driven by technological advances only 1 per cent of the world's patent grants are held by countries in the information periphery.

Satellite photography has become the spy-in-the-sky which enables the user to identify crucial details of a country from an altitude of 150 miles. Thus rich nations can learn more of what is going on in a poor nation, and more quickly, than the poor nation knows about itself. Such technology provides early warning to core nations about vital information ranging from the movement of tuna shoals off Nigeria to detecting the quality of the coffee harvest in Brazil.

Not only is the degree of available information imbalanced, so is the information *flow*. The greater part of information flow is between core nations and where the flow is between core and periphery it is substantially one-way traffic, from core to periphery. 'Estimates suggest,' writes Hamelink, 'that the flow of news from core to periphery is 100 times more than the flow in the opposite direction'.

Information gaps

There are differences too in the nature of that flow. From the periphery comes 'raw', unprocessed – and unmediated – information, while information moving from core to periphery comes packaged, with price attached. Very often that information arrives as disinformation. Hamelink stresses the capability and the will of core nations to manipulate information for political purposes:

> Both the CIA [America's secret service] and the KGB [secret service of the former Soviet Union] have elaborate networks for deliberate distortion of political information. Disinformation employs the fabrication and distortion of information to legitimate one's own operations and to delegitimate and mislead the enemy... Peripheral countries have little chance to correct or counter such disinformation.

Information flows – in their direction, volume and quality – are imbalanced and this imbalance is not to be lightly dismissed by the view that 'eventually the poor will catch up'. It is an axiom that by the time the disadvantaged have closed the information gap, the advantaged will have gone another step ahead.

The inadequate information capacities of most peripheral countries are, says Hamelink:

> a serious obstacle to their own efforts to combat poverty and other deprivations... Without information about resources, finance, and trade, peripheral countries are at a continual disadvantage in negotiations with core countries, and this jeopardises their survival as independent nations.

When so much information on poor nations is kept in data banks by information-rich countries, a 'peripheral' nation's very *sovereignty* is at risk:

information imbalance leads to the cultural integration of peripheral countries in the culture promoted by the core. Imported cultural programming encourages consumerism and individualism, and diverts attention from any regard for the long-term needs of the country.

The new consumerism and individualism also tend to accentuate divisions within a state between the haves and the have-nots: 'Internal gaps develop as urban elites become part of the international economy while the rural poor get left behind.' Economic dependency on the part of the information-poor becomes political and cultural dependency.

If a country does not have sufficient independence to nurture its own language or languages, its own forms of literary, musical and dramatic expression, its own historical and artistic heritage, then it is vulnerable to cultural invasion; and the desire for – the need for – cultural self-determination is put at risk.

Once again care must be taken to differentiate between macro-visions – often bleak, certainly disturbing – of cultural invasion of 'peripheral' by 'core' cultures, and micro-practices. We have already seen, from the research findings of Tamar Liebes and Elihu Katz published in *The Export of Meaning*,[26] that the American soap *Dallas* was read in quite different ways by people of different origins, cultures and outlooks; indeed was appropriated by them. It was *Dallas* which was dominated, not the audience for *Dallas*.

In *The Media and Modernity: A Social Theory of the Media*,[27] John B. Thompson also takes an optimistic view of the capacity of audiences worldwide to make their own meanings out of 'core' nation texts. He talks of an 'axis of globalised diffusion and localised appropriation'. Globalisation does not eliminate the negotiation of textual meanings. 'Through the localised process of appropriation,' Thompson argues, 'media products are embedded in sets of practices which shape and alter their significance'.

Expect the unexpected

John Keane in *Tom Paine: A Political Life*[28] – a book strongly recommended to readers interested in campaigning journalists of the past – quotes an old maxim, that the fecundity of the unexpected is more powerful than any statesman. In other words, life is prolific with the unpredictable. A glance at history will indicate to us that the volatility of change is a more common feature of existence than the *status quo*.

Today's wind of change is blowing from East to West. The traditionally 'poor nations of the East' are prospering; their goods advertised in our papers and on our TV. Their newly earned wealth is being invested in our own factories to the point when some claim to see a 'reverse colonialism' taking place.

The so-called Tiger economies of the Pacific basin – Japan, Malaysia, Taiwan and South Korea (and potentially the most powerful of them all, China) – are no longer 'developing' nations; they are competing nations and the balance of power is seen to be tilting in their direction: who will be the Third World nations of tomorrow? Arguably such matters should be the core, not the periphery of media studies in future, to gauge and analyse the 'fecundity of the unexpected' in relation to the roles, functions and performance of mass communication worldwide; not least, the part the media play in campaigning for, nurturing and protecting human rights.

═══════════════════════ **SUMMARY** ═══════════════════════

This chapter has stressed that a primary issue concerning the media, nationally and increasingly globally, is ownership and control. We have witnessed how transnational corporations have established commanding powers over the mediated experience of consumers of media globally. By controlling the means of mass communication, World Managers are in the strategic position to shape the message systems of our time which in turn define public realities.

The alliances which occur between governments, big business and the media are seen to be institutional rather than haphazard in nature. Corporatisation of cultural life is extensive, aided by general shifts towards deregulation and privatisation. Commoditised, information becomes the servant of those who produce it and, a number of commentators fear, pluralism of output is seriously at risk.

Public service communication is in retreat, its governing principles under review if not under attack. The situation has come about partly in face of privatisation policies, partly as a result of new technologies leading to the widening but also the fragmentation of audience.

The case urged at every opportunity by the transnationals, that the free market is a guarantor of democracy is seen here to be an unjustifiable and possibly dangerous assertion. Employment in the media industry has been increasingly casualised and this trend has been accompanied by drastic cost-cutting and thus the threat to quality and diversity of media output.

Also, in the so-called Information Age, attention has been drawn to the uneven distribution and flow of information. A few commentators in the late 1990s have claimed to spot signs of reverse in corporate growth; of national cultures, and cultures within those nations, beginning to reassert themselves. Who knows, perhaps Rupert Murdoch's News Corp may prove itself a dinosaur after all. Science is uncertain what factors consigned the dinosaurs to extinction and media commentators are equally uncertain as to what – other than rigorous national and international regulation – will 'tame' the Murdoch Leviathan.

Either way, the notion of the commoditisation of information is not new. The French novelist Honoré de Balzac in 1839 wrote of the press as degrading writers into becoming purveyors of commodities. The difference between Balzac's day and now is not so much attitudes, values and behaviour as their scale and their diffusion.

KEY TERMS

marginalisation ■ disinformation, distraction ■ collusion ■ deregulation
privatisation ■ public sphere ■ PSB (public service broadcasting)
corporatisation ■ appropriation ■ regulatory favours ■ producer choice
information imbalance ■ information-rich/information-poor
Core nations/periphery nations

SUGGESTED ACTIVITIES

1. Discussion
   (a) What issues concerning the media, other than those discussed in this chapter, may be considered matters of urgent concern?
   (b) How might the ambitions of transnational corporations be modified or controlled; and what would be the criteria for such controls?
   (c) How might periphery nations close the information gap?

2. Conduct a survey of the use of *product placement* in films and TV series. How often, for example, do we see cans of Coke as bit-part 'actors' in the story? What significance can be ascribed to product placement? What hidden agendas might there be – in terms of collusion between product marketing and programme production?

3. Draw up a list of references for an International Media Profile in which you plan to study all aspects of a Third World nation's media – its press and broadcasting services, its cinema industry (if it has one) and the degree to which that country 'uses' media imports from other – 'core' countries. If you have difficulty assembling sufficient information, the Internet may be your way forward.

NOW READ ON

Perhaps the most fascinating aspect of the study of media is how it impacts on culture as a whole and how culture, and cultures, respond to the part played by media in local, national and international life. Nowhere is this interplay between media and audiences more vividly at work – and more *intertextual* in nature than in advertising, particularly as the advertising industry is so closely wedded to corporate empires.

Try, then, *Advertising, The Uneasy Persuasion: its dubious impact on American society* by Michael Schudson (US: Basic Books, 1984; UK: Routledge, 1993), Armand Mattelart's *Advertising International: The Privatisation of Public Space* (UK: Comedia,

1991), translated by Michael Channan, and *Advertising and Popular Culture* by Jib Fowles (UK: Sage, 1996).

On a broader geo-cultural canvas Geoffrey Reeves' *Communications and the Third World* (UK: Routledge, 1993) is recommended, particularly for his chapter on Media imperialism. Also see two volumes from Sage, Nick Stevenson's *Understanding Media Cultures: Social Theory and Mass Communication* (1995) and *Questions of Cultural Identity* (1996), edited by Stuart Hall and Paul du Gay.

Finally, for a view of global discourse and corporate power in the form of what we eat, John Vidal offers very palatable fare in *McLibel: Burger Culture on Trial* (UK: Macmillan, 1997).

10 Prising Open the Black Box: Media Effects Revisited

AIMS

- To stress the complexity of media effects and the need, in attempting to measure them, to pay due regard to perceptual and contextual factors.
- To examine two rival approaches to the exploration of effects, the Cultivation position and the Ethnographic position.
- With reference to the impact of computer technology on so many aspects of our lives, to assess how far personal privacy is at risk; at the same time recognising how media communication has also exposed authority to public surveillance.

We enter the chief 'danger zone' of media study when we attempt to assess the effects, influence and impact of the media; and nowhere is the conditioning phrase, 'It all depends...' more apposite. This is perhaps a useful time for the reader to return to Chapter 3 to renew acquantaince with aspects of the so-termed active audience, in particular refreshing memory concerning codes of response.

Here I focus on what media commentators and researchers consider the nature and substance of effects. The contrasting Cultivation and Ethnographic positions are discussed and these viewed in the context of the sheer volume of mass communication messages we encounter every day and which, in the main, is produced by institutions whose reach is global as well as national.

The issue of violence in media is raised, again in a context dominated by institutional norms, values and aspirations. Technology has been a driving force in the creation of an Information Society but its multifarious use has also made possible a Surveillance Society, one in which, in the view of some commentators, privacy is under threat, if, in fact, it can actually be said to exist any more. The chapter closes with a brief round-up of the many effects commentators have ascribed to media.

The spectrum of effects: rival perspectives

Once upon a time there was a gigantic hypodermic needle full of highly toxic messages which Big Bad Media injected into the unresisting veins of poor Princess Audienza. Today we refer to this account of media effects as the *propaganda* or *mass manipulative* model. Effects-watchers subsequently had doubts, recognising that the mass comprises individuals who bring to media consumption their own expectations and agendas. We might refer to this as the model of *audience appropriation*. The Princess in this scenario is no pushover.

Effects can be looked at from two points of view, those inferred from media performance within contexts and those experienced by those at the receiving end of media performance, the audience within contexts. In each case, the context – of tranmission and of reception – is critical; and it is because contexts are themselves so complex that we have to gauge effects with the greatest of care.

Indeed, the challenge is to recognise the complexities of the interactions which take place between media and context, audience and media and context and audience. Are we referring to long-term or short-term effects, macro- or micro-effects; and while we are deciding, have we noticed that the cultural contexts we *thought* we were taking into consideration have themselves undergone radical changes? One thing we can be certain of: so long as there are media, so long as they play an important part in our individual and community lives, we will go on inferring effects whether we can prove them or not.

Currently we can identify two highly influential strands of enquiry, what might be classified as the *cultivation position*, where analysts perceive strong (or strong*ish*) effects and the *ethnographic position* which sees audiences as vigorously making of media messages and media influences what they will, according to personal agendas and personal lifestyles. In short, audiences are active.

Epimetheus' error

According to Roman reading of Greek legend, the first human woman was Pandora, the beautiful, all-gifted creation of the god, Vulcan. She was brought into the world on the orders of Jove, chief of the gods, in revenge for Prometheus stealing fire from heaven and giving it to humankind. Jove's wedding gift to Pandora, who married Prometheus' unsuspecting brother, Epimetheus, was a mysterious box. Against Prometheus' advice, Epimetheus opened Pandora's Box – and out flew all the evils which were to haunt the human world for ever.

What has never been fully settled is whether Hope did a runner too or remained in the box. Opening the black box of media effects clouds the air not so much with evils as questions that howl and gnaw and itch and cause at least a semblance of the confusion of Jove's Revenge. With apologies to Harold Lasswell,[1] whose 1948 model of mass communication is given a modest adjustment here, we might shake out from Pandora's Box the following questions:

What is affected
In whom

How and
To what extent
According to which timescale?

For the researcher any one of the above questions might represent a lifetime's work. Let us at least begin by touching upon what *might* be affected. The areas of effect are generally listed as being perceptions (the ways we 'see' each other and the world), opinion, attitudes, beliefs and values and, of course, behaviour – those parts of our life-view and life-performance which might be subject to influence by exposure to the media.

It might also be advisable to examine whether people are equally susceptible to influence; and whether the 'parts' of people – their opinions as contrasted with their values, for example – are equally susceptible. Patently they are not, which means that we require a clear picture of just who we are talking about.

Some investigators may concentrate on people in different social classes. They might focus on gender, race, income, education – all factors which come under the heading of *intervening variables*. The Cultivation position, most notably represented by George Gerbner and his team of researchers at the University of Pennsylvania's Annenburg School of Communication, hones in on the connection between heavy television viewing and media influence.

Researchers holding to the Ethnographic position concentrate on the ways people interact with what they are watching on TV in relation to all the other interactions and practices of their day-to-day lives. Yet the questions posed are not dissimilar: what does TV do to the members of its audiences and what does each member do *with* what he or she has been watching? Basically three things can happen: a change can take place in a member of audience as a result of exposure to media – an adjustment of attitude or of behaviour; a reinforcement or confirmation of existing perceptions, that is, a resistance to change; or no reaction occurs at all.

As we saw in looking at the multi-step flow model of communication (see Chapter 3) change and reinforcement are aided and implemented by more influences than just the media – people around us, people classifiable as significant others. Such influentials may help counter media messages or confirm them, though we should always bear in mind the fact that they, too, may be as influenced by media as we are.

The time factor in influence is very important, particularly if you are looking at the process from the point of view of one who actually *wishes* to influence others. Someone running a campaign of persuasion, say for health education, will be particularly anxious to learn how audience interest, having been aroused, can be sustained.

How immediate, then, are effects; how long-lasting? What we can say is that attitudes and opinions, unless strongly held, are likely to be more easily influenced than beliefs and values, assuming, that is, that beliefs and values exist, that they seem relevant to a particular situation and that they are not themselves vague and uncertain.

Cultivation position 1: a consumerist effects story

One thing the advocates and persuaders in society can be confident about is that we, as the public, as audience, have self-value; and if we don't have it, we ought to have it. We have needs and 'wants' closely connected with our self-value, what in Chapter 3 on audience was referred to as the *project of self*.

The advertising industry learnt long ago that to be successful it had to sell us something more than goods and services. Adpeople realised that 'wants' can be turned into needs by suggesting an absence of those needs. By cultivating dissonance, an uneasy feeling of deprivation – your skin or hair are not as beautiful as they ought to be – advertisers endeavour to cultivate in the head the image of loveliness created by the latest anti-ageing cream or hair shampoo and conditioner. A sense of consonance is restored; or at least that is the promise.

Cultivation theory takes the view that audiences have only meagre defences against the flood of consumerist propaganda, driven by the power of transnational corporate interest. In 1986, according to the Association of National Advertising, $102 billion, two per cent of the United States' gross national product, was spent on advertising. A similar amount was spent on design, packaging, marketing and product display. In the 1990s such sums have increased: have they been well spent and in what ways might advertising have altered the perceptions, attitudes, opinions and even beliefs and values of the public?

Douglas Kellner in his chapter 'Advertising and consumer culture' in *Questioning The Media*[2] writes:

> By the 1920s, corporations, advertising agencies, and market research organisations began planning ways to 'produce' consumers and to promote consumption as a way of life in the United States. Individual resistance to new products had to be broken down, and individuals had to be convinced that it was acceptable to purchase goods that they had previously produced themselves and that it was morally justifiable to consume, to spend money, and to gratify desires.

One could, from a cultivationist perspective, describe this as a form of spiritual conversion:

> Previously, puritan work and savings ethics and a morality of delayed gratification prevailed, so advertising had to convince individuals that consumption was now a morally acceptable route to happiness and satisfaction.

The cultivationist position bears witness to profound cultural changes which have taken place; and largely blames the big corporations and their acolyte media servants for the alleged 'consumerisation of society'. The implication is that the public has been lured by something resembling a conspiracy of corporate interest and media images into believing the proposition that consumption is the road to happiness; that the more individuals consume the happier they become. This results in mass enslavement to consumption.

Another writer who blows hot for the cultivationist position is Neil Postman. The title of his best-known book summarises his position concerning the media and audience: *Amusing Ourselves to Death*.[3] Postman worries that the techniques of message presentation and manipulation employed by advertising have become a model, or paradigm, for 'the structure of every type of public discourse'. 'To be effective,' writes Postman, 'every message must be snappy, entertaining and, above all, brief'. This implies characteristics of assertiveness over analysis and imaging over explanation.

Image politics

Postman argues that the television commercial 'has profoundly influenced American habits of thought'. Former US president Ronald Reagan felt no embarrassment in declaring that 'Politics is just like show business': politicians are performers on screen. The content of their message – what they stand for – is less important than how they come over; what they look like. Postman talks of 'instancy' as a dominant value which has a devastating effect upon political discourse. In what he terms 'image politics' he believes 'we are not permitted to know who is best at being President or Governor or Senator, but whose image is best in touching and soothing the deep reaches of our discontent'.

Like many other commentators Postman expresses concern about the way modern television appropriates – or in his view *mis*appropriates – the past and its meanings. In the Age of Show Business and image politics, Postman believes, political discourse is emptied not only of ideological content but of historical content as well. We are presented with fragments, yet none is 'based in a meaningful context'.

Postman's is a rather doom-laden picture; ironically his book is very entertaining to read; so entertaining that we forget for a moment that the author is basing his comments on hunch (and, yes, observation) not research. Are we as audience so vulnerable? Postman certainly thinks we are liable to deception:

> The television commercial is about products only in the sense that the story of Jonah is about the anatomy of whales, which is to say, it isn't. Moreover commercials have the advantage of vivid visual symbols through which we may easily learn the lessons of being taught. Among those lessons are that short and simple messages are preferable to long and complex ones; that drama is to be preferred over exposition; that being sold solutions is better than being confronted with questions about problems.

Whether Postman is right or not, his ideas command attention; and he has been far from alone in expressing his concern that the nature of public discourse is under threat from consumerist communication and its most powerful channel, television. The French president, François Mitterand, spoke out in 1994 on the theme that 'media marketing' endangered democracy. He was referring to the rise to political power of the Italian media mogul Silvio Berlusconi that spring and summer.

Berlusconi's media empire had provided the publicity which got Berlusconi and his right-wing associates into government. Though many media magnates have had political ambitions, and some have reached the foothills of political office, none, until Berlusconi, had actually become prime minister of their country. 'This,' Mitterand told five European publications on 25 May 1994, 'is an approach to democracy we are not used to and which appears fearsome to me... There is a serious risk of perverting democracy'.

The man or woman in the street might well greet such comments with a shrug; after all, doesn't it take millions of dollars to get elected in the United States; and couldn't that be considered a threat to democracy? Mitterand's point nevertheless deserves attention: if message systems are monopolised by the few, and if those systems emphasise, as Postman puts it, 'the pictures in your head more than words' (that is, *symbolic power*), then democracy must be on its guard.

Cultivation position 2: violence, order, control

A concern more likely to be expressed, if we were conducting some *vox pop* research,[4] would be about violence on our cinema and TV screens; a concern that sees connections between screen violence and our perceptions of violence in the real world. The argument is a simple one, and rash to dismiss without due consideration: the Cultivation position asserts that the more we see of violence, the more we might become insensitive to it, and thus eventually immune to it. Either way, it might confirm our view that out there is a dangerous and hostile world.

It has been estimated that in the United States the average American child, by the age of 18, will have witnessed 18 000 simulated murders on television. Following the screening of Michael Cimino's *The Deer Hunter* (1978), with its notorious Russian roulette scene, 35 young men in the US committed suicide in like manner.

The anecodotal evidence could fill many pages. Carrying more weight, however, are the many studies into the effects of violence which do indicate a link between images and realities. In an article 'Colours of violence' in *Index on Censorship*[5] Anne Nelson writes:

> The debate is not about dramas or documentaries which hinge on a killing; nor on the violence of war reports. Public concern focuses on the gratuitous violence of cinema and TV that makes dialogue subordinate to the shocking visual image and saturates the audience with its morbid repetition: the kind of movie violence that propels young men to stand up in their seats, jab their fists in the air and shout 'Aw-right!'

Nelson refers to a July 1993 issue of the American magazine *Mother Jones* which estimated that there had been over 80 separate research studies, all of them affirming the causal link between television violence and actual violence. However, in a letter published in a subsequent issue of *Index* (September/October 1994), the acting executive director of Feminists for Free Expression, Catherine Sieman, writes a repost to the position taken up by Nelson:

[she] perpetuates the myth that the connection between television violence and real-life violence has been established, while citing little actual evidence. The hypothesis that images of violence cause violence in real life is not supported by history.

Sieman argues that one of the most violent periods in American history was between 1929 and 1932, 'when there was no television and most people lacked regular access even to the movies'. Violence in the 19th century, says Sieman, referring in support of her point of view to the position taken up by the American National Research Council, was higher than now.

She also states that in industrialised countries with high TV-viewing figures the actual violence rates are lower than many developing nations which have 'low television viewing and very high rates of violence':

> The American Psychological Association (1993) and the National Research Council (1993) conclude that violence is caused by parental abuse, rejection and neglect, accompanied by factors such as poverty and the belief that educational or job opportunities are closed because of racial or ethnic discrimination.

Sieman is insisting that before we decide one way or another about the connection between mediated and lived violence we should hesitate before loading the blame for the perceived increase in violence in our communities upon the media. Cultivation may seem to be happening but proof that audiences are actually 'cultivated' by media rather than by circumstances unrelated to media must be more substantial, and more convincing if it is to carry weight. What is more, there is always the fear that concentrating on 'media-bred violence' will deflect attention from other sources of violence – inequality, deprivation and alienation.

Cultivating convergence

Perhaps the most extensive and long-running research into the effects of television violence on audience has been conducted, over more than three decades, by George Gerbner and his team at the Annenberg School of Communication. The assassination of President John Kennedy followed by that of his brother Robert and then of the Reverend Dr Martin Luther King led to the establishment in the United States in 1968 of the National Commission on the Causes and Prevention of Violence.

The Mass Media Task Force commissioned Gerbner to provide an analysis of violence on television. *Cultural Indicators,* the title of the research project, was to produce massive and significant data. Yet it seems that the more this research enterprise revealed, the less attention – in official and media circles – was paid to it. In a chapter entitled 'Violence and terror in and by the media' published in *Media, Crisis and Democracy: Mass Communication and the Disruption of the Social Order,*[6] Gerbner, summarising earlier work, believes that television viewing 'cultivates a commonality of perspectives among otherwise different groups with respect to overarching themes and patterns found in many programmes'.

It tends to erode 'traditional differences among divergent social groups. The outlooks of heavy viewers are closer to each other than are the outlooks of comparable groups of light viewers'. This process, as has been noted earlier, Gerbner calls *mainstreaming*. In an article, 'The "mainstreaming" of America: violence profile no. 11',[7] Gerbner, with co-researchers Larry Gross, Michael Morgan and Nancy Signorielli, writes that TV's images 'cultivate the dominant tendencies of our culture's beliefs, ideologies and world view'.

Both Right and Left in the political spectrum are cultivated into a mainstream or centre-stream position, with a latent tendency to drift towards the Right. The 'size' and 'effect' of this cultivation is far less critical 'than the direction of its steady contribution'. Gerbner's view is that exposure to violence on TV cultivates a *mean world syndrome*, a vision of 'life out there' as nasty, brutal and potentially short:

> Humankind [Gerbner writes in 'Violence and Terror in and by the Media'] may have had more bloodthirsty eras but none as filled with images of violence as the present. We are awash in a tide of violent representations such as the world has never seen. There is no escape from the massive infusion of colourful mayhem into the homes and cultural life of ever-larger areas of the world.

DEATHS BY THE DOZEN

In the first *Robocop* movie, of 1987, 32 people bit the dust compared to 81 in the 1990 *Robocop 2*. *Rambo: First Blood* of 1985 despatched 62 compared to *Rambo 3* of 1988, which had a corpse tally of 106. *Die Hard* in 1988 saw the termination of 18 lives but *Die Hard 2* bettered this in 1990 with a score of 264. The record holder, at least for a time, was *Teenage Mutant Ninja Turtles* (1990) with 133 killings per hour. When Oliver Stone's *Natural Born Killers*, taken from a story by Quentin Tarrantino (whose own *Reservoir Dogs* and *Pulp Fiction* didn't spare the gore) was released the *Guardian* film critic Derek Malcolm observed that it 'splatters the screen with as many cliches as corpses and murders truth with over-emphasis'.[8]

Anne Nelson[5] believes that the American networks continue with screen violence because they believe it is popular:

> The networks' audience share has plummeted over the past few years as a result of the massive inroads of cable, satellite and videotape. As commercial network audiences have dropped, so have their standards. In the attempt to recapture a bored, channel-hopping audience that they themselves have disaffected, the networks become ever more shrill, crude and action-orientated.

Yet Gerbner and his colleagues argue in 'The demonstration of power: volence profile no. 10'[9] that 'there is no general correlation between violence and the ratings of comparable programmes aired at the same time'. In other words, violence is not essential for programme profit, so why does it persist, why go on 'drenching nearly every home in the rapidly expanding "free world" with graphic scenes of expertly choreographed brutality'?

Violence travels well

Perceptions, however, often overrule facts. If violence is perceived to be an essential ingredient of popular programming, whether of fiction or 'tabloidised' news, then it will continue to be exploited, and to the damage of serious attempts to address all issues including that of violence. Nelson fears that the use of violence on screen is pre-empting quality programming:

> Hard news, international news, investigative journalism and analytical coverage of economic and social issues are endangered species, supplanted [in the US] by sensational sex and murder stories, 'disease of the week' scare stories and visually striking but meaningless footage of disasters. The current catchphrase of the US newsroom is: 'If it bleeds, it leads'.

She warns of complacence beyond American shores where public service regulation has traditionally resisted the excesses she describes in American film media. As deregulation and privatisation increase globally, public service broadcasters 'who have set standards of quality and suitability for the rest of the industry, will be forced to compete for audiences in new ways'. If these concern cutting production costs, offering instant gratification to the largest possible audiences, then 'new ways 'are also 'old ways':

> Violence [argues Nelson] lends itself to cheap, point-and-shoot productions to fill the caverns of airtime created by the new channels. Violence is visually commanding; as our viewer of the near future spins the 500-channel dial, violent images will register more quickly than talking heads.

> In the increasingly global broadcasting environment, violence travels well, a universal language with minimal lines to dub. The phenomenal box office success of the crudest Arnold Schwarzenegger films from Bangkok to Bratislava illustrate this point.

Affirmation of power

Behind the portrayal of violence is the principle, long enshrined in the Western film among other genres, that without violence (the power of the gun) there can be no order. Violence, cultivation theory argues, serves as a metaphor for control. There is legitimate violence and there is the violence that must be condemned. By demonstrating disorder (weapons in the wrong hands) the media (by showing weapons in the 'right' hands) confirm the rules of order.

If the portrayal of violence is deemed to be not altogether bad for business, it also has its 'up-side' in a political sense. In 'Violence and terror in and by the media' Gerbner says:

A market place is an arena of control by power. Left to itself it tends towards monopoly, or total power. Violence is a demonstration of power. Images of violence project hierarchies of power – gender, racial, sexual, class and national power – that the mass-cultural market place cultivates through its control of dramatic imagery rather than consumer choice or commercial need alone.

Violence stories threaten consensus, disturb consonance. Violence – so long as it is legitimately wielded – is the power that restores states of dissonance to states of consonance, re-establishes equilibrium. Things 'will turn out all right if we are on the right side (or look as if we were)'. Gerbner believes that 'Crime may not pay in the world of dramatic fiction, but violence always does – for the winner'.
He claims:

> the power to define violence and project its lessons, including stigmatisation, demonisation and the selective labelling of terror and terrorists, is the chief cultural requirement for social control. The ability and protected right to mass-produce and discharge it into the common symbolic environment may be a decisive (if unacknowledged) concentration of power-culture in domestic and global policy making.

Media violence is, therefore, 'a political scenario' working on several levels. As a symbolic exercise it is a demonstration of power, of who has it, who uses it, and who loses it.
Who can resist the flood? 'Few countries,' writes Gerbner, 'are willing or able to invest in a cultural policy that does not surrender the socialisation of their children and the future of their language, culture and society to "Market forces"'. Such a failure, in Gerbner's view, is more likely to 'contribute to the resurgence of chauvinism, clericalism and to neo-fascism than to open, diverse and humane democratic cultures around the world'.
'This,' Gerbner is convinced, 'is not an isolated problem that can be addressed by focusing on media violence alone. It is an integral part of a market-dominated system of global cultural commercialism that permeates the mainstream of the common symbolic environment.' The problem is pressing and it is unlikely, in Gerbner's view, to be combatted by individuals or families staking out their own agendas in face of the flood of images of violence:

> Only a new international environmental movement, a cultural environmental movement dedicated to democratic media reform, can do justice to the challenge of violence in and by the media.

Ethnographic position: resistance through appropriation

The Cultivation position is so assertively expressed and is seemingly so all-embracing that one senses the wind of it will sweep away the Ethnographic position altogether. We may even be tempted to take out a subscription to the Society for the Abolition of Mass Communication. But we have good reason to pause. Paradoxically, the more powerfully the Cultivation position is put, the more important it is not to lose sight of the value of ethnographic methods of research and the often revealing findings of that research.

Basically, advocates of the the Ethnographic position regard the cultivationists as stressing encoder-intention rather than measuring, to sufficient depth, decoder-response within contexts of reception. Thus they are in danger of underestimating, or even disregarding, the polysemic possibilities of audience response. Equally, they could be said to be prone to heaping upon media more blame for people's behaviour than mass communication deserves. After all, as far as the allegedly corrupting influence of scenes of violence are concerned, people flocked to witness public executions long before the days of Rambo and Exterminator.

John Fiske in an article 'Television, polysemy and popularity' in *Critical Studies in Mass Communication*[10] celebrates what he terms the 'semiotic democracy' in which people from a multiplex and shifting range of sub-cultures and self-formed groups construct their own meanings within an autonomous cultural economy. His viewpoint may, in the light of the Cultivationist position, seem a romantic one, but it is supported by numerous research studies into reception of media worldwide. What Fiske is saying is that despite the texts and images brought to us by corporately dominated media, and often with a manipulative intention, audiences *appropriate* those texts and images for their own purposes.

We must guard against a number of assumptions about members of audience. First, there is a temptation to view the project of self as something which, once formed, remains constant; amd equally that there is one project of self rather than several. In *Modernity: An Ethnographic Approach*,[11] Daniel Miller, investigating response patterns to media in Trinidad, speaks of 'multifaceted forms of identity' demonstrated by the subjects of his research in their use of imported goods, ideas and traditions.

Two major events on the Trinidad calendar – Carnival and Christmas – exemplify the multifaceted nature of identity: Carnival elicits responses from participants which express individuality through differences of style and self-display. The consumerism as typified by fashion is appropriated for the purposes of imaginative expression.

In contrast, Christmas, essentially an imported tradition, stresses other aspects of identity. In examining the 'Trini' Christmas, Miller identifies a second cultivationist oversimplification concerning *individuality*. The belief that individuality has been defined and nurtured by mass communication and the consumerist ethic is firmly held by cultivationists and interpreted as having the effect of undermining community.

Miller discovered that while Carnival is all about individuality (and is 'most effective' at countering the legacy of Trinidad's colonial past), the Trini Christmas emphasises 'the cult of domesticity and respectability rather than of spontaneity and display' characteristic of Carnival. Furthermore, in contrast to one of the most common assumptions made about consumption, it was found that far from being individualising, the process of consumption represented by Christmas is one of gradual but increasing incorporation of the community.

Miller argues from his research that 'the more knowledge people have of other societies, the more specific their own appears to be'. He says, 'I would argue there are positive consequences for the advent of mass consumption and plural cultures, wealth in materials and in imagery'. He is confident that 'ethnographic exploration of the strategies by which contradiction can be lived and culture appropriated may have some advantages over an endless dialectic of nihilism'.

Miller is saying 'lighten up': people will appropriate the messages and artefacts of consumerism and negotiate their own meanings. He concludes that 'One such advantage,' deriving from ethnography as academic practice, is that it 'goes beyond the abstract solutions of philosophical or political programmes, to encounter these struggles in the compromising pragmatics of everyday life'. Mediated experience does not take over from lived experience, it is absorbed, adopted and transformed by it.

Perchance to dream

A similar argument, that people are more appropriating than appropriated, is put by Colin Campbell in *The Romantic Ethic and the Spirit of Modern Consumerism*.[12] Campbell usefully positions modern trends in consumerist behaviour in a historical context, arguing that modern consumerism does not represent a radical break with the past. For Campbell consumption is less about acquisition (thus fulfilling corporate targets) and more about providing the material for internalised fantasy or daydreaming (thus fulfilling personal agendas). Such responses come under the heading of hedonistic behaviour; hedonism being the doctrine that pleasure is the highest good.

Campbell refers to 'the habit of covert day-dreaming'. He believes that 'individuals do not so much seek satisfaction from products, as pleasure from self-illusory experiences which they construct from their associated meanings'. This is a more complex reading of the relationship between product, image and consumer than that of the Cultivationist position. Campbell argues:

> The visible practice of consumption is thus no more than a small part of a complex pattern of hedonistic behaviour, the majority of which occurs in the imagination of the consumer... the 'real' nature of products is of little consequence compared with what it is possible for consumers to believe about them, and hence their potential for 'dream material'.

The key to understanding 'modern consumerism and, indeed, modern hedonism generally,' writes Campbell is the 'dynamic interaction between illusion and reality'.

There is not the space here to do more that pay cursory attention to this affirmation of audience's power to consume the messages, images and artefacts of the dominant and appropriate them in imaginative ways, but the work of Campbell and other ethnographically sympathetic commentators deserves to be analysed alongside those who fear the all-embracing influence of corporate culture. Campbell declares that 'no two individuals' experience of the product will be the same, just as no two people ever read the same novel'.

Potential for difference

Worries voiced by cultivationists about how electronic media are – in Marshall McLuhan's words – turning the world into a 'global village'[13] must not be lightly dismissed. The expression suggests cultural *homogeneity*, that is, sameness; and the inference is that this homgeneity is another way of describing the 'Americanisation' of cultures worldwide. Ed Turner, Head of News at CNN was not merely showing a talent for metaphor when he stated, 'We are the town-crier in the global village'.[14] He was recognising a partial truth; and declaring an intent.

A book edited by Tony Dowmunt, *Channels of Resistance: Global Television and Local Empowerment*,[15] sets out to prove – as Dowmunt's Introduction explains – that 'there is no single, homogenised global village'. The evidence of the essays published in the volume 'challenges the picture of a single all-inclusive "global village", suggesting instead a diversity of smaller "villages"' all containing 'distinct communities which relate to each other, and to the television available to them, in varied ways'.

Channels of Resistance spotlights a number of cultures worldwide. Contributors examine the ways in which the people in those cultures cope with the challenges posed by Western, particularly American dominance and respond by creating their own media programmes. Dowmunt argues that despite many problems:

> The same thirst for cultural self-expression is evident in the work of indigenous people's organisations around the world: the Inuit in the Canadian Arctic, the Indian peoples in Brazil and Bolivia, Maori in New Zealand, Aboriginal people in Australia and Native American Indians are all engaged with video and television in a variety of ways.

Domestication

Whether peoples are consuming cultural artefacts or actually producing them, a process of *domestication* seems to take place. We have already seen from the work of Tamar Liebes and Elihu Katz (see Chapter 9, Note 26) how people of different cultural orgins read the same texts differently. Research findings by Akiba A. Cohen and Itzhak Roeh published in *Mass Media Effects Across Cultures*[16] indicate that the domestication process – of adapting to local perceptions, needs and requirements – works along a continuum with strong intervention (or domestication) at one end and weak intervention at the other. While fiction can be located at or near the 'weak' intervention end of the continuum, imported news material is at the 'strong' end:

> From the start and throughout all stages of the process [of news broadcasting] there is organised and institutionalised mediation... Although the global market applies pressure toward uniformity, by providing the same material to all its subscribers, the individual stations press for parochialism in terms of language, culture, ideology, politics, and censorship.

Fictional content is subject to less intervention. Obviously imported programmes may have to be translated into the language of the home country and thus the scope for 'reconstruction' of texts is greater than if the original text were screened or broadcast in its original form. Selection and scheduling are other forms of intervention. 'However,' say Cohen and Roeh, referring to imported fiction programmes, 'the main burden of domestication...is borne by the recipients. Viewers intepret the messages according to their predispositions, schemas, repertoires, social locations, and life history.'

The authors believe researchers ought not to view effects from a strong-weak perspective but should take 'a rather "weak" culture-bound "circular" view, where the process of media production and consumption are necessarily contextualised':

> Message analysis, both in fiction and news, must be done in a dynamic contextual framework, taking into account the sociocultural ecology where meaning is produced and reproduced.

Global-local axis

Effects theory all too often seems to accentuate the negative, proffering a cast of characters limited to exploiters and exploited. Yet there are undoubted effects which deserve at least a cautious degree of celebration. One of these is posed by John B. Thompson in *The Media and Modernity: A Social theory of the Media*[17] and which he terms *symbolic distancing*. In a chapter 'The globalisation of communication' Thompson refers to the 'axis of globalised diffusion and localised appropriation' which is a key feature of the electronic age. He believes that as the 'globalisation of communication becomes more intensive and extensive, the significance of this axis increases'.

Consumers of media are both citizens of the world and of their locality: as the global becomes available to us, we render it local – *domesticate* it, and very often make meaning out of the global within our own lived contexts. Thompson writes:

> As symbolic materials circulate on an ever-greater scale, locales become sites where, to an ever-increasing extent, globalised media products are received, interpreted and incorporated into the daily lives of individuals.

Consequently, 'The appropriation of symbolic materials enables individuals to take some distance from the conditions of their day-to-day lives – not literally but symbolically, imaginatively, vicariously'.

Thompson refers to work done by James Lull in his study of the impact of TV in China.[18] For many of the Chinese interviewed by Lull in Shanghai, Beijing, Guangzhou and Xian symbolic distancing was a critical aspect of their lives. Television made available to them new vistas, lifestyles and ways of thinking. Lull quotes a 58-year-old accountant from Shanghai: 'TV gives us a model of the rest of the world'.

Such images of how other people live, says Thompson, 'constitute a resource for individuals to think critically about their own lives and life conditions'. The author does not pretend that this or other forms of appropriation do not have their own problems. Nor does he deny that they can work as much against as for individuals and communities. Localised appropriation of globalised media products is plainly a 'source of tension and political conflict'. However, Thompson seeks to stress that 'given the contextualised character of appropriation, one cannot determine in advance which aspect (or aspects) will be involved in the reception of a particular symbolic form'.

A harnessing of approaches

Advocates of the Ethnographic position would be unlikely to disagree with those of the Cultivationist position on at least one indisputable feature of societies worldwide – unequal distribution of power, influence and resources. As Stuart Hall reminds us, the cultures to which most of us belong are 'structured by power and differences'.[19]

Even one of the most noted pioneers of the ethnographic, micro-focused approach to audience research, David Morley, concedes that the polysemic possibilities of audiences are limited. In a *Journal of Communication* article, 'Active audience theory: pendulums and pitfalls,'[20] Morley writes:

> The power of viewers to reinterpret meanings is hardly equivalent to the discursive power of centralised media institutions to construct the texts that the viewer then interprets, and to imagine otherwise is foolish.

Morley suggests that the rival positions discussed here would benefit from working cooperatively. We no longer subscribe to notions of a 'mechnically imposed dominant ideology', says Morley; influence is more subtle than that, though no less pervasive. Better ways must be found to 'articulate the micro and macro levels of analysis, not to abandon either pole in favour of the other'.

The point is reinforced by Michael Morgan and James Shanahan, writing in *Mass Media Effects Across Cultures*[21] when they say:

> A challenging and fruitful area for future research would be to explore the links between microlevel cultural practices and macrolevel media effects, especially within a comparative framework.

Technology, surveillance and privacy

So far we have explored media as a force for influencing the public in more or less recognisable ways. Few people would deny that the media have a potential hold over us. They are as much a part of our lives as the weather; in fact they even tell us how the weather is going to turn out. Yet we paying attention to *them* is but one side of the coin of mass communication exchange.

Details about ourselves as citizens, voters and consumers have, thanks to computer technology, become a public commodity. Privacy, it could be claimed, met its Waterloo with the introduction of the switchcard, the modern version – some commentators claim – of the notorious Panopticon proposed by Jeremy Bentham (1748–1832), philosopher, political writer and penologist.

The Panopticon – the one that sees all – was Bentham's idea for prison design: a watchtower would be placed in the centre of an encircling building. This would enable the prisoners to be watched at all times without surveillance being obtrusive. The *knowledge* of being watched would, Bentham believed, lead to *self-regulation* on the part of the watched. In other words, they would come to submit willingly to surveillance. For prison, read society.

Each time we draw out money, pay for goods, order tickets for a pop concert using our Panopticon-alias-switchcard, the all-seeing, all-remembering computer eye adds to its already teeming bank of information about us. Surveillance, by state and by commerce, is these days more like the Invisible Man than the shadow-casting Panopticon, but it is no less powerful as people who have suffered from computer error in financial and other arrangements will testify.

Bentham's Panopticon was essentially concerned, as an idea, with correction, that is, turning the wrongdoer into a reformed person living according to pre-established social norms. The Panopticon was a normalising machine; that is, through surveillance and thus force for correction, it both defined the norm and, once the wrongdoer had accepted this, returned him or her to a kind of freedom. What the Panopticon obviously lacked to be effective was technology sophisticated enough to record information on those under surveillance.

Discipline of the norm

With the coming of what the French philosopher Michel Foucault has called the 'technologies of power',[22] Bentham's dream would appear to be closer to realisation. Mark Poster in *The Mode of Information: Poststructuralism and Social Context*[23] comments that 'The population as a whole has long been affixed with numbers and the discipline of the norm has become second nature'. He is of the view that 'Today we have a Superpanopticon, a system of surveillance without walls, windows, towers or guards'.

Yet technological change is only part of the process. Poster fears that the 'populace has been disciplined to surveillance and to participating in the process' willingly, without coercion:

> Social security cards, drivers' licences, credit cards, library cards and the like – the individual must apply for them, have them ready at all times, use them continuously. Each transaction is recorded, encoded and added to databases. Individuals themselves in many cases fill out the forms; they are at once the source of information and the recorder of the information.

Home networking constitutes 'the streamlined culmination of this phenomenon: the consumer, by ordering products through a modem connected to the producer's database, enters data about himself or herself directly into the producer's database in the very act of purchase'. In this sense, the population participates in 'the disciplining and surveillance of themselves as consumers'.

Yet for Poster the new technology, working with and within the Superpanopticon, contributes to a more far-reaching control – the shaping of language itself. He argues that the Superpanopticon 'imposes a new language situation that has unique, disturbing features'. Just as the introduction of telegraphy flattened out the idiosyncracies – the indulgencies of language – in the interest of brevity, so digitalised language 'for all its speed, accuracy and computational power, incurs a tremendous *loss* of data, or better, imposes a strong reading on it'. The subtleties of language, of emphasis, nuance, inflexion are not easily translated into digits:

> Writing accomplishes an infinite expansion of its encoding capacity by the ability of one word to have many meanings. In digital encoding no such capacity exists. In fact digital encoding derives its peculiar strength from the degree to which it restricts meaning and eliminates ambiguity or 'noise'.

Database language in Poster's opinion 'imposes a new language on top of those already existing' and it is 'an impoverished, limited language, one that uses the norm to constitute individuals and define deviants'. Databases reduce life to lists and categories, all of them arbitrary. Our whole lives can be reassembled through bits of computer information – what we read, what we buy, what political party we belong to; and the assembled bits comprise an identikit.

Poster argues that 'the structure or grammar of the database *creates* relationships among pieces of information that do not exist in those relationships outside the database'. In a sense, then, databases actually 'constitute individuals by manipulating relationships between bits of information'. This amounts to what Foucault, in *Discipline and Punish*,[22] terms 'a subtle, calculated technology of subjection'. Poster writes:

> Foucault taught us to read a new form of power by deciphering discourse/practice formations instead of intentions of a subject, or instrumental actions. Such a discourse analysis yields the uncomfortable discovery that the population participates in its own self-constitution of the normalising gaze of the Superpanopticon.

Poster's view may seem a trifle melodramatic until we begin to track through our lives and realise how much is known about us and in so many ways, and that all this information can be used to measure us, predict us, classify us, remind us, deny us while at the same time providing us with little or no information as to what information is kept on us, who keeps it, why, and how it is used.

Audience under surveillance

We are subject to surveillance as citizens and as audience. In an article 'Tracking the audience' by Oscar Gandy Jr in *Questioning Media: A Critical Introduction*,[24] the author remarks how the fragmentation of audience for media, rendered possible by new technology, has resulted in a desperation among programme-makers which has led to two strategies aimed at survival. These Gandy identifies as *rationalisation*, that is 'the pursuit of efficiency in the production, distribution, and sale of goods and services'; and *surveillance* which 'provides the information necessary for greater control'. Increasingly, says Gandy, 'the surveillance of audiences resembles police surveillance of suspected criminals' and people are less and less aware that their behaviour as audience is being measured.

Gandy expresses concern similar to that of Poster:

> Perhaps the greatest threat these computer-based systems for audience assessment represent is their potential to worsen the balance of power between individuals and bureacratic organisations. Personal information streams out of the lives of individuals much like blood out of an open wound, and it collects in pools in the computers of corporations and government bureacracies.

Resistance to the powers of the Superpanopticon is, in Gandy's view, 'almost nonexistent, and what little there is may be seen as passive and defeatist'. While recognising that a 'nearly invisible minority simply refuses to enter the system of records, giving up the convenience of credit cards and acquiring goods and services under assumed names or aliases' he fears that 'to escape the information net means to become a nonperson'. It is a high risk, for one 'maintains privacy through the loss of all else'.

Visibility works two ways

If the idea that all our private affairs are under constant surveillance by the Superpanopticon of computer databases is disturbing, we can take some comfort from the fact that another form of 'visibility' encompasses the Superpanopticonists themselves. Politicians, civil servants, business people whose activities have traditionally been shielded from public gaze are now more *visible* to the public than ever before. Once again we turn to John Thompson to edge us a step back from the pessimism which seems a professional hazard of the media critic.

In *The Media and Modernity* he calls into question the notion of the modern Panopticon:

> Whereas the Panopticon renders many people visible to a few and enables power to be exercised over the many by subjecting them to a state of permanent visibility, the development of communication media provides a means by which many people can gather information about a few and, at the same time, a few can appear before many; thanks to the media, it is primarily those who exercise power, rather than those over whom power is exercised, who are subjected to a certain kind of visibility.

We as the public may, through the computer data systems which threaten our privacy, feel vulnerable, but, Thompson believes, the visibility made possible by communication media makes it 'more difficult for those who exercise political power to do so secretively, furtively, behind closed doors'. What Thompson refers to as the 'uncontrollable character of mediated visibility' gives rise to 'a new kind of *fragility* in the political sphere'.

Scandal and sleaze bedeck the front pages of the press: on our TV screens we watch our leaders wriggle and squirm. Such visibility does not further conditions which encourage decisive political leadership. On the contrary, Thompson worries, such conditions 'may lead to weakened government and political paralysis, and which may nourish the suspicion and cynicism which many people feel towards politicians and political institutions'.

Equally they are the conditions which could provide 'fertile ground for the growth of a new kind of demagoguery [mob leadership]... rooted in part in a pervasive sense of disaffection and distrust'. In such circumstances, of course, the notion of the Panopticon/Superpanopticon could make a vengeful comeback. Bentham's model prison/society, however, relied for its success on a community being unaware that it is being watched; and incapable of counteracting surveillance. Today the keys to information control no longer hang on the belt of the jailer: they are in code and there are potentially as many code-breakers (or code-makers) as there are computers, a point which will be returned to in Chapter 11.

Strictly limited

The Autumn 1993 edition of the *Journal of Communication*, containing Part 2 of a survey entitled 'The future of the field', published contributions made in response to a call for views on media effects as 'the perennial black box of communications research'. Herbert J. Gans of Columbia University in 'Re-opening the Black Box: toward a limited effect theory' poses a number of *limiting factors* and argues how difficult it is to be certain when and how effects have taken place.

He contends that much media content 'goes in one eye or ear and out the other, at least judging by how well people remember commercials or the names of high federal officials'. Gans' case is basically that while researchers have had plenty of access to the producers of media, and know a lot about media objectives and media production, they know far less about the response patterns of audience. They remain largely ignorant of:

> the processes by which people choose what to consume in the various media; how they consume it, with what levels of comprehension, attention, and intensity of effect; what, if anything, they talk about while using the media at home; whether and how their uses of various media connect to other aspects of their lives – and which; and what kind of traces, if any, these media leave in their psyches and lives, and for how long.

Gans also makes the useful point that media researchers, possessing more than average interest in the media, may as a result 'be more affected by the media than anyone else, and it is possible that they project the effect on the "normal" consumers of media content'. The case is being made for the ethnographic approach to audience research. It is slow, Gans argues, and expensive; but essential, for:

> while content analysis can report what analysts see in the content, and sample surveys, focus groups, and laboratory experiments can result in neat, bounded answers, these all maintain some distance from people and from the lived world of media use.

Gans concludes:

> Until researchers enter and understand that world sufficiently, and provide a bedrock of interview and enthnographic findings, media researchers cannot judge the validity and reliability of the more distanced methods. Nor can they begin to develop a proper assessment of the true effects of the media.

SUMMARY

This chapter has briefly examined the rival claims concerning media effects of two 'positions' on the strong-effect/weak-effect spectrum, the Cultivation position and the Ethnographic position. 'Cultivationists' such as George Gerbner and his team of researchers are of the view that in an age in which culture is dominated by big business, subject to corporatisation, audiences for television in particular are affected according to the amount of TV they watch.

The Ethnographic position, while acknowledging the assembled powers of media instititutions to dominate mass communication – by setting the agendas, for example, by emphasising the criteria of consumerism and by legitimising violence by portraying it as a necessary adjunct to authority – regards audience as resistive and selective.

The chapter also touches upon less overt influences exerted in the Information Age: an alternative tag of contemporary life is the Surveillance Society and comparison is made between Jeremy Bentham's notion of the Panopticon and the ubiquitous switchcard. Some critics believe that computer surveillance is inexorably destroying privacy, while Mark Poster fears that digitalisation might not only help create a Superpanopticon, it will have a profound effect upon the nature of language itself. In contrast the point is made that communication media have rendered people in authority more 'visible' than ever before.

These are themes the student of media will need to follow up, question, debate and research, for the effects of media on audience will always be of headline interest to the media itself, to media analysts and to all those who have any interest in public opinion, including government and the great institutions which operate nationally and internationally. Questions concerning effect draw attention to such major issues as media imperialism, the manufacture of consent, the upholding and maintenance of hegemony, deviance definition, the legitimisation of violence and the undermining of national sovereignty.

What needs to be avoided is a 'narrowcast' approach focusing solely on media-encoding/audience-decoding: attention must be paid to broader contexts of influence. As Colleen Roach summarises the matter in *Communication and Culture in War and Peace*,[25] 'it is no longer possible to speak of the power of the media without also referring to the power of culture'. This chapter concludes with a round-up of some of the theories of effect which readers will encounter in their studies; and may recognise from personal observation and experience.

A BRIEF ABC OF PERCEIVED EFFECTS

Agenda-setting effect

The media rank events in a hierarchy of importance; encouraging people not so much what to think but what to think about.

Alienation effect

Notion that the mass character of media creates in audiences feelings of isolation; disengagement from membership of the community and therefore a sense of alienation, or estrangement, from society's values.

Amplification effect

By giving intensive cover to certain stories and issues, their importance is amplified in importance.

Boomerang effect

When media coverage backfires and achieves contrary responses or reactions from the public than those desired by the media.

Catharsis effect

The word *catharsis* comes from the Greek, meaning 'purification' or 'purgation'. Today it is defined as emotional release. We watch a play, film or TV drama and its humour, tragedy or violence triggers release of our emotions. Some commentators believe that watching screen violence has a cathartic effect. It releases tensions which in some circumstances might be expressed through real violence. In other words, fictionalised violence may head-off real violent behaviour.

Cognitive complexity effect

Media contribute to the complex mental awarenesses we have of our environment and the schemata with which we interpret that environment.

Confirming effect

What we expect or suspect concerning realities, the media confirm as true.

Copy-cat effect

What people experience through the media may stimulate copy-cat behaviour; acts of individual violence, for example, or street rioting.

continued

Desensitising effect

Over-exposure to violence or suffering might make us 'hardened' to what we see; blasé even. This has been related to what has been termed 'compassion fatigue'.

Displacement effect

This happens between media; for example the arrival of television, while not eclipsing radio certainly displaced it, shifting it towards the margins of audience use in comparison with its former dominant position.

Distraction effect

Usually relates to the ways in which the media often distract public attention from important issues by concentrating on other, usually more entertaining stories.

Enlargement effect

Capacity to expand people's knowledge and system of beliefs.

Hastening effect

When media coverage of events hastens the development of those events and responses to them, usually on the part of those in authority. Media publicity on health hazards may hasten government legislation.

Inoculation effect

Flu jabs inject a mild dose of the flu virus into the bloodstream thereby serving to built up resistance to contagion; the same goes for the media 'bug'.

Mainstreaming effect

Part of Cultivation theory; the nature of media coverage tends to create a convergence of political attitudes towards a mainstream position, but one which drifts rightwards. Coverage *blurs*, *blends* otherwise divergent groups and then *bends* the mainstream 'in the direction of the medium's interests in profit, populist politics and power'.[26]

continued

Narcoticising dysfunction effect

The media has the effect of drugging people, leading to mass apathy and general passivity.[27]

No previous knowledge effect

Where audience is uninformed about matters it is more likely to believe what the media tell them.

Reciprocal effect

Coverage affects and changes the nature of what is covered. A game such as darts, traditionally a bar-room game to accompany the pints, has through TV coverage become a spectator sport; and particularly suited to television. Equally, a party political conference, traditionally an occasion for chewing the political fat and permitting ordinary party members to get things off their chests is – once covered by TV – turned into a political spectacle governed by propriety and propagandist imagery.[28]

Reinforcement effect

Opinions, attitudes, beliefs, prejudices are deemed more likely to be reinforced than changed by media coverage.

Spill-over effect

When people outside the intended target audience are affected by the communication.

Third-person effect

Perception of effects on 'others'; thus fears about the effects of the portrayal of violence relate for example to children or teenagers rather than those actually doing the perceiving.

Trivialising effect

Charge made against television that it trivialises most of the matters it deals with out of a need to retain audience attention.

KEY TERMS

cultivation position, ethnographic position ■ intervening variables
significant others ■ dissonance, consonance ■ mainstreaming
image politics ■ polysemy (many meanings) ■ semiotic democracy
symbolic invasion ■ appropriation ■ domestication
surveillance society ■ panopticon, superpanopticon ■ rationalisation
symbolic distancing ■ visibility

=========================== **SUGGESTED ACTIVITIES** ===========================

1. Discussion
   (a) What do you consider to be the key powers of media?
   (b) Examine with examples what might be described as 'ideologies of entertainment'. How might entertainment be arguably more influential in terms of audience perceptions and attitudes, than information or education?
   (c) How have the media helped and hindered social and ethnic equality?
   (d) Discuss the possibilities of audience resistance to media influence.

2. You are part of a small publicity firm which has been asked by local government to recommend a communications strategy that will *effect* changes in public attitudes. Select one of the themes listed below and draw up such a strategy. Prepare a treatment – a recommendation – in which each media form is to be used to maximum effect.

Themes

- Community acceptance of new immigrants.
- Greater tolerance in the workplace and in social contexts of sufferers from AIDS.
- The building of a new sports stadium and leisure park on a green site of outstanding natural beauty. How should the local authority go about creating a positive public response to their plans?

3. Conduct a survey of members of the public asking two questions: what book, films, plays, pieces of music, radio or TV programmes have a) made you think differently and b) act differently? A third question should be waiting in the wings – about *feeling* differently about things; and a fourth might be, and how long did the effect last?

4. Draw up a list of the *types* of violence we see daily on cinema or TV screens and the *contexts* in which that violence takes place. Give each type which you identify a classifying title. What are the criteria which seem to operate within those classifications?

Arising from your analysis, what recommendations would you make to a panel of the wise and the good empowered to consider censoring screen violence more rigorously than it has been censored in recent years?

NOW READ ON

The student of media is too familiar with sensationalist headlines not to be affected, even modestly, with the 'whiff' of strong effects theory. It is dramatic (sometimes melodramatic) and often has headline quality in its own right, so a cautionary volume by Guy Cumberbatch and Dennis Howlett is recommended as initial reading: *A Measure of Uncertainty: The Effects of the Mass Media* (UK: Broadcasting Standards Council/John Libbey, 1989). A recent contribution to the study of audience perceptions of violence on TV is an article by Ingo Sander in the *European Journal of Communication*, March 1997, 'How violent is TV violence? An empirical investigation of factors influencing viewers' perceptions of TV violence', drawn from Sander's master's thesis for the Ohio State University. Try also *Ill-effects: The Media Violence Debate* (UK: Routledge, 1997) edited by Julian Petley.

A broad view of the whole field of effects research is offered by Shearon A. Lowery and Melvyn L. DeFleur in *Milestones in Mass Communication Research: Media Effects* (US: Longman, 1995).

If readers have not yet read any Raymond Williams this is a timely moment to tune in to the work of this highly influential British academic. *Television, Technology and Cultural Forms* (UK: Fontana, 1974) will feature on most course booklists.

The following volumes cover a range of perspectives on effect:
The Power of the Image: Essays on Representation and Sexuality by Annette Kuhn (UK: Routledge, 1985); *Impacts and Influences: Essays on Media Power in the Twentieth Century* edited by James Curran, Anthony Smith and Pauline Wingate (UK: Methuen, 1987); *Impact of Mass Media* by Ray Eldon and Carol Reuss (UK: Longman, 1988) and *Why Viewers Watch: A Reappraisal of Television's Effects* by Jib Fowles (US: Sage, 1992).

For studies in global effects, try *Media Effects Across Cultures* (see Note 16), *Media, Communication, Culture: A Global Approach* by James Lull (UK: Polity Press, 1994); *Undoing Culture: Globalisation, Postmodernism and Identity* by Mike Featherstone (1995) and Hamid Mowlana's *Global Communication in Transition* (1996), both from Sage. For broad contextual pictures, see Samuel P. Huntington's *The Clash of Civilisations And The Remaking of the World Order* (US: Simon & Shuster, 1997) and *World Communication: Disempowerment and Self-empowerment* (UK: Zed Books, 1996) by Cees Hamelink.

11 Cyberspace Calling?

AIMS

- To present a brief overview of the possibilities, particularly for research, global and interactive, presented by the Internet.
- To outline the claims made by enthusiasts for the Net in relation to the opening of new frontiers of communication.
- To temper visions of revolutionary change with the caution that new technology is as likely to be adapted to old habits as create new ones.
- To discuss issues concerning the nature and impact of simulated, or Virtual Reality.

Nowhere, except in dreams, have reality and fantasy contended for our attention than 'on the Net'. This chapter acknowledges the potential for imaginative, if not fantastic, surfing of the Net while at the same time confirming for the student of communication, and indeed the media practitioner, the remarkable research opportunities the Internet and its myriad associated services provide.

For students and journalists of today and tomorrow the Net is potentially the college library or the newpaper's clippings files multiplied several-fold in volume of information and speed of retrieval.

Cyberspace for the student researcher is chiefly to be entered and left for the purposes of gathering or exchanging information, and as a means of contacting fellow researchers in the field. For others cyberspace is 'where things are at', an alternative reality, the psycho-socio-cultural context of the future: only the 'real' world is 'virtual'.

In Chapter 10 reference was made to the ongoing debate over strong/weak effects; a similar debate is taking place over the power cyberlife may have over our real lives, cybercommunities over real communities, cybernature over real nature. Our surfboard is at the ready; and fear not, with cybersurf there is no danger of getting wet.

Global opportunities: research and the Internet

The word 'cyberspace' seems to have been first used by William Gibson in his novel *Neuromancers* published in America by Ace Books in 1984, though to locate the origin of cybernetics – the study of feedback systems – we need to go back as far as 1949 to Norbert Weiner's *Cybernetics; or Control and Communication in the Animal and the Machine*.[1] Gibson describes cyberspace as 'a consensual hallucination... [People are] creating a world. It's not really a place, it's not really space. It's notional space'.

In this notional space we can all be cybernauts, potentially free agents who by pressing computer keys, by grace of a modem and telephone line, can take off into the stratosphere of infinite knowledge instantly accessed. To borrow the words from the title of J. C. Herz's book, we can exhilaratingly surf on the Internet.[2] From a sitting position we can talk to the world: we can e-mail the president of the United States; we can drop an e-line to Bill Gates, one of the richest men on earth, Lord of Microsoft; and, of course, we can play mesmerising computer games such as *Dungeons and Dragons*, *Mortal Kombat* or *Comanche Maximum Overkill*.

The Internet, with its associates and rivals, offers to the computer-explorer a new future which is with us now for a monthly rental less than that of a TV set. I may have to wait half-an-hour for a bus to get me to work but via the modem I can be exchanging data with Sleepless in Seattle within seconds, checking the strength of the market in Tokyo or booking myself a holiday for two in the Carribean.

I can 'speak' with the Library of Congress or put out an SOS on the network for information, advice, contacts or e-friends. Boundaries of time and space suddenly mean nothing. I can 'visit' by 'image' every country on earth (at least those 'imaged' through the Net); I can obtain information from the Net about my own contexts – local or national, when other sources are closed to me, either through regulation or bureacratic decision.

They are dumping some sort of toxic waste just down the road – is it dangerous? At the council offices, they're cagey. I tune into the Net, give the details of the waste: someone somewhere will be able to identify it or direct me to where I can find the data I want; and somewhere too there will be a group of protesters who have had similar toxins dumped outside their door.

Interactivity

Students of media communication, concerned as they are for most of their work with developments and issues which are recent and increasingly global in significance, can use the Net to find the very latest information. Most of the sources quoted in this book have been drawn from the 'old' technology of print publication. I have been unable, because of the limitations of this one-way mode of communication of books, periodicals and academic papers, to 'talk' with the experts I have quoted; unable to check with them what their very latest ideas are, what new perspectives their latest research has turned up.

With the assistance of the Net feedback becomes possible; interaction a very likely bonus. The student preparing an essay or a dissertation on some aspect of violence in the media can now go direct, as it were, to the horse's mouth, and make on-line enquiries with scholars throughout the world.

Specificity

Perhaps the Net's most precious gift to the student researcher is its capacity to be specific: you wish to look up an exact item within a particular field of information. The dictionaries and reference books have given you a modest start but to acquire the amount of information you need you would have to search many volumes, some of them either difficult or impossible to obtain; and always there is the critical timelag: you have a deadline to meet.

Your problem might not be scarcity of information but too much of it. Where do you start and how do you reduce the vast information available to the specific requirements of your research task? In each case the key is *specificity*. We may not require, for example, access to the whole gamut of research findings on the perceived effects of screen violence on audience. Our interest may stress particular types of violence and modes of their portrayal in relation to segments of audience.

By being fed with key words, the computer does our selecting for us and at a speed unmatched by any other research method. Tim Miller in an article 'The database revolution' in the *Columbia Journalism Review*[3] cites an example of the advantage the database has over a publication:

> Take for example, *Who's Who in America*. In the print version each word in the two volume set is bound to one place only on a sheet of paper; the 75,000 biographies are arranged alphabetically.

> Thus we can find Caspar Weinburger in the Ws. In the computerised version, by way of contrast, each word swims in a digital soup ready to be dipped out in accordance with almost any criterion the researcher wants to specify.

'Digital soup' is one of the more memorable metaphors to be found in the steamy kitchen in which the media researcher and the journalist have to work. Miller goes on to prove the point of specificity:

> ... last year, when librarians at the *San Francisco Chronicle* wanted to find members of the secretive, men-only Bohemian Club, they went to the on-line version of *Who's Who* offered by Dialog Information Services, a vendor of more than 300 data bases. Within seconds the computer located the word 'Bohemian' each time it appeared in an entry. Among the club members found: Secretary of Defense Caspar Weinburger.

> A Search of this kind in the print version of *Who's Who* would have taken a reporter approximately eight years, not counting coffee breaks.

Sometimes of course specificity is not necessarily the key to research. The Net's facility of providing Bulletin Boards allows researchers to put out general calls for help and assistance. Two of my own students were preparing an international media profile on the press in Kenya. They soon discovered the predominant ethnocentricity of libraries and traditional databases. Information on our own press is vast but on that of Africa as a whole it was found to be meagre and largely out of date. An SOS on the Net prompted informative correspondents, including a Kenyan journalist.

It is not only the abundance of available information which can threaten to be overwhelming, but its diversity. Tom Koch in *Journalism in the 21st Century: Online Information, Electronic Databases and the News*[4] summarises how the formidable can become manageable:

> To search only newspapers for stories on, say addiction and habituation would, using traditional methods, requires months. To absorb the technical literature on the causes of drug abuse might require weeks. The legal issues involved would demand weeks more for those unused to the very specific bibliographic system used in traditional law libraries.

> The mass of potential data is overwhelming. But the fears of some that computerised information would merely overwhelm the writer with extraneous information have been balanced by the system's inherent capability to tailor information retrieval to very specific requests.

For the student of media, and for the student of media with an eye on a professional future in journalism, this 'inherent capability' may be seen as a prime feature in the future accessing and management of information. The on-line mode potentially liberates the researcher from traditional, usually restricted and often highly controlled sources of information while at the same time offering a plurality of sources manageable through specificity.

INFORMAL INFORMATION SOURCES

SIGS (Special Interest Groups) are systems of data storage and communication in which individuals sharing interest in or concern about a specific subject area can exchange information, or question others with expertise in that area, hold 'on-line conferences' and store files of stories, programs or graphics for use by the forum's membership...

Each interest group has a specific electronic area on the service and a specific area within the CompuServe computers that includes a 'library' for longer files a member may wish to have stored in a digital form for future communal use. There is also a 'message board' on which members post comments or statements for others to read and comment on at some future time and a Citizens' Band radio-like electronic available for real-time discussion should two or more members wish to use their computer terminals to communicate directly with other members of the group.

Finally, any SIG may host a 'conference' in which a guest (usually an authority in the field) will be available to answer questions as forum members plug into the system on their computer keyboards.

Tom Koch[4]

Cybervisions: new frontiers, new worlds

The notion of a 'new world' awaiting new-age exploration is a dominant metaphor among Net enthusiasts and commercial enterprises alike. A Boston software computer firm has claimed in its advertising, 'Sir Francis Drake was knighted for what we do every day… The spirit of exploration is alive at The Computer Merchant'.[5] Imagination, in the realm of simulated or *virtual reality*, recognises no limits, as Henry Rheingold, an apostle of the Net, states in *Virtual Reality*.[6] The author speaks of:

> my own odyssey to the outposts of a new scientific frontier… and an advanced glimpse of a possible new world in which reality itself might become a manufactured and metered commodity.

The attraction seems to be that the Net offers us psychological space which both in mental and physical terms seems in the real world to be more and more restricted. In a conversation between two American academics, Henry Jenkins and Mary Fuller, published in *CyberSociety: Computer Mediated Communication and Community*,[7] Jenkins is of the opinion that the fervour with which many Americans have taken to the Net and to new frontier-type virtual reality games, is a response 'to our contemporary sense of America as oversettled, overly familiar and overpopulated'.

Jenkins argues that space is the organising principle of computer games: a succession of new spaces, reached and conquered by skill and know-how, determine rather than are determined by the narrative. This view tunes in to Michel De Certeau's assertion in *The Practice of Everyday Life*[8] that 'Every story is a travel story – a spatial practice'.

The Jenkins-Fuller dialogue draws connections between the visions and practices of Renaissance explorers, and the narratives written by them and about them, and the New World exploration of Nintendo games. Jenkins says:

> Our cultural need for narrative can be linked to our search for believable, memorable, and primitive spaces, and stories are told to account for our current possession or desire for territory.

Computer games of the Nintendo variety are, believes Jenkins, a 'playground for our world-weary imagination'. He adds:

> Nintendo takes children and their own needs to master their social space and turns them into virtual colonists driven by a desire to master and control digital space.

These 'spatial stories' as De Certeau calls them, are therefore part of a long tradition of storytelling no doubt originating long before the epic journeying of Odysseus recounted by the blind poet, Homer. The intriguing irony, Jenkins points out, is that it is Japanese games creators and manufacturers, keying in to essentially Western – American – tales, embellishing them with 'eye candy' (graphics to dazzle 'world-weary imagination') who are narrating stories of modern-age exploration and colonisation.

In such cases, who is doing what and to whom? Henry Jenkins concludes an intriguing exchange by asking:

Does Nintendo's recycling of the myth of the American New World, combined with its own indigenous myths of global conquests and empire building, represent Asia's absorption of our national imagery, or does it participate in a dialogic relationship with the West, an intermixing of different cultural traditions that insures their broader circulation and consumption?

Such a question prompts another, 'In this new rediscovery of the New World, who is coloniser and who the colonist?'

Bullets and bulletins

In Chapter 8 research was classified as being far more than an academic exercise: it may prove instrumental in the process of change. Equally, electronic networking has the capability to mobilise information and ideas in the cause of change. The Net is a potentially powerful agent for the assertion of, and struggle for, civil rights, cultural identity and political independence, bypassing traditional local and national boundaries and controls.

A story in the British *Independent* (7 March 1995), written by Leonard Doyle, is headed 'Rebels use Internet to argue case'. In Mexico the Zapatista National Liberation Army was continuing revolution against what it saw as government tyranny in the age-old way, waging war from jungle hideouts and using rusty old rifles. But they had a new weapon – the laptop computer; and a new battleground – cyberspace. Doyle writes:

> Marcos, the Mexican rebel leader, carries a laptop computer in a backpack and plugs the machine into the cigarette-lighter of a pick-up truck before tapping out his now famous communiqués. Copied onto floppy disks the statements are taken by courier to supporters who transmit them by telephone to computer bulletin boards.

Doyle quotes a rebel spokesman as saying, 'What governments should really fear is a communications expert'. Suddenly the events within one country are potentially and instantly common knowledge. Networks of sympathisers across the nation, across the continent and across the globe can transmit essential information and in turn transform that information into 'bullets' which at the very least alert the many to the abuses of the few.

When Mexican president Ernesto Zedillo launched a military offensive aimed at capturing Marcos, an 'urgent action' alert was transmitted to sympathisers worldwide, and this included the president's own fax number and that of his interior minister. Doyle again:

> As a result of the campaign the president's fax machine either burnt out or was switched off according to Mariclaire Acosta, head of a Mexican human rights group.

Doyle refers to Harry Cleaver of the University of Texas at Austin. Cleaver had become a key link in the rebels' information chain. In 1994 he used hundreds of people linked by Internet to organise the translation of the book *Zapististas! Documents of the New Mexican Revolution*; it was completed in three weeks.

Cyberspace and chips

The claim that the Net is a political force, one that might further the cause of civil liberties across national boundaries, was given top-of-the-agenda confirmation in the first edition of *Wired UK* published in March 1995. On the cover was a picture of Tom Paine (1737–1809) and a resounding quotation from this great English advocate of human rights: 'We have it in our power to begin the world over again'.

Paine is awarded the cyberaccolade of 'Digital Revolutionary'. The creative director of the magazine, Tony Ageh, talked to Jim McClellan of the *Observer*,[9] saying:

> The key word here is 'world'. It's not just about computers connected to telephones. It's about a new way of thinking. It's now no longer about who you know. It's about what you know. In a small period of time the window's been blown open. Everything's up for grabs. What we are doing is pulling people in and saying 'get a piece of this!'

Ageh echoes the sentiments of Michael Benedikt in *Cyberspace: Some Proposals*[10] when he writes, 'We are contemplating a new world'. In fact, the 'new world' of *Wired UK* survived only till March 1997 when the magazine ceased publication. The ideas of Ageh and Benedikt are the stuff of romance, at once challenging cynics while making them extra cautious. What some commentators claim is happening is that control, traditionally exercised by governments and powerful groups such as the transnational corporations, is shifting away from centres to peripheries, from organisations to individuals forming their own, hierarchy-free associations.

Certainly there is plenty of evidence that in some countries of the world the electronic highway is perceived as a threat to hierarchy and authority; and hegemony itself is undermined. In India there are huge licence fees for bulletin board owners. In Iran, Saudi Arabia, Qatar and Indonesia unauthorised import of satellite dishes is a criminal offence punishable by prohibitive fines.

In Hong Kong in March 1995 police raided seven of the eight local Internet providers and shut them down, varyingly claiming that they were unlicenced or guilty of software piracy. In 1996 Singapore's Minister of Information and the Arts announced that Internet service providers and content producers would in future require licences. In Laos the Internet is banned altogether.

The open frontiers and new worlds of exploration made possible by the Net have prompted people in authority to respond to the technology of openness with the technology of closure, or censorship. In Chapter 10 mention was made of the Superpanopticon, the all-seeing one, electronic version of Jeremy Bentham's Panopticon. In recognition of the fact that in computer technology small is beautiful, the Superpanopticon has taken the form of the so-called clipper chip.

Fitted into every new computer – the initial intention of the United States government – the chip would, in the words of Howard Lake reporting in *Amnesty* magazine[11] on human rights and networking, 'allow, by means of an electronic back-door, government agencies to snoop on data passing into and out of that computer'.

Mercifully the White House shelved such plans, at least partly as a result of over 45 000 'virtual' signatures of protest from cybernauts across the globe. That was the good news. The bad news was that with the V (for violence) chip, the micro-sized Superpanopticon was to have a screen future with television.

In February 1996 President Bill Clinton signed a Telecommunications Act requiring that from 1998 all TV sets with a screen size of 13 inches and more must be fitted with V-chips. In the same month the European parliament voted for a similar measure for every TV set to be sold in the European community. These far-reaching exercises in electronic control have largely gone unchallenged in the national media, possibly because violence on TV, while tolerated, has few public advocates and because the V-chip purports to be a device confined to parental control of the viewing habits of their children.

Very laudable, but the obvious dangers are twofold: the V-chip will be capable of censoring more than violence; and, with the convergence of technologies, TV sets are being linked to modem and telephone line so that the spy in the screen will also be the spy on the wires. Of course while *encryption* – 'scrambler-coding' to protect unwanted intrusions upon data – becomes more sophisticated and more in demand as the Net widens, so does the capacity of cybernauts to navigate new routes through regulation and control, whether this is political, economic, scientific or technological in nature.

Governments, however, are unlikely to rest easy at the prospect of people other than themselves possessing data security, especially their citizens. In a tome which is itself a heady voyage into cybergraphics, *Imagology: Media Philosophy,*[12] Mark C. Taylor and Esa Saarinen suggest that we make the best of cyberfreedoms while we may:

> Who writes the rules and establishes the laws that govern cyberspace? So far, the regulations in this strange world are surprisingly few. Entering cyberspace is the closest we can come to returning to the Wild West. Console Cowboys roam ranges that seem to extend forever. But as feuds break out, fences are built, cut and rebuilt. Eventually, governments will step in and mess up everything. The wilderness never lasts long – you had better enjoy it before it disappears.

Personal encounters in cyberspace

Internet and related cyberspace information services are, it would seem, creating a new kind of population, dedicated to data exchange, 'chat-lining' and bulletin boarding, conscious of a freedom of 'movement' through global contact which is all the more amazing when the communicator/receiver need not move from the magic screen, except occasionally to reposition his or her weight from one buttock to the other.

There are varying claims as to the size of the population of cyberspace using the World Wide Web, Cix (Compulink Information Exchange), The Well (Whole Earth 'lectronic Link) or CompuServe with its 2000 different services. User-promoters estimate tens of millions, cynics believe that such a claim is an exaggeration.

It is easy to work up a head of steam, for or against, the potentialities of cyberspace as a socio-cultural environment. Let us take as an example the availability of seemingly limitless helplines: you have a problem, a concern – about illness, sexual abuse, stuttering; your marriage is heading for the rocks; you want to form a self-help group across cyberspace? Then post your message, day or night. Global counselling is only a finger-touch away.

In a sense a new 'nation' is in the offing, or at least an electronic city, a 'Netropolis' as Christine McGourty, technology correspondent of the *Daily Telegraph* puts it in an article, 'Highway to the global Netropolis'.[13] And, as in every large city, McGourty recognises, there is the risk of crime as well as the benefits of community.

As we sit sipping an uneloctronic cup of coffee in cybercafés in London, Lisbon, Lahore or LA, and contemplate making use of the on-site facility to connect with Tomsk, Tahiti or Tasmania, we may wish to ponder on notions of superhighway robbery, of system tampering – called hacking – and the vast possibilities the 'openness' of the Net allows for messages of hate as well as for peace and succour.

In the 'good, the bad and the ugly' scenario, Sadie Plant is an optimist as a *Guardian* public lives article 'Deadlier than the e-mail' by Linda Grant makes plain.[14] At the time of the interview a lecturer in Cultural Studies at the University of Birmingham, Plant is described as a 'cyberfeminist'. She challenges the assumption that computers (with their buttons, wires and technical jargon) are male territory.

Man, woman or dragon?

The computer, like weaving, in which women have traditionally always excelled (Freud declared that women had invented nothing – except weaving), is female, 'instinctive' and 'intuitive to use'. Says Plant, 'There's something almost uncanny in the way it's in tune with the way your mind works'. She believes that computers have the potential for dismantling patriarchal structures in society and existing gender relations.

For example, she points out the large number of men who key into the Net as women: is this a move not only to reshape knowledge and the channels of communication but also to experiment with gender exchange? Plant states:

> The classic explanation [of why men log on the network as women] is that it's a way of accessing female talk. But I think there's something a lot more interesting going on. There was a recent experiment done with a new virtual space in which you could choose to be male, female or a dragon. There were five men and five women to start with in the real world and when they'd made their choices, it turned out there were nine women and one dragon.

Plant's conclusion seems to be that in the particular environment in which the exchange was taking place males were unhappy with their maleness. She concedes that what is happening here might be 'just men playing around' and that this does not alter existing power structures, existing partriarchy, but the trend is there:

> 'The Net' has been developed in a piecemeal way and that shift is closely related to the philosophical underpinnings of patriarchy and gender relations. The masculine has associated itself with centralised control and women and machines in the past

have had a function through the top-controlling function of the male. We are moving away from that to a creeping, growing-from-the-bottom, grassroots network notion, which in itself is a feminist notion, of women organising themselves away from these top-down power structures.

While Sadie Plant confesses a glimmer of doubt concerning a cyberworld equally divided between men and women, Cheris Kramarae, in 'A backstage critique of virtual reality' in *CyberSociety: Computer Mediated Communication and Community*[15] is several shades more cynical about the egalitarianism of the simulated society.

Boyland?

Kramarae argues that 'Cyberspace, like earthspace, is not developed as a viable place for women'. She talks about 'malestream publications and other forums' and views 'cybersex' as something where game, play and match will continue to reflect sexist attitudes and behaviour.

She notes how in many virtual reality games the essential aim of winning is control; and in some virtual realty scenarios 'a man may create his ideal female and then shape her responses at will'. 'Sex will (has?) become another sport,' worries Kramarae, 'like hunting and shooting tanks and hostile aliens'. She quotes Mike Saenz who created *MacPlaymate* for the Apple Macintosh computer:

> I have a very silly idea for a product called Strip Teacher. She goes 'Tell me the name of the thirteenth president of the United States and I'll show you my tits'.

Kramarae comments, 'I'll venture that he's not thinking of this product as primarily an educational experience'; and her position is backed up by J.C. Herz in *Surfing the Internet*[2] who talks about her own experience of being 'chatted up' in cyberspace. Herz believes that the Net 'is more saloon than salon':

> Not too many women in these parts, scant discussion of philosophy and impressionist paintings, and no tea and sandwiches: Someone should nail up a sign 'Now entering the Net. Welcome to Boyland'.

In cyberspace, nothing need be what it seems or claims to be. Men log on as women, women log on as men: gender becomes cyberconfused. Herz says:

> Some of the Net dudes are actually dudettes. And vice versa. In fact, there's so much gender confusion on the Net that paranoia surrounds anyone claiming to be female. Consequently women are sometimes treated like lab specimens of alien life, subject to a torrent of prurient 'scientific' inquiries.

Digital mating

Plainly postings in cyberspace are far from exclusively those of information exchange, addressing only cognitive needs: the *affective domain*, of feelings, senses, relationships, is being energetically cultivated. Alix Kirsta in the UK's *Mail on Sunday*[16] writes of love on the Internet:

In the intimate atmosphere of a Soho café a romance is blossoming. Outside the rain is falling. But inside the lights are dim, the cappuccino steaming and the conversation romantic. She murmurs her love for him and he responds. They might be inches apart, their hands touching across the table. But they are not. Because while she is in London, he is in New York. And their sweet nothings are not whispered into the ear but relayed through the computer network linking millions of people worldwide – the Internet.

The Net, says Kirsta, has blossomed into a global unofficial dating agency combining the old-fashioned romance of the love letter with an 'anonymous high-tech world': 'it means there's no embarrassment if you are rejected – and you have thousands of potential partners'. For women (and men too) the Net offers 'anonymity, which opens the way to romantic – even erotic – experiences of a kind normally impossible because of the risks'.

Kirsta's story begins at this point to lose a touch of its romancing. She quotes Dr Avodah Offit, New York's first psychiatrist specialising in Internet relationship problems. Offit says:

> I have met people who are addicted to the Internet and spend up to 18 hours on-line pursuing an endless series of flirtations. I've counselled women who, when they met the man they had been corresponding with were dumped because their appearance failed to live up to expectations. I've also met four women who were duped into accepting marriage proposals from the same man.

Diablo in distress

The paradox of networking is that what to the sender/receiver of postings may be personal, indeed intimate in nature, is also nakedly public; and there are risks attached to the public display of intimate concerns. Kim Neely in a *Guardian* article 'Suicide on the Net. Cyberspace – anarchy in action or Big Brother in waiting?'[17] describes how a maverick user of the Net, Cornell University student Matt Mihaly, posting his messages under the name Diablo, was arrested, handcuffed and finished up for two days under mental supervision in the Soldiers and Sailors Memorial Hospital in Penn Yan, Ithaca, New York State.

The story raises questions concerning the use by individuals of the Net and their human rights when authorities key in to message postings and arrive at the messenger's real (not virtual) front door with anything but virtual handcuffs. Prior to his arrest, Diablo had done some fairly provocative political messaging on the Net, but it was this particular message which proved to him that a high-tech world offers no guarantee of anonymity in space:

Subject: Deadly drugs
From: Diablo
Date: 13 March 1994 09:12:35 GMT
I am planning on killing myself, and I want some information on drugs that can induce a relatively painless death. Preferably these drugs should not be impossible to obtain.

Diablo then asks if anyone knows 'how many sleeping pills a 165-pound person would have to take to ensure death'. He says he does not want any 'stuff about how I shouldn't do it'. Ironically Matt Mihaly had pulled out of his depression by the time a Net user had alerted Cornell's computer services department. Though he was arrested, Diablo was never charged with any offence, but the shadow of the event, suggests Kim Neely, falls upon cyberspace's reputation for 'dazzling lawlessness'.

Postings made in hell

It ought be acknowledged that while Matt Mihaly was 'brought to book' the Internet largely remains a venue for unchecked messages of hate as well as love. The prospect of postings which are at once public and global in the sending, and private in the receiving, unregulated by law, has proved a temptation for those eager to test the limits of freedom of expression, in sexual and in political terms. Inevitably networks of pornography and pornographers, of fascist groups dedicated to linking their hate politics worldwide, will take advantage of the absence of regulation.

Throughout America and Europe neo-fascist/white supremacist groups have spawned on the Net. In Germany the Thule Network has at least 14 linked bulletin boards. Two of these, in Frankfurt and Kassel, were shut down in October 1994 and their equipment confiscated by the authorities. The Thule Network operates surveillance on anti-fascists, publicises demonstrations and most significantly links with fascist groups worldwide, including the US-based NSDAP-AO.

In Sweden there is the Storm Network, in Norway the Nasjonal Allianse. In the UK the British National Party is active on the Net. In the USA the Ku-Klux Klan holds subscriptions on commercial on-line services such as CompuServe and American Online (AOL). Other Net users on the extreme Right are the Institute for Historical Review, Canada, a key voice in the denial of the Holocaust; in the USA, Christian Patriots and a number of right-wing Militias whose activities provoked widespread media attention following the Oklahoma bombing in 1995. Others to tread wary of are California's White Aryan Resistance, the Nation of Islam, Stormfront and Cyberhate.

Pale and male

If the impression given from examples cited here is that interaction on the Net has a Men Only feel about it, research findings offer little support so far for the optimism expressed by Sadie Plant. The first user survey of the World Wide Web, conducted by James E. Pitkow and Mimi Recker, identified a profile which is essentially 'pale and male'.[18] Of the 4000 respondents to the survey, over 90 per cent of users were professional, caucasian and male. If this is the case, what price the so-called global village, where we are all neighbours, interacting by sight and sound, and with equality at least within conceptual reach?

Numerous commentators take the view that the Net is unlikely to be a bridger of the gap between information-rich and information-poor, that it is failing to redress the balance between core and periphery; and some are of the opinion that cyperspace is largely off-limits to the poor, the ill-educated and the unemployed.

We need to recognise that while the privileged are almost invariably first to sample the newest technology, the less privileged eventually catch up – buying radio sets, TVs, computers in their turn. It is doubtful whether the gap could ever be fully closed, though some comfort may be drawn from the fact that children of the electronic age generally outdo their elders in computer know-how. This arguably promises a degree of empowerment for the future especially when we consider that navigating the superhighways does not require a licence and, once the basics are learnt, requires neither numerical nor literary sophistication.

Virtual reality and real world dilemmas

Planners at New York's University of Columbia, needing an extension to the institution's Law Library, decided on a 'virtual' alternative to building the extension in bricks, mortar, concrete and glass. They invested in a 'virtual extension', purchasing a supercomputer and appropriate software linked to user-friendly interfaces.

This initiative might well be seen to put at risk the future of stone quarrying and brick-making. Future architects could find themselves designing what Jim McClellan, in an *Observer* article, 'End of the stone age', describes as 'Soft cities'.[19] The subhead to McClellan's article suggests a vision of the future: 'Jim McClellan paces the digital streets and cyber malls of tomorrow's virtual city'.

As happens so often, life imitates art, though in this case life imitates the computer game, for the notion of virtual city-building was already pre-empted by *SimCity* a software toy from Maxis, created in 1987 by Will Wright. The Maxis Software Toy Catalogue of 1992 explains:

> SimCity makes you Mayor and City planner, and dares you to design and build the city of your dreams... Depending on your choices and design skills, Simulated Citizens (Sims) will move in and build homes, hospitals, churches, stores and factories, or move out in search of a better life elsewhere.

In constructing the new, *SimCity* does not fail to incorporate the ideology of the old, working on the assumption, which the games player is expected to take on board, that low taxes encourage growth and high taxes expedite recession: whoever claimed that computer games were not educational? Ted Friedman, in *CyberSociety: Computer Mediated Communication and Community*,[20] writes of the ideological positions vested in *SimCity*:

> These are not *flaws* in the game – they are its founding principles. They can be engaged and debated, and other computer games can be written following different principles. But there could never be an 'objective' simulation free from 'bias'; computer programs, like all texts, will always be ideological constructions.

The Columbia idea has not been lost on other educationalists. Mark C. Taylor and Esa Saarinen in *Imagology: Media Philosophy*,[12] believe that 'The "place" of the postmodern university is cyberspace' and 'within the constantly changing dataspace of the postmodern multiversity, all education is international'. Architecture will become 'electrotecture' and learning will take place in a 'global classroom'.

'When wired,' say Taylor and Saarinen, 'a person can work or even teach a class simultaneously in New York, Helsinki and Tokyo while living in the remote mountains of Massachusetts'. Yet for such changes to come about there will have to be radically new structures and regulations to administer the 'cyberversity':

> Old models that privilege institutional autonomy and national identity will be displaced by forms of cooperation and exchange that previously have been unimaginable.

If you are a teacher or a student in one of those old portable classrooms, with the door half off its hinges and water leaking down the electric light cable, all this cyberdreaming can have its raw edge. Cheris Kramarae[15] fears for the real ecology when we spend so much time in cyberecology. She links those fears to gender roles:

> I worry about the programs that encourage us to leave for extended periods the dirt and water of the actual places we live in… I can imagine the man of the house putting on his gloves and headset and visiting Costa Rica while the woman of the house stays in the real house, changing the diapers and fixing meals.

She asks whether all this means turning our backs on 'the messes we've made' in the real world.

Reality and illusion: the blurring of boundaries

Virtual reality is not merely an electronic simulation of the realities we are already familiar with. It is perceived as a new reality – a new world – in its own right. Indeed according to technovisionaries real life is when you switch on the machine not when you switch it off. Simulation, in virtual reality terms, is what is real; at least what is meaningful.

In *War of the Worlds: Cyberspace and the High-Tech Assault on Reality*,[21] a polemical tract which does not hesitate, at least metaphorically, to empty both barrels into the claims of the technovisionaries, Mark Slouka writes:

> Instead of exploring a local farm pond (or catching praying mantises in the park) today's eight-year-old can explore on her computer. Instead of keeping and taking care of a pet, she can spend time with her electronic pet on her computer. Instead of visiting real animals at a zoo (itself already a kind of simulation) she can visit the dodo and the passenger pigeon…

> All this may have its advantages – no smashed aquariums, no dog hair on the sofa – but what it lacks is inestimable: in a word reality.

Slouka deplores the 'ease with which these games blur the line between appearance and reality, the ease with which they are able to capture their users' emotions'; and what is significant 'is not the simulation [for most computer games are 'less interested in growing things than in skewering them'] but our willingness 'to buy into it':

whether we're growing tomatoes or slicing our way through a crowd with a chainsaw, after all, we're buying into a fake, and that says something about our relationship to reality.

The attention of the student of media has constantly been drawn in this book to the role the media play in defining realities. Slouka's argument about the 'assault on reality' which he perceives as happening both in cyberspace and out of it, thus deserves discussing and exploring; for, he claims, 'reality… is beginning to lose its authority'.

DIGITAL FISH

Such is the lifelike quality of computer-simulated fish available through the Aquazone program that 'owners' treat them as the real thing. The virtual fish grow, mate and reproduce. They are fed, and can be overfed. You can't (as yet) touch them. But, writes Mark Slouka,[21] 'this did not seem to matter much to the couple who called the company in tears when their fish, as the saying goes, bought the farm.

'For them, as for many if not all the 30000 other Aquazone hobbyists who didn't necessarily mourn their virtual guppies but only talked about them, fed them, and rejoiced at the birth of their fishy babies, these fish were real'.

Slouka asks, does this matter? And answers his question by saying, 'Of course it does, and in more ways than one'. If counterfeit technologies 'were limited to the world *inside* the computer, if dealing with them meant no more than dealing with the psychological side effects of raising virtual fish or virtual kids, or living in virtual communities… they'd be less of an issue'. He fears that 'the illusioneers or imagicians or whatever we choose to call them are introducing their hallucinations into the culture at large'.

Faking realities

To illustrate what he terms the 'culture of simulation' – aided, abetted and perfected through the technology of digitalisation – Slouka refers to a photograph tacked to the wall above his desk. It is a reprint of a famous and historical picture of President Roosevelt, Prime Minister Churchill and Comrade Stalin, taken at Yalta in 1945. And standing in shirt-sleeves immediately behind them is – Sylvester Stallone. Slouka keeps the picture above his desk as a reminder of 'the increasingly slippery world we inhabit', a world in which the most remarkable fact about reality is the ease with which it can be faked.

Slouka readily admits that photography has since its birth been 'fakeable', that propaganda is 'as old as language' and that the 'original photograph at Yalta was staged':

> But it's one thing to leave something out, or rig the meaning of an image by presenting it in a particular way; it's quite another to recreate the image itself.

The reality the image presents to us – in an age so dominated by the visual image – is being tampered with; and if the image can be so easily manipulated, so can public perceptions of it, believes Slouka. We become accomplices in illusion-making:

> Though aware, for example, of the inherently manipulative power of advertising, or the extent to which so-called reality-based television programmes are rigged, we nonetheless seem willing to buy the products (and the realities) they sell. Though aware that the photo-op of the candidate washing dishes at a homeless shelter or gazing admiringly at a redwood is staged – even directly contrary to his or her actual policies – we vote as though the images actually had some bearing on reality.

This 'indicates 'the enormous and abiding power of the visual sense' which more than any other 'compels our faith. We want and need to believe what we see':

> The problem with this is that our instinctive allegiance to the things our eyes show us has been transferred, largely if not entirely, to images of things as well... [and image manipulation techniques] carry the threat of manipulating not only the images we consume, but the world we inhabit. They threaten, in other words, to make our world virtual to an extent unimaginable outside science fiction.

The manipulated image undermines our trust in all representations, says Slouka, and consequently our trust in all mediated information. He believes – and it is up to the student of media to scrutinise this view with care as well as scepticism – that 'the threat inherent in image-manipulation techniques is the threat of authoritarianism, of information control'. Why? – because public belief in the veracity of some, if not all information, must be supported by a measure of conviction, otherwise a community risks 'nothing less than the kind of institutionalised cynicism found under authoritarian regimes'.

Slouka refers to the 'blurring of fiction and reality' so characteristic of public communication in the former Eastern bloc which 'spawned a culturewide and pervasive cynicism towards all official information':

> And exposing the frauds, I suspect, even if it becomes possible, will be of little help; once the public's faith in images is shaken, cynicism will spread like a contagion to *all* sources of information.

Slouka advocates a firm grip on real – unmediated – life, for all its drawbacks; and he advises the reader to resist claims of the 'inevitablity' of the virtual world taking over from the real:

> If we don't, we'll grow increasingly frightened of unmediated reality; more and more isolated, we'll come to depend, first for our comfort and eventually for our very sanity, on the technologies and the people behind them who offer to stand between us and the hostile world we inhabit, who offer us platitudes, fictions, and

out-and-out lies on which we've come to depend, who shield us from the increasingly terrifying aura of first hand experience.

Strong words but thought-provoking; sentiments in a modest way shared by Camilla Berens in a *New Statesman Diary* note:[22]

> Maybe I'm just a boring old technophobe, but I've got this vision of millions of people happily surfing the Internet while the world crumbles outside their windows.

Networking and the vulnerability of data

On the Net nothing belongs to anyone; and no text is safe from mediation. Once posted, a message becomes like Chinese Whispers, subject to appropriation. As Taylor and Saarinen[12] confirm, 'In the absence of the author it is no longer clear who owns the text'. The integrity of a text can be abused – facts and emphases altered – to the point when even the *preferred reading* can no longer be identified.

Data of every kind is vulnerable, not the least from cyberburglars called hackers who tap in to electronic treasure islands located in the 'secret' databases of big business, industry and government. It is now possible to rob a bank without leaving your swivel chair; and as the world now knows, it is possible for a juvenile to hack in to the nuclear systems of the most powerful nation on earth.

Practically every major company in the world has been assaulted by hackers. The Pentagon has suffered 250 000 attempts to penetrate its computers. Peter Popham in an article, 'The wild frontier', part of an *Independent on Sunday* series on techno-developments of the future,[23] writes that tomorrow's global village won't be some cosy idyll. International cyberspace will be like the Old West: a lawless zone.

Criminals of all sorts are already exploiting it: 'Earlier this year [1996], the *Sunday Times* claimed that 40 financial institutions in the City had been attacked since 1993; in the biggest single sting £13m was paid into an offshore account to buy off further attacks, and a total of some £400m is believed to have been paid out'. Then there are the viruses that transform vastly expensive data systems into gibberish:

> ... computer systems all over the world are infested with some 8500 viruses – software programmes that destroy valuable data; up to 2000 new strains are released every month...

The fastest-growing crime is stealing the semiconductors which are the computers' brains: 'Thefts of chips are estimated to have cost British industry £1bn last year [1995]; the biggest single incident was a theft estimated to have cost £750 000.'

The damage caused to companies by such thefts 'is often disastrous, as they spend weeks unable to function normally. According to a study carried out by Loughborough University, 70 per cent of firms that suffer computer failure go out of business within 18 months'.

Warring by software

'Bombing' the system is not confined to hackers, as a BBC Horizon programme, *The I-Bomb*,[24] illustrated. In the Gulf War of 1991, Allied software was the first and most deadly weapon, 'bombing' Saddam Hussein's information system before the real blitzkrieg began. Future wars, it would seem, will be won and lost at the console. The programme left the viewer wondering whether computer games have already moved from the realm of the virtual to that of the real in information-age combat.

Ongoing questions, ongoing issues

The thought of millions of people sitting in the solitary confines of their screen-sphere 'talking' globally while relating little and less to the people around them is disturbing. This is perhaps why the adfolk when marketing new multimedia technology tend to show a happy family enjoying personal interactions of which the TV screen is only the focus. Selling the solitary might be deemed antisocial.

The confirmed cybernaut will respond to such expressions of concern by saying that not only does the Net alter the nature of knowledge, it transforms human relationships too. Why must we always judge the present and future through – to quote Marshall McLuhan – a 'rear-view mirror'; or to be more precise, why is face-to-face communiciation considered to be the model against which other modes of communication should be measured? Taylor and Saarinen write of how their students appeared to grow in communicative confidence on the Net, trusting themselves to express matters more readily *because* they were not in face-to-face situations.

Yet it is fair argument to say that no-one is entirely liberated from the rear-view mirror syndrome: after all, the Net casts us back to Gutenberg and Typographical Man/Woman: messages in cyberspace are *written*; and every student of communication knows that what is said or written is only part of the communication story. Advocates of virtual reality will say that reaching out and touching people in cyberspace is only an electronic headset away. We may not need 'real' life at all, except to eat, sleep and relieve ourselves.

The case holds good until the virtual dream of a date with Miss World/Mister Universe or conversation with the US president, the Pope or with a 'virtualisation' of Joan of Arc is succeeded by a sudden pain in the chest: is there anyone out there to come and give the kiss of life? (Perhaps in future multimedia packages will come complete with life-support machines.)

Speed: at or on?

In *Imagology: Media Philosophy* Taylor and Saarinen take us on a conceptual roller-coaster through cyberspace. Chief among its essential characteristics they say is *speed* (of the non-chemical variety). 'Power,' they declare, 'is speed' and the 'swift shall inherit the earth'. Are we witnessing here a reassertion of Darwinism, of the 'power of the fittest to survive'? Possibly. Yet the authors also seem to be recycling an old McLuhanism, that the medium is the message. If power lies in speed, what price *content*?

Taylor and Saarinen quote in support of their case the Futurist artist, Filippo Marinetti (1876–1944), who celebrated, even glorified speed. 'Marinetti's future,' write the authors, 'has become our present'. Now Marinetti, in addition to – in the words of art historian Herbert Read – spouting much which was 'breathless and incoherent', also glorified war. He proclaimed that it was 'the only health giver of the world – militarism, patriotism, the destructive arm of the Anarchist, the beautiful Ideas that kill, the contempt for women'.[25] Given the chance to play the 'gender game' on the Net, would Marinetti have elected to be the dragon? Perhaps we should be concentrating more on perspective than speed. In any case, speed, the advocacy of it, is surely conditional upon being 'wired up' with enough creature comforts – decent pay, no creditors banging on the door – to provide unstressed opportunities to envision the future. To those on hospital waiting lists, those alone and without company from day to day and week to week, to the homeless counting the tedious hours till dawn rises over the Manhattan skyline, Waterloo Bridge or the satellite-dish roofs of Calcutta, speed is an irrelevance if not an insult.

Cyberspace and corporate ambitions

In Chapter 8 attention was paid to the dangers arising from the corporatisation of communication systems. The Net does not elude the interest of the transnationals; indeed in a sense it is their 'final frontier' in a game where digital domination leads to the profitable enclosure of communicative spaces.

The Winter 1996 edition of the *Journal of Communication* publishes a substantial symposium on the Net. The most important contribution in support of the point being made here about corporate cyberambition is by Robert W. McChesney in 'The Internet and US communication policy-making in historical and critical perspective'.

The news, according to McChesney – once very much an enthusiast for the potential egalitarianism of computer technology – is not good. He sees a formidable convergence of media ownership and computer technologies, predicting that there will be as few as six to ten 'colosssal conglomerates dominating global communications', with control of the Internet high on their agendas. McChesney writes:

> Virtually all known theories of political democracy would suggest that such a concentration of media in a handful of mostly unaccountable interests is little short of an unmitigated disaster.

Government in the United States, it would seem, has not merely stood by, it has been pushed into accelerating the process of concentration with the Telecommunications Act of 1996:

> Perhaps one of the most corrupt pieces of legislation in US history, the bill was effectively written by and for business. Much is made of the new law's competitive markets. This is, in fact, a euphemism for a deregulation that almost certainly will

lead to increased concentration...The effect of the... Act... is to assure that the market, and not public policy, will direct the course of both the Internet and the information highway.

McChesney says, describing a 'gloomy scenario', 'The new world order of communication tends to be uncritical of capitalism and commercialism and to be preoccupied with satisfying the needs of the relatively affluent, a minority of the world's population'.

Public service: quality: access

Fundamental questions can be raised here but not answered: how far, for example, can the Net preserve public sphere communication independent of conglomerate and state control? Without the support of authority, and the protective powers of regulation, can such a public space ensure the quality of communication (against the threat of pollution by cyberporn and cyberhate) and how might that first principle of public interest communication, *universal* access, be preserved?

Perhaps most seriously in the light of what has been said in this chapter concerning the fear that *virtual* community might undermine real community, does the atomisation of the sending/receiving process of the Net make communities more or less vulnerable to the allurements of the new, all-smiling, all-dancing Big Brother, corporate enculturalisation?

Is McChesney in total despair? No. He is of the view that the 'current promarket policies are going to be little short of disastrous for the quality of life for the majority of people both in the United States and globally'.

At all levels of society questions will be asked, trends challenged as the tension between democracy and capitalism becomes increasingly evident. Government itself, and how it operates, will be in the dock and under the spotlight: if the systems of communicative dominance are to change, to become democratised, so must government. In fact the first will be a condition of the second.

Scholars: free agents or corporate servants?

Among the advocates for such strategies of change are the universities and scholars of media communication. The irony is that universities, desperate for funding, are surrendering academic objectivity, grounded in principles of public interest, for the hard-cash charms of corporatised research.

McChesney's warning is addressed to schools of communication in American universities but it surely must be relevant to media communication scholars worldwide:

> Although cultivating ties to the capitalist communication sector may appear a logical management move, it will probably lead to the demise of communication as a viable discipline.

It is a timely reminder of the purpose and significance of our studies. Wherever scholars pursue the *critical* path of media (as contrasted with the *institutional*

path), they have in McChesney's words 'no alternative...but to do honest independent scholarship and instruction, with a commitment first and foremost to
democratic values'.

NO PLUG, NO WIRES, NO RIVALS

This was the title of an article by Simon Jenkins in the UK *Times* (4 January
1997) and it referred to the Internet's main rival – the *book*. Jenkins writes:
'Had the book come after, not before, the screen, I lay money the pundits
would have declared the Internet a passing and costly fad. Out would go the
dirty, eye-tiring screens with their plugs and wires and inconvenient sockets.
In their place would be books, objects of beauty customised to the needs of
the mobile leisure classes. Governments would subsidise school libraries
and set up bookshops on every street corner. Teachers would be retrained
to read... Books, being cheap, would liberate the poor and be the salvation
of culture'.

Jenkins is not whistling in the dark. He quotes a Policy Studies Report
detailing increased spending on books, more titles published, more copies
sold: 'The public loves books and has thumbed its nose at the much-hyped
revolution – or at least regards it has having nothing to do with books'. The
author is confident that 'The Internet will strut an hour upon the stage, and
then take its place in the ranks of lesser media'.

===== **SUMMARY** =====

The potential of the Net for the accessing and exchange of information, ideas and
arguments has been made manifest here. For the student researcher and for the
journalist the Net adds richly to the diversity of information sources, and these are
time-saving, global in scope and – currently at least – generally free of institutional
filtering and control. Essentially the Net should be regarded as an addition to existing
modes of information access and delivery, not a replacement.

The Net has also to be viewed, and ideally sampled, as a cultural experience. The
transforming power of metaphor has succeeded in turning one person at a keyboard
and computer screen into the equivalent of an astronaut, a surfboarder, a free spirit
roaming the ether, creating relationships across space and time, and encountering
and interacting with a limitless number of other free spirits.

For some, if not a New Jerusalem, a new – and better – reality has been born, one
in which physical presence, has become, as it were, optional. Cyperspace has created
its own priesthood of experts; their visions are of a new stage in human evolution, in

which the *virtual* has taken over from the real to the extent that experience is not experienced until it has been electronically simulated.

To the cynic, all this is definitely pie in the sky; and there is definitely a whiff of born-again gospelism about some of these claims. If, as Mark Slouka claims in *War of the Worlds*,[21] this New Age is carrying us 'on the road to unreality', it certainly has plenty of people ready to tread that road. It is a relief, then, to take a walk into town – and find the streets are not empty because the population is in front of its cyberscreen; a relief to discover people still attached to their real bodies in real time and real places; and heartwarming, as Simon Jenkins implies, to see people still sampling technology's greatest contribution to civilisation, the book.

Perhaps for a while at least we can suspend judgment over Slouka's claim, arising as it does, of course, from an American not a European, Australian, African, Middle Eastern or Far Eastern context, that 'firsthand experience has joined the list of endangered species'.

KEY TERMS

cybernetics, cybernauts ■ virtual reality ■ spatial stories
patriarchal structures ■ gender exchange ■ encryption
information-rich, information-poor ■ core, periphery ■ cognitive needs
affective domain ■ convergence

SUGGESTED ACTIVITIES

1. Discussion:
   (a) Consider the opportunities and the dangers of virtual reality.
   (b) What are the arguments for and against 'policing' the Internet?
   (c) How far should parents worry about the freedom of their children to wander the streets of the Netropolis?
   (d) In what ways will the the growing popularity of the Net worldwide affect modes of mass communication such as the press, TV and the cinema?
   (e) How might corporate giants appropriate the Net?

2. You have been asked by your college to produce a beginner's guide to the Internet, entitled, *Researching the Net*. The chief aim is to enable students to swiftly and comprehensively to summon up relevant research data for the study of media.

This may involve finding out about:

- Media legislation in the United States and Britain.
- State involvement in press and broadcasting in a number of African or Far Eastern countries.
- The current position in the European Community concerning home-grown and imported TV programmes.
- The present state of media ownership in Australia.
- The degree to which state control of the media has been relaxed in the former Soviet Union.

How might a student get started on such important enquiries?

3. Conduct a study of the ways in which *alternative media* – those free from state or corporate control – use the Net to further their activities. You will probably need to use the Net to identify what these alternative media are, and where and how they operate. Such a study would also have to include the use by such alternative media groups of video and satellite.

NOW READ ON

In reading about the claims and counterclaims for the Net and the world of cyberspace we should not forget historical perspectives on the impact of new technology on modes of cultural exchange. Look up the work of two major contributors to our thinking on society and technology, Harold Innes and Marshall McLuhan. Then try Joshua Mayrowitz's *No Sense of Place: The Impact of Electronic Media on Social Behaviour* (US: Oxford University Press, 1979).

In order of publication, the following are recommended:

Writing Space: The Computer, Hypertext and the History of Writing by Jay David Bolter (UK: Lawrence Erblaum & Associates, 1990); *Being Digital* by Nicholas Newgroponte (UK: Hodder & Stoughton, 1995) and three books from Sage, *Cultures of Internet: Virtual Space, Real Histories, Living Bodies* by Robert Shields, *Cyberspace/Cyberbodies/Cyberpunk: Cultures of Technological Embodiment* edited by Mike Featherstone and Roger Burrows (UK: 1996) and *Virtual Culture: Identity and Communication in Cybersociety* (US: 1997), edited by Steven G. Jones.

Concluding Remarks

In the study of media communication there can be few conclusions. Essentially our voyage takes us to the frontiers of meaning and, wherever meaning is confronted, there is doubt and debate, discourses and counter-discourses. The 'truth' about cyberspace, the 'power' of media and the capacity of audiences to resist or reject that power; the 'inevitability' of technological change, the 'victory' of capitalism over communism, of the private over the public, of individualism over community are ongoing issues, not certainties or inexorable trends.

While sharpening and practising our critical faculties as observers of media we need to remember to smile as well as to frown, to recognise in much media performance, and in countless media artefacts, artistry and delight, the capacity of media to stimulate, to enlighten, to reveal, to make us wonder, to make us laugh and to create in us both a relish for our own individuality and a sense of community.

We can be sure that those in control of, or with influence over, media communication systems will take pains (and sometimes cause pain) in order to stay in control. They will use communication for that purpose, which makes it all the more important that we recognise communication as a force for change; that we understand the strategies which are employed to defend privilege, assert inequality, deny freedoms, censor truth.

If, as James Carey has said, communication and culture are interchangeable,[1] then we might argue that communication and democracy are equally so: the one creates, supports, furthers and protects the other. We blur the connection at our peril.

Notes

Chapter 1: Setting the Scene: Media in Context

1. Krishan Kumar, 'Sociology' in *Exploring Reality* edited by Dan Cohn-Sherboh and Michael Urwin (UK: Allen & Unwin, 1987).

2. Philip M. Taylor, *Munitions of the Mind: A History of Propaganda from the Ancient World to the Present Day* (UK: Manchester University Press, 1995).

3. John B. Thompson, *The Media and Modernity: A Social Theory of Media* (UK: Polity, 1995).

4. Louis Althusser, 'Ideology and ideological state apparatuses' in *Lenin and Philosophy and Other Essays* (UK: New Left Books, 1971).

5. Pierre Bourdieu, *Distinction: A Social Critique of the Judgment of Taste* (US: Harvard University Press, 1984).

6. The Pilkington Committee Report on Broadcasting (1962) came down hard on the sort of programmes broadcast by commercial TV: 'Our conclusion is that triviality is a natural vice of television, and that where it prevails it operates to lower standards of enjoyment and understanding'. 'Prolefeed' was the rubbishy entertainment brought to the mass of the people, the proletariat, by the ruling party of Oceania in Orwell's *1984*.

7. Power Elite. Term employed by C. Wright Mills in *Power, Politics and People* (UK: Oxford University Press, 1963) to describe those members of society who possess power and influence, and who do so either on the public stage, like politicians, or behind the scenes, like leaders of industry or commerce; or simply people at the top of social hierarchies with influence through wealth or personal contacts. In short, the Establishment; specifically that part of it which influences decision-making at all levels of society.

8. Antonio Gramsci, *Selections from the Prison Notebooks* (UK: Lawrence & Wishart, 1971).

9. V.L. Allen, *Social Analysis: A Marxist Critique and Alternative* (UK: Longman, 1975).

10. Alan O'Connor, 'Culture and communication' in John Downing, Ali Mohammadi and Annabelle Srebemy-Mohammadi (eds) *Questioning the Media: A Critical Introduction* (US: Sage, 1990).

11. Gregory McLennan, *The Power of Ideology* (UK: Open University, 1991).

12. Glasnost: Russian, meaning 'openness'. The word became universal currency following Mikhail Gorbachev's accession to the position of President of the Soviet

Union (from 1988) and Communist Party leader (from 1985). Linked with glasnost was *perestroika*, 'restructuring'.

13. Todd Gitlin, 'Prime time television: the hegemonic process in television entertainment' in Horace Newcomb (ed.) *Television: The Critical View* (US: University of Oxford Press, 1994).

14. Herbert I. Schiller, *Culture Inc. The Corporate Takeover of Public Expression* (US: Oxford University Press, 1989).

15. Adrian Searle, 'Shopped', *Guardian* 13 August 1996.

16. James W. Carey, *Communication as Culture: Essays in Media and Society* (UK: Routledge, 1992); his chapter 'Technology and ideology'.

17. Martin F. Typper, *Prime* (1875), (see Note 16).

18. Clipper chip, or V-for-violence chip, is the spy in the computer, the 'sleeping policeman on the superhighway of information'. In February 1996 the American president, Bill Clinton signed a Telecommunications Bill requiring that from 1998 all TV sets with a screen size of 13 inches or more to be fitted with a V-chip. In the same month the European parliament voted in favour of a similar measure – the insertion of V-chips into every new TV set sold in Europe under the Television Without Frontiers directive.

19. Hans Verstraeten, 'The media and the transformation of the public sphere: a contribution for a critical political economy of the public sphere', *European Journal of Communication*, September 1996.

20. Majid Tehranian, 'Ethnic discourse and the new world dysorder' in Colleen Roach (ed) *Communication and Culture in War and Peace* (UK: Sage, 1993).

21. Postmodernist ideas have had a considerable impact on the ways modern cultures and communities are perceived and interpreted. The precursor to postmodernism, *modernism*, was characterised by an optimistic belief in progress. The machine-age was welcomed and new materials, new technologies employed to make grand statements in art, architecture and design.

Modernism is typified by skyscrapers of steel and glass as proud as Gothic cathedrals. Postmodernism has largely rejected the optimism of modernism and has backed away from 'grand truths'; indeed postmodernists question whether there are any such thing as truths.

Postmodernism is characterised by doubts, uncertainties and a reluctance to see any line of progress that is meaningful. Architecture of the period defies historical sequences by borrowing styles as if they were off-the-peg clothes (though curiously a great deal of Postmodernist architecture is a pleasure to look at). For a quick (and hopefully succinct) summary of these ideas see the 4th edition of *A Dictionary of Communication and Media Studies* (UK: Arnold, 1996) by James Watson and Anne Hill.

Chapter 2: The Language of Study

1. John Durham Peters, 'Tangled legacies', an introduction to a Symposium tracing the evolution of mass communication research published in the *Journal of Communication*, Summer 1996. The 'scholarly talent' chased out of Nazi Germany included academics of the Social Institute for Research, later called the Frankfurt

School of Theorists, such as Theodor Adorno and Herbert Marcuse. The philosopher Hannah Arendt was another scholar who crossed the Atlantic and established a world reputation with her writings.

2. C.E. Shannon and W. Weaver, *Mathematical Theory of Communication* (US: University of Illinois Press, 1949).

3. Norbert Wiener, *Cybernetics; or Control and Communication in the Animal and the Machine* (US: Wiley, 1949).

4. Wilbur Schramm, 'How communication works' in Schramm (ed.) *The Process and Effects of Mass Communication* (US: University of Illinois Press, 1954).

5. Harold Lasswell, 'The structure and function of ideas' in Lyman Bryson (ed.) *The Communication of Ideas* (US: Harper and Row, 1948).

6. George Gerbner, 'Towards a general model of communication' in *Audio-Visual Review* 4 (1956).

7. Ferdinand de Saussure's *Course in General Linguistics* (UK: Fontana, 1974). The first edition, in French, was published after de Saussure's death. A translation by W. Baskin appeared in the US in 1959. De Saussure is generally acknowledged as a founding-father of *Structuralism*.

8. C.S. Peirce, *Collected Papers 1931–58* (US: Harvard University Press).

9. C.K. Ogden and I.A. Richards, *The Meaning of Meaning. A Study of the Influence of Language upon Thought and of the Science of Symbolism* (UK: Routledge & Kegan Paul, 1923; 10th edn, 3rd impression, 1953).

10. John Fiske, *Introduction to Communication Studies* (UK: Methuen, 1982, 2nd edition, 1990, reprinted 1995).

11. Edmund Leach, *Culture and Communication* (UK: Cambridge University Press, 1976).

12. Gillian Dyer, *Advertising as Communication* (UK: Methuen, 1982 and subsequent editions).

13. John Fiske, *Television Culture* (UK: Routledge, 1987).

14. Roland Barthes, *Mythologies* (UK: Granada/Paladin, 1973 and subsequent editions).

15. Erving Goffman, *The Presentation of Self in Everyday Life* (US: Anchor, 1959; UK: Penguin, 1971).

16. Madan Sarup, *Introductory Guide to Post-Structuralism and Postmodernism* (UK: Harvester Wheatsheaf, 1993).

17. Jean Baudrillard, a leading light in the so-termed Postmodern movement, has argued that truth, or meaning, are notions which can be dispensed with altogether as a result of the signifier, in the modern world of image-bombardment and image-recycling which audiences are subjected to, being detached from that which is signified. Basically he is saying that anything can be made to mean anything. See Nick Stevenson's Chapter 5, 'Baudrillard's blizzards' in Stevenson, *Culture: Social Theory and Mass Communication* (UK: Sage, 1995) where he is critical of 'Baudrillard's irrationalism'.

Also, see Baudrillard's *Selected Writings* (UK: Polity Press, 1988) edited with an introduction by Mark Poster, and *Symbolic Exchange and Death* (UK: Sage, 1993), translated by Iain Hamilton Grant with an introduction by Mike Gane.

18. Robert Hodge and Gunther Kress, *Social Semiotics* (UK: Polity Press, 1988).

19. Gunther Kress, *Linguistic Processes in Sociocultural Practices* (UK: Edward Arnold, 1977).

20. Stanley Cohen and Jock Young (eds), *The Manufacture of News* (UK: Constable, 1973), one of the seminal texts of the period.

21. Frank Parkin, *Inequality and Political Control* (UK: Paladin, 1972).

22. Aberrant decoding. Umberto Eco, 'Towards a semiotic enquiry into the television message' in *Working Papers in Cultural Studies* No. 3 (UK: Birmingham University Centre for Contemporary Culture Studies, 1972).

Chapter 3: Audience: the Uses We Make of Media

1. Peter Collett and Roger Lamb, *Watching People Watching Television* (UK: IBA Report, 1985).

2. Frankfurt school of theorists. When the Institute for Social Research returned from New York to Frankfurt in 1949, Herbert Marcuse stayed in America, writing a number of influential books, the best known of which is *One Dimensional Man* (UK: Sphere Books, 1968). See *The Frankfurt School: Its History, Theories and Political Significance* (UK: Polity paperback, 1995) by Rolf Wiggershaus, translated by Michael Robertson.

3. Jay Blumler and Elihu Katz, *The Uses of Mass Communication* (US: Sage, 1974).

4. Denis McQuail, Jay Blumler and J.R. Brown (eds), *Sociology of the Mass Media* (UK: Penguin Books, 1972).

5. Tamar Liebes and Elihu Katz, *The Export of Meaning: Cross-cultural Readings of Dallas* (US: Oxford University Press, 1990; UK: Polity, 1993).

6. Sandra J. Ball-Rokeach and Melvyn DeFleur, 'A dependency model of mass media effect' in G. Gumpert and R. Cathcart (eds) *Inter-Media: Interpersonal Communication in the Media* (US: Oxford University Press, 1979).

7. Hans Magnus Enzensburger, 'Constituents of a theory of the media' in Denis McQuail (ed.) *Sociology of Mass Communication* (UK: Penguin Books, 1972). Enzensburger's chart is taken from Sven Windahl, Benno Signitzer and Jean T. Olson's *Using Communication Theory: An Introduction to Planned Communication* (UK: Sage, 1992), itself derived from Enzensburger's 'Bankassten zu einer Theorie der Medien' in D. Prokop (ed.) *Medienforschung* vol. 2 (Frankfurt: Fischer, 1985).

8. Neil Postman, *Amusing Ourselves to Death* (UK: Methuen, 1986).

9. Greg Philo, *Seeing and Believing: The Influence of Television* (UK: Routledge, 1990).

10. Retention concerning people and places is stronger than recall of causes and consequences according to researches conducted by O. Findake and B. Hoijer summarised in 'Some characteristics of news memory comprehension', in *Journal of Electronic and Broadcasting Media* **29**(5) (1985).

11. L.A. Festinger, *A Theory of Dissonance* (US: Row Pearson, 1957).

12. Self-fulfilling prophesy. Occurs when the act of predicting certain behaviour helps cause that behaviour to take place. *Labelling* people – as educational failures, for example – can be the first step in prompting a self-fulfilling failure. At the *intrapersonal* level of communication we, as individuals, decide whether we are

going to conform to, or reject, the expectations about us of others; and much depends upon the influence over us of *Significant Others*; and their power to impose their judgments upon us. The self-fulfilling prophecy has much to do with *negative* feedback, for few of us are so confident that criticism, especially if it is sustained, does not have impact on our self-view. This condition also applies to groups within society and within cultures.

13. Paul Lazarsfeld *et al.*, *The People's Choice* (US: Duell, Sloan & Pearce, 1944).

14. John B. Thompson, *The Media and Modernity: A Social Theory of the Media* (UK: Polity, 1995).

15. John Fiske, *Reading the Popular* (US: Unwin Hyman, 1989).

16. *Resistance Through Rituals: Youth Sub-cultures in Post-war Britain* (UK: Methuen, 1975), edited by Stuart Hall and Tony Jefferson.

17. Dick Hebdige, *Subculture: The Meaning of Style* (UK: Methuen, 1979).

18. Ien Ang, *Desperately Seeking the Audience* (UK: Routledge,1991).

19. Herbert J. Schiller, *Culture Inc. The Corporate Takeover of Public Expression* (US: Oxford University Press, 1989).

20. Ien Ang, 'Global village and capitalist postmodernity' in David Crowley and David Mitchell (eds) *Communication Theory Today* (UK: Polity, 1994).

21. Michel de Certeau, *The Practice of Everyday Life*, translated by Steven Rendell (US: University of California Press, 1984).

Chapter 4: Media in Society: Purpose and Performance

1. Directed in 1941 for RKO pictures, *Citizen Kane* is the most famous 'media picture' and in the view of many critics one of the best films ever made. It is the story of a newspaper tycoon, John Foster Kane, an alias for the American newspaper baron, William Randolph Hearst (1863–1951). It is a film which according to Leonard Maltin's *Movies and Video Guide* (UK: Penguin, published annually) 'broke all the rules and invented some new ones'.

2. For an analysis of Silvio Berlusconi's impact on broadcasting in Italy, see Paul Statham's article 'Television news and the public sphere in Italy: conflicts at the media/politics interface' in *European Journal of Communication*, December 1996.

3. Henry Porter, 'The keeper of the global gate', *Guardian* 29 October 1996.

4. Denis McQuail, *Mass Communication Theory: An Introduction* (UK: Sage, 1983).

5. In 1972, the general Conference of the United Nations Educational, Scientific and Cultural Organisation (UNESCO) reported with concern how the media of the richer nations were not only increasingly dominating world opinion but were too often 'a source of moral and cultural pollution'. Six years later UNESCO set up an international commission for the Study of Communication Problems under the chairmanship of Sean MacBride, former secretary-general of the International Commission of Jurists.

   The MacBride Commission's remit was to investigate the media information interaction between Western and Third World nations. The 484-page report arising from MacBride's 16-strong commission (which included the Columbian novelist Gabriel Garcia Marquez and Marshall McLuhan, the Canadian media guru), urged a strengthening of Third World independence in information-gathering and transmission and measures to protect national cultures against the one-way flow of information and entertainment from the West.

The aim was to create a New World Information Order, which would entail a degree of 'control' over 'freedom'; and which, predictably, got a very bad press in the West. Out of MacBride emerged the International Program for the Development of Communication (IPDC), which was – again predictably – to prove a frail defensive wall against the floodtide of Western media imperialism.

6. John Hartley, *The Politics of Pictures: The Creation of the Public in the Age of Popular Media* (UK: Routledge, 1992).

7. Richard V. Ericson, Patricia M. Barnak and Janet B.L. Chan, *Representing Order: Crime, Law and Justice in the News Media* (UK: Open University Press, 1991).

8. Edward S. Herman and Noam Chomsky, *Manufacturing Consent: The Political Economy of the Mass Media* (US: Pantheon, 1988).

9. Herbert J. Gans, 'Reopening the black box: toward a limited effects theory' in *Journal of Communication,* Autumn 1993.

10. D.R. LeDuc, 'Deregulation and the dream of diversity' in *Journal of Communication,* **32**(4) (1982).

11. Harold Innes. See *The Bias of Communication* (Canada: Toronto Press, 1951) and *Concepts of Time* (Canada: Toronto Press, 1952).

12. John Fiske, *Reading the Popular* (US: Unwin Hyman, 1989).

13. J.H. Boyer, 'How editors view objectivity' in *Journalism Quarterly,* **58** (1981).

14. Denis McQuail, *Media Performance: Mass Communication and the Public Interest* (UK: Sage, 1992).

15. McQuail, 'Mass media in the public interest' in James Curran and Michael Gurevitch (eds), *Mass Media and Society* (UK: Edward Arnold, 1991).

16. John Keane, 'The crisis of the sovereign state' in Marc Raboy and Bernard Dagenais (eds) *Media, Crisis and Democracy: Mass Communication and the Disruption of Social Order* (UK: Sage, 1992).

17. Leviathan. John Keane refers to 'the secretive and noisy arrogance of the democratic Leviathan'. Originally 'leviathan' was the Hebrew name for a huge sea monster, of terrible strength and power. It was adopted as a metaphor for the power of the state. The English philosopher Thomas Hobbes (1588–1679) gave his most notable treatise the title of *Leviathan* (1651). He argued that only absolutist government could ensure order and security. However, though the population were required to demonstrate total obedience to their monarch, they had the right to his/her protection in return.

18. Nick Stevenson, *Understanding Media Cultures: Social Theory and Mass Communication* (UK: Sage, 1995).

Chapter 5: The News: Gates, Agendas and Values

1. Herbert J. Gans, *Deciding What's News* (US: Pantheon, 1979).

2. Allan Bell, *The Language of News Media* (UK: Blackwell, 1991).

3. Stanley Cohen and Jock Young (eds), *The Manufacture of News: Social Problems, Deviance and Mass Media* (UK: Constable, 1973).

4. Philip M. Taylor, *War and the Media: Propaganda and Persuasion in the Gulf War* (UK: Manchester University Press, 1992).

5. Denis McQuail and Sven Windhal, *Communication Models for the Study of Mass Communication* (UK: Longman, 1986; 2nd edition, 1993). This book should be on the shelf of every student of media and communication. It identifies the models, describes their function and offers a critical appraisal of each one.

6. Gunther Kress, *Linguistic Processes in Sociolcultural Practice* (Australia: Deakin University Press, 1985).

7. Ito Youichi, 'The future of political communication research: a Japanese perspective' in *Journal of Communication*, Autumn 1993.

8. Walter Lippmann, *Public Opinion* (US: Macmillan, 1922).

9. Johan Galtung and Mari Ruge, 'The structure of foreign news: the presentation of the Congo, Cuba and Cyprus crises in four foreign newspapers', in *Journal of International Peace Research*, 1 (1965), reprinted in Stanley Cohen and Jock Young (eds) *The Manufacture of News* (see Note 3).

10. Marc Raboy and Bernard Dagenais (eds), *Media, Crisis and Democracy: Mass Communication and the Disruption of Social Order* (UK: Sage, 1992).

11. Bernard Berelson and G.A. Steiner, *Human Behaviour: An Inventory of Scientific Findings* (US: Harcourt, Brace, World, 1963).

12. Christopher P. Campbell, *Race, Myth and the News* (US: Sage, 1995).

13. Anthony Smith, *The Geopolitics of Information* (UK: Faber, 1980).

14. Jeremy Tunstall, *Journalists at Work* (UK: Constable, 1971).

15. David Barsamian, *Stenographers to Power: Media and Propaganda* (US: Common Courage, 1992).

16. Jörgen Westerståhl and Folke Johansson, 'Foreign news: news values and ideologies' in *European Journal of Communication*, March 1994.

17. Chechen war coverage. Another – essentially political – reason why the civil war was under-reported was that the governments of nation states themselves tended to 'look the other way', considering the conflict to be an internal matter, the business of Russia and her former satellites and not affecting the interests of the international community.

18. Philip Schlesinger, 'Newsmen in their time machine' in *British Journal of Sociology*, September 1977.

Chapter 6: Narrative: the Media as Storytellers

1. Arthur Asa Berger, *Narratives in Popular Culture, Media, and Everyday Life* (US: Sage, 1997).

2. Walter R. Fisher, 'The narrative paradigm: in the beginning' in *Journal of Communication*, Autumn 1985.

3. George Herbert Mead, 'The nature of aesthetic experience' in *International Journal of Ethics*, **36** (1926).

4. Jerome Bruner, *Actual Minds, Possible Worlds* (US: Harvard University Press, 1986).

5. Peter Dahlgren and Colin Sparks (eds), *Journalism and Popular Culture* (UK: Sage, 1992).

6. Roland Barthes, *Mythologies* (UK: Paladin, 1973).

7. Robert C. Allen (ed.), *Channels of Discourse: Television and Contemporary Criticism* (UK: Routledge, 1987).

8. Bryan Appleyard, 'If there's too much soap, it won't wash', *Independent* 11 July 1996.

9. Robert C. Entman, 'Framing: toward clarification of a fractured paradigm' in *Journal of Communication,* Autumn 1992.

10. Binary frames. Arthur Asa Berger (see Note 1) refers to 'central oppositions' and these relate back to ideas posed by the Swiss linguist Ferdinand de Saussure in *A Course in General Linguistics* translated into English and published after his death by McGraw-Hill in 1966. Meaning, believed de Saussure, is derived from relationships, of one feature set against another, of one term set against another.

    'The most precise characteristic' of concepts, de Saussure believed, 'is in being what the others are not.' Berger quotes Jonathan Culler's *Structuralist Poetics: Structuralism, Linguistics, and the Study of Literature* (US: Cornell University Press, 1975) which discusses de Saussure's ideas in detail and those of the linguist Roman Jakobson from whom structuralists have taken 'the binary opposition as a fundamental operation of the human mind basic to the production of meaning'. Berger follows this up by saying, 'That is why when we read or hear the word *rich*, we automatically contrast it with *poor* and when we read or hear of the word *happy* we think of the word *sad*. If everyone has a great deal of money, *rich* loses its meaning; *rich* means something only in contrast to *poor*'.

11. Jasper Rees, 'Slap "n" tickle', *Independent* 30 July 1996.

12. Roland Barthes, *S/Z* (UK: Jonathan Cape, 1975).

13. Vladimir Propp, *Morphology of the Folk Tale* (US: University of Texas Press, 1968).

14. Richard V. Ericson, Patricia M. Baranak and Janet B.L. Chan, *Visualising Deviance: A Study of News Organisation* (UK: Open University, 1987).

15. John Hartley, *The Politics of Pictures: The Creation of the Public in the Age of Popular Media* (UK: Routledge, 1992).

16. Milly Buonanno, 'News values and fiction-values: news as serial device and criteria of "fiction worthiness" in Italian television fiction' in *European Journal of Communication*, June 1993.

17. Adrian Tilly, 'Narrative' in David Lusted (ed), *The Media Studies Book: A guide for teachers* (UK: Routledge, 1991).

18. Lesley Henderson, *Incest in Brookside: Audience Responses to the Jordache Story* (UK: Channel Four Television/Glasgow University Media Group, 1996).

19. Justin Lewis, *The Ideological Octopus: An Exploration of Television and Its Audience* (UK: Routledge, 1991).

20. Daniel C. Hallin, 'Sound-bite news: television coverage of elections, 1968–1988' in *Journal of Communication*, Spring 1992.

21. John Fiske, *Reading the Popular* (US: Unwin Hyman, 1989).

Chapter 7: Pressures and Constraints in Media Production

1. John B. Thompson, *The Media and Modernity: A Social Theory of the Media* (UK: Polity, 1995).

2. G. Maletzke, *The Psychology of Mass Communication* (Germany: Verlag Hans Bredow-Institut, 1963).

3. John Pilger, *Heroes* (UK: Pan Books, 1986, new edition, 1995).

4. Allan Bell, *The Language of News Media* (UK: Blackwell, 1991).

5. Colin Sparks, 'Popular journalism: theory and practice' in Peter Dahlgren and Colin Sparks (eds) *Journalism and Popular Culture* (UK: Sage, 1992).

6. Reporters Sans Frontières, *Report* (UK: John Libbey, 1994).

7. Barbie Zelizer, 'Has communication explained journalism?' in *Journal of Communication*, Autumn 1993.

8. Jo Bardoel, 'Beyond journalism: a profession between information society and civil society', *European Journal of Communication*, September 1996.

9. Philip Schlesinger, *Putting 'Reality' Together: BBC News* (UK: Constable, 1978; Methuen, 1987).

10. Philip M. Taylor, *Law and the Media: Propaganda and Persuasion in the Gulf War* (UK: University of Manchester Press, 1992).

11. David Miller, 'The Northern Ireland Information Service and the media. aims, strategy, tactics' in John Eldridge (ed.), *Getting the Message: News, Truth and Power* (UK: Glasgow University Media Group/Routledge, 1993).

12. Eamon Hardy, '"Primary Definition" by the state - an analysis of the Northern Ireland Information Service as reported in the Northern Ireland press' (Unpublished dissertation, Queen's University, Belfast, 1983).

13. Eamon Hardy speaking on Channel Four's *Hard News,* 19 October 1989.

14. Tom Koch, *Journalism in the 21st Century: Online Information, Electronic Databases and the News* (US: Adamantine Press, 1991).

15. Koch, *The News as Myth: Fact and Context in Journalism* (US: Greenwood Press, 1990).

16. Liesbet van Zoonen, *Feminist Media Studies* (UK: Sage, 1994).

17. See van Zoonen, 'Professional socialisation of feminist journalists in the Netherlands' in *Women's Studies in Communication,* **12**(3) (1989) and 'Rethinking women and the news' in *European Journal of Communication,* March 1988.

18. Sue Curry Jansen, 'Beaches without bases: the gender order' in George Gerbner, Hamid Mowlana and Herbert I. Schiller (eds) *Invisible Crises: What Conglomerate Control of the Media Means for America and the World* (US: Westview Press, 1996). The title of Jansen's article is a play on what in her notes the author calls a groundbreaking work, Cynthia Enloe's *Bananas, Beaches and Bases: Making Feminist Sense of International Studies* (US: University of California Press, 1989).

19. Robert W. Connell, *Gender and Power* (US: Stanford University Press, 1987).

20. Tuen van Dijk, *Racism and the Press* (UK: Routledge, 1991).

21. Karen Ross, *Black and White Media: Black Imagery in Popular Films and Television* (UK: Polity, 1996).

22. Jeremy Tunstall, *Television Producers* (UK: Routledge, 1993).

Chapter 8: In the Wake of Magellan: Research as Exploration

1. Ien Ang, *Watching 'Dallas': Soap Opera and the Melodramatic Imagination* (UK: Methuen, 1985).

2. Brenda Dervin, 'The potential contribution of feminist scholarship to the field of communication' in *Journal of Communication*, Autumn 1987.

3. Angela McRobbie, '"Jackie": an ideology of adolescent femininity' in B. Waites, T. Bennett and G. Martin (eds) *Popular Culture: Past and Present* (UK: Croom Helm, 1982). See also McRobbie's *Feminism and Youth Culture: From 'Jackie' to 'Just Seventeen'* (UK: Macmillan, 1991).

4. Glasgow University Media Group: *Bad News* (UK: Routledge & Kegan Paul, 1976); *More Bad News* (UK: Routledge & Kegan Paul, 1980); *Really Bad News* (UK: Writers and Readers' Cooperative, 1982); *War and Peace News* (UK: Open University Press, 1991).

5. Data on the Cultural Indicators research programme are quoted by George Gerbner in Note 1 of his article 'The hidden side of television violence' published in *Invisible Crises: What Conglomerate Control of Media Means for America and the World* (US: Westview Press, 1996) edited by Gerbner, Hamid Mowlana and Herbert I. Schiller.

6. George Gerbner, Larry Gross, Michael Morgan and Nancy Signorielli, 'The "mainstreaming" of America: violence profile no. 11', *Journal of Communication*, Summer 1980.

7. Carolyn D. Smith and William Kornblum (eds), *In the Field: Readings on the Field Research Experience* (US: Praeger, 1989).

8. Liesbet van Zoonen, *Feminist Media Studies* (UK: Sage, 1994).

9. Valerie Walkerdine, 'Video replay: families, films and fantasy' in Victor Burgin, James Donald and Cora Kaplan (eds) *Formations of Fantasy* (UK: Methuen, 1986).

10. Shaun Moores, *Interpreting Audiences: The Ethnography of Media Consumption* (UK: Sage, 1993).

11. James Lull, 'The social uses of television' in *Human Communication Research*, 6(3) (1980). See also Lull's 'How families select television programmes: a mass observation study' in *Journal of Broadcasting and Electronic Media*, 26(4) (1982). In 1988 Lull edited *World Families Watch Television* (UK: Sage) and in 1990 published *Inside Family Viewing: Ethnographic Research on Television's Audience* (UK: Routledge).

12. Janice Radway, *Reading the Romance: Women, Patriarchy and Popular Literature* (US: University of North Carolina Press, 1984).

13. Edmundo Morales, 'Researching peasants and drug producers' in Smith and Kornblum, see Note 7.

14. John Corner, 'Meaning, genre and context: the problematics of "public knowledge" in the new audience studies', in James Curran and Michael Gurevitch (eds), *Mass Media and Society* (UK: Edward Arnold, 1991).

15. Justin Lewis, 'Decoding television news' in Phillip Drummond and Richard

Paterson (eds) *Television in Transition: Papers from the First International Television Studies Conference* (UK: British Film Institute, 1985).

16. Justin Lewis, *The Ideological Octopus: An Exploration of Television and its Audience* (UK: Routledge, 1991).

17. David Morley, *The 'Nationwide' Audience* (UK: BFI, 1980).

18. Charlotte Brunsdon and David Morley, *Everyday Television: 'Nationwide'* (UK: BFI, 1978).

19. David Morley, *Family Television* (UK: BFI, 1985).

20. Greg Philo, *Seeing & Believing: The Influence of Television* (UK: Routledge, 1990).

21. Lesley Henderson, *Incest in Brookside: Audience Responses to the Jordache Story* (UK: Channel Four Television, 1996).

22. Tamar Liebes and Elihu Katz, *The Export of Meaning: Cross-cultural Readings of Dallas* (US: Oxford University Press, 1990; UK: Polity Press, 1993).

23. Richard Dyer, Introduction to Dyer *et al.* (eds) *Coronation Street* (UK: BFI, 1981).

24. Dorothy Hobson, *'Crossroads': The Drama of a Soap Opera* (UK: Methuen, 1982).

25. Ann Gray, *Video Playtime: The Gendering of a Leisure Technology* (UK: Routledge, 1992). See also 'Video recorders in the home: women's work and boys' toys', a paper presented by Gray to the Second International Television Studies Conference, London 1986; 'Behind closed doors: video recorders in the home' in Helen Baehr and Gillian Dyer (eds), *Boxed In: Women and Television* (UK: Pandora, 1987) and 'Reading the readings: a working paper' presented in 1988 to the Third ITS Conference, London.

26. Cynthia Cockburn, *Machinery of Dominance: Women, Men and Technical Know-How* (UK: Pluto Press, 1985).

27. Roger Silverstone, 'Television and everyday life: towards an anthropology of the television audience' in Marjorie Ferguson (ed.), *Public Communication: The New Imperatives* (UK: Sage, 1990).

28. Silverstone and Eric Hirsch (eds), *Consuming Technologies: Media and Information in Domestic Spaces* (UK: Routledge, 1992).

29. The so-termed *4 Cs* (cross-cultural consumer categories) was prevalent in the ad business in Britain in the 1980s. Much the largest category was Mainstreamers, gauged as 40 per cent of the market. Aspirers were the young and upwardly mobile section of the consuming population. Succeeders had already arrived socially and economically while the smallest group, Reformers, were nevertheless – because of their education and commitment to the quality of life – the most articulate in expressing their needs and wielding influence.

30. Arnold Mitchell, *The Nine American Lifestyles* (US: Macmillan, 1983).

31. Hakuhodo Institute of Life and Living, 'Hitonami: keeping up with the Satos' (Japan: PHP Research Institute, 1982).

32. John Eldridge (ed.), *Getting the Message: News, Truth and Power* (UK: Routledge, 1994).

33. Larry Gross, 'Out of the mainstream: sexual minorities and the mass media' in Ellen Seiter, Hans Borchers, Gabriele Kreutzner and Eva-Maria Warth (eds) *Remote Control: Television, Audiences & Cultural Power* (UK: Routledge, 1991).

34. Rita Grosvenor and Arnold Kemp, 'Spain's Falling Soldier really did die that day', *Observer*, 1 September 1996.

Chapter 9: Ownership and Control: Ongoing Issues

1. *The Good, the Bad and the Ugly* (1967), a 'spaghetti western' directed by Sergio Leone, with Clint Eastwood, Lee Van Cleef and Eli Wallach; probably the best of Leone's 'Dollars' trilogy.

2. Robin Anderson, 'Oliver North and the news' in Peter Dahlgren and Colin Sparks (eds) *Journalism and Popular Culture* (UK: Sage, 1992).

3. Roland Barthes, *Mythologies* (UK: Paladin, 1973).

4. Robert W. Connell, *Gender and Power* (US: Stanford University Press, 1987).

5. Sue Curry Jansen, 'Beaches without bases' in George Gerbner, Hamid Mowlana and Herbert I. Schiller (eds) *Invisible Crises: What Conglomerate Control of Media Means for America* (US: Westview Press, 1996). In her Notes, Jansen refers the reader to Abuoali Farmanfarmaian's 'Sexuality in the Gulf War: did you measure up?' in *Genders*, **13**, Spring 1992.

6. Scott Inquiry: *Report of the Inquiry into the Export of Defence Equipment and Dual-Use Goods to Iraq and Related Prosecutions (1996)*. See *the Scott Report and its Aftermath* by Richard Norton-Taylor, Mark Lloyd and Stephen Cook (UK: Gollancz, 1996).

7. Richard Norton-Taylor, 'Scott free?' *Guardian*, 14 August 1996.

8. Phil Gunson, *Guardian*, 10 May 1994.

9. Sykes Committee. Appointed in April 1923 by the Postmaster General to review the status and future of 'broadcasting in all its aspects'; chaired by Sir Frederick Sykes, the Committee met on 34 occasions. As well as recommending public rather than a commercial service, the Sykes Committee proposed a single receiver licence of ten shillings to be paid annually.

10. Christopher Browne, *The Prying Game: The Sex, Sleaze And Scandals of Fleet Street And The Media Mafia* (UK: Robson Books, 1996).

11. Nicholas Coleridge, *Paper Tigers: The Latest, Greatest Newspaper Tycoons and How They Won the World* (UK: Heinemann, 1993).

12. E.M. Rogers and J.W. Dearing, 'Agenda-setting: where has it been, where is it going?' in *Communication Yearbook*, **11** (US: Sage, 1987).

13. John Fiske, *Reading the Popular* (US: Unwin Hyman, 1989).

14. Robert W. Chesney, 'Critical communication research at the crossroads' in *Journal of Communication*, Autumn 1993.

15. Herbert J. Schiller, *Culture Inc.* (US: Oxford University Press, 1989).

16. Everette E. Dennis, *Of Media and People* (US: Sage, 1982).

17. Jeremy Tunstall and Michael Palmer, *Media Moguls* (UK: Routledge, 1991).

18. James Curran and Michael Gurevitch (eds), *Mass Media and Society* (UK: Edward Arnold, 1991).

19. Jay Blumler, 'Meshing money with mission: purity versus pragmatism in public broadcasting' in *European Journal of Communication*, December 1993.

20. Denis McQuail, *Media Performance: Mass Communication and the Public Interest* (UK: Sage, 1992).

21. Nicholas Garnham, *Capitalism and Communication: Global Culture and the Economics of Information* (UK: Sage, 1990).

22. Barbara A. Thomass, 'Commercial broadcasters in the member states of the European Community: their impact on the labour market and working conditions' in *European Journal of Communication*, December 1994.

23. Nicholas Garnham, 'The media and the public sphere' in Peter Golding, Graham Murdock and Philip Schlesinger (eds) *Communicating Politics: Mass Communications and the Political Process* (UK: University of Leicester Press, 1986).

24. Richard J. Barnet and Ronald E. Müller, *Global Reach. The Power of the Multinational Corporations* (UK: Cape, 1975).

25. Cees Hamelink, 'Information imbalance: core and periphery' in John Downing, Ali Mohammadi and Annabelle Srebemy-Mohammadi (eds), *Questioning The Media: A Critical Introduction* (US: Sage, 1990).

26. Tamar Liebes and Elihu Katz, *The Export of Meaning: Cross-cultural Readings of Dallas* (US: Oxford University Press, 1990; UK: Polity Press, 1995).

27. John B. Thompson, *The Media and Modernity: A Social Theory of the Media* (UK: Polity Press, 1995).

28. John Keane, *Tom Paine: A Political Life* (UK: Bloomsbury, 1995).

Chapter 10: Prising Open the Black Box: Media Effects Revisited

1. Harold Lasswell's actual model of 1948, posed in 'The structure and function of communication in society' in Lyman Bryson (ed.) *The Communication of Ideas* (US: Harper & Row, 1948), asks five vital questions:

   Who
   Says *what*
   To *whom*
   In which *channel*
   With what *effect*?

2. Douglas Kellner, 'Advertising and consumer culture' in John Downing, Ali Mohammadi and Annabelle Srebemy-Mohammadi (eds) *Questioning the Media: A Critical Introduction* (US: Sage, 1990).

3. Neil Postman, *Amusing Ourselves to Death* (UK: Methuen, 1986).

4. *Vox pop*, from the Latin *vox populi*, the voice of the people. To 'vox pop' is to research into the opinions of 'Joe Public'.

5. Anne Nelson, 'Colours of violence' in *Index on Censorship* May/June 1994. Catherine Sieman's retort is published in Letters: V for viewing in the September/October edition of *Index*.

6. George Gerbner, 'Violence and terror in and by the media' in Marc Raboy and Bernard Dagenais (eds) *Media, Crisis and Democracy: Mass Communication and the Disruption of the Social Order* (UK: Sage, 1992).

7. George Gerbner *et al.*, 'The "mainstreaming" of America: violence profile no.11'

in *Journal of Communication*, Summer 1980. The belief in a causal link between video violence and child behaviour was given weight in a report by Professor Elizabeth Newson, *Video Violence and the Protection of Children* (1994), signed by 25 leading child psychologists and psychiatrists.

The view expressed in the report was that many experts in the field had understated the effect of violence on children, and they 'underestimated the degree of brutality and sustained sadism that film-makers were willing to portray'. The report was deemed 'reckless' by Guy Cumberbatch at the University of Aston, himself a noted researcher into media effects.

8. Derek Malcolm, 'Faster Oliver - kill! kill!' in *Guardian*, 23 February 1995.
9. George Gerbner *et al.*, 'The demonstration of power: violence profile no. 10' in *Journal of Communication*, Summer 1979.
10. John Fiske, 'Television, polysemy and popularity' in *Critical Studies in Mass Communication* 2(2) (1986).
11. Daniel Miller, *Modernity: An Ethnographic Approach. Dualism and Mass Consumption in Trinidad* (US: Berg, 1994).
12. Colin Campbell, *The Romantic Ethic and the Spirit of Modern Consumerism* (UK: Blackwell, 1987).
13. Marshall McLuhan and Bruce Powers, *The Global Village: Transformation in World Life and Media in the 21st Century* (US; Oxford University Press, 1987).
14. Ed Turner, Head of News at CNN in an interview for *Distress Signals* a Canadian TV documentary made by Orbit Films, Toronto, 1990.
15. Tony Dowmunt (ed.), *Channels of Resistance: Global Television and Local Empowerment* (UK: British Film Institute/Channel Four TV, 1993).
16. Akiba A. Cohen and Itshak Roeh, 'When fiction and news cross over the border: notes on differential readings and effects' in Felipe Korezenny and Stella Ting-Toomey (eds), *Mass Media Effects Across Cultures* (US: Sage, 1992).
17. John B. Thompson, *The Media and Modernity: A Social Theory of the Media* (UK: Polity Press, 1995). On the theme of 'globalised diffusion and localised appropriation' see also James Gifford's chapter, 'Travelling cultures' in *Culture Studies* (US: Routledge, 1992), edited by Laurence Grossman, Cary Nelson and Paula A. Treichler. Gifford writes of cultural *hybridity* brought about by the movement – the journeying – of peoples and of cultural expression. Gifford speaks of 'dwelling-in-travel' and believes 'We are seeing the emergence of new maps [of cultural analysis]: borderland cultural areas, populated by strong diasporic ethnicities unevenly assimilated to dominant nation states'. His advice to the researcher is to focus 'on any culture's farther range of travel while *also* looking at its centres, its villages, its intensive field states'. The notion of *travelling by media* is hinted at by Gifford and taken up by Josefa Loshitzky in 'Travelling culture/travelling television' in *Screen*, Winter 1996.
18. James Lull, *China Turned On: Television, Reform, and Resistance* (UK: Routledge, 1991).
19. Stuart Hall, 'Ideology and communication theory' in B. Devlin *et al.* (eds), *Rethinking Communication: Paradigm Examplars* vol.3 (UK: Sage, 1989).

20. David Morley, 'Active audience theory: pendulums and pitfalls' in *Journal of Communication*, Autumn 1993.

21. Michael Morgan and James Shanahan, 'Cooperative cultivation analysis: television and adolescents in Argentina and Taiwan' in Korezenny and Ting-Toomey (see Note 16).

22. Michel Foucault is among the most notable writers to emphasise the connection between control (political, economic, social and cultural), language as a definer and technology as a reinforcer; and his application of the notion of the modern-day Panopticon has had considerable influence. See *Discipline and Punish* (US: Pantheon, 1990).

23. Mark Poster, *The Mode of Information: Poststructuralism and Social Context* (UK: Polity, 1990).

24. Oscar Gandy Jr, 'Tracking the audience' in *Questioning Media: A Critical Introduction* (see Note 2).

25. Colleen Roach (ed.), *Communication and Culture in War and Peace* (US: Sage, 1993).

26. George Gerbner in an article 'Television's populist brew: the three "Bs" ' in *Etcetera*, Spring 1987.

27. View expressed by P.H. Lazarsfeld and R. Merton in 'Communication, taste and action' in Lyman Bryson (ed.) *The Communication of Ideas* (UK: Harper & Row, 1948). The authors believed that 'Mass communication may be included among the most respectable and efficient social narcotics'.

28. See K. and G.E. Lang, 'Some observations on the long-range effects of television' in S. Ball-Rokeach and M.G. Cantor (eds), *Media, Audience, and Social Structure* (US: Sage, 1986).

Chapter 11: Cyberspace Calling?

1. Norbert Weiner (1894–1964), father of cybernetics. Weiner acknowledged that the word *cybernetics* had already been used by the French physicist André Marie Ampère. Wiener's book, *Cybernetics; or Control and Communication in the Animal and the Machine* (US: Wiley, 1949), combines 'under one heading the study of what in a human context is sometimes loosely described as thinking and in engineering is known as control and communication'; in short, response or feedback systems. In his later, more accessible work, *The Human Use of Human Beings: Cybernetics & Society* (US: Anchor, 1954) Weiner says that 'Society can only be understood through a study of the communication facilities which belong to it'.

2. J.C. Herz, *Surfing the Internet* (UK: Abacus, 1995).

3. Tim Miller, 'The data-base revolution', *Columbia Journalism Review*, September/October 1988.

4. Tom Koch, *Journalism in the 21st Century: Online Information, Electronic Databases and the News* (UK: Adamantine Press, 1991).

5. The Computer Merchant ad appeared in *Boston Computer Currents*, September 1991.

6. Henry Rheingold (ed.), *Virtual Reality* (US: Simon & Shuster, 1991).

7. Mary Fuller, Assistant Professor of Literature, Massachusetts Institute of Technology (MIT) and Henry Jenkins, director of film and media studies at MIT,

'Nintendo@ and New World travel writing: a dialogue' in Steven G. Jones (ed.) *CyberSociety: Computer Mediated Communication and Community* (US: Sage, 1995).

8. Michel De Certeau, *The Practice of Everyday Life* (US: University of California Press, 1984).

9. Tony Ageh is quoted by Jim McClellan in 'It's a wired world', *Observer/Life*, 19 March 1995.

10. Michael Benedikt (ed.), *Cyberspace: Some Proposals* (US: Simon & Shuster, 1991).

11. Howard Lake, 'Wipeout in cyberspace' in *Amnesty*, November/December 1994.

12. Mark C. Taylor and Esa Saarinen, *Imagology: Media Philosophy* (UK: Routledge, 1994).

13. Christine McGourty, 'Highway to the global Netropolis' in *Daily Telegraph*, 4 May 1994.

14. Linda Grant, 'Deadlier than the e-mail' in *Guardian*, 30 November 1994.

15. Cheris Kramarae. 'A backstage critique of virtual reality' in Steven G. Jones (ed.) *CyberSociety: Computer Mediated Communication and Community* (see Note 7).

16. Alix Kirsta, 'Love bytes. How romance is blossoming for women on the information superhighway' in the *Mail on Sunday*, 29 January 1995.

17. Kim Neely, 'Suicide on the Net. Cyberspace – anarchy in action or Big Brother in waiting?' in the *Guardian*, 6 January 1995 and reprinted from *Rolling Stone Magazine*, May 1994.

18. James E. Pitkow and Mimi Recker, *The First World Wide Web User Survey*, based upon over 4000 responses (1994), conducted on behalf of the Graphics, Visualisation and Usability Centre (GVU) of the Georgia Institute of Technology; the first of regular surveys of the use of the Web.

Other research bodies surveying use and users of the Net are the Finnish company Mika Rissa and the California-based SRI International.

19. Jim McClellan, 'End of the stone age' in *Observer/Life*, 19 February 1995.

20. Ted Friedman, 'Making sense of software: computer games and interactive textuality' in Jones (ed.) (see Note 7).

21. Mark Slouka, *War of the Worlds: Cyberspace and the High-Tech Assault on Reality* (US: Basic Books, 1995).

22. Camilla Berens, 'diary', *New Statesman & Society*, 3 March 1995.

23. Peter Popham, 'The wild frontier', *Independent on Sunday*, 13 October 1996.

24. BBC *Horizon* programme, 'The I-Bomb', 27 March 1995.

25. Herbert Read, *A Concise History of Modern Sculpture* (UK: Thames & Hudson, 1964). The first so-termed Futurist manifesto was signed by Marinetti alone and published in *Le Figaro*, Paris, on 20 February 1909. It was, as Read puts it, 'full of sound and fury'.

Concluding Remarks

1. James W. Carey, *Culture as Communication: Essays on Media & Society* (US: Unwin Hyman, 1989; UK: Routledge, 1992).

Glossary of Terms

Aberrant decoding Wrong or mistaken but only in the sense that it does not accord with the **preferred reading** of the encoder.

Absence In news, for example, that which is excluded, off the agenda, gatekept. That which is absent may still be significant, and significant *because* of its absence.

Active audience Rather than merely accepting what it is told, the active audience is capable of thinking for itself, making its own interpretations, **appropriating** for its own purposes media messages.

Agenda A list of items – news stories – placed in order of importance in relation to **news values.**

Agora An open space where matters concerning the community are discussed. The Greek *agora* was the true 'marketplace' where ideas were exchanged and decisions made concerning the affairs of state.

Amplitude Size; a core news value according to Galtung and Ruge, yet depending on other values such as **proximity**.

Analogue See Digital/Analogue.

Anchorage A newspaper photograph is 'anchored' by its caption. Anchorage is a customary way of ensuring a preferred reading of the text. The voice-over in a narrative – feature film or documentary – serves a similar purpose.

Appropriation Taking over, making use of; for example corporations, through sponsorship, appropriating culture to further corporate interests.

Attribution Information is attributed to sources, some – such as people in authority – carrying more weight than others. If the attribution of information links to an elite source that information is more likely to be considered newsworthy.

Authoritarian press theory Operates in totalitarian regimes where the media are servants of authority, and its voice.

Bricolage Term referring to style, generally in self-presentation; the elements of that style being gleaned from other styles and modes of expression; bits and pieces from disparate origins assembled, often in defiance of convention.

Channel The physical/technical means by which a message is transmitted. In interpersonal communication the channel may be the body and the voice. The channel in television comprises the TV set, wires etc. The word channel has however been used more generally to refer to operational structures (for example Channel 4).

Citizenship entitlements Another term for human rights – the right, for example, to be told the truth, without bias.

Closure Refers to the closing down of meaning; to communication which is closed rather than open ended. In interpersonal terms, also refers to the 'closing down' of an interaction.

Code A set of rules by which **signs** are meaningfully assembled. There are arbitrary or fixed codes such as Morse Code and varyingly arbitrary codes such as those of presentation and behaviour; and more open codes such as aesthetic codes. Messages are **encoded** and **decoded**.

Cognitive, affective Aspects of thought, understanding, working-out, problem-solving are cognitive in nature; aspects of feeling, sensitivity – the emotional side of our personalities – are affective.

Cognitive dissonance A feeling of unease, of discomfort arising from our expectations failing to be met; or where there is discrepancy between principle and behaviour. Relates to congruity, that is, information or a situation which fits in to patterns of expectation; where this does not occur, dissonance is experienced, and a possible response is one of avoidance or rejection.

Coin of exchange Cultural experiences – like last night's episode of a popular soap – become topics of conversation, in the family or in the workplace, and represent a valuable ingredient of social interaction.

Commanders of order An alternative term for the *power elite* or the Establishment.

Commercial *laissez-faire* model of effects Poses a counter-argument to 'strong effects' theory; maintaining that media are produced for commercial reasons alone and that profit is the chief motive for media production, not ideology.

Commonality Describes those things a community holds in common; their shared culture, values, attitudes and so on.

Connotation The level of analysis in which meaning is encountered and addressed.

Consensus/dissensus Where the majority agree/disagree. The media claim to know when there is public consensus, though actual proof is difficult if not impossible to come by. However, by publishing or broadcasting that there is consensus may help create or reinforce it.

Consonance Where expectations are met; where what happens or how a person behaves falls in with our expectations, leaving us with a sense of cognitive satisfaction.

Consumerisation Where the dominant socio-cultural emphasis is on consuming to the point where this rules over other, non-monetary values.

Context The situation – cultural, social, historical, economic, political and environmental – in which acts of communication take place.

Convergence Coming together, a meeting in the centre. In terms of computer technology many formerly separate modes of information converged into central hardware. Convergence also refers to media ownership which converges into the hands of fewer and fewer owners.

Coorientation Occurs where a person is orientated both to another person and to an issue, the one proving an influence, upon the other. For example, if two people like each other and agree on an issue (or another person) then they can be in a state of consonance; in balance.

Core, periphery In terms of political, cultural or economic power, and in relation to the degree to which nations are **information-rich**, or **information-poor**, they are often divided into core (important, centrally significant) nations and periphery (nations at the margins of global importance).

Corporate intrusion Describes the way large corporations exert, through advertising or patronage, influence over culture; often intrusively in terms of using cultural artefacts to market their own image, products and services.

Counterframing Dominant forces – the power elite – in society command agendas and 'frame' the news; such framing is based upon the ideology of those setting the frame. Those in society with alternative standpoints in turn attempt to promote their own agendas with counterframing.

Crisis definition A function of media generally is defining realities; in this case media are in a position to identify – and amplify – crisis.

Cultivation theory Media expose audiences to attitudes, realities, ideologies and in the process, cultivate the nature and pattern of responses.

Cultural apparatus Those elements in society which contribute to the process of enculturalisation, of cohesiveness-making – education, the arts, media.

Cultural capital Our education, knowledge of the arts or of history provides us with a form of currency on which we might capitalise socially or professionally.

Cybernetics The scientific study of feedback systems in humans, animals and machines.

Deconstruction Analysis as dissection; the taking apart of elements of a text and subjecting them, and their relationship to other textual elements, to critical scrutiny.

Democratic-participant theory One of a number of normative theories of media; very much an ideal, and rarely to be found in the real world, in which the public has access to, involvement in and a degree of control over media communication.

Demonisation The media often use scare tactics to label certain public figures or groups within society as deviant. The intended effect is to persuade the public to reject what the 'demons' stand for, their ideas, what they say or do.

Denotive, Connotative Orders of meaning or signification. Basically the denotive concerns the level of identification and description, the connotative the level of analysis and interpretation.

Dependency theory Focuses on the degree to which audiences are dependent on media for their information about the world; concerns the impact the media have on our perceptions and attitudes. How far do we look to the media for confirmation?

Deregulation The policy of reducing, or eliminating altogether, regulations concerning, in particular, public service broadcasting. Regulation, for instance, might govern the amount of imported programmes a network is permitted to show or insist that lighter entertainment is balanced by more serious programmes.

Development theory A normative function of media relating to the purposes and practices of media in developing or so-termed Third World countries; recognising the delicacy of economic progress and the risk to that progress of 'bad news' stories.

Diachronic structure According to sequencing (for example A to B to C), as contrasted with **synchronic** structures built up through comparison. Diachronic linguistics is the study of language through history; synchronic linguistics works from a point in time, comparing and contrasting.

Diffusion The spreading of information or ideas through the social system. Diffusion studies focus on the processes by which the channels of communication, from mass media to interpersonal contact, operate and interact in broadening public awareness. In turn reception studies analyse what the public makes of diffusion processes.

Digital/analogue Terms describing how information is processed by machine, essentially the computer. Digital operates by numbers – 'digits', and is a binary system, making use of two digits only, 0 and 1. In contrast, the analogic system works by measuring variation. T. F. Fry in *Beginner's Guide to Computers* (UK: Newnes Technical Books, 2nd edn, 1983) illustrates the analogue process by referring to the car speedometer: 'Here the position of a needle relative to a dial represents the speed of the car in kilometres or miles per hour but is arrived at not by computing numbers but by a continuous monitoring of shaft revolution speeds and a conversion of this through the device's physical properties, gears and cables, to give the dial reading'; in other words, by analogy. By transforming all data into numbers the digital system has vast potential for information storage and lends itself more effectively to editing. Digitalisation of communication systems has enabled the **convergence** of communication forms to take place and facilitated multimedia operations.

Discourse A mode of communication which is socially constructed and is both a vehicle of debate and explanation.

Disinformation Aspect of propaganda, tailoring information to mislead, either by selection, economising with the truth or just plain lies.

Dissonance A sense of uneasiness or discomfort resulting from situations in which expectations are not fulfilled; when we find perception and reality in conflict.

Diversity May refer to diversity of media source, channels or programmes. In a **pluralist** society diversity is seen as a key criterion, in particular diversity in media ownership and control.

Domestication The practice of localising media artefacts – news or fiction – from across national or cultural borders; appropriating them for local consumption.

Emancipatory/repressive use of media The first envisages a public for media which has rights of access and participation; the second closes down both the operation and consumption of media to one of top-down control; essentially restrictive; media used as agents of order.

Empowerment Refers to the part media might play in giving power/influence to audience.

Encrustation Images as they pass through time and public experience acquire fresh associations which, by a cumulative process, alter or modify their original meanings.

Encryption Coding communicative signals so that access is restricted to those with the appropriate decoding device.

Ethnographic analysis Investigates the uses made of media by audiences in their own contextual settings, social and cultural.

Exchange   Refers to the reciprocal nature of communication, where the decoder contributes to meaning-making on an equal footing, and interactively.

Extracted information   That which audiences derive from their **lived experience**. This is matched up to **mediated experience**.

Fictionworthiness   Parallels newsworthiness in that news to a degree fulfils criteria appropriate to fictional, or story, narratives.

Field of experience   Where our life experiences overlap or have features in common, meaningful communication is most likely to occur.

Fragmentation   Of audience; brought about by the diversification of modes of media consumption such as cable, video, satellite.

Frames; schemata   Our reception of media messages is conditioned by the 'mind sets', sometimes called frames or schemata, which influence our perceptions and the process of interpretation.

Free press theory   Normative theory of media in which the basic principle is freedom from legal restriction.

Frequency   Term of varying use; frequency is a criterion for newsworthiness: events likely to fit in with the frequency of news schedules (hourly, daily) are more likely to be included than others which do not, like stories which take a long time to unfold.

Gatekeeping   Restricting access to people or information; in news terms, a process of selecting/rejecting information for onward transmission.

Gender   Categorisation, culturally defined and referring to the attitudes, perceptions, values and behaviour of males and females in relation to socio-cultural expectations.

Genre   Mode of classification in which certain characteristics of form and style are identifiable and generally constant. TV soaps constitute a genre.

Glasnost   Opening up; specifically refers to the greater freedom of expression permitted in the Soviet Union from 1989.

Hegemony   In society an overarching form of power/control created and sustained through popular consent.

Hermeneutic   Concerns understanding, revelation, making things clear. Barthes' Hermeneutic Code of narrative operates to unravel enigmas, solve mysteries.

Hierarchy   Classification, social, political and so on in graded subdivisions, the most powerful, influential sectors at the top. A social hierarchy – traditionally – would constitute upper, middle and lower classes.

Hitonami **consciousness**   Japanese term, meaning to align oneself to other people (for example keeping up with the Joneses or, viewed from Tokyo, the Satos).

Homo narrens   Latin, for man the storytelling animal.

Horse-race journalism   In which political issues, particularly at election time, are presented in terms of winners and losers.

Hypodermic needle 'theory'   As the metaphor suggests, the media's message – according to this 'hunch' theory – is injected into a docile and accepting audience. Also termed the **Mass manipulative theory**.

Iconic, indexical, symbolic   Classifications or types of sign. Iconic resembles, represents the original; the indexical sign works by association and the symbolic sign 'stands for' something else, the result of consent and general application. The alphabet is made up of symbols whose connection with the sounds they stand for is arbitrary.

Identification Various applications: may be a stage in the process of accepting ideas or modes of conduct; or relate to the way audiences identify with characters, real or fictional, in books, films or broadcasting.

Ideological state apparatus The family, education, culture and the media constitute ISAs as contrasted with the RSAs, repressive state apparatuses such as the military, police and the law.

Ideology The public dimension of values; the manifestation of the ideal through social, cultural, political and economic discourses.

Immediacy A news value characteristic of the Western media and relating to the dominance of deadlines. The more swiftly the news can be reported the more it fulfils the value of immediacy.

Impartiality Not taking sides.

Information model, story model Relate to the gathering, assembly and presentation of news; the one works on the assumption that the news is centrally a mode of transmission of information, the other that news itself is a cultural artefact with narrative traditions linking it closer to fiction – of construction – than fact.

Intertextual The positioning of one text against another, spatially or temporarily, deliberately or by accident can have an interactive effect in which one text plays off or plays against another, making possible new insights, new 'readings'.

Knowns, unknowns In TV news coverage, Knowns in society such as leading public figures are several times more likely to have their activities, and what they say, reported on, than Unknowns such as ordinary members of the public.

Kuuki Japanese, describing a climate of opinion influential in the relationship between public and media.

Labelling Relates to definitions of deviance; those defined as deviant by the media are seen to carry the 'label' of their deviance and the label continues as reinforcement of the definition.

Langue* and *parole de Saussure identified *la langue* as the overall language system, while *la parole* is the manifestation of the system in action, in speech and writing.

Mainstreaming Effects of TV viewing, particularly heavy viewing, in which views from the political right and left converge into a more centrist position though the shift is, over a period, deemed to be towards the right.

Media imperialism Power, exported through modes of communication, from a dominant country to others, affecting social, cultural, political and economic situations in the recipient culture or country; 'conquest' by cultural means.

Mediation Process of representing, defining and interpreting reality on the part of media and on behalf of audience; between actuality and reception is what is termed mediated experience brought to us by newspapers, radio, TV, film and so on.

Message What an act of communication is *about*; that which is deliberately conveyed by the encoder to the decoder.

Metaphor Figure of speech which works by transporting qualities from one plain of reality to another, such as sporting contests being reported in the language of war. The simile *compares*, the metaphor *becomes*, hence its potential power when effectively used in media practice.

Metonym The use of a specific term to describe a generality; thus Fleet Street was generic for the British press as a whole; by drawing diverse elements under a single umbrella term, metonym risks being a process of oversimplification and stereotyping.

Mobilisation The stirring up by the media of public interest in and subsequently support for a cause or issue.

Moral economy A dimension of consumer products used in the home – such as TVs, videos and computers – where values and judgments are located; concerns choices made within the family and who makes choices in terms of the use of those products.

Myth In relation to media, process of rendering as self-evident socio-cultural, political or economic 'truths' which careful analysis usually identifies as being justifications of the underpinnings of bourgeois, middle-class society.

Narrative codes Instrumental in the creation of stories, influencing form and content and operating in relation to character, action, situation, the unfolding of mystery and story resolution.

New World Information Order Proposed by United Nations Educational, Scientific and Cultural Organisation in order to ensure balanced and objective news reporting on a global scale.

Noise Any impediment which gets in the way of clear communication. This can take three main forms, **technical/mechanical** (physical noise or discomfort; distraction), **semantic** (difficulty over meaning) and **psychological**.

Normative functions Media operate according to norms, or rules, arising from particular social and political situations. Among a number of normative theories of media are the **Free Press theory** and the **Development theory**. The term *performative* is used to describe what actually happens rather than what is supposed to happen. See Chapter 4.

Objectivity In a journalistic sense, reporting matters without taking sides or expressing opinion; free of subjective values.

Open, closed texts Terms referring to the degree of leeway a text permits the decoder. A closed text is designed to close down the reader's scope for interpretation; open texts, such as works of art, permit a plurality of responses.

Overt, covert Overt is open, above board, intentionally obvious activity; covert is indirect or hidden.

Panopticon The all-seeing; a **metaphor** for control, originating with the 19th-century philosopher Jeremy Bentham who proposed a prison in which a central tower permitted **surveillance** of prisoners who would be placed in cells arranged around the tower: they would behave as required because they knew they were being watched. Some critics perceive electronic technology as being the modern version of the Panopticon, or as Mark Poster prefers to call it, the **Superpanopticon**. See Chapter 10.

Paradigm, Syntagm Syntagms are elements, or working details, within the broad categorisation of a paradigm. A *genre* is paradigmatic; its syntagmic elements those features of process – in which the genre is created.

Performatives Words to describe how things are said with regard to news events, such as *announce, assert, declare, insist*, each use carrying with it an evaluative, judgmental capacity. *Say* or *said* are neutral performatives unless they are linked with other performatives which are not value-free. For example, 'Management say there is no extra money, but unions demand the money be found'; the one being presented in a good light, the other not.

Periodicity Term describing the time-scale or a news organisation's schedules. A 24-hour periodicity such as that of a newspaper will favour news events which occur within that range of time – like a murder or a sudden disaster, thus it serves as a *news value*. See Chapter 5.

Personalisation A familiar media practice in reporting issues and events is to present them through the image of a leading player in those events. It is more convenient, if simplistic, to praise or blame an individual rather than a group; and makes livelier journalistic copy.

Photographic negativisation Portraying through media texts and images the positive norm through contrast, that is by its opposite, just as a photo-negative is instrumental in producing the finished picture.

Pluralism Many faceted, a state of affairs in which many opinions are tolerated; hence the term pluralist society.

Polysemy Describes a communicative situation where there are potentially many meanings; that is, texts can be decoded in a number of ways by different audiences within the contexts in which those texts are experienced.

Postmodernism Reaction to modernist views concerning the inevitability of progress; sees contemporary life as essentially problematic, fragmentary; pulling back from grand theories explaining the nature of society and culture.

Power elite Those persons within a culture in a position to influence, directly or indirectly political and economic decision-making. Sometimes referred to as the Establishment. Drawn from the highest echelons of society, business, the law, the military and so on.

Preferred reading Preferred, that is, according to the sender or encoder of the message; where the decoder by intent or accident 'misreads' the intended message, the result is deemed to have been **aberrantly** decoded.

Privatisation The shift from public ownership of the media to private ownership and control.

Propaganda The process by which ideas are propagated; term used to describe persuasion which is blatant, unashamed, vigorous.

Proximity Nearness, cultural or geographical. Proxemics is the study of spatial relationships at the level of interpersonal communication. In terms of mass communication, proximity is seen as a news value.

PSB Public Service Broadcasting.

Public sphere The arena, or space in which the public as citizens communicate and in theory contribute to the decision-making and running of their community; a place of debate and discourse which in real terms is a media space.

Redundancy The 'slack' which is built into communicative exchanges; that which is strictly not necessary for a message to be grasped but serves to ensure that in an exchange the message, or essential part of it, has not been lost.

Resistive responses Linked with notions of audience **empowerment**, responses on the part of the reader, listener or viewer which, to a degree, resist or deny the **preferred reading**; countering the impression of the audience as merely reactive and accepting.

Rhetoric Persuasion by means of presentational devices; classically, defines the skills of persuasion but in modern parlance has come to mean communication that is declamatory but without substance.

Salience Meaningfulness; of special importance.

Segmentation The division of audience and/or consumers into segments considered appropriate for programming or sales; traditionally based upon differences of class and income, latterly on perceived differences of lifestyle and expectations.

Self-censorship Not communicating a message/conveying information/expressing opinion in order to head off the risk of censorship further up the line of communication.

Self-fulfilling prophesy Usually results from the process of **labelling**. Persons or groups classified as failures or troublemakers may behave in such a way as to confirm predictions, that is fulfil the expectations others hold of them.

Semiology/Semiotics The study of **signs** and sign systems within socio-cultural contexts.

Semiotic power The use of signifiers (such as dress, appearance) as forms of self or group expression, denoting an independent, even resistive use of the products of mass consumption.

Sign The smallest element of the communicative process, a letter of the alphabet, a single musical note, a gesture. The sign is assembled according to **codes** and depends for its meaning on its relation to other signs.

Signal The initial indicator of the communication process, like establishing eye contact before speaking, or the ringing of the telephone.

Significant others People of our acquaintance or in public life whose opinion about matters is important to us. People of influence.

Sound-bite A segment of a news bulletin, of very short duration. In a general sense communication using such segments, where the assertive prevails over the explanatory or analytical.

Source The origins from which information on a news story arises; the majority of news tends to come from official sources.

Spiral of silence Where in the public arena the holding of opinions threatens to isolate the communicator, there will be a tendency for such opinions to enter a spiral leading to silence; in effect, self-censorship will occur.

Storyness The characteristics of an act of communication, or communication process (like the news) which resembles a story, employing narrative forms and techniques.

Surveillance Overseeing, watching, on the look-out. An important use to which audiences put the media in their capacity as watchdog and 'windows on the world'. Equally those is authority exercise surveillance, today chiefly by electronic means, over the public.

Tabloidese Language of the tabloid press – succinct, dramatic, emotive, sensationalised, personalised and often even poetic. The key linguistic device of the tabloids is the pun.

Text In the study of communication a text is that which is produced – a photograph, a cartoon, a novel, a movie; equally a person may be described as a text in that he/she communicates by personal appearance, body language, speech and behaviour. Barthes differentiates between the *work* (that which has been encoded) and the *text* (that which is decoded).

Transmission The process by which a sender transmits a message to a receiver; generally seen as a one-way operation.

Transaction Indicates that communication is an interactive process in which the meaning of a communicative exchange is something transacted or negotiated between encoder and decoder.

Uses and Gratifications Theory targeted on the uses audiences make of media in order to satisfy, or gratify needs.

Visions of order Refers to the perceived purpose of the mass-produced textual or pictorial image, that is to affirm on behalf of authority the nature of order and control.

Watchdog/guard dog Contrasting roles of the media in society; the watchdog role sees the media performing in the interests of the public; the guard dog role serving to protect those in authority.

Index

References are to the main body of the text. However, occasionally the reader's attention is drawn to the Notes, pages 282–97. In this case the reference will begin with 'n', followed by the chapter number and the page number in the Notes. For example: New World Information Order, n5Ch4 (286).

A

aberrant decoding, 54, 68
aberrant news values, 122
action code, 138, 140
advertising, 142, 160, 161, 171,
    198–200, 221, 231, 236, 173, 175
Ageh, Tony, 264
agenda setting, 112–16, 225
agora, 99, 201, 213, 218, 225
Allen, Robert, 134
alliances of influence, 116
Althusser, Louis, 15, 19
amplification, 113
amplitude, 118–19, 160
anchorage, 45
Anderson, Robin, 208–9
Ang, Ien, 76–8, 79, 180, 195
Annenberg School of Communication,
    67, 183, 235, 239
Appleyard, Brian, 135–6, 141
Assis, de, Machado, 10
attribution, 123
audience
    active/resistive, 68–71, 75–6, 190–2,
        194, 217–18, 243–7
    appropriation of media by, 23, 24,
        197, 243–7
    as consumers, as citizens, 77

as mediators of news, 109
attention span, 69
cognitive and affective needs of, 69
communicator's image of, 157–8
critical response of, 193
cultivation theory, 67–8
cultural divergence, 194
dependency theory, 65–6
emancipatory use of media, 66–7
ethnographic position on audience,
    74–6
fragmentation of, 77–8
frames of reference, referential and
    critical, 71
Frankfurt school of media analysts,
    61–2
identifying, 61–2
image of the communicator, 159
information retention/recall of, 69,
    146, 251, n10Ch3(285)
minorities, 201–2
pleasure of audience recognised, 194
project of self, 73–4
response codes, 54
response to Jordache Story, 146–6
segmentation of, 17, 161, 198–200
'semiotic resistance', 226–7
technology, use of 195–8
uses and gratifications theory, 62–5

B

balance, 97–98
Ball-Rokeach, Sandra J. and Melvyn De
    Fleur, 65
Bardoel, Jo, 160
Barnet, Richard and Ronald Muller,
    224–6

Barsamian, David, 123
Barthes, Roland (1915–80) 40, 44, 51–3, 133, 138–40, 209
Bass, A.Z., 110
Baudrillard, Jean, 50, n17Ch2(284)
BBC (British Broadcasting Corporation), 28–9, 50, 51, 87, 163–5, 213, 222, 223
Beaverbrook, Lord (1879–1964), 84
Bell, Allan, 107, 121, 123, 126, 155, 165–6
Bell, Martin, 163
Benedikt, Michael, 264
Bentham, Jeremy (1748–1832), 247–8
Berelson, B. and G.A. Steiner, 120
Berens, Camilla, 174
Berger, Arthur Esa, 131, 137
Berlusconi, Silvio, 85, 214, 237
Berry, Colin, 69
binary framing, 137, n10Ch6(289)
Birt, John, 88, 222
Blumer, Herbert, 189–90
Blumler, Jay, 62, 221, and Elihu Katz, 62
Borman, Ernest, 133
boundary event, journalistic event, 168
Bourdieu, Pierre, 16
broadcasting, public service (PSB), 28, 86–9, 91, *see also* BBC
Brookside, 136; Jordache story, 145–6, 193–4
Brottons, Mario, 203
Browne, Christopher, 214
Bruner, Jerome, 132
Brunsdon, Charlotte, 190
bulletin boards, 260–1
Buonanno, Milly, 143–4
'bystander journalism', 163

C
Campaign for Press and Broadcasting Freedom (UK), 66
Campbell, Christopher P., 120
Campbell, Colin, 244
Capa, Robert, 203
Carey, James W., 26, 31, 281
censorship, 92, 96, 111–12, 156, 160, 162, 164, 219, 221, 247–9, 264–5, 268, 276

Centre for Contemporary Cultural Studies (CCCS), University of Birmingham, 53, 190
Chartists, the, 100
Chomsky, Noam and Edward Herman, 96
Citizen Kane, 85, n1Ch4(286)
citizenship entitlement, 101–2
Cleaver, Harry, 263
clipper (or V-) chip, 264–5
closure, 45, 70, 134, 140, 149
Cockburn, Cynthia, 196
codes, 43–4, 51
    of narrative, 138–40
    of response *see* response codes
cognitive, affective, 55, 69, 135, 140, 267
cognitive dissonance, 69–70, 189
Cohen, Akiba and Itzhak Roeh, 245–6
Cohen, Stanley and Jock Young, 54, 107
Coleridge, Nicholas, 214
Collett, Peter and Roger Lamb, 61, 197
commonality, 13
Connell, Robert W., 171, 209
consensus, 96
consent, manufacture of, 96
consonance, hypothesis of, 120
consumer categories *see* Four Cs
consumerisation, 23, 236
convergence, 26–7, 183, 200, 221
core, periphery nations, 227–8, 270
Corner, John, 188
Coronation Street, 195
corporate control, 22, 78, 89, 115, 163–5, 276
corporate sponsorship, 219–20
Cosby Show, 189
countermodernisation, hypermodernisation, demodernisation, postmodernisation, 29–30
crisis definition, 96
Crossroads, 195, 196
Culler, Jonathan, n10Ch6(289)
cultivation, ethnographic position, 234
cultivation theory, 198, 234–42
culture
    commodification of, 22

consumerisation of, 23–4, 248
corporatisation of, 22–3, 212–26,
    276–7
global-local axis, 246
hegemony, 18–24
hierarchy, 16–17
power forms of, 14–15
racism, 174–6
simulation of, 270
cultural apparatus, 15, 19, 115
    capital, 16
    hybridity, n17Ch10(295)
    Indicators programme, 183, 239
    invasion, 229
    orientation of news, 106
    proximity, 119
    ritual, 106
    technology, impact of, 24–7
Curran, James, 100, 221
cybernetics, 36–7, 259
cyberspace, 8, Ch11; and gender,
    266–8

D
Dahlgren, Peter, 132
Dallas, 180, 194, 195, 229
Darwinism, 275
de Certeau, Michel, 79, 262
democracy, 30–1, 153, 158, 224–6,
    237–8, 273, 277, 278, 281
denotation, connotation, 2, 51–2, 141
Dennis, Everette, 219
dependency theory, 65–6
deregulation, 220, 276, *see also*
    regulation
Dervin, Brenda, 181–2
de Saussure, Ferdinand (1857–1913),
    40, 41, 44, n10Ch6(289)
development theory, 92, n5Ch4(286)
deviance definition, 95
Diablo, 268
diachronic structure, 146
digitalisation *see* technology
digital mating, 267–8
digital soup, 260
Dijk, Tuen van *see* van Dijk, Tuen
discipline of the norm, 248
discourse, 51, 115–16, 131, 182, 224,
    227, 248–9

disinformation, 167, 208–9, 228
dissonance, 154
distancing, symbolic, 246
domestication, 245–7
dominant, negotiated, oppositional, 54
Dowment, Tony, 245
Doyle, Leonard, 263
Dyer, Gillian, 42
Dyer, Richard, 145

E
Eastenders, 50
Eco, Umberto, 9, 54
effects of media, 191–3; Ch10
    brief ABC of effects, 253–5
Eldridge, John, 200–1
empowerment, 75, 100, 171, 181, 270
encryption, 265
enculturalisation, 78–9, 220, 277
enigma (or hermeneutic) code, 138–9,
    140, 146, 203
Enloe, Cynthia, n18Ch7(290)
Entman, Robert, 136
Enzensburger, Hans Magnus, 66–7
equality, 77, 100, 196, 227, 166–7
Ericson, Richard V., Patricia Barnah
    and Janet B.L. Chan, 95, 142–3
ethnocentrism, 106, 119, 174, 261
ethnography, 74–6, 242–7

F
faking realities, 272–4
Falklands War (1982), 111
Farmanfarmaian, Abouali, n5Ch9(293)
Federal Communications Commission
    (USA), 87, 214, 220
feedback, 36–7
fields of experience, 37–8, 137
Fisher, Walter, 131
Festinger, Leon, 69–70
fiction *see* narrative
First Amendment (of the American
    Constitution), 97, 224
Fiske, John, 41, 43, 52, 75–6, 98,
    148–9, 217–18, 226–7, 243
Foucault, Michel, 248, 249
Four Cs (consumer categories),
    n29Ch8(292)

frames of reference, 71
  binary frames, n10Ch6(289)
Frankfurt school of theorists, 61–2,
  n1Ch2(283), n2Ch3(285)
freedoms, the five, 100
Friedman, Ted, 270
frequency, 118

G

Galtung, Johan and Mari Ruge,
  117–26, 143
Gandy, Oscar Jr, 249–50
Gans, Herbert, 97, 107, 126, 251
Garnham, Nicholas, 221, 223
gatekeeping, 137–8
gender representation and the media,
  169–72
genre, 137–8
Gerbner, George, 38–40, 67–8, 183–4,
  235, 239–42
Gibson, William, 259
Gifford, James, n17Ch10(295)
Gitlin, Todd, 21–2
Glasgow University Media Group, 145,
  166, 182–3, 192, 200–1
glasnost, 20, n12Ch1(282–3)
globalisation, 175, n17Ch10(295)
Goffman, Erving, 44–5
Gramsci, Antonio (1899–1937), 19
Grant, Linda, 266
Gray, Ann, 195–6
Gregory, Martyn, 222
Gross, Larry, 201–3
group dynamics, 155
guard dog, watchdog, 94
Guerin, Veronica, 158
Gulf War (1991), 111, 119, 126, 166,
  209, 210, 275
Gunson, Phil, 211–12
Gutenberg, John of (c.1400–68), 6, 15,
  27, 275

H

hacking, 266, 274
Hakuhodo Institute of Life and Living,
  199
Hall, Stuart, 53–4, 117, 124, 247; and
  Tony Jefferson, 75
Hallin, Daniel, 147–8, 153

Hamelink, Cees, 227–8
Hardy, Eamon, 167
Hartley, John, 94, 96, 142–3
Hearst, William Randolph
  (1863–1951), 85
Hebdige, Dick, 75
hegemony, 18–24, 51, 264
'hegemonic masculinity', 171, 209
Henderson, Lesley, 145–6, 193–4
Herman, Edward and Noam Chomsky,
  96
hermaneutic (or enigma) code of
  narrative, 138–9, 146
Hertz, J.C., 259, 267
HICT (Household Uses of Information
  and Communication Technologies)
  Project, 197
hierarchy, of access (to news sources),
  166–7
'hitonami consciousness', 200
Hobbes, Thomas (1588–1679),
  n17Ch4(287)
Hobson, Dorothy, 195, 196
Hollywood narrative mode, rhetorical
  mode, 134
Hodge, Robert and Gunther Kress, 51
homo narrens, 131
'horse-race journalism', 148, 153
Howard, Richard, 138
hybridity, n17Ch10(295)
hypodermic needle 'model' of mass
  communication effect, 7, 243
hypothesis of consonance, 120

I

iconic, indexical, symbolic, 42–3
ideological state apparatuses (ISAs),
  repressive state apparatuses (RSAs),
  15, 19
ideology, 19–20, 51, 52, 116, 124,
  182–3, 213, 220, 222, 224, 225,
  247, 270
ideology of mass culture, ideology of
  populism, 195
image politics, 237
immediacy as a news value, 126, 160
impartiality, 97–8, 165
information
  disinformation, 167, 208, 228

extracted, 116
flow of, 169, 228
gaps, 228–9, 270
global imbalances of, 227
information-rich, information-poor,
    227
mediated, 109, 228, 273–4
New World Information Order,
    n5Ch4(286)
privatisation of, 219
vulnerability of data, 274–5
Innes, Harold, 97
instancy, 237
interactivity, 259–60
invisibility as an issue, 174
Internet, 89, 168, 231, Ch11
intertextuality, 49, 143, 221
intervening variables, 56, 113, 146, 235
intrusion, 159
Iran–Contra hearings, 208–9

J
Jakobson, Roman, n10Ch6(289)
Jansen, Sue Curry, 170–1, 209
Jenkins, Henry and Mary Fuller, 262–3
Jenkins, Simon, 278
Jordache story, 145–6, 193–4

K
Keane, John, 101, 229
Kellner, Douglas, 236
Kirsta, Alex, 267–8
knowledge, institutional, ethnographic,
    77
knowns, unknowns, 107, 109
Koch, Tom, 168–9, 261
Kornblum, William, 184–5
Kramarae, Cheris, 167, 271
Kress, Gunther, 116
Kumar, Krishan, 12–13
kuuki, 116

L
Lake, Howard, 260
langue la, parole la, 44
Langer, John, 132
language *see* codes, discourse, narrative,
    signs, text
Lasswell, Harold, 38, 234

Lazarsfeld, Paul, 72–3
Leach, Edmund, 42
Le Duc, D.R., 97
leviathan, 101, n17Ch4(287)
Lewin, Kurt, 108–9
Lewis, Justin, 146–7, 188
Liebes, Tamar and Elihu Katz, 64–5,
    71, 194, 229, 245
Lippman, Walter, 117
Loshitzky, Josefa, n17Ch10(295)
Lull, James, 187, 246
Lusted, David, 144

M
MacBride Commission (1978),
    n5Ch4(295)
Madonna, 75, 76, 141
Magellan, Ferdinand (1480–1521), 6
magic bullet theory of mass
    communication effects, 7
mainstreaming, 67–8, 183, 240
Maletzke, G., 153–62
Marinetti, Filippo (1876–1944), 276
Martín-Barbero, Jésus, 17
mass communication models *see* models
    of mass communication
mathematical theory of communication,
    34–35
McChesney, Robert, 218, 276–8
McClellan, Jim, 264, 270
McCullin, Don, 112
McGorty, Christine, 266
McLuhan, Marshall, 26, 217, 245, 275,
    286
McNelly, J.T., 109
McQuail, Denis, 39, 62, 90–4, 98–9,
    100, 221; and Sven Windahl, 114
McRobbie, Angela, 182
Mead, George Herbert, 132
mean world syndrome, 240
media
    alliances in, 116
    barons, 84–6, 213–15, 237
    boundary event, journalistic event,
        168
    'bystander journalism', 163
    casualisation of labour in, 223
    control features, 164
    control function of, 133

corporate power and, 216–26, 241
correspondence as news value, 120
credibility of, 116
crisis definition, 95–6
cross-media ownership, 220
effects of, 191–3, Ch10
ethnic imbalance, 172–6
gender representation in, 169–72
'horse-race journalism', 148, 153
imperialism, 232, 245, 252
manufacture of consent, 96
new values, 117–126
New World Information Order,
  n5Ch4(286–7)
normative theories, 90–4
objectivity, balance, impartiality,
  97–9, 100
ownership and control of, 212–26
pressures and constraints, Ch7, 223
professionalism, 162–5
public sector, private sector, 212–13
racism and, 120, 172–6
representatives of order, 95
sexism in, 170–1
'stenographers to power', 123
Third world and, 92, n5Ch4(286–7)
travelling by, n17Ch10(295)
violence and, 238–42
mediation, Ch5, 159, 160, 180, 182,
  208–9, 245, 273, 274
Mercurio, El, 90, 91
metonym, metaphor, 45–9, 121, 217,
  260
Miller, Daniel, 243
Miller, David, 166–7
Miller, Tim, 260
mimetic plain, 141
miners' strike (UK), 1984, 191–3
Mitchell, Arnold, 199
mobilisation, 92, 93, 95–6
models of mass communication
  Bass's 'double action' model (1969),
    110–11 (Figure 5.3)
  commercial *laissez-faire*, 86
  Galtung and Ruge's model of
    selective gatekeeping (1965), 117
    (Figure 5.7)
  Gerbner's model (1956), 39 (Figure
    2.3)
  Lasswell's model (1948), 38

Maletzke's model of mass
  communication, 153–62 (Figures
  7.1 and 7.2)
McCombs and Shaw's agenda-setting
  model (1976), 112–13 (Figure
  5.4)
McNelly's model of news flow
  (1958), 110 (Figure 5.2)
one-step, two-step, multi-step flow
  model of communication, 72
  (Figure 3.1), 235
propagandist or mass manipulative
  model, 34, 84–6, 234
public service model, 86–9
Rogers and Dearing's model of
  agenda-setting process (1987),
  114 (Figure 5.5), 216
transmission model, 34–40, 135
tripolar model of agendas, 115
  (Figure 5.6), 216 (Figure 9.2)
Schramm's model (1954), 37–8
  (Figure 2.2)
Shannon and Weaver's model
  (1949), 34–6 (Figure 2.1)
Westerståhl and Johansson's model
  of news factors in foreign news
  (1994), 124 (Figure 5.8)
White's gatekeeping model (1950),
  108–9 (Figure 5.1)
Moores, Shaun, 186–7, 191, 197
'moral economy', 197
Morales, Edmundo, 188
Morgan, Michael and James Shanahan,
  247
Morley, David, 190–1, 197, 247; and
  Sonia Livingstone, Andrea Dahlberg
  and Eric Hirsch, 197
'Mr. Gate', 108
Murdoch, Rupert, 86, 89, 213–15
myth, 52–3, 133, 163–5, 208–9, 214,
  217, 226, 239, 263

N
narrative
  binary framing, 137, n10Ch6(289)
  characters in, 141–2
  closure, 134, 140, 149
  codes of, 138–40
  computer games, 262
  disequilibrium, equilibrium, 132, 135

frames of, 142, 145
Hollywood narrative mode, rhetorical mode, 134
information model, story model, 132
gender coding, 140–1
genre, 137–8
news as, 142, 146–7
probability, fidelity, 131–2
rhetorical fantasies, 133
schemata, 136–7
soap narratives, 135
story level, meaning level, 141
symbolism, 132–4
time and, 135
topicality, 144
Nationwide, 190–1
Neely, Kim, 268
Neighbours, 63
Nelson, Anne, 238, 240–1
Netropolis, 266
networking, electronic, 263
networks of control, 89
news
    aberrant news values, 122
    agenda-setting, 112–16, 168
    amplification of issues, 113
    as construct, 107
    as discourse, 115–16
    as narrative, 146–9
    attribution as news value, 123
    boundary event, journalistic event, 168
    corporate agendas and, 115
    crisis as news value, 119
    cultural orientation of, 106
    'double action' process of news flow, 110
    gatekeeping, 108–112, 160
    ideology and, 124–6
    immediacy, 126
    influence on fiction modes, 142–4
    knowns, unknowns, 107
    levels of value, 124
    'maleness' of, 170–2
    management, 166–69
    negativity, 122
    personification and news values, 121–2

proximity as news value, 106, 119, 123–4, 144
    ritualistic nature of, 132
    selection, distortion, replication, 122
    soundbite news, 147–8
    source, 107, 123, 165–9
    technology and news narrative, 147–8
    values, 117–26
    violence as news value, 125
    visions of order, 142
Newson, Elizabeth, n7Ch10(295)
Nineteen Eighty-Four (1949), 13
noise, 35–6
normative, performative, 87
normative theories of media, 90–4
North, Oliver, 208–9
Northcliffe, Lord (1865–1922), 85
Norton-Taylor, Richard, 210; with Mark Lloyd and Stephen Cook, n6Ch9(293)

O
objectivication, 197–8
objectivity, 97–9, 100, 148–9, 155, 162–5, 180, 270
O'Brien, James Bronterre, 84
Offit, Avodah, 268
O'Kane, Maggie, 159
open, closed texts, 45
order, visions of, 142
Orwell, George (1904–50), 13, 17
ownership and control, 112, Ch9 narrowing basis of, 213–14

P
Packer, Kerry, 213
Paine, Thomas (1737–1809), 164
panopticon, superpanopticon, 247–9, 264
paradigm, syntagm, 44
parasocial interaction, 63
Parkin, Frank, 54
participant observation, 74, 184–7
Peirce, Charles (1834–1914), 41, 42
percept, 39–40
personification/personalisation, 96, 121, 209, 211

Peters, John Durham, 34
Philo, Greg, 69, 70, 191–3
photographic negativisation, 94
Pilger, John, 155
Pilkington Committee Report on Broadcasting (1962), 17, n6Ch1(282)
Pitkow, James E. and Mimi Recker, 269
Plant, Sadie, 266–7, 269
plurality, 87, 91, 94, 96, 221, 230
Poor Man's Guardian, 84
Popham, Peter, 274
Porter, Henry, 86
Poster, Mark, 248–9
Postman, Neil, 68, 236–8
postmodernism, 30, n21Ch2(283)
power elite, 18, 21, 51, 54, 87, 88, 99, 121, 123, 124, 169, n7Ch1(282)
power forms, 14
power value, 79, 96, 106, 241–2
preferred reading, 54, 68, 115, 134, 190, 227, 274
press/printing
    and racism, 172–5
    deviance definition, 95
    Fourth Estate, 83
    Koenig steam press, 25
    normative theories of press, 90–4
    Poor Man's Guardian, 84
    press advertising, 85
    radical press, 84, 99
    tabloids, 46–9
    Thunderer, The, 46
    Yellow Press, 85
prior restraint, 156
producer choice, 223
project of self, 73–4, 99, 153, 236, 243
propaganda, 13–14, 21, 34, 45, 53, 84, 166, 273
Propp, Vladimir, 141–2
public service broadcasting (PSB), 28–9, 86–9, 91, 102, 212–13, 233
public sphere, 4, 99, 213, 217, 221, 223, 277

R
Raboy, Marc and Bernard Dagenais, 119
Radway, Janice, 188
Read, Herbert, 276

redundancy, 35, caption, Figure 2.1, 36
Rees, Jasper, 137
referential (or cultural) code, 139
regulation, 88, 91, 213, 214, 220, 241, 269, 277
regulatory favours, 220
researching media
    Blumer's five principles of research, 189
    consumer research, 198–200
    content analysis, 182–3
    ethnographic research, 184–90
    focus groups, 190–4
    HICT Project, 197–8
    insider contacts, 188
    Internet and research, 258–62
    networks of friendship, 188
    qualatitive, quantative, 184–98
    research approaches: convergence, 200
    research as change agent, 201
    specifity, 260–1
    VALS typology, 199
response codes, 54
Rheingold, Henry, 262
rhetorical fantasies, 133
right of reply, 94
Roach, Colleen, 252
Ross, Karen, 175–6

S
Saatchi & Saatchi, 211–12
Saenz, Mike, 267
Sarup, Madan, 49
Saussure, de, Ferdinand *see* de Saussure
Schiller, Herbert, 22–3, 78, 219–20, 224
Schlesinger, Philip, 126, 163–5
scholars of media, 277
Schramm, Wilbur, 37–8, 137
Scott Report (UK), 209–11
Searle, Adrian, 23
Seiter, Ellen, 202
segmentation, 17, 161, 198–200
selection, distortion, replication, 122
self-fulfilling prophecy, 71, 120, n12Ch3(285–6)
semiology/semiotics, 40–6
'semiotic democracy', 243

semiotic power, 76
Shannon and Weaver *see* models of
    mass communication
showbusiness, age of, 237
Sieman, Catherine, 238–9
significant others, 44, 71–2, 235
signification, orders of, 51–2
signifier, signified, 40–2
signs, 40–2
SIGS (special interest groups), 261
Silverstone, Roger, 197
SimCity, 270
Slouka, Mark, 271–4, 279
Smith, Anthony, 122
Smith, Carolyn, 185
soaps, 50, 63–4, 135–6, 141, 148–9,
    161, 180, 193–4, 229
soft cities, 270
Solidarity (Poland), 123–4
soundbite news, 147–8
source, 165–9
sovereignty, 228–9, 252
Sparks, Colin, 157–8
specificity, 260
speed as power, 275
spin doctoring, 166–7, 211–12
Steiler, Kaspar, 117
stereotyping, 45, 120, 168, 172–4
Stevenson, Nick, 101–2, n17Ch2(284)
story level, meaning level, 141
storyness, 132
surveillance, 64–5, 106, 186, 227,
    247–51
Sykes Committee Report on
    Broadcasting (1923), 87, 212–13
symbolic
    code of narrative, 139–40
    convergence theory, 133
    distancing, 246

T
Taylor, Mark C. and Esa Saarinen, 265,
    274, 275–6
Taylor, Philip M., 14, 111, 166, 270–1
technology
    and audience measurement, 78
    and the news, 147–8, 160
    audience use of, 195–8

channel 'dearth', channel 'plenty', 88
    convergence of, 26–8
    democratising potential of, 218
    digitalisation, 27, 88, 160, 249, 252,
        272
    diversification, 213
    HICT (Household Uses of
        Information and Communication
        Technologies) Project, 197
    Internet, Ch11
    'moral economy' constituents of,
        197–8
    online data collection, 169
    setmeter, peoplemeter, 78
    socially situated, 196
    steam press of Frederick Koenig, 25
    surveillance, 247–51
    telegraphy, 25, 248
    V-chips, 265
    vulnerability of data, 274
    warring by software, 275
Tehranian, Majid, 29–30
Telecommunications Act 1996 (USA),
    265, 276
text, 2, 44–5
Thatcher, Margaret, 13
Thomass, Barbara, 223
Thompson, John B., 14–15, 24, 73–4,
    80, 153, 229, 246–7, 250–1
tiger economies, 24, 229
Tilly, Adrian, 144
Tunstall, Jeremy, 123, 126; and Michael
    Palmer, 220
Turner, Ed, 215 (Figure 9.1), 245

U
UNESCO (United Nations
    Educational, Scientific and Cultural
    Organisation), n5Ch4(286–7)
uses and gratifications theory, 62–5, 135

V
VALS typology, 199
van Dijk, Tuen, 172–5
van Zoonen, Liesbet, 169–70, 185
Verstraeten, Hans, 28
Vietnam War, 125

virtual reality, 258, 262, 267, 2704
violence in the media, 125, 238–42, 265
visibility, 250–1

W
Walkerdene, Valerie, 186–7
watchdog, guard dog, lapdog, 94, 100, 211, 225
Watson, James and Anne Hill, n21Ch1(283)
wedom/theydom, 96, 142
Weiner, Norbert, 36–7, 259, n1Ch11(296)

Westerståhl, Jörgen and Folke Johansson, 124–5
White, David M., 108
Wright Mills, C., 18

Y
Yellow press, 85
Youichi, Ito, 116

Z
Zeliger, Barbie, 159
Zoonen, Liesbet van see van Zoonen